Deference to the Legislature in WTO Challenges to Legislation

Global Trade Law Series

VOLUME 26

KLUWER LAW INTERNATIONAL

Deference to the Legislature in WTO Challenges to Legislation

Daniel Lovric

Wolters Kluwer
Law & Business

AUSTIN BOSTON CHICAGO NEW YORK THE NETHERLANDS

Published by:
Kluwer Law International
PO Box 316
2400 AH Alphen aan den Rijn
The Netherlands
Website: www.kluwerlaw.com

Sold and distributed in North, Central and South America by:
Aspen Publishers, Inc.
7201 McKinney Circle
Frederick, MD 21704
United States of America
Email: customer.service@aspenpublishers.com

Sold and distributed in all other countries by:
Turpin Distribution Services Ltd.
Stratton Business Park
Pegasus Drive, Biggleswade
Bedfordshire SG18 8TQ
United Kingdom
Email: kluwerlaw@turpin-distribution.com

Printed on acid-free paper.

ISBN 978-90-411-3145-4

Printed in Great Britain.

This Book is dedicated to my parents
Ivan Lovric and Irja Lovric.

Table of Contents

List of Abbreviations

ALOP	Appropriate level of protection
Anti-Dumping Agreement	*Agreement on the Implementation of Art. VI GATT* 33 ILM 1144 (1994)
API	*Agreement on Pre-shipment Inspection* 33 ILM 1144 (1994)
ATC	*Agreement on Textiles and Clothing* 33 ILM 1144 (1994)
BVerfG	Bundesverfassungsgericht (German Federal Constitutional Court)
BVerfGE	Bundesverfassungsgerichtentscheidung (judgment of the German Federal Constitutional Court)
DSB	Dispute Settlement Body of the WTO
DSU	*Understanding on Rules and Procedures Governing the Settlement of Disputes* 1869 UNTS 401; 33 ILM 1226 (1994)
EC	European Communities
ECHR	European Convention on Human Rights
ECJ	European Court of Justice
EEC	European Economic Community
ECtHR	European Court of Human Rights
Enabling Clause	*Decision on Differential and More Favourable Treatment, Reciprocity, and Fuller Participation of Developing Countries*, GATT Document L/4903, 28 November 1979, BISD 26S/203
EU	European Union
GATT	*General Agreement on Tariffs and Trade 1994* 1867 UNTS 187; 33 ILM 1153 (1994)

GATS	*General Agreement on Trade in Services* 33 ILM 1167 (1994)
ICJ	International Court of Justice
ILC	International Law Commission
IMF	International Monetary Fund
ITC	International Trade Commission of the US
ITLOS	International Tribunal for the Law of the Sea
Licensing Agreement	*Agreement on Import Licensing Procedures* 33 ILM 1144 (1994)
MERCOSUR	Mercado Común del Sur (Southern Common Market)
MFN	Most-favoured-nation
NAFTA	*North American Free Trade Agreement* 32 ILM 605 (1993)
OECD	Organization for Economic Cooperation and Development
PCIJ	Permanent Court of International Justice
SCM Agreement	*Agreement on Subsidies and Countervailing Measures* 33 ILM 1125 (1994)
SPB	Policies Regarding the Conduct of Five-year ('Sunset') Reviews of Antidumping and Countervailing Duty Orders, *United States Federal Register*, Vol. 63, No. 73 (16 April 1998), p. 18871.
SPS	Sanitary and Phytosanitary
SPS Agreement	*Agreement on the Application of Sanitary and Phytosanitary Measures*, 1867 UNTS 493; 33 ILM 1153 (1994)
TBT Agreement	*Agreement on Technical Barriers to Trade* 33 ILM 1144 (1994)
TRIMS	*Agreement on Trade-Related Investment Measures*, 1868 UNTS 186; 33 ILM 1125 (1994)
TRIPS	*Agreement on Trade Related Aspects of Intellectual Property Rights* 1869 UNTS 299; 33 ILM 1197 (1994)
UN	United Nations
VCLT	*Vienna Convention on the Law of Treaties*, 23 May 1969, 1155 UNTS 331; 8 ILM 679 (1969)
USTR	United States Trade Representative
WTO	World Trade Organization
WTO Agreement	*Marrakesh Agreement Establishing the World Trade Organization*, 15 Apr. 1994, 33 ILM 1144 (1994)

Preface

This book deals with the way in which international courts deal with challenges to domestic legislation, with a particular focus on the World Trade Organization (WTO). The aim of the book is to describe the current actual practice of WTO tribunals in this area. Such a description could be important for future work on setting a normative basis for such practice.

This book examines the case law of the WTO. The WTO is a natural reference point for analysing international challenges to legislation. It is the only global institution that regularly hears challenges to legislation in a judicial manner. Of course, other international courts (in particular the European Court of Human Rights) also hear challenges to legislation, and the book makes frequent reference to their decisions.

A study of international challenges to legislation indicates how far international tribunals have deferred to the opinions of domestic parliaments. This is a critical issue for the future development of international law. International tribunals need to have a clear idea of how far they have deferred to domestic parliaments in the course of their past legal analysis – this will aid them, and aid those parliaments, in setting levels of deference in the future.

In the past, international deference to the domestic legislature was procedural in nature, revealed in restrictions on jurisdiction and remedy. Now deference has moved on to substantive issues, focusing on the way legislation is characterized against relevant international obligations. Thus there is a shift from procedural to substantive deference in international challenges to legislation. This shift is revealed in the nature of legislative characterization by international tribunals. This shift has not been examined in depth previously, which, given the importance of the topic, is a surprising omission.

A good way of examining this deference is to look at three kinds of characterization by international tribunals; factor characterization, proportionality characterization and certainty characterization. Proportionality characterization involves familiar issues of effectiveness, optimality and balance, while factor characterization involves the weighing and balancing of legislation's legal and practical operation, its legislative purpose, and external standards. WTO case law in these areas reveals a careful and differentiated degree of deference to the domestic legislature, although there are a number of outlying cases that show a markedly intrusive approach. The third type of characterization – certainty characterization – is relatively rare in domestic constitutional law, but is a common feature of international challenges to legislation. It involves determining the certainty with which domestic legislation operates consistently with international obligations. WTO case law about certainty characterization represents a fairly intrusive approach, and thus represents a relatively low level of deference.

This book represents my personal views only.

Acknowledgements

Thank you to:

Professor Hilary Charlesworth, for her encouragement in helping me complete the thesis that formed the basis of this book.
Professor Philip Kunig, for making it possible for me to study for a semester at the Free University in Berlin.

Thank you to everyone working with Kluwer, for helping to improve this book.

Thank you Christiane for supporting me, and for encouraging me to start this project in the first place.

Prelude: A Brief History of International Challenges to Legislation

International challenges to legislation can trace their heritage at least as far back as the nineteenth century. The earliest signs are apparent in the activities of the first modern arbitral tribunals, following on from the Jay Treaty.[1]

An interesting question is why international challenges to legislation did not make an earlier appearance. The answer seems to be twofold; before the nineteenth century, there was probably not enough legislation to stimulate disputes, and there was certainly not a developed system of international adjudication. Far back in history, before the establishment of sovereign States, there was no regulatory legislation as such. What legislation there was tended to be ad hoc responses to particular problems, rather than comprehensive regulation along the lines of modern legislative schemes. In the feudal system, public power was distributed in such a way that there was limited scope for regulation by statutes. However, in the beginnings of the modern age, legislation began to play a more important role. International arbitration, in contrast, enjoyed some popularity in the Middle Ages.[2] Still, there was little scope for it to be applied to what scarce legislation existed. With the development of the modern state, increasing amounts of public regulation were achieved by statutes. Only at the end of the eighteenth century did the first modern codifications of the civil law world appear. The statutes of the common law world remained a sideline to the main business of the common law until quite recently. However, by the nineteenth century, legislation had become a central element of government in all major developed States.

---

1. Treaty of Amity, Commerce and Navigation (1794), Martens R2, vol. 5, 640.
2. W. Grewe, *The Epochs of International Law*, trans. M. Byers (Berlin & New York: Walter de Gruyter, 2000), Ch. 3.

Coinciding with the increasing importance of legislation was an increased interest in international arbitration. The Jay Treaty[3] between Britain and the United States is considered 'the historical landmark from which the trend which was to lead to the establishment of a true international judicial system is usually dated'.[4] Interestingly, the Jay Treaty arbitrations included a legislation-related issue. The Second Jay Commission dealt with claims by British creditors for compensation for losses suffered as a result of US State legislation. That legislation released US debtors from British debts if the amounts of the debts were paid into the State treasury. The disputes were eventually resolved by a special treaty in 1802, under which the United States paid a bulk sum to cover the 'confiscated debts'.[5]

Following the relative success of the Jay Treaty, international arbitration began to take off in the nineteenth century.[6] This coincided with the increasing importance of domestic legislation. Inevitably, international disputes connected to domestic legislation began to arise. The famous *Caroline* dispute (1840)[7] was resolved by the enactment of the US Habeas Corpus Act of 1842, which was intended to prevent the recurrence of the problem.[8] The CSS (Confederate States ship) *Alabama* Claims Arbitration (1870–1871) also touched on legislative matters, as Britain claimed that its domestic legislation prevented it from complying with relevant international obligations.[9] A number of international disputes over legislation are also recorded for the early years of the twentieth century. A dispute between the United States and Japan in 1906 over California's discriminatory education policies was resolved by changes to Californian legislation.[10] Better known is the Panama Canal Tolls dispute. In 1913, Britain claimed that a US statute regulating tolls on the Panama Canal was incompatible with the Hay-Pauncefoot Treaty.[11] The dispute played out through exchanges of diplomatic correspondence and was noted in the *American Journal of International Law* of

3. Treaty of Amity, Commerce and Navigation (1794), Martens R2, vol. 5, 640. See H. Schlochauer, 'Jay Treaty', in *Encyclopedia of Public International Law*, ed. R. Bernhardt, vol. 3 (Amsterdam: Elsevier, 1997), 1140, 4–7.
4. Zafrulla Khan, *ICJ Yearbook* (1971–1972), 130, quoted in Schlochauer, above n. 3, 6.
5. Schlochauer, above n. 3, 6.
6. Grewe, above n. 2, Ch. 6.
7. Moore, *Digest of International Law*, vol. 6 (1906), 30.
8. Noted in D. Shelton, *Remedies in International Human Rights Law* (Oxford: Oxford University Press, 1999), 128.
9. This claim failed, as would be expected under the modern principle that a State cannot plead its domestic law as a defence to an international claim. See R. Jennings & A. Watts (eds), *Oppenheim's International Law*, 9th edn (Essex: Longman's, 1992), 84; S. Bhuiyan, *National Law in WTO Law* (New York: Cambridge University Press, 2007), 34.
10. As noted by the International Law Commission, 'Draft Articles and Commentaries on Responsibility of States for Internationally Wrongful Acts', *Report of the International Law Commission*, 53rd session, Doc. A/56/10 (2001), Commentary to Art. 32, para. 3.
11. *Panama Canal Tolls* case, Hackworth, *Digest*, vol. 6, 59; see also R. Ago, 'Sixth Report on State Responsibility', Doc. A/CN.4/302, in *Yearbook of the International Law Commission*, vol. 2, Part 1 (1977), 16, para. 34.

the day.[12] The dispute was eventually settled when the United States agreed to amend the relevant legislation.

These developments in State practices were accompanied by some deeper academic thinking about the relationship between international obligations and domestic legislation. Most notably, in 1899, the prominent German scholar Triepel wrote extensively about this relationship.[13] He distinguished between so-called internationally relevant domestic law and other law (internationally irrelevant domestic law). The basis of this distinction was as follows:

> Internationally relevant domestic law is all public law, the introduction or maintenance of which indicates the exercise of an international law authority or the fulfilment or violation of an international law duty of the State.[14]

From this distinction, Triepel built up a series of sub-classifications:[15]

(1) Internationally relevant domestic law was divided between domestic law in violation of international law and domestic law consistent with international law.
(2) Domestic law consistent with international law was further divided into domestic law allowed by international law and domestic law required by international law.
(3) Domestic law required by international law was further divided into directly ordered law and internationally necessary law. Directly ordered law is domestic law that international law expressly requires to be in existence (e.g., when a treaty expressly requires a particular kind of domestic legislation to be in place). Internationally necessary law is domestic law that is not expressly required by international law, but is nevertheless necessary to achieve the result required by international law (e.g., when a treaty requires the protection of aliens, but the only way to achieve this is to enact domestic legislation).[16]

---

12. Editorial Comment, 'The Panama Canal Act', AJIL 6 (1912): 978; J. Latane, 'Panama Canal Act and the British Protest', AJIL 7 (1913): 17.
13. H. Triepel, *Völkerrecht und Landesrecht* (Leipzig: Hirschfeld, 1899). Writing in the context of the recently unified Germany, Triepel was concerned to rebut the argument that public international law (rather than domestic German law) regulated relationships between the German *Länder* (States) and the German federal entity. *Völkerrecht und Landesrecht* became a landmark in the evolution of the dualist theory of international and domestic law.
14. Triepel, above n. 13, 272.
15. *Ibid.*, 272, 299.
16. Triepel wrote that:

> [Internationally necessary law] is indeed established in consideration of an international duty, but it is a duty which in itself leads to something other than the formation of this legal rule. The State establishes the law here, because, if it did not do so, it would not, *under domestic law*, be in a position to fulfil an international duty, for example a duty to punish . . . thus, the legislator is moved to act not by *international law*, but by *domestic law*. In directly ordered law, the act that the State was ordered to perform by international law consisted in creating law; here the State puts itself in a position, with regard to *its own* law,

Although international lawyers have not taken up Triepel's terminology, his work has influenced all subsequent thought on this topic and has a continuing relevance for modern challenges to legislation. The timing of Triepel's work was excellent, as the following years showed a gradual growth in such challenges.

The period 1920–1939 saw the first regular trickle of cases involving challenges to legislation and an increased interest in the issue by States. In 1930, the Preparatory Committee of the Conference for the Codification of International Law (under the auspices of the League of Nations) raised in a general fashion the issue of legislation as breaching international obligations. The Committee asked a number of States to answer the following questions:

> Does the State become responsible in the following circumstances:
>
> Enactment of legislation incompatible with the treaty rights of other States or with its other international obligations? Failure to enact legislation necessary for the purpose of implementing the treaty obligations of the State or its other international obligations?[17]

These questions were not answered in any authoritative way.[18] However, several States gave considered responses, suggesting that the responsibility of the State

---

> and through the new law, to perform an act ordered by international law. In the former case, the fact of not legislating or of repealing the law was itself already contrary to the law; in this case, the breach of the law results from the fact that the State has not performed the act which the law authorizes it to perform, or that it has performed the act which the State authorizes it not to perform.

Ibid., 299; cited in Ago, above n. 11, 14, at fn. 58. The translation is that given by Ago, with some minor changes.

The two kinds of 'domestic law required by international law' are the most puzzling of Triepel's concepts, but perhaps also the most rewarding for modern international lawyers. The critical question in many challenges to legislation is whether particular legislative provisions are truly *required* to meet international obligations, or are merely one of a range of measures available to a State in meeting its international obligations. The answer to this question is fairly easy in the case of directly ordered law, as the relevant international obligation will expressly set out the need for the legislation. However, such international obligations are fairly rare. The question of whether domestic legislation is internationally *necessary* law is thus of great practical importance. In setting this question, Triepel identified two factors of importance in challenges to legislation: first, the nature of what the international obligation requires, and second, the effect of the domestic legal system on the operation of domestic legislation. The second factor is of particular importance to modern international lawyers. It implies that the effect of the domestic legal system on domestic legislation needs to be considered on the international legal plane. As we will see in Ch. 8, these issues are central to what I call 'certainty characterization' of legislation.

17. League of Nations, Conference for the Codification of International Law, Bases of Discussion for the Conference Drawn up by the Committee, vol. III: Responsibility of States for Damage caused in their Territory to the Person or Property of Foreigners, Doc. C.75.M.69. 1929.V, 25, quoted in Ago, above n. 11, 6.
18. According to the International Law Commission's Special Rapporteur on State Responsibility at the time, the answers given to the question 'were bound to be influenced on this point by the rather superficial manner in which the question was drafted'; Ago, above n. 11, 15, para. 33. In any case, the resulting Codification Conference at the Hague in 1930 'ended in almost

in such cases would depend on the nature of the international obligations concerned.[19] In other words, the questions would have to be answered on a case-by-case basis.

Arbitral tribunals made a number of important decisions around this time. In the *Norwegian Shipowners* case (1922),[20] the tribunal dealt with US legislation requisitioning shipping-related material during World War I. The tribunal held that it could not entirely disregard the content of the legislation, but rejected the US argument that its reasoning should be governed by US statute law.[21] In the *Mariposa* case (1933),[22] the US-Panama General Claims Commission emphasized the value of an international court waiting for domestic implementation of legislation before resolving a challenge to the legislation.[23] It argued that judicial resolution of disputes should be deferred when possible, so as to give diplomats the maximum chance to resolve the issue by negotiation.

More important than arbitral tribunals in this period, however, was the activity of the Permanent Court of International Justice (PCIJ). This was the first major standing international court, and it had a wide jurisdiction (for the times) over specific and general international law issues. The PCIJ's activity concentrated on the international law relationships in Europe arising out of the post-war division of Europe.[24] Within that framework, it decided a number of cases concerning domestic legislation.[25] Of particular importance was the *Danzig Legislative*

---

unmitigated failure'; R. Jennings, 'What Is International Law and How Do We Know It When We See It?', reproduced in M. Koskenniemi (ed.), *Sources of International Law* (Aldershot: Ashgate Publishing Company, 2000), 66.

19. Ago, above n. 11, 15, para. 33.
20. *Norwegian Shipowners (Norway/USA)*, UNRIAA, vol. I, 307 (1922), reproduced in part in L. Green, *International Law through the Cases* (Toronto: Carswell, 1978), 3.
21. Green, *ibid.*, 5. (The Tribunal quoted Lammasch, *Die Rechtskraft internationale Schiedssprüche* (1913), 37.) This argument arose from the wording of the Special Agreement setting up the Tribunal, which provided that 'The Tribunal shall examine and decide the aforesaid claims in accordance with the principles of law and equity.' The Tribunal interpreted the phrase 'the principles of law and equity' as referring to international law. The Tribunal concluded that there was nothing in the legislation that was contrary to international law, in the special circumstances concerned.
22. 6 RIAA 338, 341; see also Ago, above n. 11, 17, para. 35.
23. The Commission held as follows:

> The Commission does not assert that legislation might not be passed of such a character that its mere enactment would destroy marketability of private property, render it valueless, and give rise forthwith to an international claim, but it is the opinion of the Commission that ordinarily, and in this case, a claim for expropriation of property must be held to have arisen when the possession of the owner is interfered with and not when the legislation is passed which makes the later deprivation of possession possible.

United Nations, *Reports of International Arbitral Awards*, vol. VI. (United Nations Publication, Sales No. 1955.V.3), 340–341 (quoted in Ago, above n. 11, 17, para. 35).

24. H. Meyer, *The World Court in Action: Judging among the Nations* (New York, Oxford: Rowman & Littlefield Publishers, 2002).
25. For example: *German Settlers in Poland* (1923) P.C.I.J., Series B, No. 6; *Acquisition of Polish Nationality* (1923) P.C.I.J., Series B, No. 7; *Nationality Decrees Issued in Tunis and Morocco*

Decrees case, which Lauterpacht called 'the first instance of international judicial review of a national enactment in the sphere of fundamental human rights'.[26]

Following World War II, the PCIJ was replaced by the International Court of Justice (ICJ). In contrast to the PCIJ, the ICJ has heard only a limited number of challenges to legislation.[27] This can be explained by a number of factors. The greater number and diversity of litigating States (as compared to the PCIJ) may have removed a degree of political consensus that allowed such challenges to proceed. Furthermore, many disputes involving challenges to legislation – particularly in the fields of human rights and international trade – are not heard by the ICJ, but are heard by specialist tribunals instead. We will come back to these tribunals shortly, after examining some significant developments in the way international lawyers have viewed challenges to legislation since World War II.

International lawyers began to look more deeply at challenges to legislation when the International Law Commission embarked on its project on State responsibility for internationally wrongful acts.[28] Inevitably, the Commission's project touched on the issue of consistency between domestic legislation and public international law. In 1977, the second Special Rapporteur for the project, Ago, published his study of the subject.[29] Ago proposed a basic framework for looking at State responsibility for domestic legislation, based on the nature of the relevant international obligation. He wrote that:

> [T]he existence of two kinds of international obligations may be noted. In carrying out some of them, the State may employ only certain specific means; in carrying out others, it can choose from among a variety of means.[30]

Ago called the first kind of obligation an obligation of conduct, and the second kind an obligation of result.[31] The conduct/result distinction could readily be

---

(1923) P.C.I.J., Ser. B., No. 4; *S.S. Wimbledon* (1923) P.C.I.J., Series A, No. 1; *Factory at Chorzów* (1928) P.C.I.J., Series A, No. 17; *Lotus* (1927) P.C.I.J., Series A, No. 10; *Free Zones of Upper Savoy and the District of Gex* (1932) P.C.I.J., Series A/B, No. 46; *Consistency of Certain Danzig Legislative Decrees with the Constitution of the Free City* (1935) P.C.I.J., Ser. A./B., No. 65; *Minority Schools in Albania* (1935) P.C.I.J., Ser. A./B., No. 64; *Phosphates in Morocco* (1938) P.C.I.J., Series A/B, No. 74.

26. *Consistency of Certain Danzig Legislative Decrees with the Constitution of the Free City* (1935) P.C.I.J., Ser. A./B., No. 65. See H. Lauterpacht, *The Development of International Law by the International Court* (Cambridge: Cambridge University Press, 1934 (reprinted 1982)), 107, at fn. 50.
27. Examples include *Rights of Nationals of the United States of America in Morocco* (1952) ICJ Reports 176 (concerning a particular application of a general statute) and *Application of the Convention of 1902 Governing the Guardianship of Infants* (1958) ICJ Reports 55. See also Bhuiyan, above n. 9, 128.
28. See International Law Commission, above n. 10.
29. Ago, above n. 11.
30. Ago, above n. 11, 4, para. 4.
31. To support this idea, Ago cited Triepel's distinction between directly ordered law and internationally necessary law, as well as the writings of the Italian lawyers Anzilotti and Donati (Ago, above n. 11, 4, para. 4, fn. 3). Ago had also put this idea many years before, in his pre-war Hague lectures (R. Ago, 'Le delit international', *Recueil des Cours* 68 (1939): 508).

applied to challenges to legislation, according to Ago.[32] The conduct required by an obligation of conduct could be the enactment or repeal of legislation.[33] Similarly, the result required by an obligation of result could also be achieved by such enactment or repeal.[34] Ago's ideas formed the basis of the Commission's treatment

---

32. Ago, above n. 11, 15, para. 32. He claimed that the existing body of writing on the subject was consistent with these principles, and cited a number of sources for the claim. He gave numerous examples of State practice to back up his theory, while at the same time admitting that there was a paucity of express statements of position on the issue (Ago, above n. 11, 16, para. 33). It is useful to examine Ago's list of secondary sources on this issue. They were:

    - Triepel's *Völkerrecht und Landesrecht*, above n. 13.
    - Ago's previous writings on the issue (R. Ago, *'Le delit international', Recueil des Cours* 68 (1939): 508).
    - Books on state responsibility for legislation: A. Bilge, *La responsabiliti internationale des Etats et son application en matiere d'actes legislatifs* (thesis no. 471, Tsitouris, Istanbul, 1950); E. Vitta, *La responsibility internazionale dello Stato per atti legislativi* (Milan: Giuffre, 1953). Unfortunately, neither of these sources were readily available to me (or not translated), and thus could not be considered for the purposes of this book.
    - Extracts from monographs on the general subject of state responsibility or international law generally: I. Brownlie, *Principles of Public International Law*, 2nd edn (Oxford: Oxford University Press, 1973), 435–436; C. de Visscher, *'La responsibilité des Etats', Bibliotheca Visseriana*, vol. II (Leyden: Brill, 1924), 97; U. Scheuner, *'L'influence du droit interne sur la formation du droit international', Recueil des Cours* 68 (1939): 95; Bin Cheng, *General Principles of International Law as Applied by International Courts and Tribunals* (London: Stevens, 1953); P. Guggenheim, *Traité de droit international public* (Geneva: Georg, 1954); P. Reuter, *'La responsabilité internationale', Droit international public* (Paris: Les Nouvelles Institutes, 1955–1956); G. Schwarzenberger, *International Law*, vol. 1, 3rd edn (London: Steven and Sons, 1957); A. Sereni, *Diritto internazionale* (Giuffre: Milan, 1962); G. Morelli, *Nozioni di diritto internazionale*, 7th edn (Padua: CEDAM, 1967); E. Jimenez de Arechaga, 'International Responsibility', in *Manual of Public International Law*, ed. Sørensen (London: Macmillan, 1968), 547–548; J. Verzijl, *International Law in Historical Perspective*, vol. 6 (Leyden: Sijthoff, 1973); A. Fabre, *Principes du droit des gens* (Paris: Librairie de droit et de jurisprudence, 1974).

    This list illustrates the limited amount of theorizing that had been done at the time in relation to State responsibility and challenges to legislation. The quantity and coverage of these sources was limited. Most were works dealing with larger questions of State responsibility, rather than the legislative inconsistency issue in particular, and are usually only a couple of pages in length. Those few works that focused on the legislative issue (e.g., Vitta and Bilge) were rather dated, even when Ago's Sixth Report was issued in 1977. With the exception of the brief comments of a few authors (e.g., Brownlie, although one could also mention here one brief discussion by a British lawyer not cited by Ago: G. Fitzmaurice, 'The General Principles of International Law Considered from the Standpoint of the Rule of Law', *Recueil des Cours* 92 (1957): 1), there was no contribution from a lawyer specialized in the common law tradition. The lack of North American contribution was noticeable, as was the lack of contribution from the third world. Of course, this is not to disparage the quality of Ago's sources. A number of the authors were international lawyers of the highest standing, including a number of current or future World Court judges (including Ago himself).
33. Ago, above n. 11, 5, paras 5–6.
34. *Ibid.*, 13, para. 27:

    > Let us take the case of an international obligation which allows the State to achieve the required result by whatever means it prefers, that it to say, either by promulgating a law, or by passing an act or issuing administrative regulations, or by following established

of domestic legislation for the next two decades,[35] and its influence can still be seen in the Commission's final Draft Articles on the Responsibility of States for Internationally Wrongful Acts (2001).[36] However, in the end, the distinction between obligations of conduct and of result was abandoned.[37] Various influential States had made it clear to the Commission that the distinction was too abstract and was liable to cause confusion.[38]

---

practice or adopting a new practice, or by some other means. It seems obvious that, when an international obligation is of this nature, the State's choice of the means to be employed can in no case constitute the breach of the obligation.

35. At one stage, the International Law Commission's Draft Articles on State Responsibility provided as follows (see International Law Commission, Report on the work of its 48th Session, *Yearbook of the International Law Commission*, vol. II, Part 2 (Doc. A/51/10) (1996), 60):

> *Article 20*
>
> *Breach of an international obligation requiring the adoption of a particular course of conduct*
>
> There is a breach by a state of an international obligation requiring it to adopt a particular course of conduct when the conduct of that State is not in conformity with that required of it by that obligation.
>
> *Article 21*
>
> *Breach of an international obligation requiring the achievement of a specified result*
>
> 1. There is a breach by a State of an international obligation requiring it to achieve, by means of its own choice, a specified result if, by the conduct adopted, the State does not achieve the result required of it by that obligation.
> 2. When the conduct of the State has created a situation not in conformity with the result required of it by an international obligation, but the obligation allows that this or an equivalent result may nevertheless be achieved by subsequent conduct of the State, there is a breach of the obligation only if the State also fails by its subsequent conduct to achieve the result required of it by that obligation.

36. Document A/56/10. The Draft Articles and Commentary are available on the Commission's web site; <http://untreaty.un.org/ilc/texts/9_6.htm> (visited 29 Apr. 2007).

37. In the Commission's Commentary to the final form of the Draft Articles, it noted as follows (International Law Commission, above n. 10, Commentary to Art. 12, para. 11):

> In practice, various classifications of international obligations have been adopted. For example a distinction is commonly drawn between obligations of conduct and obligations of result. That distinction may assist in ascertaining when a breach has occurred. But it is not exclusive, and it does not seem to bear specific or direct consequences as far as the present Articles are concerned.

The Commission also cited a decision of the ECtHR to support the proposition that '[t]he distinction between obligations of conduct and result was not determinative of the actual decision that there had been a breach' (*Colozza and Rubinat v. Italy* (1985) ECHR, Series A, No. 89. See International Law Commission, above n. 10, Commentary to Art. 12, para. 11).

38. Politically, the conduct/result distinction was not well received by States. J. Crawford, 'Second Report on State Responsibility', Doc. A/CN.4/498, in *Yearbook of the International Law Commission*, vol. 2, Part 1 (1999), para. 56 noted the following comments by States:

> – The distinctions developed in Chapter III 'do not appear to have any bearing on the consequences of their breach as developed in Part Two'. (Denmark)

The final form of the Draft Articles suggests a different analytical method from Ago's for identifying conflict between international obligations and domestic legislation. Basically, the Draft Articles suggest a cautious, case-by-case approach. For example, the wording of Article 12[39] (which establishes the basic nature of a breach of an international obligation) was consciously designed to cover situations in which the enactment of legislation would amount to a breach of an international obligation.[40] Under this article, the existence of a breach depends on the particular facts of the situation and the particular legal rules involved. As the Commission noted:

> [I]n the final analysis, whether and when there has been a breach of an obligation depends on the precise terms of the obligation, its interpretation and application, taking into account its object and purpose and the facts of the case.[41]

This suggests a very cautious method for dealing with challenges to legislation. Indeed, the Commission appeared to suggest that the best that could be done was to deal with such situations on a case-by-case basis.[42]

- The provisions relate to 'rules of substantive law, which classify primary obligations'; such provisions have 'no place in a draft of this kind and should be deleted'. (France)
- There is a certain danger in establishing provisions that are too abstract in nature, since it is difficult to anticipate their scope and application. Such provisions, rather than establishing greater legal certainty, might be abused as escape clauses detrimental to customary international law. They may also seem impractical to States less rooted in the continental European legal tradition, because such abstract rules do not easily lend themselves to the pragmatic approach normally prevailing in international law . . . In sum, the German Government is not quite sure whether the complicated differentiations set out in Articles 20, 21 and 23 are really necessary, or even desirable. (Germany)
- The fineness of the distinctions drawn between different categories of breach may exceed that which is necessary, or even helpful, in a statement of the fundamental principles of State responsibility [and] that it may be difficult to determine the category into which a particular conduct falls. (United Kingdom)

39. Article 12 provides:

> There is a breach of an international obligation by a State when an act of that State is not in conformity with what is required of it by that obligation, regardless of its origin or character.

40. International Law Commission, above n. 10, Commentary to Art. 12, paras 2 and 12.
41. *Ibid.*, para. 1.
42. *Ibid.*, para. 11:

> The question often arises whether an obligation is breached by the enactment of legislation by a State, in cases where the content of the legislation prima facie conflicts with what is required by the international obligation, or whether the legislation has to be implemented in the given case before the breach can be said to have occurred. Again, *no general rule can be laid down applicable to all cases.* Certain obligations may be breached by the mere passage of incompatible legislation. Where this is so, the passage of the legislation without more entails the international responsibility of the enacting State, the legislature itself being an organ of the State for the purposes of the attribution of responsibility. In other circumstances, the enactment of legislation may not in and of itself amount to a breach,

As we will see in the remainder of this book, this is perhaps an over-cautious approach. Some general principles can be identified regarding international challenges to legislation. But why did the Commission not go further to examine the possibility of such principles? The answer lies, in part, in the relative scarcity of tribunal decisions that were available at the time. However, in recent days, the creation of specialist international tribunals dealing with human rights and trade has been the trigger for an explosion in the number of challenges to legislation. The most important of these tribunals are the European Court of Human Rights (ECtHR) and the tribunals of the World Trade Organization (WTO).[43]

The ECtHR is a regional court that has compulsory jurisdiction over human rights matters in Europe. Individuals have standing to challenge particular applications of domestic legislation. As a result, the ECtHR has dealt with an enormous number of challenges to legislation in the past few decades.[44] Not surprisingly, it has developed a sophisticated and relatively settled approach to dealing with such challenges.[45]

The WTO system was created in the mid-1990s to replace the limited system under the General Agreement on Tariffs and Trade (GATT) of 1947. The main innovation of the WTO system was to allow its tribunals virtually automatic jurisdiction over challenges to legislation (although, unlike the ECtHR, only States and similar entities can initiate such challenges in the WTO). The WTO system is almost universal, and is thus distinguished as the only truly global institution that regularly hears challenges to legislation.

The future promises further growth in the number of international challenges to legislation. As more aspects of regulation become internationalized, more aspects of domestic regulation will come up for international scrutiny. An important part of that scrutiny will be from international tribunals.

This raises the question of how international tribunals can deal with those challenges in a legal manner, without becoming overtly politicized. The only way for them to do so is to apply a legal method. Yet, the basis of such a method, beyond the identification of international rules and the interpretation of treaty text, is still in an undeveloped state – even the International Law Commission resigned itself to dealing with such challenges on a case-by-case basis. Nevertheless, the recent

---

> especially if it is open to the State concerned to give effect to the legislation in a way which would not violate the international obligation in question. In such cases, whether there is a breach will depend on whether and how the legislation is given effect. [emphasis added, footnotes omitted]

43. The European Court of Justice also has an active jurisdiction here, but only in the field of European Union law.
44. There are too many examples to list comprehensively here. An impression of the volume of cases here can be gained from the Council of Europe's Lists of General Measures Adopted to Prevent New Violations of the European Convention on Human Rights, <www.coe.int/t/e/human_rights/execution/02_Documents/MGindex.asp#TopOfPage> (visited 21 Mar. 2007).
45. The ECtHR's approach to challenges to legislation would be an interesting study in itself, but is outside the scope of this book.

flood of WTO case law may allow the development of a less modest conceptual approach. Can one find some hints of a more general method in this case law?

This book is not concerned directly with the issue of how international tribunals *should* deal with challenges to legislation. Rather, it is focused on how they have actually done so in recent WTO practice. Survey work of this nature is a vital preliminary step towards building a future legal doctrine about international challenges to legislation. In this regard, we are fortunate, as it is only in the last fifteen years that a large body of case law has become available from a truly global adjudicative system – the WTO.

Chapter 1
Introduction

1.1. THE SUBJECT OF THIS BOOK

Surprisingly, there are no highly developed principles of international law specifically about international challenges to domestic legislation – but there should be. In the past, international challenges to legislation were rare; however, in the last twenty years or so, conditions have changed and such challenges are common. The underlying causes for the increase in such challenges are expanded jurisdiction and strengthened remedies in several international tribunals, particularly in the fields of trade and human rights. Challenges to domestic legislation in international tribunals are here to stay, in increasing numbers, and with increasing demands. The task for international lawyers is to make order out of a hurly-burly of new cases.

Creating legal order from a large new body of case law demands preliminary surveys and descriptive work. This book aims to contribute to this preliminary work. The book examines recent practices in the World Trade Organization (WTO) legal system, with a view to building up analytical systems for viewing current practices in international challenges to legislation. I do not intend to examine how international tribunals *should* treat such challenges, nor do I try to suggest any norms that govern such treatment. Rather, this book has the more modest goal of identifying patterns in current case law, to the extent that such patterns can be found. This kind of analysis does not aim to illustrate binding rules or principles in international adjudication – although it can form the basis for future work in this regard.

This kind of descriptive work cannot be done in an abstract space – rather, it must be done with an eye on certain realities and political arguments lying behind technical legal arguments. These realities include the strong legitimacy of most domestic legislatures, the limited mandate of international tribunals, and the need for international judges to argue persuasively. In short, any survey of case law here needs to account for the struggle between domestic and international actors, and in particular, between domestic legislatures and international tribunals.

Therefore, the central issue dealt with in this book is deference. How far do international tribunals defer to the opinions of domestic legislatures? Deference is built into the structure of legal review of legislation, and it is the key element of such review. Although deference is often expressed in different ways, it is an essential element in every international challenge to legislation.

In earlier times, deference was expressed in procedural ways. Tribunals exercising procedural deference decided that they had no jurisdiction to hear a challenge. They declined jurisdiction on discretionary grounds. Remedies were weak or vague. However, now the environment has changed, and treaties have forced international tribunals to accept jurisdiction, and to grant more specific remedies. Procedural deference is on the retreat. Yet, as procedural deference declines, other forms of deference advance. The new deference in international challenges to legislation is substantive. Tribunals now hear such challenges on their merits, and it is mainly on the merits that tribunals express deference to domestic legislatures.

Thus, much of this book is about the practice of substantive deference in international challenges to legislation. To some extent, this issue is a familiar one in public international law, namely, how to resolve domestic sovereignty with international authority. The issue of deference is a basic theme in public international law. Yet, deference in challenges to legislation raises its own special issues. An international tribunal may give one kind of deference to administrative decisions and a different kind of deference to legislative decisions. This is because of the different expertise and authority held by the executive branch of government as opposed to the legislative branch. In particular, the legislative branch is uniquely placed (at least in the case of democratically elected legislatures) to make judgments about the culture and perceptions of the population. International tribunals are not well placed to make such judgments and therefore show a degree of deference to legislative decision-making in this area.

This reminds us of the analogy between international law and domestic constitutional law.[1] In many ways, international tribunals perform tasks similar to those of domestic constitutional courts when they review legislation. Of course, the international legal system is not a full-blown constitutional system. However, one can make many useful parallels between international challenges to legislation and domestic constitutional law. Most noticeably, legal concepts developed through the immense experience of domestic constitutional courts can be a useful inspiration in examining the jurisprudence of international tribunals.

In dealing with substantive deference in challenges to legislation, one needs an organizing principle to deal with the mass of cases that have been decided. For this

1. D. Cass, 'The Constitutionalization of International Trade Law: Judicial Norm-Generation as the Engine of Constitutional Development in International Trade', EJIL 12 (2001): 39; M. Krajewski, *Verfassungsperspektiven und Legitimation des Rechts der Welthandelsorganisation* (Berlin: Duncker & Humblot, 2001).

book, the organizing principle is a concept familiar to domestic constitutional lawyers, namely, characterization. According to this concept, international tribunals need to determine the character of legislation in light of relevant international obligations. Characterization is an essential element of any legal system involving judicial review of legislation. Without principles of characterization, a constitutional-type text is half complete.[2]

Characterization is familiar to lawyers in federations as a means of dividing competences between federal and regional units. However, the concept has a much broader application than the division of competences and extends to any relationship between higher-level norms and lower-level measures of general application. The lower-level measures need to be characterized in light of the higher-level norms – thus, domestic legislation needs to be characterized in light of international rules.

Admittedly, there may be other organizing principles for describing deference in international challenges to legislation.[3] For example, one could also choose to describe case law according to the status of the legislation in the domestic legal hierarchy, or according to whether the relevant legislature is elected or appointed. These would be legitimate focal points for a study on international challenges to legislation. To pursue these points here, however, would demand a much longer book than this one. Using the principle of characterization is a helpful starting point in this new field, and it leads to some helpful generalizations about deference in international challenges to legislation. Nevertheless, issues of the domestic legal hierarchy and of democratic legitimacy lie in the background here, and they will be discussed in this book at times.

Characterization in international challenges to legislation can be divided into three broad categories:

- characterization of the nature of legislation according to its formal legal features and surrounding background facts (factor characterization);
- characterization of the proportionality of domestic legislation as measured against international obligations (proportionality characterization); and
- characterization of the certainty with which domestic legislation operates in a manner consistent with international obligations (certainty characterization).

The first two classes of characterization are familiar to constitutional lawyers – perhaps not in name, but in substance. Many domestic constitutional law cases concern factor characterization. Here, the court examines the various features of the legislation to determine whether it falls within a particular constitutional concept. If a constitutional norm requires the court to look at the extent to which the legislation is adapted to its purpose, the court will undertake proportionality characterization. International tribunals perform very similar tasks, depending on the nature of the international obligation concerned.

---

2. G. Taylor, *Characterisation in Federations: Six Countries Compared* (Berlin: Springer, 2006), 144.
3. For discussion of one example, see Ch. 5 below, n. 10.

However, certainty characterization is a particular feature of international challenges to legislation. Here, the tribunal examines the features surrounding the legislation – such as domestic administrative practices and judicial interpretations – to determine whether the legislation is consistent with international law. This kind of review is also known to domestic constitutional lawyers. However, the international legal system encourages this kind of review. International obligations are cast broadly and thus encourage broadly drafted implementing legislation. This is the kind of legislation that attracts certainty characterization. Furthermore, international tribunals, unlike domestic constitutional courts, cannot determine the content of domestic law. International tribunals cannot as a matter of law determine how domestic legislation should be administered. They can only make findings on how domestic legislation is likely to be administered. Thus, certainty characterization is a particular characteristic of international challenges to legislation.

The three classes of characterization raise particular issues relating to deference given by international tribunals. This is most obvious in cases of certainty characterization. In such cases, the international tribunal must evaluate the actual operation of domestic law: in other words, it needs to determine the content of norms of another legal system. For an international tribunal, the issue of deference arises in dealing with domestic views about the operation of the domestic legal system. The international nature of a challenge to legislation also affects defence in proportionality characterization. Here, the core of the judicial task is to balance the purpose of the international rule and the purpose of the domestic legislation. In many cases, the international tribunal is removed from local realities, and thus is less able than a domestic court to judge the proportionality of domestic legislation. As a result, issues of deference arise in dealing with domestic views about the nature of the purpose-balancing exercise. A different kind of balance arises in factor characterization. Here, the matters to be balanced are features of the legislation that do not necessarily correspond directly with particular purposes. In carrying out factor characterization, an international tribunal must deal with claims for deference to local views about the relative weighting and relevance of these features. Thus, the characterization exercise involves different kinds of deference for each of the three types.

It is for this reason that this book examines international challenges to legislation from the perspective of these three types of characterization. Doing so is likely to reveal the ways in which international tribunals show different kinds of deference in carrying out characterization of each type.

1.2. WHY THIS SUBJECT IS IMPORTANT

Few international lawyers have chosen to write about challenges to legislation, and fewer still have focused on the topic as a specialization.[4] There is little analysis of

4. A notable exception is S. Bhuiyan, *National Law in WTO Law* (Cambridge: Cambridge University Press, 2007). Bhuiyan also notes the lack of published research in this area (pp. 6 and 121). One should also mention Ch. 10 of M. Oesch, *Standards of Review in WTO Dispute*

the topic apart from some fairly general statements in the context of the general principles of State responsibility, or in the context of the margin of appreciation[5] or standard of review.[6] Twenty years ago, this was because there were few international tribunal decisions about challenges to legislation. Today, the growth of published case law in the area demands consideration and will be of interest to actors at both the domestic and international levels.

For example, domestic legislatures are concerned with their own prerogatives, their 'safe harbour' from the interferences of international tribunals. An analysis of challenges to legislation will help to define these safe harbours. It is therefore to the advantage of domestic legislatures to promote the development of legal concepts dealing with challenges to legislation. Indeed, a failure to participate in this development will be a lost chance to influence the way in which the safe harbours will be defined.

Similarly, international tribunals have a strong interest in the analysis of international challenges to legislation. International tribunals need to develop principled jurisprudence solidly based on practice and coherent theories. This is the core of a legal approach to solving disputes. Without a demonstrably legal approach, international tribunals will have enormous difficulties in persuading States to follow their rulings. Law becomes more persuasive when it is real (based on practice) and explicable (based on coherent principles).

An analysis of challenges to legislation therefore has two aspects: it should be grounded in actual practice and should aim to develop higher-level concepts with which to view that practice. This book focuses on the former aspect. Describing current practices in an organized and rigorous way is a necessary pre-condition to developing durable higher-level concepts. This kind of descriptive work, focusing on legislation (i.e., measures of general application) is lacking in the current literature.

Assuming that durable higher-level concepts can be developed about international challenges to legislation, one can speculate on the resulting influence of these concepts on international law itself. A developing jurisprudence of challenges to legislation will, in the long term, provide a new vantage point for re-examining and refining established doctrines. Such doctrines concern justiciability (such as the reserved domain of domestic jurisdiction and the exhaustion of

---

Resolution (Oxford: Oxford University Press, 2003), which deals with the application of the WTO standard of review to domestic law.

Bhuiyan's book deals with both characterization (in Ch. 5) and deference (in Ch. 6), within a larger discussion of the general relationship between domestic and WTO law. Oesch's book deals with deference in challenges to legislation as part of a general discussion of the standard of review. In contrast with these works, this book focuses specifically on procedure, characterization, and deference, and provides a more detailed discussion on how deference has been expressed in procedure, and in substantive matters (as seen through the lens of characterization).

There is also a brief relevant discussion in S. Cottier & K. Schefer, 'The Relationship between World Trade Organization Law, National and Regional Law', JIEL 1 (1998): 83.

5. See Section 4.5.2.
6. See Section 4.6.

local remedies), remedies (in particular, the remedy of declaration), and general principles of State responsibility. Just as other specialized growth areas in international law (such as the law of the sea, individual human rights, and international criminal law) have pushed along the development of general international law doctrine, it is not unreasonable to expect a modest contribution from the area of challenges to legislation. Such developments, however, are several steps removed from the descriptive focus of this book.

1.3. WHY FOCUS ON THE WTO?

This book will examine the aforementioned issues from the perspective of the law of the WTO because the WTO is a natural reference point for analysing international challenges to legislation. It is the only global institution that regularly hears challenges to legislation in a legal manner. Admittedly, the European Court of Human Rights (ECtHR) hears more challenges to legislation than do WTO tribunals. However, the ECtHR is a regional institution, with a lesser claim to be representative of global legal practices. Of course, ECtHR practices provide a valuable context, and this book will make frequent reference to them.

Focusing on WTO challenges to legislation reveals several important insights into international challenges to legislation. Most importantly, procedural and remedial methods of expressing deference have been substantially curtailed in the WTO. Challenges to legislation are more available under WTO procedures than under previous international legal systems. WTO remedies are more specific, and they are supported by ambitious enforcement procedures. This means that deference in WTO challenges to legislation needs to be expressed in considering the substantive matters at issue. As mentioned earlier, decreasing deference in procedural and remedial matters has pushed issues of deference into issues of substance. The WTO is an ideal field to examine this process in action.

1.4. METHODOLOGY AND TERMINOLOGY

1.4.1. Methodology

Radbruch once wrote that 'Sciences which have to busy themselves with their own methodology are sick sciences.'[7] However, difficulties in substance can often be traced to underlying methodological problems, which themselves cannot be solved conclusively. It pays to be aware of these problems.

7. G. Radbruch, *Einführung in die Rechtswissenschaft*, 12th edn (Stuttgart: Koehler, 1969), 253; quoted in K. Zweigert & H. Kötz, *An Introduction to Comparative Law*, trans. J.A. Weir, 3rd edn (Oxford: Oxford University Press, 1998), 33.

Analysis of modern international economic law raises particular methodological issues. Jackson has described a number of these issues.[8] He argues that the nature of international economic law means that its study involves the following:

- the need to account for the relationship of international economic law to public international law in general;
- the need to account for the relationship of international economic law to municipal law, and in particular, constitutional law;
- the need for a strong component of multidisciplinary research and thinking, in particular, economics and political science, but also other fields such as cultural history, anthropology, and geography;
- the need for a higher than usual emphasis on empirical analysis of case studies, and the corresponding need to master a considerable amount of detail to understand broad principles;
- difficulty in obtaining information; and
- the need to account for the greater public face and consequent visible politicization of international economic law.

Analysing WTO challenges to legislation in light of all of these factors is obviously outside the scope of this book. Instead, this book focuses on the first two matters: the links between WTO law and aspects of general public international law, and the analogies between WTO law and constitutional law. Each aspect of WTO challenges to legislation needs to be placed in the wider context of public international law generally. Particular aspects of WTO doctrine often find their counterparts in principles of general public international law. The relevance of domestic constitutional law is a little more complex, involving difficult questions of comparative law. Before discussing these questions, however, I will outline my general legal method. Following this, I will explain the terminology that I use in this book.

1.4.1.1. Legal Method in General

Linking legal analysis with thought from the social sciences raises important methodological issues. It is not clear whether these kinds of linkages 'dilute' the normativity of international law.[9] This and related issues are in themselves the subject of an important body of literature. The basic approach in this book is, however, to

---

8. J. Jackson, 'Global Economics and International Economic Law', JIEL 1, no. 1 (1998): 9–10.
9. S. Krasner, 'What's Wrong with International Law Scholarship?: International Law and International Relations: Together, Apart, Together', *Chi. J Int'l. L.* 1 (2000): 93, at 98 writes:

 > [T]he methodological divide that separates political science and international law is not likely to be bridged, and that, perhaps, is not such a bad thing. The task of political scientists is primarily to explain what is and thereby to hint at what might be. The task of lawyers is more often to elucidate not what is, but what might be. If the normative project that is central to international public law were more closely linked with the empirical project of international relations scholars, both enterprises might be enriched. [footnotes omitted]

focus on *legal* concepts. One should take seriously the claim[10] that there must be (at least a degree of) separation between the questions of:

- what the law is (the positive question);
- what the history of the law is (the historical question);
- what the function of law is (the sociological and political question); and
- what the law should be (the policy question).

Isolating the first question is a conscious technique, designed to preserve the 'special quality' of law.[11] The first question provides the essential context for answering the other questions. In this book, I will not attempt to answer all of these questions but will merely focus on the first.[12] In particular, I aim to show how the law is applied in practice. However, despite this focus, the second, third, and fourth questions are useful follow-up questions, and I will therefore refer to them from time to time.

These issues lead to the broader methodological questions of international law. I do not intend to review the complex literature in the area.[13] However, I will set out my methodological assumptions, as follows:

- The four questions set out above should be kept separate, at least to some degree.[14] It may be impossible to keep them completely separate from one another, and there may be occasions when one needs to mix these questions. For example, it may be useful at times to move from a positivist view of law to a view of law as a process. However, it is important to be aware of the extent to which one is mixing the two views at any particular time, so as to preserve the normative qualities of law.
- One can adopt an eclectic approach to method, as long as one is aware that one is doing so. This could be called a conscious eclectic approach.[15]

10. G. Schwarzenberger, *The Inductive Approach to International Law* (London: Steven and Sons, 1965), 8.
11. M. Byers, 'Taking the Law out of International Law: A Critique of the Iterative Perspective', *Harv. Int'l. L.J.* 38 (1997): 201, at 204.
12. This is not to suggest that answering the fourth question is at all necessary. As M. Koskenniemi, 'Letter to the Editor of the Symposium', AJIL 93 (1999): 351, at 356, points out, an instrumentalist approach (i.e., providing policy solutions) is a product of a particular academic tradition. Other approaches, such as pointing out problems, or taking a moral point of view, are also valid. However, this book assumes that a legal analysis must at least start from the first question.
13. See generally M. Koskenniemi (ed.), *International Law* (Aldershot: Dartmouth, 1992).
14. Schwarzenberger, above n. 10, 8.
15. R. Müllerson, *Ordering Anarchy: International Law in International Society* (London: Martinus Nijhoff, 2000), 31:

> There may be, of course, objections to such a selective use of different theories. One may be accused of being eclectic. However, is eclecticism necessarily such a bad thing? If a choice of strong points from different theories is open, conscious and can theoretically be justified (e.g., if it can be shown that a phenomenon under study, or an aspect of it, can be

'Good scientists [and lawyers], like good novelists and good historians, make use of all the tools at their disposal in trying to anticipate the future. That includes not just theory, observation, and rigorous calculation, but also narrative, analogy, paradox, irony, intuition, imagination, and – not least in importance – style.'[16]

- The normative question (i.e., asking what the law is) involves an inductive approach,[17] requiring a rigorous attention to raw data. However, the inductive approach is fundamentally limited. Much important data is simply not available.[18] More importantly, the inductive approach relies on the researcher's pre-existing assumptions about the nature of the subject.[19] Therefore, the inductive approach provides only a very limited degree of objectivity. However, this limited degree of objectivity can be a useful thing when dealing with highly controversial issues.
- The language of international law is adapted to simultaneously support opposing points of view.[20] Words are given meaning by the culture of interpretive communities, rather than by their inherent content. This is not necessarily a bad thing, as long as the points of view of weak players are given some representation in international legal arguments. Developing a new legal concept should therefore involve a discussion of whose voices the new concept includes and whose voices it excludes.

Thus, the method adopted in this book is basically inductive, combined with awareness that this will inevitably favour one or another political position. While complete objectivity is impossible, it is desirable to avoid subjectivity through an inductive process based on rigour.

Nevertheless, any attempt to avoid subjectivity cannot avoid the political nature of conflicts of principles. Such conflicts cannot be resolved objectively, and no set of rules, regardless of how ingenious they are, can resolve such conflicts:

> [I]ssues of contextual justice cannot be solved by the application of ready-made rules or principles. Their solution requires venturing into fields such as

---

better explained not by a single theory but by the use of various theories), eclecticism may become a principled approach to research.

16. J. Lewis, 'International Relations Theory and the End of the Cold War', *International Security* 17 (1992): 58, quoted in R. Müllerson, *International Law, Rights and Politics: Developments in Eastern Europe and the CIS* (London: Routledge, 1994), 4.
17. G. Schwarzenberger, 'The Inductive Approach to International Law', *Harvard Law Review* 60 (1947): 539; Schwarzenberger, above n. 10.
18. O. Schachter, *International Law in Theory and Practice* (London: Martinus Nijhoff Publishers, 1991), 36.
19. W. Jenks, *The Prospects of International Adjudication* (London: Steven and Sons, 1964), 617–662. See also A. D'Amato, 'The Inductive Approach Revisited', *Indian J. Int'l. L.* 6 (1966): 509–514.
20. M. Koskenniemi, 'The Politics of International Law', EJIL 1 (1990): 4.

politics, social and economic casuistry which were formally delimited beyond the point at which legal argument was supposed to stop in order to remain 'legal'.[21]

Conflicts of principles are, in the end, resolved by political processes. Writing a legal thesis about such conflicts involves taking a political stance, whether consciously or unconsciously.

What can legal writing as such add to this political process? Many international lawyers point to the ability of international law to reduce the heat, and the resulting irrationality and destructiveness, of particular conflicts.[22] There must always be struggle when a conflict of principles is involved, but verbal conflicts are better than physical conflicts, and verbal conflicts are often better structured than unstructured. A properly structured verbal conflict allows for full expression of the underlying principles at stake – and increases the chances for persuasion and compromise (although this can never be guaranteed). Well-designed international legal analysis offers the chance for a presumption of structured verbal conflict. The danger is that badly designed structures end up repressing discussion. Legal structures should allow different voices to be heard. The task here is to develop structures in which conflicts of international and domestic rules can be played out verbally, giving voice to all with a principle at stake.

One way to develop good structures is to draw on the experience of domestic constitutional systems. Such systems have enormous experience in designing legal concepts to deal with a variety of political conflicts. However, drawing on this experience inevitably leads to problematic issues involved with comparative law and the transplanting of legal concepts.

1.4.1.2. Issues of Comparative Method

Merely examining WTO jurisprudence risks introspection. Just as a trip to a foreign country often teaches us more about ourselves than about foreigners, a trip into the jurisprudence of other legal systems gives us a clearer picture of WTO judicial review.

This book is heavily influenced by domestic constitutional law concepts. As I am trained as an Australian lawyer, many of these concepts are borrowed, consciously or unconsciously, from Australian constitutional jurisprudence. There is no point in covering up one's biases and pre-conceptions here; it is better to make them explicit. Australian jurisprudence is based on common law constitutional jurisprudence generally, and from the United States particularly. Readers familiar

21. *Ibid.*, at 31–32.
22. C. de Visscher, *Theory and Reality in Public International Law* (Princeton: Princeton University Press, 1957), 369; J. Jackson, *The World Trading System: Law and Policy of International Economic Relations*, 2nd edn (Cambridge, MA: MIT Press, 1997), 110.

with this jurisprudence will recognize, in particular, a focus on the idea of characterization of legislation, and also, on particular methods of characterization.

Nevertheless, I have made an effort to draw concepts from other jurisdictions to achieve some balance. The constitutional jurisprudence of Germany is a particularly rich source here. The concept of proportionality characterization stems originally from German jurisprudence, although the increasing popularity of the concept means that it is now a feature of common law thinking as well. The idea of certainty characterization is also related to German thinking, in particular, the idea of the *Bestimmtheitsgebot* (requirement for legal certainty). These ideas have found a secure place in the jurisprudence of the ECtHR on challenges to legislation, which is also a major source of ideas in this book.

One may disagree with this method. For example, Oesch writes of the 'irrelevance of domestic standard-of-review concepts' in dealing with the WTO standard of review:

> GATT 1947 Panels were consistently reluctant to look for guidance from domestic legal systems and to apply *mutatis mutandis* standards of review as developed in domestic administrative jurisprudence. The same observation holds true for panels and the Appellate Body, which have so far dealt with standard-of-review matters under the WTO. Albeit frequently using language which is similar to that used in certain domestic contexts, panels have deliberately avoided giving the impression that well-established standards in domestic administrative law, as shaped by the specificities of each member's legal system, could be of help in panel proceedings.[23]
>
> [T]he WTO adjudicating bodies have made it clear that they would develop their own standard-of-review principles, taking the relevant principles in the WTO agreements as their foundation. Therefore, this work refrains from analyzing domestic standard-of-review concepts.[24]

The danger that may justify Oesch's reluctance to look to other legal systems for inspiration is the transplantation problem, as popularized by Watson.[25] In essence, the problem is that legal ideas cannot simply be transplanted from one legal system to another. A legal idea needs a history, culture, political system, and economy to give it substance, and such features will vary from one legal system to another. Careless legal transplants often fail in foreign soil.

To avoid the difficulties of the transplantation problem, one needs to look to the methods of comparative law. Unfortunately, and famously, comparative law is

---

23. M. Oesch, *Standards of Review in WTO Dispute Resolution* (Oxford: Oxford University Press, 2003), 7, citing Panel Report, *US – Cotton Yarn*, para. 7.35, fn. 193.
24. *Ibid.*, 8, citing D. Cass, 'The "Constitutionalization of International Trade Law": Judicial Norm-Generation as the Engine of Constitutional Development in International Trade', EJIL 12 (2001): 39, at 59.
25. A. Watson, *Legal Transplants: An Approach to Comparative Law* (Edinburgh: Scottish Academic Press, 1974).

a discipline both limited and abused.[26] To gain the benefits of comparative law, one must be aware of both its methods and limits.[27]

It may well be that domestic constitutional rules can be transplanted into WTO law. Cass argues that '[c]onstitutional law rules, principles and doctrines are being borrowed from other constitutional domains . . . thereby leading to a closer resemblance between international trade law and constitutional law'.[28] Many of the technical problems of constitutional judicial review and international challenges to legislation are the same, at least at a broad conceptual level. Furthermore, it is impossible for international lawyers to set aside their background training in domestic constitutional law and develop new principles for the WTO from a blank page. The principles of WTO law inevitably build on a framework of the public law of the WTO members. However, it is not the purpose of this book to examine the practicalities of transplantation. To do so would require a full comparative study of challenges to legislation in WTO law and domestic constitutional law.

Rather, this book is restricted merely to using domestic constitutional law as a source of contrast and new ideas, rather than as an attempt at legal transplantation. The ideas and analysis of domestic constitutional courts provide useful points of reference for examining WTO practices. An issue in WTO challenges to legislation is likely to have arisen in a different form in domestic constitutional litigation, and domestic courts may have analysed and described the issue in a sophisticated way. This analysis may not be transplantable, but it is certainly food for thought about WTO doctrine.

Inevitably, this method may result in a degree of eclecticism – a contradiction of the basic inductive method described above. However, if one keeps in mind the limited role of domestic constitutional comparisons, this is not a major problem. It is better to gain the insights offered by these comparisons than to exclude them in zealous pursuit of an inductive method. Indeed, legal methods cannot be purely inductive; one still requires inspirations, models of thought, and sources of new ideas. Domestic constitutional law is a valuable way of giving this essential background to an inductive approach to examining international challenges to legislation.

---

26. O. Kahn-Freund, 'On Uses and Abuses of Comparative Law', MLR 37 (1974): 1.
27. If there is anything like a standard text on the methods of comparative law, it is that written by Zweigert & Kötz, above n. 7. It has been described as 'the most authoritative discussion of its kind': J. Merryman, *The Loneliness of the Comparative Lawyer* (The Hague: Kluwer, 1999), 483, fn. 12. According to Zweigert & Kötz (p. 34), the 'basic methodological principle of all comparative law is that of *functionality*'. According to *the principle of functionality*, one must not examine issues by reference to one's own legal system (or any particular legal system), but rather by reference to functions. The principle of functionality has positive and negative aspects. In its negative aspect, the principle tells the comparative lawyer to 'eradicate the pre-conceptions of his native legal system'; in its positive aspect, the principle tells the lawyer to look for aspects of foreign legal systems 'to find the analogue to the solution which interests him' (p. 35). This principle is based on the hypothesis that every society faces essentially the same problems, although they may solve these problems in different ways (but often with similar results) (p. 34). As to the actual process of comparison, Zweigert and Kötz recommend a basically inductive approach (pp. 43–46).
28. Cass, above n. 24, 51.

1.4.2. Terminology

Describing a system as complex as challenges to legislation in the WTO is bound to create risks of confusing terminology. It is probably impossible to use terms that are simultaneously readable and entirely accurate. The terminology used in this book attempts to strike a medium between readability and accuracy. What follows here is an examination of the most important of these terms used in this book.

The nature of legislation poses some difficulties with terminology. The word *legislation* itself is problematic, as there are many kinds of legislative rules in the world.[29] Some forms of rules – such as policy statements, parliamentary explanatory materials, and so on – are not, strictly speaking, legislation. This book uses the term *legislation* in a broader sense, to cover all rules of general application with legal effect. Similarly, the term *legislature* is used in a broad sense, covering all authorities that issue 'legislation'. Admittedly, in some cases, this description is not ideal. For example, it may be stretching language to describe an administrator issuing policy guidelines as a 'legislature' issuing 'legislation'. Nevertheless, this is not a significant problem if one keeps in mind the special sense in which these terms are used. As all forms of abstract rules, applicable to general situations in the future, share common characteristics, it is helpful to group them together with a label – such as *legislation.*

The WTO dispute resolution system has a number of unique characteristics that are reflected in a unique jargon. The system is composed of Panels and the Appellate Body, rather than of courts per se. Nevertheless, the Appellate Body is very similar to a court, with a standing membership including outstanding jurists. Panels are more like arbitrators, appointed on an ad hoc basis, but nevertheless, they use legal methods in making decisions. For this reason, the term *WTO tribunal* is used for both Panels and the Appellate Body. While WTO specialists use the term *dispute resolution* to describe the process of these bodies, this book sometimes employs the term *WTO litigation*, as this can give a truer flavour of the nature of proceedings. The parties to such proceedings are, strictly speaking, WTO members; a WTO member need not be a State.[30] However, this book often uses the less-accurate term *State*. This allows clearer comparisons with general international law, in which the defending party in an action is almost always a State.

This book also generally avoids technical terms for the nature of litigation, preferring instead to refer to *challenges* to legislation. The term *challenge to legislation* is a useful umbrella concept that can be applied to the WTO as well as to most other forms of international review of legislation.

29. See Section 2.2.
30. The leading example of which is the European Communities.

1.5. THE STRUCTURE OF THIS BOOK

Chapter 2 of this book sets out a broad context for describing challenges to legislation. It discusses the nature of legislation and some general concepts of public international law that relate to challenges to legislation. The chapter notes the varieties of legislation in the world. More importantly, it discusses the concept of the 'legislative environment', which covers the web of domestic laws and practices that affect the operation of legislation. The chapter also discusses the application of the inter-temporal principle to domestic legislature, as well as the relevance of certain principles of State responsibility.

The remainder of the book is dedicated to the issue of deference in international challenges to legislation. Chapter 3 discusses the notion of deference in tribunal procedures, while Chapters 4–8 discuss the notion of deference in substantive decision-making by international tribunals. It will be apparent that the second kind of deference is of particular importance.

Chapter 3 examines the ways in which procedural deference has gradually been eroded in WTO challenges to legislation. We will see here that WTO tribunals are less able to express deference in procedural matters than are other international tribunals. This diverts pressures for deference into issues of substance and heightens the importance of substantive deference.

Chapter 4 then analyses the increasingly important question of substantive deference. It begins with basic matters concerning the judicial method: fact-finding and the making of inferences from raw facts. Deference governs the way in which both matters are dealt with by tribunals. The chapter then considers the ways in which public international law in particular has regulated the degree of substantive deference in international litigation. First, it examines how international obligations contain within themselves notions of deference. Second, it considers traditional notions of deference, such as the reserved domain of domestic jurisdiction and the margin of appreciation. Finally, it describes the notion of deference in the WTO known as the 'standard of review'.

The book then turns to the issue of characterization of legislation and how the manner of characterization affects the degree of deference in challenges to legislation. This is the bulk of the book. Chapter 5 provides a general discussion of characterization and serves as an introduction to the detailed discussion in the next three chapters, which concern factor characterization (Chapter 6), proportionality characterization (Chapter 7), and certainty characterization (Chapter 8). It is in these chapters that the most important aspects of deference in modern challenges to legislation are described by reference to a large volume of WTO case law. Chapter 9 provides some concluding comments.

Chapter 2

The Nature of Legislation

2.1. INTRODUCTION

Why is a challenge to legislation different from a challenge to another measure, such as an administrative decision? One explanation is that the nature of legislation is special: legislation is different from other forms of State activity. To understand challenges to legislation, one needs to understand some basics about the nature of legislation.

It would be too ambitious for this book to survey the nature of legislation in detail. Instead, this chapter identifies some unique features of legislation and points out consequences of these features for challenges to legislation. As a preliminary matter, the chapter defines the concept of legislation as used in this book. We will see that legislation exists in many forms and that we cannot assume that it is democratic in nature, nor that it occupies a particular place in the domestic legal hierarchy. Instead, the common characteristic of legislative rules is that they usually deal with abstract, generally applicable matters.

This is the characteristic that makes challenges to legislation special: the challenge is to an abstract rule, not to a real-world action, and to a range of possible outcomes, not to a particular outcome.

Next, this chapter examines the important feature of legislation that I call the legislative environment. This term includes the clusters of legal norms surrounding and affecting particular legislation, such as legal doctrine and administrative practices. The legislative environment is often crucial to the outcome of challenges to legislation because it alters the operation of the legislation. In many cases, the legislative environment is so important that one cannot understand the real nature of challenged legislation unless one takes the legislative environment into account.

Third, this chapter looks at the temporal aspects of legislation. Legislation exists over a period of time; it does not happen in just one instant. Indeed, it is the temporal aspect of legislation that makes it different from an administrative action: while administrative acts are usually completed within a short period, legislative acts have an ongoing character. During the period in which legislation exists, surrounding legal factors – such as the content of international obligations – can change. This ongoing existence of legislation, as well as its interaction with what international lawyers call the 'inter-temporal principle', has several procedural and substantive consequences in international challenges to legislation.

These three matters have important consequences for the discussion of challenges to legislation in the rest of this book. In Chapter 3, which deals with procedural deference, we will see that the legislative environment and temporal aspects of legislation need to be taken into account in determining jurisdiction and remedies in challenges to legislation. The remaining chapters of the book, which deal with substantive deference, also build on the themes discussed in this chapter. In particular, the discussion of certainty characterization in Chapter 8 depends heavily on the nature of the legislative environment. Thus, the matters discussed in this chapter are basic concepts on which later chapters in this book are built.

2.2. THE TYPES OF LEGISLATION

The concept of 'legislation' covers a variety of instruments in the public law hierarchy. Most commonly, *legislation* refers to rules passed directly by the parliament or primary legislature of a State; namely, statutes. It would be misleading, however, to view statutes as the only kind of legislation. For the purposes of analysing international law challenges to legislation, one needs to take into account many other kinds of instruments.

These other instruments include subordinate legislation, such as regulations, rules, by-laws, and determinations. However, in many cases, a handbook, a manual, or a set of guidelines provides the vital rule affecting a situation or a person's rights. In a practical sense, therefore, one can also describe administrative statements as 'legislation'. In other cases, it is a *practice* that is the vital factor. In particular, the practice of domestic courts in interpreting legislation may be crucial. Legislation is often ambiguous, and this ambiguity is often resolved only through the decisions of the courts.

One can go further here. At one end of the spectrum, an unwritten rule may be the vital factor in the legal process. A custom, or a particular way of doing things, might have exactly the same effect as a written regulation or body of case law. At the other end of the spectrum, one could even view a constitution as legislation. This may be particularly apt if the constitution can be modified by an ordinary statute. There have been several (sometimes successful) international law challenges to constitutional provisions.[1] However, the relatively static nature of most

1. Several States have changed their constitutions to make them consistent with international treaties. For example, Germany changed its constitutional rules on military service to make

constitutions and their unique political significance make it difficult to include them as 'legislation' for the purposes of this book.

One obvious point needs to be made here: different kinds of legislation play different roles in different States. What is achieved by a statute in one State may be achieved by subordinate legislation in another State, and by administrative guidelines in yet another State. It is therefore dangerous to assume that the instrument's rank in the legal hierarchy is particularly significant in challenges to legislation. However, that rank is not irrelevant. In certainty characterization, as we will see, a high rank may give a rule a more certain operation, and therefore better protect it from challenge.[2]

The variety of legislation can sometimes make it difficult to generalize about international challenges to legislation. The greater the variety of instruments classified as legislation, the more difficult it becomes to make accurate generalizations about them. One should never lose sight of the fact that a challenge to, for example, a statute, often has a different flavour than a challenge to, for example, an administrative guideline. More importantly, legislation has a different political significance in different States. In democratic States, statutes are usually the direct expression of an elected legislature, and therefore, an indirect expression of the people. Even subordinate rules in democracies take on at least some of the democratic flavour of their empowering statutes. In some authoritarian States, statutes and other legislation may not have this democratic quality. These differences have important consequences in international challenges to legislation. For example, it is usually easier to change a regulation than a statute, and it is often easier to change legislation in an authoritarian State than in a democratic State.

Nevertheless, the variety of legislation should not be a fatal objection to the study of challenges to legislation. All kinds of legislation have features in common, stemming from their abstract, generally applicable nature (see **Box 1** for a discussion of this requirement in WTO law). These common features allow generalization across all fields of legislation. Such features, as will be discussed next, include a surrounding legislative environment and unique temporal characteristics.

Box 1. Which 'Legislative' Measures Can Be Challenged in WTO Proceedings?

In WTO litigation, it is necessary to identify a 'measure' at issue.[3] It is clear that 'acts setting forth rules or norms that are intended to have general and prospective application' are such measures, and can be challenged.[4] This means that most instruments commonly considered as 'legislation' can be covered, such as statutes and regulations.

---

them consistent with the Convention on the Elimination of All Forms of Discrimination against Women, 18 Dec. 1979, [1983] *ATS* 9 (see *BGBl.* 2000 I, 1822).

2. See Section 8.2, text at n. 34.
3. Article 3.3 DSU.
4. Appellate Body Report, *US – Corrosion-Resistant Steel Sunset* Review, para. 82.

Questions may arise if the measure is not a 'rule or norm', for example, when it is an administrative statement. A good example is the US Sunset Policy Bulletin (SPB).[5] This instrument gives 'guidance' to administrators conducting sunset review of anti-dumping measures. The Appellate Body has confirmed that it is subject to WTO challenge:

> In our view, the SPB has normative value, as it provides administrative guidance and creates expectations among the public and among private actors. It is intended to have general application, as it is to apply to all the sunset reviews conducted in the United States. It is also intended to have prospective application, as it is intended to apply to sunset reviews taking place after its issuance.[6]

Thus, 'normative value' appears to be the key requirement for challengeable legislation, which can be indicated by the creation of public expectations, and by general and prospective application. In *US – Zeroing* (*EC*), the Appellate Body set out three particular requirements for the challenging party, all of which require a high standard of supporting evidence. It held that the measure must

- be 'attributable' to the legislating Member;
- have a precise content; and
- have a general and prospective application.[7]

The 'precise content' of the measure seems to be a requirement of ascertainability. Even unwritten measures can have a precise content, although particular rigour is required in finding that this is the case. An abstract

5. Policies Regarding the Conduct of Five-year ('Sunset') Reviews of Anti-Dumping and Countervailing Duty Orders, *United States Federal Register*, vol. 63, no. 73 (16 Apr. 1998), 18871.
6. Appellate Body Report, *US – Oil Country Tubular Goods Sunset Review,* para. 187 [footnote omitted]. In *US – Corrosion-Resistant Steel Sunset Review,* The Appellate Body said (at fn. 87):

> We observe that the scope of each element in the phrase 'laws, regulations and administrative procedures' [in Article 18.4 Anti-Dumping Agreement] must be determined for purposes of WTO law and not simply by reference to the label given to various instruments under the domestic law of each WTO Member. This determination must be based on the content and substance of the instrument, and not merely on its form or nomenclature. Otherwise, the obligations set forth in Article 18.4 would vary from Member to Member depending on each Member's domestic law and practice.

7. Appellate Body Report, *US – Zeroing* (*EC*), para. 198:

> [W]hen bringing a challenge against such a 'rule or norm' that constitutes a measure of general and prospective application, a complaining party must clearly establish, through arguments and supporting evidence, at least that the alleged 'rule or norm' is attributable to the responding Member; its precise content; and indeed, that it does have general and prospective application. It is only if the complaining party meets this high threshold, and puts forward sufficient evidence with respect to each of these elements, that a panel would be in a position to find that the 'rule or norm' may be challenged, as such. This evidence may include proof of the systematic application of the challenged 'rule or norm'.

See also Panel Report, *US – Export Restraints*, para. 8.85.

principle, however, seems unlikely to be challengeable.[8] The Appellate Body has yet to rule on whether practices can in themselves be challenged.[9]

2.3. THE LEGISLATIVE ENVIRONMENT

Legislation does not exist in a vacuum. Rather, it should be seen as part of a larger regulatory environment, consisting of other legislation (whether at a higher, similar, or lower level in the legal hierarchy) and other legal acts (such as court decisions). This is the legislative environment.

A legislative provision needs to be seen in light of provisions above it in the legal hierarchy. Taking the example of a challenged statute, the provisions above it can include constitutional rules, or similar rules of law.[10] Imagine that an international tribunal is reviewing an allegedly arbitrary statute. The tribunal may find that the arbitrariness is cured by constitutional rules obliging the statute to be interpreted in a sufficiently certain manner. Clearly, the tribunal will need to take account of such constitutional rules.

The legislative environment also includes norms at the same level in the legal hierarchy as the challenged legislation. For example, a provision in a statute needs to be seen in light of other provisions in the statute. A wider aspect of the legislative environment is the entire corpus of legislation of the State. A statute needs to be seen in the context of its companion statutes, a regulation needs to be seen in the context of other regulations, and practice needs to be seen in the context of other practices. Some norms in the legislative environment are particularly important, as they affect all other legislation. For example, general statutes regulating domestic judicial and administrative review may cure the arbitrariness of particular legislation.

A legislative provision also needs to be seen in light of provisions below it in the legal hierarchy. Consider again a statute, which is, on its face, inconsistent with an international obligation. Here, subordinate legislation may cure that inconsistency by resolving ambiguities in the statute or providing detailed rules consistent with the international obligation. In other cases, the statute may be consistent on its face with an international obligation but may nevertheless violate that obligation because the surrounding legislative environment at a lower level alters the effect of the statute in practice. A statute that appears flawed on its face can be improved by subordinate legislation. A statute that looks good on paper can also be tainted by its subordinate legislation. Thus, the effects of sub-regulations, administrative guidelines, and practice can be decisive factors in challenges to legislation, especially when they are a *concretization* of an abstract legislative rule.

If the legislating State has a federal structure, matters become more complicated. The challenged legislation may be influenced by the legislation of other parts of the

8. Appellate Body Report, *US – Zeroing (EC)*, para. 198.
9. Appellate Body Report, *US – Oil Country Tubular Goods Sunset* Review, para. 220; Appellate Body Report, *US – Gambling*, para. 132. Some Panel Reports seem to indicate that practices might be challengeable: Panel Report, *US – Zeroing (EC)*, para. 7.96; Panel Report, *Turkey – Rice*, para. 7.87.
10. In some States, the operation of customary rules (e.g., common law) may be an important check on the operation of statutes.

federation. For example, the legislation at the level of central government may set out broad principles of regulation, which are concretized by more detailed regional legislation. Similarly, legislation at the level of regional government may be limited by the operation of federal legislation. In such cases, the international tribunal carrying out the review needs to look at the federal and regional legislative structure as a whole.

A final complication arises if the legislating State is part of a supranational organization (or – in the case of the European Union (EU) – is a supranational organization itself).[11] For example, in a challenge to legislation of an EU Member State, it will be important to examine relevant EU legislation. This legislation could be 'primary law' (i.e., treaty provisions, roughly equivalent to constitutional provisions) or 'secondary law' (i.e., Regulations, Directives, etc.). In addition, supranational administrative acts may be relevant to the review, in the same way as are domestic administrative acts.

We can now draw all of these aspects of the legislative environment into an illustrative example. I have deliberately chosen the most complicated situation of all, involving a federation embedded within a supranational organization. This example represents the kind of legislative environment that could arise in States such as Germany, Austria, or Belgium. In the example in Table 2.1, the challenged legislation is a domestic federal statute.

Table 2.1. The Legislative Environment for a Statute of a Federation Embedded within a Supranational Organization

<table>
<tr><td rowspan="3">Supranational Level</td><td colspan="2">Constituent Treaties</td></tr>
<tr><td colspan="2">Relevant Regulations and Directives</td></tr>
<tr><td colspan="2">Administrative acts</td></tr>
<tr><td rowspan="3">Domestic Level – Central Government</td><td>Statute under challenge</td><td>Other relevant statutes</td></tr>
<tr><td>Subordinate legislation</td><td>Subordinate legislation under other relevant statutes</td></tr>
<tr><td>Administrative practice</td><td>Administrative practice under other relevant statutes</td></tr>
<tr><td rowspan="3">Domestic Level – Regional Government</td><td colspan="2">Statutes</td></tr>
<tr><td colspan="2">Subordinate legislation</td></tr>
<tr><td colspan="2">Administrative practice</td></tr>
</table>

11. The same issue may arise in other guises elsewhere. For example, when one State is managing the affairs of another State, the legislation of the managing State may be relevant to a review of the legislation of the managed State.

In most cases, the legislative environment is not this complicated. However, even in simpler cases, the legislative environment is likely to have a major impact on the outcome of a challenge to the legislation.[12]

This impact can be felt in several ways. These relate to jurisdiction, remedy, and substance.

First, jurisdictional issues may emerge. The challenge may be framed generally, covering several elements of the legislative environment simultaneously (e.g., statute, regulations and administrative practices). Here, the tribunal may be able to define its own jurisdiction in the complaint by focusing on the particular element it finds most convenient. Alternatively, the complaint may be framed precisely against one of the elements in the legislative environment. Here, the tribunal may be able to decline jurisdiction on the basis that the correct challenge was to a different element. Historically, this has been the basis of findings that a statute could not be challenged until it had been implemented: that is, that the correct element for challenge was administrative practice, not the statute on its face. As we shall see, however, in the WTO, there is very little of this freedom for the tribunal to define or decline jurisdiction.[13]

Second, the legislative environment may influence remedies. When legislation on its face has been challenged successfully, the remedy may be not to change the legislation, but rather to change its legislative environment. For example, a statute may be rendered consistent with international law by the issuance of new subordinate legislation, or by the creation of a new administrative practice. The legislative environment could also be changed at a higher level, such as by changing constitutional practice or by issuing new supranational directives.

Third, the legislative environment may influence the course of certainty characterization.[14] If the challenge focuses on the certainty with which legislation conforms to an international obligation, the crucial issue is the legal operation of the legislation. This operation depends heavily on the legislative environment. In some cases, the legislative environment will supply the required certainty. For example, a statute on its face lacking sufficient certainty in complying with an international obligation may be given that certainty by constitutional doctrine, other statutes of general application, administrative law, subordinate legislation, administrative practice, or court decisions. Of course, these elements of the

---

12. This has been expressly recognized by the Appellate Body. In *US – Carbon Steel*, it held that, to make an objective assessment of the meaning of legislation, it was important to look at the evidence provided by 'the consistent application of such laws, the pronouncements of domestic courts on the meaning of such laws, the opinions of legal experts and the writings of recognized scholars' (Appellate Body Report, *US – Carbon Steel*, para. 157). In *Dominican Republic – Import and Sale of Cigarettes*, the Appellate Body rejected the view that the challenged legislation itself was the only relevant matter, and held instead that Panels may weigh and balance aspects of the legislative environment (Appellate Body Report, *Dominican Republic – Import and Sale of Cigarettes*, para. 112).
13. See Section 3.2, text at n. 22.
14. See Ch. 8.

legislative environment may sometimes work in the opposite way, creating confusion in a statute that is otherwise clear on its face. This confusion may in itself be the basis of a successful challenge to the legislation.

However, the legislative environment is noticeably less relevant to factor characterization[15] and proportionality characterization.[16] In these types of challenges, the exact operation of the legislation is rarely at issue. Therefore, the influence of the legislative environment on that operation is rarely relevant. In factor characterization, the challenge focuses on the legislation's legal and practical operation, and on its purpose (with varying degrees of emphasis). However, the legislative environment does not impinge here – if it is of relevance, the dispute moves into the realm of certainty characterization instead. However, the issue of the legislative environment can sometimes be at issue in proportionality characterization, where the challenge focuses on the proportionality of the legislation in achieving its purpose. For example, the legislative environment may create an operation of the challenged legislation clearly disproportionate to its purpose, when that operation is not apparent from the legislation on its face. However, this is a rare example: most often, the litigating parties in a proportionality characterization challenge agree on the legal operation of the legislation.

2.4. THE TEMPORAL ASPECT OF LEGISLATION

Legislation has a special relationship to time. It does not happen at a particular point in time, but rather exists over a period of time as a continuing and ongoing event. This distinguishes it from other forms of State action that do happen at a particular time, or over a very short period.

International law is familiar with the concept of State conduct occurring over time periods. To use the terminology of State responsibility,[17] legislation represents a continuing act. A breach of an international obligation arising from legislation may itself have a continuing character, for example, a breach arising from an act that extends over a period of time and that continues while that act remains inconsistent with the relevant international obligation.[18] In the context of challenges to

15. See Ch. 6.
16. See Ch. 7.
17. International Law Commission, 'Draft Articles and Commentaries on Responsibility of States for Internationally Wrongful Acts', *Report of the International Law Commission*, 53rd session (A/56/10) (2001), Commentary to Art. 14; see also R. Ago, 'Fifth Report on State Responsibility', Doc. A/CN.4/291, in *Yearbook of the International Law Commission*, vol. 2, Part 1 (1976), 21–24, paras 61–71 and N. Gallus, 'Recent BIT Decisions and Composite Acts Straddling the Date a Treaty Comes into Force', ICLQ 56 (2007): 491.
18. International Law Commission, above n. 17, Commentary to Art. 14, para. 7. The intellectual heritage of this concept can be traced as least as far back as Triepel, with his concept of *Dauerdelikt* (H. Triepel, *Völkerrecht und Landesrecht* (Leipzig: Hirschfeld, 1899), 289, acknowledged in International Law Commission, above n. 17, Commentary to Art. 14, para. 7).

legislation, the continuing nature of such a breach can sometimes raise tricky issues. As we will see shortly, such issues arise when the relevant international obligation arises or changes during the period of the breach, or when an international tribunal gains jurisdiction relating to the obligation during this period.[19]

Furthermore, legislation can be seen as a complex act, made up of the combination of several simple actions extending over a period of time. Merely maintaining legislation in force over a period of time is one of these actions. The 'complex' act includes other actions during that period (i.e., those actions that form the legislative environment).[20] The theory of the complex act has two important implications for the treatment of legislation under the doctrines of State responsibility. First, a breach cannot occur until the conclusion of the 'simple' act. A series of simple acts without this final concluding simple act would be merely preparatory action, and would not be a breach in itself.[21] This could mean, depending of the international obligation and the legislation in question, that mere existence of legislation might be unchallengeable. This is the basis of the common argument that any inconsistencies with international law will be

---

The final Draft Articles on State Responsibility provide:

Article 14 – Extension in Time of the Breach of an International Obligation

1. The breach of an international obligation by an act of a State not having a continuing character occurs at the moment when the act is performed, even if its effects continue.
2. The breach of an international obligation by an act of a State having a continuing character extends over the entire period during which the act continues and remains not in conformity with the international obligation.
3. The breach of an international obligation requiring a State to prevent a given event occurs when the event occurs and extends over the entire period during which the event continues and remains not in conformity with that obligation.

Article 15 – Breach Consisting of a Composite Act

1. The breach of an international obligation by a State through a series of actions or omissions defined in aggregate as wrongful, occurs when the action or omission occurs which, taken with the other actions or omissions, is sufficient to constitute the wrongful act.
2. In such a case, the breach extends over the entire period starting with the first of the actions or omissions of the series and lasts for as long as these actions or omissions are repeated and remain not in conformity with the international obligation.

19. J. Pauwelyn, 'The Concept of a "Continuing Violation" of an International Obligation: Selected Problems', BYIL 66 (1995): 415, 430, at 440–447.
20. Perhaps less arguable is the view that the complex act includes actions that occurred before the legislation came into force (such as the legislative procedure that gave rise to the legislation). Normally, the circulation of draft legislation is not inconsistent with international law (see R. Jennings & A. Watts (eds), *Oppenheim's International Law*, 9th edn (Essex: Longman's, 1992), 86, fn. 16). However, it is possible to imagine an international obligation to refrain from the 'threat' of legislating – which could theoretically cover the introduction of draft legislation into a legislature. It may also be arguable that the complex act includes actions occurring after legislation ceases to be in operation.
21. International Law Commission, above n. 17, Commentary to Art. 14, para. 13.

prevented by the legislative environment.[22] Second, the complex act theory has important implications for the rule of exhaustion of local remedies. If one believes that this rule is constitutive of breach, rather than procedural,[23] the complex act theory suggests that legislation will not breach international law until it has been interpreted by the highest courts of the State. Such judicial interpretation, if inconsistent with the relevant international obligation, would be the final 'simple' act, combining with the passage and initial implementation of legislation, to constitute a breach of the international obligation.

Another feature of the temporal character of legislation relates to the legal relationships created by the legislation. Such relationships may concern the creation of property rights, a legal status such as citizenship or refugee status, or a myriad of other juridical facts. Such juridical facts generally have a continuing character. A juridical fact can also become disengaged from the legislation that created it. For example, legislation may cease to be in operation, but the juridical facts that it created may continue in existence. As we will see shortly,[24] these matters are dealt with in public international law under the inter-temporal principle.

The temporal aspect of legislation gives rise to two kinds of procedural issues in challenges to legislation:

- jurisdictional issues – when the legislation was in force before the international obligation came into existence;
- issues of remedy – when the past implementation of the legislation creates ongoing legal relationships even after the repeal of the legislation.

These issues arise most often in two scenarios. First, and most commonly, legislation may be enacted before the time an international obligation came into existence, but continue in existence after that time. Second, legislation may be enacted and repealed before the international obligation came into existence, but juridical facts arising out of the legislation nevertheless continue in existence. These scenarios are represented graphically in Figures 2.1 and 2.2.

---

22. See generally Ch. 8 of this book and R. Ago, 'Sixth Report on State Responsibility', Doc. A/CN.4/302, in *Yearbook of the International Law Commission*, vol. 2, Part 1 (1977), 6, para. 7. Of course, some obligations of conduct could preclude this administrative practice argument. For example, Ago noted Art. 2(1)(c) CERD (International Convention on the Elimination of All Forms of Racial Discrimination, *UNTS*, vol. 660, 195), which requires the amendment or repeal of certain laws. He suggested (at 6, para. 7) that the Article would be breached by failing to amend or repeal such laws, 'even if they actually never would have been or no longer could be applied'.
23. For a discussion of this issue, see Ago, above n. 22, 20–43, paras 47–112; International Law Commission, Report of the International Law Commission, 54th session, A/57/10 (2002), 131–136, paras 150–172.
24. See Section 2.4.1.

Figure 2.1. International Obligations and Pre-existing Continuing Legislation

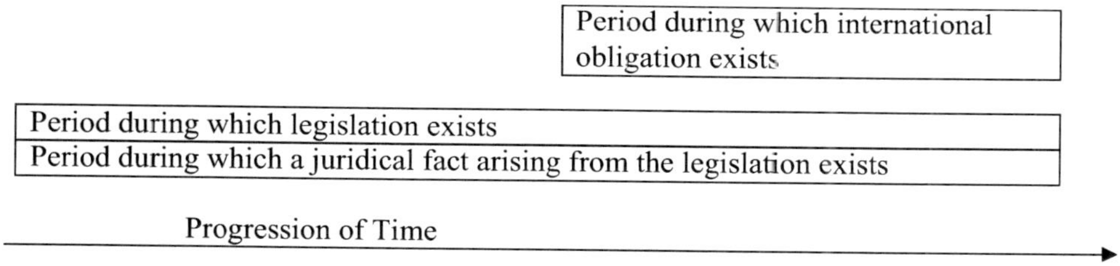

(Here the legislation and juridical facts arising from it pre-date the international obligation and continue in existence after the international obligation comes into force.)

Figure 2.2. International Obligations and Pre-existing Repealed Legislation

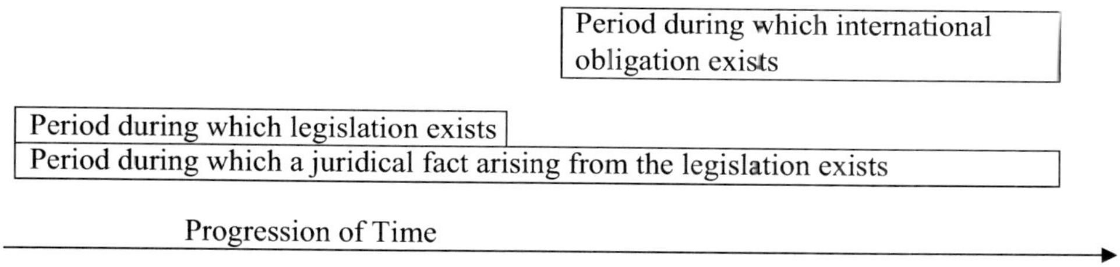

(Here the legislation and juridical facts arising from it pre-date the international obligation. However, the legislation has been repealed before the international obligation comes into force, and the juridical facts arising from the legislation continue to exist after that repeal.)

The issues arising from these scenarios are of great practical importance when international obligations are undergoing a process of reform. The changes brought about to GATT rules by the Uruguay Round, for example, created a host of temporal issues before WTO tribunals.[25] The changes flowing from the Doha Round are likely to raise these issues again. In particular, one is likely to see issues arise about the status of legislation that is inconsistent, but pre-dates, the Doha Round reforms.

Before examining WTO law in this respect, some discussion is needed about the basic rule of time in international law, namely, the inter-temporal principle.

25. For example, Appellate Body Report, *Brazil – Desiccated Coconut*, paras 179–180; Appellate Body Report, *Canada – Term of Patent Protection*, paras 71–72; Appellate Body Report, *EC – Hormones*, para. 128; Appellate Body Report, *EC – Sardines*, paras 196–216.

2.4.1. The Inter-temporal Principle

According to general principles of international law, States are not responsible for acts that are completed *before* the creation of inconsistent international obligations. Thus, Article 13 of the International Law Commission's Draft Articles on State Responsibility provides the following:

> An act of a State does not constitute a breach of an international obligation unless the State is bound by the obligation in question at the time the act occurs.[26]

Similarly, Article 28 of the Vienna Convention on the Law of Treaties (VCLT)[27] provides the following:

> Absent a contrary intention, a treaty cannot apply to acts or facts which took place, or situations which ceased to exist, before the date of its entry into force.

International law thus recognizes the principle of criminal law that an act can be punished only under law applicable at the time of the act (*nulla poena sine lege*).[28] These rules are particular expressions of the general principle of inter-temporal law.[29]

The standard statement of the inter-temporal principle is that of Judge Huber in the *Island of Palmas* case.[30] He said:

> A juridical fact must be appreciated in the light of the law contemporary with it, and not of the law in force at the time when a dispute in regard to it arises or falls to be settled.[31]

In the context of challenges to legislation, the 'juridical fact' may be the legislation itself, or an independent juridical fact arising out of the operation of the legislation. In all cases, the timing of the juridical fact is critical.

Judge Huber also drew a distinction between the creation of rights and the existence of rights. He noted that 'The existence of the right, in other words, its continued manifestation, shall follow the conditions required by the evolution of the law.'[32] One view of this distinction is that the creation of a juridical fact 'must be appreciated in the light of the [international] law contemporary with it', but that the maintenance of that fact can be affected by later developments in international law.

---

26. International Law Commission, above n. *17*.
27. *Vienna Convention on the Law of Treaties* (Vienna, 23 May 1969, 1155 UNTS 331; 8 International Legal Materials 679).
28. R. Higgins, 'Time and the Law: International Perspectives on an Old Problem', ICLQ 46 (1997): 501, at 507.
29. On the inter-temporal principle, see International Law Commission, above n. 17, Commentary to Art. 13 and literature cited therein.
30. (1949) II UNRIAA 829.
31. *Ibid.*, 845.
32. *Ibid.*

This has serious consequences for challenges to legislation when the legislation (or another juridical fact arising from the legislation) pre-dates the international obligation. The maintenance of the juridical fact may need to 'follow the conditions required by the evolution of the law', that is, be consistent with the international obligation.[33] The key point here is that the initial creation of the legislation or other juridical fact did not conflict with the international obligation when it first came into existence. However, does the later creation of the international obligation create such a conflict? Both WTO tribunals[34] and other international tribunals[35] have often dealt with this issue.

Here, the juridical fact of the creation of the legislation or other juridical fact must, in Judge Huber's words 'be appreciated in the light of the law contemporary with it'. As no relevant international obligation existed at that time, the creation of the legislation was consistent with international law. However, the situation is different when we move forward to the time when the international obligation was created. Applying Judge Huber's principle, we could conclude that the ongoing existence of the legislation is inconsistent with international law. This is consistent with a literal view of Judge Huber's distinction between 'the creation of rights' and the 'existence of rights', and with his statement that 'The existence of the right, in other words, its continued manifestation, shall follow the conditions required by the evolution of the law.'[36]

It may be dangerous, however, to take Judge Huber's distinction too literally. Doing so may jeopardize legal certainty by not meeting expectations of the validity of juridical facts created before the creation of an international obligation. Some argue that the inter-temporal principle does *not* allow a legal situation to lose its 'lawful' status if the ongoing existence of the situation later becomes inconsistent with international law.[37] For example, Higgins argues that Huber's formulation of the inter-temporal principle was closely linked to the facts of the *Island of Palmas*

---

33. As the International Law Commission, above n. 17, Commentary to Art. 14, para. 11 points out, an analogy can be made here to the view of the UN Human Rights Committee report in *Lovelace v. Canada* (Communication No. R.6/24, U.N. Doc. Supp. No. 40 (A/36/40) at 166 (1981). There, the complainant's marriage in 1970 resulted in her losing status as a registered member of an Indian group. Canada accepted the Committee's jurisdiction only in 1976. The Committee acknowledged that it was not competent to examine allegations relating to events that took place before 1976. However, the Committee recognized (at para. 11) that:

    > [T]he situation may be different if the alleged violations, although relating to events occurring before 19 August 1976, continue, *or* have effects which themselves constitute violations, after that date.

34. Appellate Body Report, *Brazil – Desiccated Coconut*, 15; Appellate Body Report, *Canada – Patent Term*, paras 71–72; Appellate Body Report, *EC – Hormones*, para. 128.
35. For example, the ECtHR in *Marckx v. Belgium* (1979) ECHR, Series A, No. 31. See also the UN Human Rights Committee in *Gueye v. France*, Communication No. 196/1985, U.N. Doc. CCPR/C/35/D/196/1985 (1989).
36. (1949) II UNRIAA 829, 845.
37. Higgins, above n. 28, 516.

case (i.e., the establishment and maintenance of territorial title).[38] Outside such situations, Huber's formulation may not always be applicable.

Nevertheless, there is something to be said for the view that the maintenance of legislation (or a situation arising from legislation) can be affected by later changes in international law. If pre-existing legislation or situations were sheltered from changes to international law, every new treaty would have to include special transitional provisions so as to affect pre-existing legislation or situations. If this were to happen, the reforming role of international law would be much reduced. Of course, some may argue that international law does not have much of a reforming role beyond implementing the exact agreements between States.

There is a middle view here, however. This view is based on the principle of res judicata; that is, the permanency of the authoritative fixing of a juridical fact, in particular, through a court decision.[39] This principle is itself a feature of the greater principle of legal certainty. Thus, if a juridical fact arising from legislation was fixed by a court before the creation of the international obligation, that juridical fact cannot later be held inconsistent with the obligation. However, the result is different if the circumstance on which the legislation operated to create the juridical fact was *not* declared as such by a court before the creation of the international obligation. If a court then purported to declare the juridical fact, based on the pre-existence of the circumstance, the declaration would be inconsistent with the international obligation. Thus, the criterion of this middle view is the existence of an authoritative judicial pronouncement of the validity of the relevant juridical fact.

The middle view has much to commend it, in terms of achieving legal certainty without hindering the effective development of international law. It is

---

38. *Ibid.*
39. The principle of res judicata was accepted and discussed by the ICJ in Application of the Convention on the Prevention and Punishment of the Crime of Genocide (*Bosnia and Herzegovina v. Serbia and Montenegro*), Judgment of 26 Feb. 2007, paras 114–120. At para. 116, it said:

    > Two purposes, one general, the other specific, underlie the principle of res judicata, internationally as nationally. First, the stability of legal relations requires that litigation come to an end. The Court's function, according to Article 38 of its Statute, is to 'decide', that is, to bring to an end, 'such disputes as are submitted to it'. Secondly, it is in the interest of each party that an issue which has already been adjudicated in favour of that party be not argued again. Article 60 of the Statute articulates this finality of judgments. Depriving a litigant of the benefit of a judgment it has already obtained must in general be seen as a breach of the principles governing the legal settlement of disputes.

    See also Appellate Body Report, *US – Shrimp* (*Article 21.5 – Malaysia*), para. 97, where the Appellate Body recognized that 'Appellate Body Reports that are adopted by the DSB . . . must be treated by the parties to a particular dispute as a final resolution to that dispute.' With respect to Panel Reports, the Appellate Body said in *EC – Bed Linen* (*Article 21.5 – India*), para. 93, that 'a panel finding which is not appealed, and which is included in a panel report adopted by the DSB, must be accepted by the parties as a final resolution to the dispute between them, in the same way and with the same finality as a finding included in an Appellate Body Report adopted by the DSB – with respect to the particular claim and the specific component of the measure that is the subject of the claim'.

broadly similar to the practice of domestic constitutional courts[40] in dealing with the consequences of declaring legislation to be unconstitutional. There appears to be a presumption that the ongoing maintenance of legislation after the creation of an international obligation is a breach of the obligation.[41] When the international obligation comes into force, the legislation must be changed if it is to conform to the obligation. Only pre-existing juridical facts arising from the legislation and declared as such by a court are protected from the new obligation.

Of course, these principles will be subject to the exact content of the international obligation. In some cases, the obligation may deal with prior legislation and juridical facts expressly. In other cases, the nature of the obligation may determine the issue.[42] As in all challenges to legislation, the features of the international obligation should be the focus.

It remains to be seen which of these approaches to the inter-temporal principle will be adopted generally in international challenges to legislation. As we will now see, the literal view mentioned above most closely reflects current practice in the WTO.

---

40. For example, this issue has been discussed in detail in German constitutional law. The Federal Constitutional Court has recognized that legislation may *become* unconstitutional some time after its creation, due to changed constitutional standards. This should not affect its valid legal operation at a time before it became unconstitutional. Nor should it affect the validity of court decisions prior to that time. However, it may affect a court decision made before that time that has not yet been enforced. The newly declared unconstitutionality of the legislation can bar the subsequent enforcement of a court decision validly made at a previous time: K. Schlaich & S. Korioth, *Das Bundesverfassungsgericht*, 7th edn (München: CH Beck, 2007), 224, para. 391; C. Pestalozza, *Verfassungsprozeßrecht*, 3rd edn (München: CH Beck, 1991), 276–280.
41. For WTO jurisprudence, see Appellate Body Report, *EC – Hormones*, para. 128; Appellate Body Report, *EC – Sardines*, para. 206. This is also the case under the ECHR. For example, in the *Marckx* case ((1979) ECHR, Series A, No. 31), Belgian legislation discriminating between marital and ex-marital children in inheritance matters pre-dated the entry into force of the ECHR for Belgium. Belgium argued that if the legislation were held inconsistent with the ECHR, the result would be 'to render many subsequent distributions of estates irregular and open to challenge before the courts' (para. 58). The ECtHR rejected this argument, noting that the principle of legal certainty would dispense the Belgian State from re-opening legal acts or situations prior to its judgment (para. 58). In other words, the *ongoing* maintenance of the legislation was inconsistent with the ECHR, but its original creation and prior application was not.

    This is also the case where the 'new' international obligation is really a new interpretation of an old obligation. This is best illustrated in the context of the ECHR. The ECtHR has clearly held that the ECHR is to be interpreted as a 'living instrument', 'in the light of present-day conditions' (*Tyrer v. United Kingdom* (1978) ECHR 2). If present-day conditions change, the legislative standards required by the ECHR may rise, and previously consistent legislation may be open to challenge. Here, the principle as expressed in *Marckx* should apply, that is, the ongoing existence of the legislation will be inconsistent with the ECHR, but only from the date on which the meaning of the ECHR changed.
42. In the WTO, the Appellate Body has been reluctant to rebut the presumption that the maintenance of pre-existing legislation can be inconsistent with a new obligation: Appellate Body Report, *EC – Hormones*, para. 128; Appellate Body Report, *EC – Sardines*, para. 206. In the former case, the Appellate Body said (at para. 128):

    > If the negotiators had wanted to exempt the very large group of SPS measures in existence on 1 January 1995 from the disciplines of provisions as important as Articles 5.1 and 5.5, it appears reasonable to us to expect that they would have said so explicitly.

2.4.2. The Inter-temporal Principle in WTO Challenges to Legislation

In general, WTO tribunals have applied Judge Huber's principle that 'The existence of the right, in other words, its continued manifestation, shall follow the conditions required by the evolution of the law.'[43] This principle has been applied by WTO tribunals to legislation as such. Thus, the ongoing maintenance of legislation that pre-dated the Uruguay Round agreements has been held to breach those agreements.[44] Also, the principle has been applied to situations arising from pre-existing legislation: WTO tribunals may examine a measure 'whose legislative basis has expired, but whose effects are alleged to be impairing the benefits accruing to the requesting Member under a covered agreement'.[45] In general, the alternative views about the operation of the inter-temporal principle mentioned earlier have failed to take hold in the WTO. Admittedly, it is too early to form a conclusive view on this matter. It may also be the case that the inter-temporal principle results in matters occurring prior to the entry into force of a treaty being given lesser weight as evidence.[46] Regardless of all these issues, the result in any given case will depend on special temporal rules (if any) in the relevant WTO obligation.

An example of such a special temporal rule was examined in the *Canada – Patent Term* case. Canadian legislation granted a term of patent protection for seventeen years from the date of granting of the patent.[47] Article 33 of the Agreement on Trade-Related Aspects of Intellectual Property Rights (TRIPS) requires a minimum period of twenty years from the date of filing the application for the patent. Canada appeared to agree that its legislation did not meet this requirement. However, Article 70.1 of TRIPS prevents relevant TRIPS obligations from applying to 'acts which occurred before the date of application of the Agreement'.[48] The challenged legislation only applied to patent applications filed before 1 October 1989, that is, before the commencement of TRIPS. In interpreting the word *acts,*

43. (1949) II UNRIAA 829, 845.
44. Appellate Body Report, *EC – Hormones*, para. 128. Under the old GATT system, this approach was subject to an express transitional rule that grandfathered pre-existing *mandatory* legislation (see S. Bhuiyan, 'Mandatory and Discretionary Legislation: The Continued Relevance of the Distinction under the WTO', JIEL 5 (2002): 571; Kwan Kiat Sim, 'Rethinking the Mandatory/ Discretionary Legislation Distinction in WTO Jurisprudence', *World Trade Review* 2 (2003): 33; Y. Naiki, 'The Mandatory Discretionary Doctrine in WTO Law: The *US – Section 301* Case and Its Aftermath', JIEL 7 (2004): 23. No such rule now exists in the WTO as a general proposition.
45. Appellate Body Report, *US – Upland Cotton*, para. 263.
46. See Gallus, above n. 17, in the context of bilateral investment treaties.
47. This seventeen-year period only applied in relation to patent applications made before 1 Oct. 1989. For later applications, a period of twenty years after the application date applied.
48. Article 70.1 of TRIPS provides:

> This Agreement does not give rise to obligations in respect of acts which occurred before the date of application of the Agreement for the Member in question.

the Appellate Body focused on the ongoing situation, not on what had taken place in the past:

> An 'act' is something that is 'done', and the use of the phrase 'acts which occurred' suggests that what was done is now complete or ended. This excludes situations, including existing rights and obligations, that have not ended.[49]

Thus, while the filing of the patents was protected from challenge, the ongoing results of such filing under the legislation could be challenged. This is broadly consistent with the general principle that pre-WTO legislation can be attacked through challenging the character of the ongoing juridical facts resulting from the legislation.[50]

The inter-temporal principle is particularly relevant in WTO challenges to legislation when the legislation has been repealed before the challenge gets underway. In general, WTO tribunals have refused to hear such challenges on the basis that the issue is moot.[51] However, they have sometimes examined repealed legislation to assist an analysis of ongoing measures, for example, by clarifying the operation of the ongoing measures.[52] In any case, some WTO obligations may require an examination of repealed legislation.[53]

Another inter-temporal issue arises when legislation is altered during the dispute resolution processes. This does not necessarily bring the legislation outside the terms of reference of the WTO tribunal concerned.[54] It is true that 'as a general

---

49. Appellate Body Report, *Canada – Patent Term*, para. 58. At para. 59, the Appellate Body continued:

> Almost any existing situation or right can be said to have arisen from one or more past 'acts'. For example, virtually all contractual and property rights could be said to arise from 'acts which occurred' in the past. If the phrase 'acts which occurred' were interpreted to cover all continuing situations involving patents which were granted before the date of application of the TRIPS Agreement for a Member, including such rights as those under [patents granted under the legislation], then Article 70.1 would preclude the application of virtually the whole of the TRIPS Agreement to rights conferred by the patents arising from such 'acts'.

50. See also Panel Report, *US – DRAMS*, para. 6.14.
51. Appellate Body Report, *US – Certain EC Products*, para. 81; Panel Report, *Dominican Republic – Import and Sale of Cigarettes*, para. 8.3. A rare counter-example is Panel Report, *US – Wool Shirts and Blouses* (in which the US measure was withdrawn after the Panel released its interim report, but the Panel nevertheless went on to release its final report). See also Appellate Body Report, *US – Upland Cotton*, para. 272, in which the Appellate Body held that the mere unavailability of the recommendation remedy for a repealed measure was not 'dispositive of the preliminary question of whether a panel can address claims in respect of that measure'.
52. Appellate Body Report, *EC – Computer Equipment*, para. 94; Panel Report, *EC – Trademarks and Geographical Indications (Australia)*, para. 7.17.
53. An example examined by the Appellate Body in *US – Upland Cotton* (para. 273) is Art. 7.8 of the SCM Agreement. This provides that a finding that 'any subsidy has resulted in adverse effects to the interests of another Member' requires the defendant Member to 'take appropriate steps *to remove the adverse effects* or . . . withdraw the subsidy' [emphasis added] The 'adverse effects' could, in theory, be effects from repealed legislation.
54. Appellate Body Report, *EC – Chicken Cuts*, para. 156.

rule, the measures included in a panel's terms of reference must be measures that are in existence at the time of the establishment of the panel'.[55] However, the Appellate Body has held that this rule does not apply in these circumstances:

- if the alteration 'does not change the essence of the identified measure'[56]; or
- if the substance of the challenge is the ongoing effect of the legislation.[57]

Similar considerations apply if a WTO tribunal declares legislation to be WTO-inconsistent and sets a deadline for removing the inconsistency. In *US – FSC (Article 21.5 – EC II)*, the legislation was repealed within such a deadline, but it was replaced with new legislation on the same subject matter that was also WTO-inconsistent. In compliance proceedings, the Appellate Body held that the original deadline also applied to the new legislation. The setting of that deadline formed 'part of a continuum of events' with subsequent compliance proceedings.[58]

These issues are closely linked to the question of content of the remedy given. In particular, this may concern the period for implementation of remedial measures (the WTO system of remedies allows a tribunal to fix a time for remedying inconsistent legislation[59]). In *US – FSC (Article 21.5 EC)*, the United States argued that it had the right to provide 'an orderly transition' for its taxpayers affected by the legislation.[60] In particular, it argued that the effect of the legislation need not stop immediately, but that a transitional period of operation could be allowed. The Appellate Body rejected this argument based on the wording of Article 4.7 of the Agreement on Subsidies and Countervailing Measures (SCM Agreement) (which requires the withdrawal of a measure 'without delay').[61] That is, there was no right to continue WTO-inconsistent legislation in operation for a transitional period to allow for an 'orderly' transition to a WTO-consistent regime.

Such temporal questions are an important part of the wider issues of jurisdiction and remedies in WTO challenges to legislation. In the next chapter, we look at these wider issues in more detail. Temporal questions will also reappear in our later examination (in Chapter 8) of substantive deference in the context of certainty characterization.

---

55. *Ibid.*
56. Appellate Body Report, *Chile – Price Band System*, para. 139.
57. Appellate Body Report, *US – Upland Cotton*, para. 263. See also Appellate Body Report, *EC – Selected Customs Matters*, para. 184.
58. Appellate Body Report, *US – FSC (Article 21.5 – EC II)*, para. 87.
59. See Section 3.3, text at n. 90.
60. Appellate Body Report, *US – FSC (Article 21.5 – EC)*, para. 224.
61. *Ibid.*, paras 229–230.

Chapter 3
Procedural Deference

3.1. INTRODUCTION

States are increasingly willing to grant jurisdiction to international tribunals, especially in the fields of international trade and human rights. Previously, this jurisdiction was granted extremely grudgingly, as was evidenced by the strict wording of jurisdictional provisions. Whatever one thought of this restricted jurisdiction as a matter of policy, it brought with it one useful device for international tribunals. Faced with very controversial disputes, such tribunals could usually find a way to decline jurisdiction. This kind of issue avoidance was (and still is) a handy method of avoiding entanglement in disputes in which the rudimentary machinery of traditional international litigation was unlikely to make a substantial positive contribution to any eventual settlement.

However, systems such as the WTO have taken a decisive step towards greater jurisdiction. WTO tribunals have 'automaticity', that is, their establishment cannot be vetoed by the defendant State, their terms of reference are largely determined by the complaining State, and their recommendations will almost certainly be formally accepted by the collective WTO membership.[1] Thus, WTO tribunals do not have the same scope as other international tribunals to avoid difficult issues by declining jurisdiction.

The increased jurisdiction of WTO tribunals means that there is limited scope to express deference to domestic authorities through jurisdictional means. However, the issue of deference does not just go away; it just reappears in other forms.

---

1. That collective membership, in the form of the DSB, can only refuse to accept a Panel or Appellate Body recommendation in the unlikely event of a consensus veto: Art. 6.1 DSU.

One way in which deference could reappear is in the system of remedies. International tribunals generally have a limited set of remedies in challenges to legislation, primary among them being the declaration of inconsistency. This remedy has a built-in degree of deference, as it leaves the defendant State considerable leeway in fashioning a response.

Yet, here too, the WTO system has progressed beyond traditional international law so as to limit the scope for deference. The declaration of inconsistency is still the main remedy (in the guise of a 'recommendation'). However, this remedy is supported by less-deferential mechanisms, such as 'suggestions', time limits, and formal compliance procedures. WTO tribunals have also expressed their reasons for decisions in such a way as to limit the leeway available to the domestic legislature in fashioning a response to a declaration.

This means that procedural mechanisms have lost much of their capacity to express deference in WTO challenges to legislation. WTO tribunals cannot easily decline jurisdiction in such challenges. The remedies they issue are more specific than those of other international tribunals, and they are backed up with unusually powerful enforcement mechanisms.

This chapter examines in detail the way in which deference can be expressed through procedural mechanisms in international challenges to legislation and describes the declining availability of these mechanisms in the WTO. It first examines the issue of *justiciability*, both in the formal and discretionary sense, and then moves on to the system of *remedies* available for successful challenges. In the WTO, the scope for procedural deference will be seen to be quite limited. This implies a greater pressure on substantive deference (which is the subject of Chapters 4–8).

3.2. JUSTICIABILITY

3.2.1. Justiciability Generally

The concept of justiciability allows a court or tribunal to refuse to hear a claim. Justiciability can be the ultimate expression of deference, as without it, a court or tribunal will refuse to hear a claim. Justiciability has been an ever-present issue in challenges to legislation, particularly at the international level.

Davey has identified most issues relating to justiciability in WTO litigation (which he calls 'issue-avoidance' techniques), as follows:

- limitations on the parties who can bring an action (e.g., 'standing' or legal interest requirements);
- restrictions limiting the time at which an action may be brought (e.g., categorizing actions as too late (mootness) or too early (ripeness or failure to exhaust other remedies));
- categorization of actions as inappropriate for judicial consideration (e.g., political questions, *non liquet*); and

– exercise of judicial economy so as to avoid considering issues (e.g., strict interpretation of terms of reference; resolution of only necessary issues).[2]

Rather than repeating Davey's analysis, I will use a simpler framework here, based on two meanings of the term *justiciability*.[3] First, the term can mean 'court or tribunal jurisdiction' in the strict sense of the term. Second, it can refer to the ability of courts and tribunals to decline to hear a case on discretionary grounds. These discretionary grounds mainly relate to 'judicial economy', although they also include other elements mentioned by Davey, such as ripeness. This chapter discusses justiciability in challenges to legislation by reference to these two kinds of justiciability.

It is important to remember that these two types of justiciability overlap to an extent. In some cases, it is unclear whether a particular issue relates to a tribunal's jurisdiction or to its discretion to refuse to hear a matter. Dividing the concept of justiciability in this way is thus not intended to describe established legal categories. It is used here simply as a useful analytical device for discussing issues of justiciability.

3.2.2. Justiciability without Discretion: Jurisdiction

The first type of justiciability, *jurisdiction* in the strict sense of the term, defines the field of matters in which a court or tribunal may legally hear and decide claims.[4] If a tribunal has no jurisdiction to hear and decide a matter, it must refuse to hear the claim. This is true even when the claim, if heard, would succeed on its merits. Without jurisdiction, the claimant must look elsewhere to enforce its rights. In the WTO, for example, the 'vesting of jurisdiction in a panel is a fundamental prerequisite for lawful panel proceedings'.[5]

Jurisdiction has been an ever-present issue in challenges to legislation. At the domestic level, the question of jurisdiction must often be resolved before a constitutional court will hear a challenge to legislation. Nevertheless, such courts often do find that they have the necessary jurisdiction. This is not so easy at the

---

2. W. Davey, 'The Authority of the WTO Dispute Settlement System', JIEL 4 (2001): 79, at 96.
3. G. Lindell, 'The Justiciability of Political Questions: Recent Developments', in *Australian Constitutional Perspectives*, eds H. Lee & G. Winterton (Sydney: Law Book, 1992), 180, at 182–191. G. Fitzmaurice, 'Law and Procedure of the International Court of Justice, 1951–4: Questions of Jurisdiction, Competence and Procedure', BYIL 34 (1958): 1, at 12 divides what I call here 'jurisdiction' into two subcategories of jurisdiction (relating to the capacity of a tribunal to deal with the relevant matters in general) and admissibility (relating to the capacity of a tribunal to deal with a particular dispute, for example, because of claims about the exhaustion of local remedies). This distinction, while important, is nevertheless not critical to the discussion here.
4. In international law, the term *jurisdiction* can also mean the field of matters within which a State may validly regulate. This book, however, is not concerned with this meaning of the term, but rather the jurisdiction of international tribunals.
5. Appellate Body Report, *US – 1916 Act*, para. 54.

international level. The jurisdiction of international tribunals is generally tightly controlled by States.

There are basically two ways in which an international tribunal can obtain jurisdiction to hear a matter. First, there can be a special agreement (a *compromis*) between States that are parties to a dispute that grants the tribunal jurisdiction to deal with the dispute.[6] In some cases, the agreement can be constructed from the conduct of the parties, through the doctrine of *forum prorogatum*.[7] Alternatively, a pre-existing treaty can contain a compromissory clause giving the tribunal jurisdiction over a range of defined matters, including the matter in dispute. The International Court of Justice (ICJ) also possesses the ability to gain jurisdiction from general declarations by States under Article 36(2) of its Statute.

For international challenges to legislation, the compromissory clause is the most important basis for jurisdiction. Although some challenges to legislation have been heard on the basis of a special *compromis*, it is far more common for an international tribunal to gain its authority from a general treaty. The main problem has been whether the compromissory clause has been sufficient in each particular case. The ICJ is the prime example in this respect, with the result that it has heard few challenges to legislation.[8]

The growth in international challenges to legislation has been possible only because of increasing State willingness to enter into compromissory clauses in treaties dealing with particular matters. These treaties cover subject matters corresponding to the growth areas in challenges to legislation, namely, human rights and international trade. The main tribunals hearing challenges to legislation, the WTO Appellate Body and the ECtHR, are supported by extraordinarily ambitious jurisdictional clauses, which are contained in the constituent treaty wording and applicable to most kinds of disputes.

It is worth describing here briefly the elements of WTO tribunals' effectively compulsory jurisdiction (also known as 'automaticity').

First, there is no formal requirement for standing. There is no express or implied need for a 'legal interest' in a dispute;[9] all that is required is that the claimant be a WTO member.[10] This can be contrasted with other international

6. I. Brownlie, *Principles of Public International Law*, 6th edn (Oxford: Oxford University Press, 2003), 683.
7. *Ibid.*, 689.
8. The ICJ has occasionally considered challenges to legislation and similar disputes. However, these cases have generally turned on matters of treaty interpretation (*Case Concerning Rights of Nationals of the United States of America in Morocco*, Judgment (1952) ICJ Reports 176) or other determinations of the content of international law (*Fisheries* case (*United Kingdom v. Norway*), Judgment (1951) ICJ Reports 116), or have foundered for jurisdictional reasons (*Fisheries Jurisdiction* case (*Spain v. Canada*), Jurisdiction of the Court, Judgment (1998), ICJ Reports 432). I am not aware of any ICJ decision that has dealt with the peculiarities of a challenge to legislation in the same detail as many decisions of WTO tribunals and the ECtHR.
9. Appellate Body Report, *EC – Bananas III*, para. 132.
10. An exception here is for disputes about pre-shipment inspection; Art. 4 API provides for an independent entity comprised of experts to hear complaints made by 'an exporter' or

courts, which generally require some connection between the claimant and the subject matter of the dispute.[11]

Second, there is no requirement that the legislating WTO member consent to the tribunal's jurisdiction. As described above, this stands in stark contrast to the jurisdictional basis of most international courts. Consent to WTO tribunal jurisdiction is given generally on accession to the WTO Agreements. WTO litigants may delay the formation of a Panel, but they cannot block it entirely.[12] The fact that a dispute concerns matters that the legislating State considers to be political rather than legal in nature cannot block Panel proceedings.[13]

One should also add to this list that there is no strict requirement in the WTO for the exhaustion of local remedies. That is, the complainant need not pursue all available domestic remedies before bringing its complaint before a WTO tribunal.[14] Other international courts (such as the ICJ[15] and the ECtHR[16]) generally require the exhaustion of local remedies before exercising jurisdiction.[17] Furthermore, a challenging State in WTO proceedings is not limited to arguments raised before domestic authorities. Indeed, there is considerable scope for raising entirely new arguments before a WTO tribunal.[18]

It is also important that the complainant has wide discretion to frame the ambit of the claim. Panels have jurisdiction over a matter referred to the Dispute Settlement Body (DSB) by the complaining State.[19] These terms of reference form the

---

'pre-shipment inspection entity' (i.e., an 'entity contracted or mandated by a member to carry out pre-shipment inspection activities': Art. 1.4 API).

11. In the ICJ, see *Barcelona Traction, Light and Power Company, Limited*, Judgment (1970) ICJ Reports 3; *South West Africa*, Second Phase, Judgment (1966) ICJ Reports 6, cited in Davey, above n. 2, 97. In the ECtHR, see C. Ovey & R. White, *Jacobs and White: The European Convention on Human Rights*, 3rd edn (Oxford: Oxford University Press, 2002), 405–407.
12. Articles 4 and 6.1 DSU.
13. Davey, above n. 2, 104–105.
14. For supporting arguments see Davey, above n. 2, 103–104. E. Vermulst, *The WTO Anti-Dumping Agreement: A Commentary* (Oxford: Oxford University Press, 2005), 239, fn. 5 suggests that this is the general view, but notes also contrary views. The general view is consistent with the Appellate Body ruling in *US – Section 211 Appropriations Act*, para. 265, that the US legislation was inconsistent with the national treatment rule in TRIPS. Although the legislation *could* allow foreigners the substantive benefits available to US nationals, the Appellate Body found that it created an 'extra procedural hurdle' for foreigners, and for this reason did not provide national treatment. Thus, there was no need to test the US assertion that foreigners could obtain the same treatment as US nationals through pursuing remedies with US authorities.
15. *Interhandel* case, Preliminary objections, Judgment (1959) ICJ Reports 6, at 27; *Elettronica Sicula S.p.A.* (*ELSI*), Judgment (1989) ICJ Reports 15, at 42, para. 50 (A treaty does not override the rule 'in the absence of any words making clear an intention to do so').
16. Ovey & White, above n. 11, 409–411.
17. There is some dispute over whether the principle of exhaustion of local remedies is a rule of procedure or of substantive law; see International Law Commission, *Report of the International Law Commission*, 54th session, A/57/10 (2002), 131–136, paras 150–172.
18. This is the case in WTO challenges to administrative action: Appellate Body Report, *Thailand – H-Beams*, para. 94; Panel Report, *Argentina – Poultry Anti-Dumping Duties*, para. 7.146. It seems probable that the same principle would apply in challenges to legislation
19. Article 7 DSU.

basis of the Panel's jurisdiction,[20] and it is allowed to consider only claims set forth in those terms of reference.[21] Nevertheless, a WTO member 'enjoys certain discretion in the identification of the specific measure at issue',[22] subject to a 'specificity requirement regarding the identification of the measures that serves the due process objective of notifying the parties and the third parties of the measure(s) that constitute the object of the complaint'.[23] The freedom of WTO complainants to set the terms of reference has significant consequences in challenges to legislation. The complainant can choose to focus on the elements of the legislative environment[24] that it chooses. That is, it can focus on statutory rules, delegated legislation, policy statements, administrative practices, or a combination of these. The WTO tribunal hearing the challenge must deal with the challenge on these terms.

The complainant's freedom to frame the ambit of the claim in WTO litigation contrasts greatly with the practice of other international tribunals. In general, the jurisdictional clauses of such tribunals do not allow the complainant freedom to choose the elements of the legislative environment to be challenged. For example, claimants before the ECtHR usually claim that their rights have been infringed upon by implementation of legislation; it is only in rarer cases that the court allows challenges to legislation as such.[25] In cases before the ICJ, the Court itself determines the real dispute that has been submitted to it.[26] If the ICJ's jurisdiction is based on an acceptance of its compulsory jurisdiction, the legislating State will often have submitted reservations to this acceptance.[27] If that jurisdiction is based on a special agreement, the legislating State will similarly be involved in defining the Court's jurisdiction.

In sum, WTO tribunals are in the unusual position of being unable to refuse jurisdiction to hear a challenge to legislation and of being obliged to hear the challenge on the terms chosen by the complainant. Unlike other international tribunals, WTO tribunals cannot express deference by denying jurisdiction. Their jurisdiction over challenges to legislation is virtually automatic. However, they still feel pressure for deference to the domestic legislature. Inevitably, that deference reappears in other guises, such as in claims for discretionary rulings on justiciability or claims for deferential remedies. We now look at the first of these issues, namely, discretionary justiciability.

---

20. Appellate Body Report, *Brazil – Desiccated Coconut*, 22; Appellate Body Report, *India – Patents (US)*, paras 92–93. In *Mexico – Corn Syrup (Article 21.5 – US)*, para. 36, the Appellate Body stated that 'Panels are required to address issues that are put before them by the parties to a dispute'.
21. Appellate Body Report, *India – Patents (US)*, paras 92–93.
22. Appellate Body Report, *EC – Selected Customs Matters*, para. 149.
23. *Ibid.*, para. 152.
24. See Ch. 8.
25. Ovey & White, above n. 11, 406–407.
26. *Maritime Delimitation and Territorial Questions between Qatar and Bahrain*, Jurisdiction and Admissibility, ICJ Reports (1995), 24–25; *Fisheries Jurisdiction Case (Spain v. Canada)*, ICJ Reports (1998), 432, at 449, para. 31.
27. For example, see the *Fisheries Jurisdiction Case (Spain v. Canada)*, Jurisdiction of the Court, Judgment, ICJ Reports (1998), 432, at 438, para. 14.

3.2.3. Discretionary Justiciability: Judicial Economy

The most important element of discretionary justiciability in WTO litigation is the principle of *judicial economy*. According to this principle, WTO tribunals 'may exercise judicial economy and refrain from addressing claims beyond those necessary to resolve the dispute'.[28] In *Mexico – Taxes on Soft Drinks*, the Appellate Body held that:

> [P]anels have 'a margin of discretion to deal, always in accordance with due process, with specific situations that may arise in a particular case and that are not explicitly regulated'.[29] For example, panels may exercise judicial economy, that is, refrain from ruling on certain claims, when such rulings are not necessary 'to resolve the matter in issue in the dispute'.[30] The Appellate Body has cautioned, nevertheless, that '[t]o provide only a partial resolution of the matter at issue would be false judicial economy'.[31]

Thus, judicial economy has a criterion of necessity: WTO tribunals have the power to refuse to hear claims that are unnecessary to resolve the dispute. Not surprisingly, there is some tension between the requirement for judicial economy and the requirement for WTO tribunals to resolve disputes before them.[32] This tension surfaces when the parties disagree about the necessity for a WTO tribunal to resolve a claim.

Disputes about the necessity to resolve a claim have a special relevance in challenges to legislation. This is usually because of the existence of the legislative environment surrounding the legislation under challenge. Typically, the legislating State claims that the legislation under challenge can be made to operate consistently with international obligations, if one takes the legislative environment into account. It goes on to claim that the dispute is better resolved by domestic processes, thereby taking advantage of that legislative environment. For example, it may claim that domestic courts will interpret the legislation in a way consistent with international obligations, and that it is premature for international tribunals to

28. Appellate Body Report, *US – Upland Cotton*, para. 718; Appellate Body Report, *Canada – Wheat Exports and Grain Imports*, para. 133.
29. [original footnote] Appellate Body Report, *EC – Hormones*, fn. 138 to para. 152. See also Appellate Body Report, *US – FSC (Article 21.5 – EC)*, paras 247–248.
30. [original footnote] Appellate Body Report, *US – Wool Shirts and Blouses*, 19, DSR 1997:I, 323, at 340 [remainder of original footnote omitted].
31. [original footnote] Appellate Body Report, *Australia – Salmon*, para. 223.
32. Appellate Body Report, *Mexico – Taxes on Soft Drinks*, para. 51. The requirement to help resolve disputes arises under Art. 11 DSU (A WTO tribunal must 'make an objective assessment of the matter before it' and 'make such other findings as will assist the DSB in making the recommendations or in giving the rulings provided for in the covered agreements'). Vermulst, above n. 14, 258, suggests that judicial economy 'is a relic from the diplomacy-based GATT dispute settlement system, which should not have a place in the judicialized two-layered WTO system'. However, this statement goes too far, given the recognized role of domestic courts – and of international courts such as the ICJ – of minimizing controversial decision-making by focusing on what is *necessary* to decide a case.

hear the challenge.[33] Alternatively, it may claim that domestic authorities will exercise their discretion under the legislation consistently with international law.[34] Inherent in these claims is an argument that the international tribunal should exercise judicial economy in the matter. In many international tribunals, these kinds of arguments succeed, for example, on the grounds of failure to exhaust local remedies,[35] or because the tribunal finds that there is no crystallized breach until the legislation is actually implemented (i.e., the challenge is not yet ripe).[36]

In the WTO, however, there is a reduced scope for such arguments. There is no formal recognition of the rule of exhaustion of local remedies.[37] WTO members are free to draft their claims against a particular implementation of the legislation, or the legislation as such, or both.[38] That is, they may define the scope of the dispute in their own terms. In doing so, they can set the playing field for arguments about necessity and the application of judicial economy. To give an obvious example, if a challenge is framed against the legislation as such,[39] the tribunal must hear the challenge even in the face of counterarguments about the effect of the legislative environment. It is necessary to hear the challenge to resolve the dispute. It is probably for this reason that the Appellate Body has called for WTO members to exercise 'especial diligence' in framing claims against legislation: the automaticity of the claim requires a corresponding degree of clarity in its expression.[40]

As a result, judicial economy is rarely, if ever, a useful outlet for pressure over deference in challenges to legislation. WTO tribunals cannot decline to hear a challenge to legislation as such. This means that the pressure for deference must find different outlets. In the examples noted above regarding the legislative environment, this outlet appears in substantive issues, in particular, in certainty characterization. The procedural issue of judicial economy is transformed into the substantive issue of whether the legislation operates with enough certainty to achieve WTO-consistent results. This is discussed in detail in Chapter 8. First, however, some discussion is needed of decreasing procedural deference with respect to remedies.

---

33. For example, Panel Report, *Argentina – Textiles and Apparel*, paras 6.66–6.69; Appellate Body Report, *Argentina – Textiles and Apparel*, para. 54.
34. See Section 8.4, text at n. 128.
35. See above, text at n. 14.
36. Davey, above n. 2, 101–103.
37. See above, text at n. 14.
38. This is subject to the requirement that the legislation being challenged is identified without ambiguity. However, this identification need not be of particular legislative provisions: Appellate Body Report, *US – Oil Country Tubular Goods Sunset Review*, paras 168–173.
39. There is a minimum requirement that a request for the establishment of a Panel must 'identify the specific measures at issue and provide a brief summary of the legal basis of the complaint sufficient to present the problem clearly': Art. 6.2 DSU; Appellate Body Report, *US – Carbon Steel*, para. 125. However, a mere reference to domestic legislation 'as such' in such a request seems to be sufficient to incorporate a challenge to the legislation: Appellate Body Report, *US – Oil Country Tubular Goods Sunset Review*, para. 165.
40. Appellate Body Report, *US – Oil Country Tubular Goods Sunset Review*, para. 173.

3.3. REMEDIES

As with all issues concerning challenges to legislation, the issue of remedies is intertwined with issues of deference. International tribunals (and domestic courts) must show deference to domestic legislatures in granting remedies for legislation breaching international obligations. It is not a judicial function to draft amending legislation; this remains the function of the legislature. The question then becomes, What kind of deference is involved in remedies in challenges to legislation?

This section begins with a general discussion of remedies, with a focus on remedies in challenges to legislation, and moves on to such remedies in public international law generally. While there are no rigid rules here, there appears to be a general trend to use a particular remedy in challenges to legislation, namely, a declaration of inconsistency. A declaration of inconsistency has the great advantage of leaving the details of compliance to the legislature, and therefore it has an inbuilt measure of deference. Of course, this degree of this deference depends on the specificity of the reasoning underlying the declaration.

WTO law follows this general approach. The main remedy in WTO challenges to legislation is a recommendation, which is roughly equivalent to a declaration of inconsistency. However, the WTO remedial system contains several modifications. For example, WTO tribunals can make specific suggestions for remedial action, provide for rulings on exact time frames for compliance, allow follow-up WTO litigation to test compliance measures, and provide in the end for countermeasures. These modifications reduce the degree of deference inherent in the declaration of inconsistency. Unlike general public international law, the granting of a WTO remedy in a challenge to legislation can lead to significant constrictions on the freedom of legislative choice. As a result, the deference is pushed out of the realm of procedure and, instead, into the realm of substance.

3.3.1. Remedies Generally

It seems that all legal systems contain some kind of system of remedies. Indeed, some legal systems appear to have grown out of systems of remedies. Common law may be an example of this, with general legal principles gradually emerging from a mass of individual actions pursuing particular remedies.[41]

In many developed legal systems, the system of remedies is complete and sophisticated. International law, by contrast, is still in the process of building such a system. Some progress has been made: the International Law Commission has defined a set of acceptable responses to breaches of international obligations. In its Draft Articles on State Responsibility, the Commission outlined broad principles on the consequences of such breaches. In general terms, the Commission

41. P. Glenn, *Legal Traditions of the World*, 2nd edn (Oxford: Oxford University Press, 2004), 242.

stated that a breach attracts a duty of cessation and non-repetition[42] and a duty to make full reparation via 'restitution, compensation and satisfaction, either singly or in combination'.[43] However, one should keep in mind that the Draft Articles deal with the general consequences of breaches, and not with the power of international tribunals to issue remedies under specific international regimes.[44] As most challenges to legislation occur under such regimes, this is the issue that we are most concerned with here.

Even for international tribunals, there is no coherent system of applicable principle in contemporary public international law. Gray concluded her comprehensive study of the issue with the observation that the ICJ, at least, 'is some way from creating an international law of remedies'.[45] Crawford noted that the ICJ rarely if ever talked of remedies, and, indeed, that the (common law) concept of remedy is difficult to translate into different legal systems.[46] He did note however, that the ICJ has recently begun to issue 'remedies' as such.[47]

Obviously, the problem of remedies in international law is connected with the problem of enforcement. International courts have no police and no army to enforce their judgments, and States can still defy their orders if they choose (whatever may be said about the effectiveness or morality of such defiance). Defiance to judicial authority is a feature of an underdeveloped legal system.[48] International tribunals face the daunting prospect of such defiance.

The problem of defiance is linked to the issue of deference. On the one hand, international tribunals should not issue remedies that attract zero levels of compliance. On the other hand, they should not fail to grant remedies when necessary;

---

42. International Law Commission, 'Draft Articles and Commentaries on Responsibility of States for Internationally Wrongful Acts', *Report of the International Law Commission*, 53rd session (A/56/10) (2001), Art. 30.
43. *Ibid.*, Arts 31 and 34.
44. *Ibid.*, Commentary to Art. 37, para. 6.
45. C. Gray, *Judicial Remedies in International Law* (Oxford: Oxford University Press, 1987), 107.
46. J. Crawford, '*Marbury v. Madison* at the International Level', *Geo. Wash. Int'l. L. Rev.* 36 (2004): 505, at 514.
47. Crawford, *ibid.*, citing *LaGrand* (*Germany v. U.S.*) (2001) ICJ Reports 466; see also *Arrest Warrant of 11 April 2000* (*Congo v. Belgium*), Judgment (2002) ICJ Reports 3, at 32, para. 76.
48. The situation is analogous to the early days of the US federation:

> One popular technique for dealing with unpopular decisions has been defiance. During Andrew Jackson's presidency, the states sometimes defied Supreme Court decisions, such as when Georgia went through with the execution by hanging of a Cherokee named Corn Tassels in the face of a Supreme Court order not to do so. Jackson was thought to lack the will to enforce federal court mandates. In another Cherokee controversy with Georgia, Jackson reputedly said, 'John Marshall [Chief Justice of the Supreme Court] has made his decree, now let him enforce it.'

B. Friedman, 'Attacks on Judges: Why They Fail', *Judicature* 81 (1998): 150, at 153 (reproduced at <www.ajs.org/cji/cji_attacks.asp> (visited 9 Apr. 2008)). Even in developed legal systems, problems of defiance arise, for example, in the area of labour law or fundamental social change. For examples, in the United States and Germany, see R. Rogowski & T. Gawron (eds), *Constitutional Courts in Comparison: The U.S. Supreme Court and the German Federal Constitutional Court* (New York: Berghahn Books, 2002).

indeed, remedies incorporating a degree of deference may increase the chances of compliance. The question therefore is, as with all issues of deference in challenges to legislation: What level of deference do such tribunals apply in practice?

3.3.2. Remedies for Challenges to Legislation: The Declaration of Inconsistency

Crawford has pointed out the importance of the declaratory remedy in international law:

> The international legal system is in the process of making links between declarations, jurisdiction, and remedies, thereby more broadly affirming the declaratory tradition. This is why, in my opinion, 'judicial review' in the declaratory mode is not merely useful but inevitable.[49]

The remedy of declaration[50] is perhaps the remedy most generally used by international tribunals. A declaration states a legal situation, for example, that a particular course of conduct is inconsistent with a particular international obligation. Gray concluded that the most common form of awards of the Permanent Court of International Justice (PCIJ) and the ICJ has been declarations (although such awards by arbitral tribunals have been more rare).[51]

The remedy of declaration was also specifically mentioned by the International Law Commission in its commentary on the Draft Articles on State Responsibility. Noting that reparation for breaches could take the form of 'satisfaction',[52] the Commission went on to say:

> One of the most common modalities of satisfaction provided in the case of moral or non-material injury to the State is a declaration of the wrongfulness of

49. Crawford, above n. 46, 514.
50. See I. Zamir & J. Woolf, *The Declaratory Judgment* (London: Sweet & Maxwell, 1993); P. Young, *Declaratory Orders* (Sydney: Butterworths, 1984).
51. Gray, above n. 45, 96–97:

> In the decisions of the Permanent Court of International Justice and of the International Court of Justice the declaratory judgement is the commonest type of award . . . the declaratory judgement was not used by international arbitral tribunals as a remedy for breaches of international law; that is, with very few exceptions – comprising awards of nominal damages, which could possibly be represented as declaratory judgements, and the grant of satisfaction in the form of a declaratory judgement – arbitral tribunals were not requested simply to declare that there had been a breach of international law and did not in fact make such declarations. The same is largely true of the practice of the Permanent Court of International Justice; it gave declaratory judgements mostly for the purpose of interpreting a treaty or contract or settling a question of territorial sovereignty. Obviously there can be no absolutely clear-cut distinction between such a judgement and a declaration that there has been a violation of international law, but the form of the judgement is different. [footnotes omitted]

52. International Law Commission, above n. 42, Arts 34 and 37.

> the act by a competent court or tribunal. . . . Any court or tribunal which has jurisdiction over a dispute has the authority to determine the lawfulness of the conduct in question and to make a declaration of its findings, as a necessary part of the process of determining the case. Such a declaration may be a preliminary to a decision on any form of reparation, or it may be the only remedy sought.[53]

As noted earlier, the remedy of declaration is common in ICJ practice. It is also a feature of several other international courts and tribunals, such as the ECtHR.[54] As we will see, it is also a feature of the WTO tribunal system.

Of course, there are many other forms of remedy available to international tribunals. The International Law Commission's Draft Articles on State Responsibility mentions that, even in the absence of an international tribunal, a State in breach of an international obligation has a duty of cessation and non-repetition,[55] and a duty to make full reparation via 'restitution, compensation and satisfaction, either singly or in combination'.[56] If that State refuses to fulfil these duties, an injured State may have access to countermeasures.[57] International tribunals often have the power to order one or more of these remedies. In some challenges to legislation, these other remedies (e.g., restitution[58]) may be appropriate.

Nevertheless, the remedy of declaration has particular usefulness in most challenges to legislation. In granting a declaration, the international tribunal merely states that the legislation is inconsistent with the relevant obligation. This is a declaration of inconsistency. The method of removing the inconsistency is left to the domestic legislature. For this reason, a declaration of inconsistency strikes a nice balance between legality and deference. The fact of the breach is left in no doubt. Yet, the legislature is given considerable room to move in fashioning a response. The value of a declaration of inconsistency in challenges to legislation has been recognized by many States, which have given their own constitutional

53. *Ibid.*, Commentary to Art. 37, paras 6 and 7.
54. Ovey & White, above n. 11, 417.
55. International Law Commission, above n. 42, Art. 30.
56. *Ibid.*, Arts 31 and 34.
57. *Ibid.*, Arts 49–54.
58. The International Law Commission noted that:

> The term 'juridical restitution' is sometimes used where restitution requires or involves the modification of a legal situation either within the legal system of the responsible State or in its legal relations with the injured State. Such cases include the revocation, annulment or amendment of a constitutional or legislative provision enacted in violation of a rule of international law, the rescinding or reconsideration of an administrative or judicial measure unlawfully adopted in respect of the person or property of a foreigner or a requirement that steps be taken (to the extent allowed by international law) for the termination of a treaty. [footnotes omitted]

Ibid., Commentary to Art. 35, para. 5.

courts power to issue such a declaration about domestic legislation, particularly in relation to guarantees of human rights.[59]

Of course, the discretion of the legislature in this regard is affected by the degree of specificity of the reasoning underlying the declaration. The way in which an international tribunal sets forth its reasoning is crucial to setting the freedom of action for a domestic legislature. While the declaration establishes the inconsistency, the detailed reasoning reveals the extent of the inconsistency. The passages in the tribunal's ruling in which it applies the international obligation to the substance of the legislation are critical. Any remedial legislation needs to take account of the detailed reasoning of the international tribunal. It is this reasoning that allows room to manoeuvre for a domestic legislature.

A useful example of such reasoning comes from outside the arena of the WTO. *Ammur v. France* was a challenge to legislation ruled upon by the ECtHR. It concerned French legislation authorizing detention in the international zone of a French airport. The facts of the case clearly revealed a deprivation of liberty under Article 5 of the European Convention on Human Rights (ECHR), and the only real issue was the justification for that deprivation of liberty. The ECtHR found the French law to be deficient in this regard, as it did not provide adequate protection against arbitrariness. The crucial passage in the judgment gave the reasons as to *why* the law failed to give such protection. The ECtHR stated that the law did not:[60]

- allow the ordinary courts to review the conditions under which aliens were held;
- if necessary, allow the ordinary courts to impose a limit on the administrative authorities as regards the length of time in which aliens were held;
- provide for legal, humanitarian, and social assistance; and
- specify procedures and time limits for access to such assistance so that asylum seekers could take necessary steps to get such assistance.

The room to manoeuvre for the French legislature was apparent from this reasoning. Two basic options were available:

(1) address each of the factors listed by the ECtHR (in which case the chances of a continuing violation would be very low); or
(2) address some of those factors, and perhaps also provide other safeguards (in which case there would be some chance of future challenges to the legislation under the ECHR).

Thus, the ECtHR's declaration of inconsistency did not give a blank cheque to the legislature as to the means of amending the offending legislation. The Court's

59. A good example in the civil law system is the system of constitutional remedies in Germany (see E. Benda & E. Klein, *Verfassungsprozeßrecht*, 2nd edn (Heidelberg: C.F. Müller, 2001), Ch. 5). In the common law world, this is particularly noticeable in the process of adopting Bills of Rights, for example, in the United Kingdom (Human Rights Act 1998, Section 4).
60. (1996) 22 ECHR 533, para. 53.

underlying reasoning set the real limits on the legislature's response to the declaration. We will come back to this point in the context of WTO remedies.[61]

Let us make a short diversion to consider the relevance of the dialogue theory in relation to judicial declarations.[62] One reason given in domestic systems for the declaration of inconsistency in challenges to legislation is to create a dialogue between the courts and the legislature. The declaration starts such a dialogue, which is continued by a legislative response. The dialogue may continue if that response is met with another declaration of inconsistency, and a further response, and so on. The dialogue theory is one way of reconciling the respective roles of the legislature and the judiciary.

The dialogue theory is taken a step further in systems that allow judicial 'suggestions' for the way in which legislation should be amended.[63] An example of such a system exists in Germany. There, many lawyers speak of the 'request decision' (*Appellentscheidung*), whereby the constitutional court makes an appeal to the legislature to amend or enact legislation according to certain criteria. As we will see later,[64] there is a rough analogy to the request decision in the WTO in the form of 'suggestions'.

It is an interesting question whether or not the dialogue theory can be extended to dialogues between international tribunals and domestic legislatures. One factor working against such a dialogue is the relative infrequency of international challenges to legislation. Only the ECtHR and the European Court of Justice (ECJ) come close to domestic courts in the numbers of cases with which they deal. Here, dialogues have occurred.[65] Nevertheless, one can see such dialogues occurring in the WTO arena as well. A well-known example is the *US – FSC* case, in which the US legislation underwent several revisions in response to a series of WTO tribunal rulings.[66] Dialogues may also take place between international tribunals and treaty drafters. For example, one might expect that the jurisprudence of the Appellate Body will have an impact on the drafting of the Doha Round text.[67] These speculations are nevertheless outside the scope of this book.

---

61. See Section 3.3.3.3.1.
62. See generally K. Roach, 'Dialogue or Defiance: Legislative Reversals of Supreme Court Decisions in Canada and the United States', *Int'l. J. Constitutional Law* 4 (2006): 347, who examines such dialogues in Canada and the United States.
63. In the United States, the best-known example is the *Miranda* decision, in which the Supreme Court set out standards by which it would judge future legislation dealing with the requirement to give suspects of offences notice of the right to remain silent. See *ibid.*, 351–356.
64. See Section 3.3.3.3.3.
65. See the discussion of Irish abortion legislation, as amended after decisions of the ECtHR and the ECJ, in V. Jackson & M. Tushnet, *Comparative Constitutional Law* (New York: Foundation Press, 1999), 174–180.
66. See Appellate Body Report, *US – FSC (Article 21.5 – EC II)*, paras 1–11.
67. Several Panel decisions under the old GATT system had a direct impact on the drafting of WTO provisions. For example, the Panel decision in *US – Imposition of Countervailing Duties on Certain Hot-Rolled Lead and Bismuth Carbon Steel Products Originating in France*, 15 Nov. 1984, GATT Doc. SCM/185 (unadopted) influenced the drafters of the SCM Agreement to insert in the definition of 'subsidy' a requirement for government contribution: see M. Matsushita,

We now return to our main point, which is that a declaration of inconsistency provides an inbuilt degree of deference in challenges to legislation. To this extent, a declaration of inconsistency provides an extra pressure valve in the procedural stages of many international challenges to legislation. However, the situation is somewhat different in the WTO. There, the system of remedies is more specific than in general public international law. As a result, the pressure valve of a declaration of inconsistency is less available than in other international systems. The pressure is diverted to substantive issues instead. This point is explored in detail below.

3.3.3. WTO Rules on Remedies

The WTO system has a fairly well-developed system of remedies.[68] I will only give a bare outline here, as the details are available elsewhere.[69]

3.3.3.1. Outline of WTO Rules on Remedies

The main remedy is a 'recommendation', under Article 19 of the Dispute Settlement Understanding (DSU). Once a Panel has made a recommendation, the litigating WTO members are able to lodge an appeal with the Appellate Body. If they do not lodge an appeal, or if the Appellate Body confirms the recommendation, the DSB will almost certainly adopt the recommendation.[70] The defendant WTO member must then report on its intentions to bring its offending measure into compliance with WTO rules.[71]

Failing sufficient efforts to modify the measure, WTO complainants are able to bring a formal claim of insufficient compliance.[72] Eventually, the complainants

---

T. Schoenbaum & P. Mavroidis, *The World Trade Organization: Law, Practice, and Policy* (Oxford: Oxford University Press, 2003), 267.

68. P. Grane, 'Remedies under WTO Law', JIEL 4 (2001): 755; S. Cho, 'The Nature of Remedies in International Trade Law', *U. Pitt. L. Rev.* 65 (2004): 763. On the binding nature of WTO rules, compare J. Bello, 'The WTO Dispute Settlement Understanding: Less Is More', AJIL 90 (1996): 416 with J. Jackson, 'The WTO Dispute Settlement Understanding-Misunderstandings on the Nature of Legal Obligations', AJIL 91 (1997): 60.
69. D. Palmeter & P. Mavroidis, *Dispute Settlement in the World Trade Organization: Practice and Procedure* (The Hague: Kluwer Law International, 1999).
70. Technically, the DSB adopts the Panel Report rather than the recommendation as such, and makes its own recommendation: see Art. 16.4 DSU.
71. Article 21.3 DSU.
72. The DSU contains an express procedure for dealing with suspected non-compliance. This procedure is a further Panel hearing, to determine whether compliance has been achieved. Art. 21.5 DSU provides:

> Where there is disagreement as to the existence or consistency with a covered agreement of measures taken to comply with the recommendations and rulings such dispute shall be decided through recourse to these dispute settlement procedures, including wherever possible resort to the original panel.

may call for compliance deadlines,[73] and, in the most difficult cases, for authorization to implement countermeasures in the form of suspension of trade concessions.[74] Nevertheless, the power of WTO countermeasures often lies more in the threat than in the reality of retaliation. Hudec wrote that GATT retaliation (the predecessor to WTO retaliation) was rather symbolic, with a purpose 'largely fulfilled by the fanfare which surrounds the formal decision authorizing it'. He added that actual retaliation 'tends to be something of an anti-climax'.[75] Indeed, the authorization of retaliation may act as a spur to legislative change by the defendant WTO member, but the actual imposition of trade sanctions may stiffen the resistance to change.[76]

3.3.3.2. Recommendations as Declarations of Inconsistency

A recommendation has obvious similarities to a declaration of inconsistency. A recommendation is made if a measure is *not* in conformity with a WTO rule.[77] The typical order in a successful challenge to legislation reads as follows:

> The [WTO tribunal] *recommends* that the Dispute Settlement Body request the [legislating WTO member] to bring [the legislation], found in this Report,

---

WTO tribunals hearing a compliance dispute make recommendations and suggestions in a similar way as do Panels in 'original' proceedings. That is to say, Art. 21.5 DSU compliance tribunals made declarations of inconsistency in the form of a recommendation, with the option of making an express suggestion for implementation. However, their nature as a tribunal of compliance influences the nature of the ruling. Although they are not restricted to considering the reasoning in the 'original' tribunal report, their 'recommendation' is focused on whether the 'measures taken to comply with the [original DSU] recommendations and rulings' are consistent with WTO rules.

73. See Section 3.3.3.3.2.

74. The WTO treaties have 'contracted out' of the general international law regime on countermeasures, and provided specific procedures for trade retaliation (J. Pauwelyn, 'Enforcement and Countermeasures in the WTO', AJIL 94 (2000): 335). While there is at least a theoretical possibility that a particularly severe breach of WTO rules would trigger general rules on State responsibility, this possibility has not yet arisen as a substantial issue.

    The WTO system of countermeasures is centred around the concept of retaliation. If parties to a dispute cannot agree to any suitable compensation for an unremedied breach of WTO law (Art. 22.1 DSU), the complaining party can request the WTO DSB to authorize the suspension of concessions or obligations under the covered agreements as against the defendant WTO member (Art. 22.2 DSU). Retaliation is nevertheless seen as a last resort (Art. 3.7 DSU), and the preferred outcome under the DSU is a withdrawal of the offending measure (Art. 3.7 DSU). The defendant WTO member can complain about the level or manner of retaliation to a WTO arbitrator (Art. 22.6 DSU). The level of trade retaliation is measured in monetary terms, either on the basis of 'nullification and impairment' of WTO benefits, or in subsidy cases as 'appropriate': M. Matsushita, T. Schoenbaum & P. Mavroidis, *The World Trade Organization: Law, Practice, and Policy*, 2nd edn (Oxford: Oxford University Press, 2006), 180–195.

75. R. Hudec, *The GATT Legal System and World Trade Diplomacy*, 2nd edn (Butterworths, 1990), 196–197.

76. R. Hudec, 'The New WTO Dispute Settlement Procedure: An Overview of the First Three Years', *Minn. J. Global Trade* 8, no. 1(1999): 115.

77. A different set of DSU provisions applies to the so-called non-violation complaints; see Matsushita, Schoenbaum & Mavroidis, above n. 74, 121–122.

> to be inconsistent with the [relevant WTO Agreement], into conformity with its obligations under that Agreement.

Thus, the making of a recommendation is equivalent to declaring that the legislation is inconsistent with a WTO member's international obligations.

There has been some debate over whether a recommendation obliges the legislating WTO member to repeal the legislation.[78] In *US – Uruguay Round*, the Panel ruled that the 'focus of WTO dispute settlement' is on withdrawal of measures.[79] This is certainly the case with prohibited subsidies, as Article 4 of the SCM Agreement requires the tribunal to recommend withdrawal of such subsidies. However, the stronger view for most WTO obligations is that the legislating WTO member has discretion as to the means of curing the inconsistency. The Panel in *US – Section 301 Trade Act* stated:

> The obligation on Members to bring their laws into conformity with WTO obligations is a fundamental feature of the system and, despite the fact that it affects the internal legal system of a State, has to be applied rigorously. At the same time, enforcement of this obligation must be done in the least intrusive way possible. The Member concerned must be allowed the maximum autonomy in ensuring such conformity and, if there is more than one lawful way to achieve this, should have the freedom to choose that way which suits it best.[80]

Furthermore, in *EC – Hormones* (*Article 21.3*(*c*)), Arbitrator Lacarte-Muró stated:

> Although withdrawal of an inconsistent measure is the *preferred* means of complying with the recommendations and rulings of the DSB in a violation case,[81] it is not necessarily the only means of implementation consistent with the covered agreements.[82]

Importantly, Article XVI(4) of the WTO Agreement obliges each WTO member to 'ensure the conformity of its laws, regulations and administrative procedures with its obligations as provided in the annexed Agreements'. It does not go so far as to require the repeal of inconsistent legislation.

---

78. The text of the WTO treaties is not conclusive here. Certainly, the DSU envisages that some disputes will be resolved by mutual agreement, without a withdrawal of the offending measure. Even without such agreement, 'the first objective of the dispute settlement mechanism' is merely 'usually' to secure the withdrawal of the offending measure (Art. 3.7 DSU). Of course, compromise solutions such as compensation 'should be resorted to only if the immediate withdrawal of the measure is impracticable and as a temporary measure pending the withdrawal of the measure which is inconsistent with a covered agreement' (Art. 3.7 DSU).
79. Panel Report, *US – Section 129(c)(1) URAA*, para. 3.88. At least in the area of subsidies, the obligation to withdraw a measure is somewhat clearer. Article 7.8 SCM Agreement provides that the defendant WTO Member shall take 'appropriate steps to remove the ... subsidy'.
80. Panel Report, *US – Section 301 Trade Act*, para. 7.102.
81. [original footnote] By contrast, in a non-violation case, brought under Art. XXIII(1)(b) of the GATT 1994, Art. 26.1(b) DSU states explicitly that 'there is no obligation to withdraw'.
82. *EC – Hormones (Article 21.3(c))*, para. 38.

The main discretion left to the domestic legislature here is thus the choice between repealing or amending the legislation, or altering the legislative environment. The legislature also has some choice as to the manner of making such changes. Repeal is a straightforward matter, but it is often a difficult political task to achieve if the legislation is a statute. The amendment of a statute poses similar political problems. Thus, the inconsistency can often only be removed by altering the legislative environment, such as by changing regulations or administrative practices. In any case, the way in which this is done is left to the discretion of the domestic legislature.

Nevertheless, the WTO remedial system limits this discretion, and in doing so, prevents an expression of deference through the remedy of a declaration of inconsistency. There are various ways in which this discretion is limited.

3.3.3.3. Limits to Deference to the Legislature in the WTO Remedial System

The WTO remedial system, based on recommendations, has features that limit deference in the same way that a declaration of inconsistency limits deference in other legal systems. As mentioned earlier,[83] the underlying reasoning of courts that issue such declarations can limit the ways in which domestic legislatures can respond to an unfavourable ruling. The same point applies in the WTO. When a WTO tribunal issues a recommendation in a challenge to legislation, its underlying reasoning shapes the ultimate legislative response to the ruling. Such reasoning can point out substantive or procedural flaws in the process of making legislation, leading to different kinds of responses.

The WTO remedial system has two additional features that further limit deference to domestic authorities. These are the availability of time limits and express suggestions. As we will see in the following pages, these features are useful tools for the WTO system, if used carefully and with restraint. Nevertheless, they further reduce the narrow freedom of action available to a domestic legislature faced with a WTO recommendation about inconsistent domestic legislation.

3.3.3.3.1. Limited Deference by Underlying Reasoning

As mentioned earlier,[84] the underlying reasoning of courts places substantial limits on the freedom of a domestic legislature to remedy legislative inconsistency. In the process of characterizing legislation as inconsistent with a WTO obligation, a WTO tribunal will give reasons as to why there is inconsistency. WTO tribunals have wide discretion as to the extent to which they give detailed reasons for their decisions and thereby guide remedial action. There is no abstract 'minimum standard' of reasoning.[85] A tribunal's reasons set the degree of the legislating State's freedom to respond to the recommendation.

83. See Section 3.3.2, text after n. 59.
84. See Section 3.3.2, text after n. 59.
85. Appellate Body Report, *Korea – Alcoholic Beverages*, para. 168.

There are many examples of this kind of reasoning and the accompanying restrictions on legislative responses. One example is the question in *US – FSC* as to whether the subsidy provided by the legislation was export contingent and therefore prohibited by Article 3.1(a) of the SCM Agreement. In the original proceedings, the Panel[86] gave its main reasons as to why the subsidy was export contingent, as follows:

> The subsidy is only available with respect to 'foreign trading income'; foreign trading income arises from the sale or lease of 'export property' or the provision of services relating to the sale or lease of export property; and export property is limited in effect to goods manufactured, produced, grown or extracted in the United States which are held for direct use, consumption or disposition outside the United States. Thus, the existence and amount of the subsidy depends upon the existence of income arising from the exportation of US goods or the provision of services relating to the exportation of such goods.[87]

From this reasoning, the parameters of remedial action were apparent. The Panel implied that the subsidy, if it were to cease to be an export subsidy, must no longer relate to goods produced domestically *and* used outside the United States. In response, the US Congress passed amending legislation. However, in later compliance proceedings, the Appellate Body held that the amending legislation did not meet the required parameters:

> It may also be recalled that the measure at issue in the original proceedings in *US – FSC* contained an almost identical condition relating to 'direct use... outside the United States' for property produced in the United States. In that appeal, we upheld the panel's finding that the combination of the requirements to produce property in the United States and use it outside the United States gave rise to export contingency under Article 3.1(a) of the SCM Agreement. We see no reason, in this appeal, to reach a conclusion different from our conclusion in the original proceedings. [88] [footnotes omitted]

In this way, the US freedom of action in remedying the inconsistency was limited. Any remedial action had to be tailored to satisfy the underlying reasoning of the WTO tribunal.

The potential of this kind of underlying reasoning to limit deference is clear. Although a declaration of inconsistency appears to give wide discretion to the domestic legislature, the declaration must always be seen in the context of the underlying reasoning.

Nevertheless, the most important limits to procedural deference in the WTO remedial system do not come from this kind of reasoning. Rather, they arise

86. This finding was not appealed.
87. Panel Report, *US – FSC*, para. 7.108.
88. Appellate Body Report, *US – FSC* (*Article 21.5 – EC*), para. 118.

through some express features of the DSU relating to time limits and judicial suggestions. The remainder of this chapter deals with these features.

3.3.3.3.2. Limited Deference by Time Limits

One of the features of the legislative process is its slowness. In dealing with conceptually or politically complex issues, legislatures need time to discuss all relevant points. Furthermore, there are often time-consuming but important procedural steps that need to be followed in passing legislation. For example, in the case of statutes, time frames need to be based on legislative timetables, obligatory consultation and debate periods, and quality-control processes. These processes cannot take place overnight.

International tribunals need to take into account these time factors in issuing remedies in challenges to legislation. Until recently, this has not posed a significant practical problem for tribunals, as international law remedial systems have not posed tight time limits on compliance.

However, the WTO remedial system stands out in international law because of its tightly controlled system of time limits for compliance. These time limits greatly restrict the amount of deference given to domestic legislatures in complying with declarations of inconsistency.

At first glance, the general principles of WTO law in this regard are fairly flexible. WTO members have a 'reasonable period' in which to comply with recommendations and rulings. Article 21.3 of the DSU provides (in part):

> If it is impracticable to comply immediately with the recommendations and rulings, the Member concerned shall have a reasonable period of time in which to do so.

Such a reasonable period may be proposed by the defendant WTO member or agreed upon between the litigating parties.[89]

The strictness of the system becomes apparent when there is a dispute as to what is a 'reasonable' period of time for compliance. In such cases, the length of a reasonable period of time can be set by arbitration.[90] Article 21.3(c) of the DSU also gives guidelines to arbitrators on this matter, based on a maximum of fifteen months.[91] Furthermore, Article 21.1 of the DSU provides that 'prompt compliance with recommendations or rulings of the DSB is essential in order to ensure effective resolution of disputes to the benefit of all Members'. Also, Article 21.3 of the

---

89. Article 21.3(a) and (b) DSU.

90. Article 21.3(c) DSU provides for:

> [A] period of time determined through binding arbitration within 90 days after the date of adoption of the recommendations and rulings [of the DSU]. [footnote omitted]

91. 'In such arbitration, a guideline for the arbitrator should be that the reasonable period of time to implement panel or Appellate Body recommendations should not exceed 15 months from the date of adoption of a panel or Appellate Body Report. However, that time may be shorter or longer, depending upon the particular circumstances.' [footnote omitted]

DSU appears to suggest that immediate implementation is preferred, because the 'reasonable period' provision applies only if immediate implementation is impracticable.

From these clues in the treaty text, arbitrators have inferred the principle that a reasonable period of time should be 'the shortest period possible within the legal system of the member to implement the relevant recommendations and rulings of the DSB', in light of the 'particular circumstances' of the dispute.[92] In the first such arbitration (*Japan – Alcohol*), the United States argued that Panels should undertake a technical inquiry into the domestic legislative system and disregard domestic political, economic, and social considerations.[93] The arbitrator in that case did not address this argument. However, later arbitrators have taken into account the following factors in setting a time limit for remedying a breach in a challenge to legislation:

(1) The degree of complexity of the Appellate Body (or Panel) decision leading to the declaration of inconsistency.[94]
(2) The intricacy of the law-making process.[95]
(3) The flexibility of the law-making process.[96]
(4) If relevant – the legislating WTO Member's inaction (or insufficient action) in the first months following adoption of the WTO tribunal report by the DSB.[97]
(5) Pre-legislative activities, such as 'consultations within government agencies as well as with the affected sectors of society' as 'a concomitant of law-making in contemporary polities'.[98]
(6) If relevant – the 'unique impact' of a proposed measure on the society of the defendant WTO Member (but not its mere 'domestic contentiousness' or 'political sensitivity').[99] This unique impact could be evidenced by:
    (a) the longstanding nature of existing legislation;[100]
    (b) the fundamental integration of existing legislation into central policies of the defendant WTO member;[101]

---

92. Award of the Arbitrator, *EC – Tariff Preferences*, para. 26, citing Award of the Arbitrator, *Chile – Price Band System*, para. 34, Award of the Arbitrator, *US – 1916 Act*, para. 32 and Award of the Arbitrator, *US – Offset Act (Byrd Amendment)*, para. 42. See also Award of the Arbitrator, *US – Oil Country Tubular Goods Sunset Review*, para. 25.
93. Award of the Arbitrator, *Japan – Alcoholic Beverages (Article 21.3)*, para. 13.
94. Award of the Arbitrator, *Chile – Price Band System (Article 21.3)*, para. 37.
95. Award of the Arbitrator, *Chile – Price Band System (Article 21.3)*, para. 38, citing Award of the Arbitrator, *EC – Bananas III*, para. 19; Award of the Arbitrator, *US – 1916 Act*, paras 38–39.
96. Award of the Arbitrator, *Chile – Price Band System (Article 21.3)*, para. 39, Award of the Arbitrator, *EC – Tariff Preferences (Article 21.3)*, para. 36, citing Award of the Arbitrator, *US – 1916 Act*, para. 39; Award of the Arbitrator, *Canada – Patent Term*, paras 63 and 64.
97. Award of the Arbitrator, *Chile – Price Band System (Article 21.3)*, para. 43.
98. *Ibid.*, para. 42.
99. *Ibid.*, para. 47. Award of the Arbitrator, *EC – Tariff Preferences (Article 21.3)*, para. 56.
100. Award of the Arbitrator, *Chile – Price Band System (Article 21.3)*, para. 48.
101. *Ibid.*

(c) the 'price-determinative regulatory position' of existing legislation;[102] and
(d) the intricacy of existing legislation.[103]

(7) If relevant – any practice of advance publication of legislative measures, prior to their enforcement.[104]
(8) If relevant – the need to translate legislative measures into various official languages.[105]
(9) If relevant – the operation of verification procedures for the fulfilment of requirements of the legislative process.[106]

Thus, domestic political, economical, and social considerations are not seen as decisive criteria in setting time limits; they are merely matters to be taken into account. This is a major limit on deference in setting time limits. The business of the legislature is to balance and resolve political and policy interests – the core of which is made up of such considerations. There is some scope for such considerations to be taken into account in the context of 'unique impact' mentioned above. Yet, domestic political, economical, and social considerations do not take a central place in setting remedial time frames. The general, 'one-size-fits-all' time frame of fifteen months highlights this fact.

The lack of deference here is emphasized by the principle that WTO members 'must take advantage of the flexibility and discretion available within its legal and administrative system to implement the recommendations and rulings of the DSB as speedily as possible'.[107]

In other words, WTO members must take advantage of discretionary domestic mechanisms to speed up legislative responses. However, they do not have the right to apply discretionary domestic mechanisms to slow down these responses – even if this may be desirable from the point of view of transparency in the law-making process.[108]

These limits to deference in setting time frames have the inevitable outcome that remedial action often comes too late. There are numerous examples of legislative responses that come too late, particularly when the legislature is a complex body, such as the US Congress, or an organ of the European Communities.[109]

---

102. *Ibid.*
103. *Ibid.*
104. Award of the Arbitrator, *EC – Tariff Preferences* (*Article 21.3*), para. 51, citing Award of the Arbitrator, *Korea – Alcoholic Beverages* (*Article 21.3*), para. 47 and Award of the Arbitrator, *EC – Bananas III* (*Article 21.3*), para. 19.
105. Award of the Arbitrator, *EC – Tariff Preferences* (*Article 21.3*), para. 53.
106. Award of the Arbitrator, *EC – Tariff Preferences* (*Article 21.3*), para. 53.
107. Award of the Arbitrator, *US – Oil Country Tubular Goods Sunset Review*, para. 27; Award of the Arbitrator, *Canada – Patent Term*, paras 63 and 64; Award of the Arbitrator, *US – Offset Act* (*Byrd Amendment*), para. 64 (referring to Award of the Arbitrator, *US – Section 110(5) Copyright Act*, para. 39 and Award of the Arbitrator, *US – 1916 Act*, para. 39).
108. However, in *US – Oil Country Tubular Goods Sunset Review*, para. 51, Arbitrator Ganesan appeared to take account of the need for transparency and efficiency in setting a time limit for compliance.
109. For example, *US – Section 211 Appropriations Act*; *US – Section 110(5) Copyright Act*; *EC – Bananas III*; *EC – Hormones*. For a personal view on compliance issues from the Director of

Of course, merely extending time limits may not solve this problem, and in some cases may even exacerbate it. Nevertheless, the lack of WTO deference in this regard is established. As a result, pressures for deference are pushed into the substantive aspect of challenges to legislation.

3.3.3.3.3. Limited Deference by Express Suggestions

As mentioned earlier, German courts sometimes deal with challenges to legislation by the means of an *Appellentscheidung* (request judgment).[110] Here, a court makes an express suggestion as to the kind of legislative remedial action that is required or desirable. These kinds of suggestions obviously attempt to limit legislative discretion in fashioning that remedial action. A declaration of inconsistency allows a wide range of responses from the legislature. An *Appellentscheidung* attempts to narrow that range according to the nature of the express suggestion made.

The WTO remedial system contains a mechanism that is similar in many respects to an *Appellentscheidung*. This is the remedy of 'suggestion'. Article 19.1 of the DSU provides (in part):

> In addition to its recommendations, the panel or Appellate Body may suggest ways in which the Member concerned could implement the recommendations.

It is clear that Article 19.1 suggestions do not impose binding obligations on defendant WTO members. Article 19.1 is not phrased in the imperative in this respect; it only mentions suggestions for 'ways' in which the defendant WTO member 'could' implement the recommendation.[111] It

---

the Legal Affairs Division of the WTO Secretariat, see W. Wilson, 'Compliance by WTO Members with Adverse WTO Dispute Settlement Rulings: The Record to Date', JIEL 10 (2007): 397. Wilson (p. 397), considers that virtually all WTO breaches lead to an indication that the breach will be remedied. However, he notes that legislative compliance is less rapid than administrative compliance, and that the United States and the European Communities 'have experienced some residual compliance difficulties in a small number of cases'.

110. C. Pestalozza, *Verfassungsprozeßrecht*, 3rd edn (München: CH Beck, 1991), 289, fn. 75. Pestalozza (at 288–289) distinguishes between various kinds of comments in decisions: 'advisory' grounds (*beratende Nebengründe*), 'warning' grounds (*warnende Nebengründe*), 'documenting' grounds (*dokumentierende Nebengründe*) and 'storing' grounds (*bevorratende Nebengründe*). He locates the *Appellentscheidung* in the 'warning' grounds class.

111. Not every kind of suggestion can be made under Art. 19.1 DSU. Only suggestions as to 'ways in which the Member concerned could implement the recommendations' are allowed. Since the recommendation itself is focused on bringing an offending measure 'into compliance' with WTO rules (or, in the case of certain subsidies, 'withdrawal' of the measure), the suggestion too must focus on compliance (or withdrawal).

In *Brazil – Aircraft* (*Article 21.5 – Canada*), Canada asked the Panel to suggest the creation of mechanisms to allow *verification* of compliance with the original recommendation. The Panel did not think a suggestion on surveillance of compliance was allowable:

> In our view, Article 19.1 appears to envision suggestions regarding what could be done to a measure to bring it into conformity or, in case of a recommendation under Article 4.7 of the SCM Agreement, what could be done to 'withdraw' the prohibited subsidy. It is not

does not mention 'the ways' in which the member must implement the recommendation.[112]

The potential for Article 19.1 suggestions to reduce deference in WTO remedies is obvious. The more specific and more exclusive a suggestion becomes, the less freedom a domestic legislature has to fashion a legislative response. If used carelessly, a suggestion could remove the flexibility inherent in a declaration of inconsistency. For this reason, Article 19.1 suggestions are rarely made.[113] Even when the complainant expressly requests a suggestion, WTO Panels have often refused to do so.[114] Panels generally are careful not to issue a suggestion unless there are clear reasons for doing so.[115]

The potential for Article 19.1 suggestions to limit deference to domestic legislatures can be seen from a few examples. In *Guatemala – Cement I*, the Panel suggested that 'Guatemala revoke the existing anti-dumping measure on imports of Mexican cement, because, in our view, this is the only appropriate means of implementing our recommendation.'[116] This 'mandatory' form of suggestion purports to define the only response available to the legislature. Still, the Panel expressly held that, in general, the modalities of implementing a recommendation are for the relevant WTO member to determine.[117]

A limit on deference can also be seen in cases in which suggestions are not phrased in mandatory terms. In the *US – Offset Act* (*Byrd Amendment*) case, the Panel made the following suggestion:

> Although there could potentially be a number of ways in which the United States could bring the CDSOA into conformity, we find it difficult to conceive of any method which would be more appropriate and/or effective than the

---

> clear if Article 19.1 also addresses issues of surveillance of those steps. That said, any agreement that WTO Members might reach among themselves to improve transparency regarding the implementation of WTO obligations can only be encouraged.

Panel Report, *Brazil – Aircraft* (*Article 21.5 – Canada*), para. 7.3. This view was confirmed in by the Panel Report in *Canada – Aircraft* (*Article 21.5 – Brazil*), para. 6.4.

112. For a more comprehensive analysis, see P. Mavroidis, 'Remedies in the WTO Legal System: Between a Rock and a Hard Place', EJIL 11 (2000): 763, 784–788.
113. Matsushita, Schoenbaum & Mavroidis, above n. 67, 80.
114. For example: Panel Report, *EC – Tube or Pipe Fittings*, para. 8.11; Panel Report, *US – Steel Plate*, para. 8.8; Panel Report, *US – DRAMS*, para. 7.4.
115. Matsushita, Schoenbaum & Mavroidis, above n. 67, 80–81, explain the lack of 'suggestions' as resulting from a desire on the part of Panels not to 'rock the boat':

> The WTO dispute settlement system favours a practice whereby panels stick to recommendations without suggestions. . . . Traditionally, panellists are divided between among 'governmentalists' and 'non-governmentalists' (in the GATT/WTO parlance), the former being preferred to the latter in the overwhelming majority of the cases. Practical considerations are more prevalent in the minds of governmental panellists, who know and understand political concerns. Practical considerations generally disfavour remedies that might 'rock the boat'. [footnotes omitted]

116. Panel Report, *Guatemala – Cement I*, para. 8.6. See also Panel Report, *Guatemala – Cement II*, para. 9.5 and Panel Report, *US – Cotton Yarn*, para. 8.5.
117. Panel Report, *Guatemala – Cement I*, para. 8.3.

> repeal of the CDSOA measure. For this reason, we suggest that the United States bring the CDSOA into conformity by repealing the CDSOA.[118]

Although the Panel did not purport to identify the *only* appropriate response, the wording of the suggestion was quite specific: the legislation should be repealed.

Some WTO tribunals have been careful to word their suggestions to preserve the discretion of domestic legislatures. For example, the Panel, in *US – 1916 Act (Japan)*, made the following suggestion:

> [W]e are of the view that, in order to bring the 1916 Act as such into conformity with its WTO obligations, the United States would probably have to amend that law to such an extent that it may no longer have a number of its current main features.[119]

The Panel then suggested that 'one way for the United States to bring the 1916 Act into conformity with its WTO obligations would be to repeal the 1916 Act'.[120] It did not purport to identify the *only* means of remedying the inconsistency.

The Panel in *EC – Bananas III (Article 21.5 – Ecuador)* went even further in this respect by identifying a range of options for remedial action. It stated that the European Communities had 'at least' three options for bringing its offending measures into WTO compliance and described these options in detail.[121] This was a clear attempt by the Panel to emphasize the ultimate discretion of local authorities to design changes to the offending measure (within the broad limits provided by WTO rules).

In sum, one can see a differentiated approach from WTO tribunals in dealing with the suggestion remedy. On the one hand, there are signs of a less-deferential approach in the decisions in *Guatemala – Cement I* and *US – Offset Act (Byrd Amendment)*. On the other hand, some Panels have stressed the non-exclusive nature of suggestions, and there has also been a general reluctance to provide suggestions at all.

This differentiated state of the case law can be understood better if we take a brief detour from a descriptive approach and examine the policy question of whether suggestions are a good idea at all. In my view, Article 19.1 suggestions have some value as remedies in challenges to legislation. If a suggestion is not too tightly worded and avoids an arrogant tone, it may be successful in setting the boundaries of a productive domestic debate.[122] It may be particularly useful if opposing domestic lobbies are fairly evenly balanced; a gentle push can tip the

---

118. Panel Report, US – Offset Act (Byrd Amendment), para. 8.6.
119. Panel Report, *US – 1916 Act (Japan)*, para. 6.302.
120. *Ibid.*
121. Panel Report, *EC – Bananas III (Article 21.5 – Ecuador)*, paras 6.155–6.158.
122. Panels seem more willing to make suggestions if the defendant WTO member has not implemented a recommendation within the allowed time limits. In Panel Report, *EC – Bananas III (Article 21.5 – Ecuador)*, the Panel held as follows (para. 6.154):

> Panels have not often made suggestions pursuant to Article 19.1. While Members remain free to choose how they implement DSB recommendations and rulings, it seems appropriate, after one implementation attempt has proven to be at least partly unsuccessful.

scales in the desired direction. This was probably the intention of the Panel in *EC – Bananas III* (*Article 21.5 – Ecuador*). Most Panellists will be aware of the power of suggestions in this respect.[123]

3.4. CONCLUDING REMARKS

In earlier times, international challenges to legislation often focused on procedural issues, such as the ripeness of the challenge, the need to wait for actual implementation of legislation, and the content of vague remedies. However, procedural deference in international challenges to legislation generally is on the decline, both in terms of jurisdiction and of remedy.

This decline is especially marked in the WTO. Jurisdiction in WTO tribunals is virtually automatic. Furthermore, complainants can choose which aspects of a domestic measure will be the subject of a challenge, and the tribunal often has little discretion to avoid difficult issues by focusing on aspects of the legislative environment. In addition, the WTO system reduces procedural deference by providing special remedies in the form of suggestions for legislative changes and binding time limits for such changes. Procedural deference in the WTO has been reduced to relatively insignificant levels.

Yet, the issue of deference to domestic legislatures does not simply disappear: there is a constant – and legitimate – demand for such deference. This demand needs to be satisfied through the substantive aspects of challenges to legislation. These aspects do not deal so much with jurisdiction and remedy as they do with the question of whether challenged legislation is actually consistent with the relevant international obligation. In the WTO, one can assume that jurisdiction will be established and that remedies will be available. The main question is whether legislation breaches an international obligation in a substantive way.

The rest of this book discusses these substantive aspects of international challenges to legislation. The next chapter deals with the basic building blocks of deference in international litigation and, in particular, in international challenges to legislation. Chapter 5 then establishes a framework for analysing the substantive aspects of a challenge to legislation, namely, the framework of legislative characterization. Chapters 6–8 then examine three different types of characterization in light of the basic building blocks of deference, with a view to discovering how much substantive deference WTO tribunals actually show to domestic legislatures.

---

that an Article 21.5 panel make suggestions with a view toward promptly bringing the dispute to an end.

123. One should also consider that WTO tribunals can use the Art. 19.1 suggestion to create 'safe harbours' for domestic legislative action. Thus, Mavroidis argues that compliance with a Panel's suggestion should raise an irrebuttable presumption of compliance with WTO rules (Mavroidis, above n. 112, 781). There is much to be said for this argument. An irrebuttable presumption here would provide a clear benefit for a legislating WTO member – and clear compensation for the limits on its discretions created by the suggestion.

Chapter 4
Substantive Deference

4.1. INTRODUCTION

Decreasing deference in procedural matters in WTO challenges to legislation means that WTO tribunals need to exercise deference more and more in matters of substance. In this chapter, we turn to the nature of substantive deference in challenges to legislation. Substantive deference concerns issues of raw fact-finding as well as the making of inferences from such facts. It is influenced by general principles such as the margin of appreciation (in European law) and the standard of review (in WTO law). In examining these matters, this chapter describes certain practical aspects of deference, which underlie the more detailed descriptions of WTO tribunal practices in the later chapters of this book.

Deference to the legislature is a common feature with all courts dealing with challenges to legislation, whether at the international or domestic level. Creating legislation is the job of the legislature, not of the courts.[1] Therefore, courts should defer to the legislature in the design of such rules, to the extent allowed by constitutional or international law. This judicial deference is connected to fundamental legal and constitutional principles, such as the rule of law, the separation of powers and (in democracies), the democratic mandate of legislatures.[2] Most constitutional and international law rules allow legislatures wide discretion in

---

1. According to the US Supreme Court in *Rodriguez v. United States* (1987) 480 US 522 at 525–526:

> Deciding what competing values will or will not be sacrificed to the achievement of a particular objective is the very essence of legislative choice – and it frustrates rather than effectuates legislative intent simplistically to assume that whatever furthers the statute's primary objective must be the law.

2. See K. Schlaich & S. Korioth, *Das Bundesverfassungsgericht*, 7th edn (München: CH Beck, 2007), Ch. 7.

balancing competing political interests and values. The courts do not, and should not, engage in this kind of balancing without clear constitutional or international law authority.

Substantive judicial deference is expressed through various legal principles in different courts. The principles have various labels, such as 'the reserved domain of domestic jurisdiction',[3] '*in dubio mitius*',[4] 'subsidiarity',[5] 'margin of appreciation',[6] 'political question',[7] 'judicial self-restraint',[8] 'standard of review',[9] 'core of legislative power',[10] 'justiciability',[11] 'intensity of judicial control'[12] and 'freedom of legislative design and expression'.[13]

The underlying reasons for judicial deference are varied, but all reflect the need for courts to present themselves in political disputes as neutral. In other words, deference results from courts refusing to balance political interests, so far as this is possible. Deference helps to protect the courts from accusations of partisanship. Deference is also a kind of judicial comity, which recognizes the different roles played by the courts and the legislature.[14]

International tribunals need to be particularly aware of the need for deference.[15] To the extent that they cease to be objective, they cease to be legitimate, especially as they are established and maintained through diplomatic means (and are therefore not directly subject to control by domestic legislatures). Like many domestic courts, they hold no popular mandate. Instead, they gain their legitimacy from the persuasiveness, coherence, and objectiveness of their reasoning. According to one view, international courts are legitimate only because States have delegated their own functions to the international level because of some failure in domestic political processes.[16] If so, international tribunals need to be careful not to act beyond

3. See Section 4.5.1.
4. See Section 4.4, text at n. 70.
5. A. Estella, *The EU Principle of Subsidiarity and Its Critique* (Oxford: Oxford University Press, 2003).
6. See Section 4.5.2.
7. Brennan J, *Baker v. Carr* (1962) 369 US 186, 217.
8. Schlaich & Korioth, above n. 2, 281, para. 505.
9. See Section 4.6.
10. Consider the dictum of US Chief Justice Marshall in *M'Culloch v. Maryland* (4 Wheat.) 316 (1819), at 421:

> Let the end be legitimate, let it be within the scope of the Constitution, and all means which are appropriate, which are plainly adapted to that end, which are not prohibited, but consist with the letter and spirit of the Constitution, are constitutional.

11. Schlaich & Korioth, above n. 2, 281–291 (using the German term *Verfassungsgerichtsbarkeit*).
12. *Ibid.*, 293–296 (using the German term *Kontrolldichte*).
13. *Ibid.*, 291–292 (using the German term *Gestaltungsspielraum*).
14. Y. Shany, 'Toward a General Margin of Appreciation Doctrine in International Law?', EJIL 16 (2006): 907, at 921.
15. C. Arup, 'The State of Play of Dispute Settlement the World Trade Organization', *Journal of World Trade* 37 (2003): 897, at 915.
16. See M. Pollack, *The Engines of European Integration* (Oxford: Oxford University Press, 2003), Chs 1–2.

their delegation, and to restrict themselves to activity that will actually help to remedy the domestic political failure. This is particularly true in cases of challenges to legislation, when rulings by international tribunals can be very politically sensitive at the domestic level.[17]

It is important to remember that all concepts of deference in challenges to legislation are applied in the context of relevant constitutional or international law rules.[18] That is, one cannot apply a ready-made general concept of deference in the abstract. The application of any principle of deference will differ according to the wording and context of the particular substantive provision involved, as well as the factual background. In the WTO context, the volume of relevant rules – hundreds of pages – can make it difficult to generalize about WTO law as a whole so as to extract a universal standard of deference. It is dangerous simply to assume that principles of deference will be applied in exactly the same way in all cases. The Appellate Body's striking image of an 'accordion' (used in the context of the concept of 'likeness' of products) is also relevant here: particular concepts expand and contract according to their context.[19] While general concepts of deference are important in challenges to legislation, they will always be subject to the content of the relevant international obligations.

Nevertheless, general principles about deference do exist. I do not intend here to make a survey of these principles, or to examine in more detail the theoretical basis for judicial deference. That has been done often in the past.[20] Instead, this chapter will examine practical aspects of deference in the context of international challenges to legislation.

---

17. According to the Appellate Body:

> '[A]s such' challenges against a Member's measures in WTO dispute settlement proceedings are serious challenges. By definition, an 'as such' claim challenges laws, regulations, or other instruments of a Member that have general and prospective application, asserting that a Member's conduct – not only in a particular instance that has occurred, but in future situations as well – will necessarily be inconsistent with that Member's WTO obligations. In essence, complaining parties bringing 'as such' challenges seek to prevent Members *ex ante* from engaging in certain conduct. The implications of such challenges are obviously more far-reaching than 'as applied' claims.

Appellate Body Report, *US – Oil Country Tubular Goods Sunset Review*, para. 172.

18. Looked at another way, the *lex generalis* of general concepts of deference may be modified by the *lex specialis* of the relevant international obligations. Admittedly, it is far from clear that general principles of deference are *law* as such. Nevertheless, such principles may have a practical effect similar to a binding legal principle.
19. Appellate Body Report, *Japan – Alcoholic Beverages II*, 114:

> The concept of 'likeness' is a relative one that evokes the image of an accordion. The accordion of 'likeness' stretches and squeezes in different places as different provisions of the WTO Agreement are applied.

20. Schlaich & Korioth, above n. 2, Ch. 7; C. Pestalozza, *Verfassungsprozeßrecht*, 3rd edn (München: CH Beck, 1991), Ch. 1; H. Abraham, *The Judicial Process*, 5th edn (Oxford: Oxford University Press, 1986), 368–395; M. Cappelletti, *The Judicial Process in Comparative Perspective* (Oxford: Oxford University Press, 1989), Ch. 1.

First, this chapter examines how deference is involved in fact-finding in challenges to legislation and in making inferences from the facts. There is an important distinction between deference given in finding raw evidence and the factual conclusions that are subsequently drawn from the raw evidence:

> The former concerns the issue as to how meticulously a panel should examine the scope and appropriateness of the relevant factual evidence. It is closely related to the role which panels play in undertaking and controlling the process of fact-finding; this role can be characterised by either an adversarial or an inquisitorial technique.[21] [footnotes omitted]

Findings of raw facts arise simply from gathering data (such as statistics), with little or no judgment involved. On the other hand, making inferences from such facts involves a degree of judgment. For example, price and sales volume data for two kinds of products are raw facts, but the 'fact' that those products are 'like' or 'not like' can only be found as an inference from those raw facts. In the former case, issues of deference concern the admissibility of evidence and the scope of the factual inquiry. In the latter case, these issues concern the extent to which an international tribunal may use its judgment in making inferences from the facts. Domestic legislatures guard jealously their prerogatives to assess the nature of problems and how best to solve them. Yet, international tribunals must draw inferences from raw facts to apply international law to those facts.

This chapter then goes on to examine how the content of international obligations can determine the applicable degree of deference. This can occur in two ways. First, international obligations can allow States some discretion in interpreting and applying such obligations. Alternatively, the content of an international obligation can be determined to an extent by domestic law.

This chapter then turns to three recognized concepts of deference in public international law generally:

- the reserved domain of domestic jurisdiction;
- the margin of appreciation; and
- the standard of review.

The first two concepts have been recognized to an extent in public international law generally, while the third concept is the main measure of deference in the WTO. We will see that the first concept is rather dated and of limited practical use, while the second concept has mainly been developed in the context of European law. The WTO standard of review has mainly been applied in the context of challenges to administrative actions, but it is still in a rather undeveloped state in its application to challenges to legislation.

In sum, general measures of deference in public international law provide limited concrete guidance to WTO tribunals in dealing with domestic legislation. It is for this reason that later chapters in this book examine how such tribunals have

21. M. Oesch, 'Standards of Review in WTO Dispute Resolution', JIEL 6 (2003): 635, at 640.

dealt with deference in particular challenges to legislation, through the lens of legislative characterization.

4.2. RAW FACTS DEFERENCE

The raw facts in challenges to legislation can be a variety of matters, including the following:

- the content of the legislation itself;
- the surrounding legislative environment, such as other legislation, subordinate legislation, administrative practices, and domestic jurisprudence; and
- other matters, such as economic or political data.

Deference in determining raw facts in challenges to legislation concerns the extent and procedure of an international tribunal's fact-finding exercise. The extent of the fact-finding exercise depends on how many of the raw facts are taken into account in a challenge to legislation. This may be constrained by timing factors or other matters. The procedure of the fact-finding exercise is determined by the way in which international tribunals receive evidence about these matters. In the following section, we consider these matters in detail.

4.2.1. Procedures in Fact Finding: Deference as to Gathering Raw Facts

A critical factor in international challenges to legislation is the procedure by which the tribunal informs itself about the relevant legislation. Clearly, the parties themselves will present whatever information will aid their own case. Sometimes, however, the tribunal may wish to gather its own evidence. In practice, the legislating State will enjoy considerable deference here, particularly regarding sensitive security or commercial-in-confidence information. This deference is increased by the burden of proof placed on a complaining State to establish underlying facts.[22] These facts take on a special significance in challenges to legislation in cases in which the dispute focuses on the operation of the legislative environment.

One might expect international tribunals to defer to the parties to the dispute by refraining from gathering information independently. However, international tribunals generally have wide inherent discretion in the kinds of evidence they can gather and consider.[23] Thus, the ICJ, the ECtHR and WTO Panels may commission

---

22. Appellate Body Report, *US – Carbon Steel*, para. 157.
23. According to Kazazi:

> The fact-finding power of international tribunals appears to be inherent and thus even in cases where it is not specifically referred to in their rules of procedure, international tribunals are entitled to require parties to produce evidence and to investigate the disputed

independent expert reports related to factual matters.[24] Nevertheless, there are some basic tensions here between adversarial and investigative methods of litigation, which are yet to be fully resolved. Indeed, there are limits to the independent fact-finding capacity of international tribunals. At the most basic level, some kinds of facts can be gathered only with the consent of States, such as national security information and information about the internal workings of government. These kinds of information aside, there may be limits to the gathering of commercial-in-confidence information[25] or other types of information not in the public domain.

This situation greatly increases the importance of the burden of proof. When insufficient evidence exists to establish the existence of particular matter, the question of who bears that burden can be the decisive issue. Generally speaking, this burden rests with the party who asserts the existence of that matter.[26] In the case of international challenges to legislation, the challenging State needs to show that the legislation is inconsistent with the international obligation, and it needs to do so to an adequate standard. Without such evidence, the challenge will fail at the first stages. This can be illustrated by WTO practice. WTO tribunals have sometimes dismissed challenges to legislation simply on the grounds of insufficient material brought into evidence.[27] Furthermore, a WTO challenge to legislation can be dismissed if the complainant simply submits raw evidence

---

> facts at their own initiation. Theoretically, the parties always remain empowered to agree to the contrary in order to limit the fact finding power of a tribunal if they so choose. In practice, however, such instances are rare and parties usually emphasize the power of the tribunal.

M. Kazazi, *Burden of Proof and Related Issues – A Study on Evidence before International Tribunals* (The Hague: Kluwer, 1995), 166.

24. Kazazi, *ibid.*; J. Pauwelyn, 'Evidence, Proof and Persuasion in WTO Dispute Settlement – Who Bears the Burden?', JIEL 1 (1998): 227.
25. R. Behboodi, ' "Should" means "Shall": A Critical Analysis of the Obligation to Submit Information under Article 13.1 of the *DSU* in the *Canada – Aircraft* Case', JIEL 3 (1998): 563.
26. Appellate Body Report, *US – Carbon Steel*, para. 157:

> The party asserting that another party's municipal law, as such, is inconsistent with relevant treaty obligations bears the burden of introducing evidence as to the scope and meaning of such law to substantiate that assertion. Such evidence will typically be produced in the form of the text of the relevant legislation or legal instruments, which may be supported, as appropriate, by evidence of the consistent application of such laws, the pronouncements of domestic courts on the meaning of such laws, the opinions of legal experts and the writings of recognized scholars. The nature and extent of the evidence required to satisfy the burden of proof will vary from case to case.

See also Appellate Body Report, *US – Wool Shirts and Blouses*, 337; Panel Report, *US – Section 129(c)(1)* URAA, para. 6.28.

27. An interesting example is the *US – Gambling* dispute, where the original Panel and Appellate Body report found that the United States had not produced enough evidence to prove that various US statutes were consistent with the chapeau to Art. XIV GATS. In subsequent compliance proceedings, the United States attempted to produce new evidence to prove that consistency, without amending the statutes. The compliance Panel rejected the argument, using an argument similar to res judicata in relation to previous proceedings (Panel Report, *US – Gambling* (*Article 21.5 – Antigua and Barbuda*), paras 6.83–6.84).

without linking that evidence to arguments related to the relevant international obligation.[28]

These limits to fact-finding are relevant for challenges to legislation in the same way that they are for other kinds of international litigation. Yet, challenges to legislation raise particular issues about the way in which facts are found about the legislative environment. In such challenges, the text of the challenged legislation is always in evidence,[29] as is as the text of relevant subordinate legislation and policy statements. However, other aspects of the legislative environment may be less apparent (such as the influence of domestic jurisprudence on the operation of a statute).

When such evidence is difficult to get, international tribunals have to grapple with claims for deference by the legislating State. Such claims are especially powerful when they concern the effects of domestic legislation (such as the effects of a body of domestic case law or other aspects of the legislative environment). In principle, international law has tended to downplay such claims by treating domestic law as an issue of fact. As the PCIJ famously said:

> From the standpoint of International Law and of the Court which is its organ, municipal laws are merely facts which express the will and constitute the

28. In *US – Gambling*, paras 140–141, the Appellate Body said:

> A *prima facie* case must be based on 'evidence *and* legal argument' put forward by the complaining party in relation to *each* of the elements of the claim. A complaining party may not simply submit evidence and expect the panel to divine from it a claim of WTO-inconsistency. Nor may a complaining party simply allege facts without relating them to its legal arguments. . . . The evidence and arguments underlying a *prima facie* case, therefore, must be sufficient to identify the challenged measure and its basic import, identify the relevant WTO provision and obligation contained therein, and explain the basis for the claimed inconsistency of the measure with that provision. [footnotes omitted]

See also Appellate Body Report, *US – Zeroing (EC)*, para. 217. An example of this can be seen in WTO challenges to anti-dumping measures:

> For applicants challenging an anti-dumping measure, the burden of proof may constitute a more formidable hurdle than in other areas of WTO law. This is for two reasons. First, these types of cases are fact-rich and often fact-decisive. At the same time, the respondent, i.e., the WTO member that imposed the measure, often has a monopoly position as the possessor of *all* facts because of the confidentiality systems that prevail in most jurisdictions.

E. Vermulst, *The WTO Anti-Dumping Agreement: A Commentary* (Oxford: Oxford University Press, 2005), 252.

29. It seems legally impossible to consider a challenge to legislation as such without admitting the text of the legislation. However, particular action under that legislation could be challenged without admitting the text of the legislation as evidence: for example, the particular provision of a financial benefit could be made under general appropriations legislation, but the generality of an appropriations clause would make it irrelevant to a challenge to the administrative action of providing the benefit.

activities of States, in the same manner as do legal decisions and administrative measures.[30]

Thus, international tribunals are theoretically allowed to review facts about legislative environments. However, when the parties to the dispute have already presented such facts, international tribunals have no duty to verify them (unlike a domestic court, which may well have such a duty). Indeed, an international tribunal that undertook such a verification process could be perceived as doubting the parties' veracity – which would be an extreme result. One can conclude that international tribunals are unlikely to engage in independent fact-finding about legislative environments.[31] This, combined with the burden of proof on the complaining State, gives the legislating State considerable advantage in the process of determining raw facts about the legislative environment. The resulting deference in the substantive aspects of a challenge to legislation is discussed in more detail in Chapter 8 (certainty characterization).

4.2.2. The Extent of Fact-Finding: Deference as to Admissibility of Raw Facts

A legislating State sometimes claims that only certain kinds of raw facts can be considered by an international tribunal. In some cases, this claim may be that the inter-temporal principle makes certain facts irrelevant to the international law status of legislation. For example, the claim may be that the relevant facts are only those that were available to the legislator during the process of legislating.[32]

30. *Certain German Interests in Polish Upper Silesia* (1926) PCIJ., Series A, No. 7, 19, quoted in Appellate Body Report, *India – Patents (US)*, para. 65 and by ITLOS in M/V 'SAIGA' (*Saint Vincent and The Grenadines v. Guinea*) (No. 2), Provisional Measures, Order made on 11 Mar. 1998, [1998] ITLOS Reports 24, para. 120. The reason for this treatment of domestic legislation is to avoid international courts appearing to make binding interpretations of domestic law (e.g., see *Malone v. The United Kingdom*, 2 Aug. 1984, Series A, No. 82, para. 79) and to allow the application of rules of evidence (in particular, the burden of proof) in the process of making findings (Panel Report, *US – Section 301 Trade Act*, para. 7.18, citing the PCIJ's decision in *Brazilian Loans*, PCIJ, Series A, Nos 20/21, 124 and the ICJ's decision in *Elettronica Sicula S.p.A., Judgment* (1989) ICJ Reports 47, para. 62). However, a failure to make a correct finding of fact can amount to an error of law by an international tribunal. This is particularly relevant in the WTO system, with its two-tier system: as a result, the Appellate Body may review a Panel's characterization of domestic legislation. Otherwise, international tribunals without a general fact finding mandate, such as the Appellate Body, would be unable to characterize the factual background to legislation: *EC – Hormones*, Appellate Body Report, para. 132.
31. This may not apply in relation to facts that stand outside the direct legislative environment, such as market conditions, etc. These kinds of facts do not concern the *legal* effect of domestic legislation, and are thus less susceptible to claims for deference.
32. A similar argument has been made in WTO challenges to administrative action, in relation to the facts available to domestic authorities when granting trade remedies: Ehlermann & N. Lockhart, 'Standard Of Review In WTO Law', JIEL 7 (2004): 491, at 505.

However, this argument is unlikely to succeed unless the particular terms of the international obligation give it clear support.[33]

A more significant claim here relates to the nature of the facts that are admissible. This may happen in two kinds of cases. First, the legislating State may claim that only the legal operation of legislation should be taken into account – but not its practical operation or its legislative environment. This may be the case when the legislation is consistent with the international obligation on its face, but its operation in the context of the facts of the real world is inconsistent with the obligation.[34] Alternatively, the legislating State may claim that the practical operation of the legislation and the legislative environment *should* be taken into account, and that the international tribunal should not focus on the text of the legislation in the abstract. This is the case when the consistency of the legislation with the international obligation depends on the interaction of the legislation with the legislative environment or other facts. As we will see in Chapter 8, this arises in cases of certainty characterization.

This aspect of the extent of the fact-finding exercise is well known to international lawyers through the distinction between characterization de jure and characterization de facto. Characterization de jure involves an assessment of the rights, duties, privileges, powers, and prohibitions created by the challenged legislation. Characterization de facto, in contrast, involves an assessment of how the legislation actually relates to its factual background. As we will see later in our discussion of characterization, this has also been described as the distinction between legal operation and factual operation.[35]

The distinction may be made clearer by an example. In WTO law, legislation creating a subsidy may be export contingent by reason of law (de jure) or by reason of fact (de facto). The Appellate Body has held that de jure export contingency must be demonstrated on the basis of the words of the relevant legal instrument, but de facto contingency 'must be inferred from the total configuration of the facts constituting and surrounding the granting of the subsidy'.[36] For example, a statute that grants money for the export of a product would be characterized as a de jure

33. Support for this position could be extracted by analogy with the inter-temporal principal: see Section 2.4.1.
34. For example, the famous wine gallon case: *Schieffelin & Co. v. United States* 424 F.2d 1396 (1970).
35. See Section 6.2.
36. Appellate Body Report, *Canada – Aircraft*, para. 167. In Appellate Body Report, *Canada – Autos*, para. 100 the Appellate Body said:

> The simplest, and hence, perhaps, the uncommon, case is one in which the condition of exportation is set out expressly, in so many words, on the face of the law, regulation or other legal instrument. We believe, however, that a subsidy is also properly held to be *de jure* export contingent where the condition to export is clearly, though implicitly, in the instrument comprising the measure. Thus, for a subsidy to be *de jure* export contingent, the underlying legal instrument does not always have to provide *expressis verbis* that the subsidy is available only upon fulfillment of the condition of export performance. Such conditionality can also be derived by necessary implication from the words actually used in the measure.

export contingency. By contrast, a statute that grants money for the manufacture of a product for the domestic market, where the factual background shows that the product is an important input for the manufacture of an export product, may be characterized as a de facto export contingency.

The relevant question here is how international tribunals respond to claims for deference by the legislating State – through demands for characterization de jure or characterization de facto. This is discussed in detail in Chapter 6 (factor characterization). However, a few basic observations should be made here.

First, the content of the legislation itself may be so clear that reference to other facts may be unnecessary. The text of legislation is usually the most important fact in any challenge to the legislation; indeed, the text may be a conclusive factor that makes any other facts unnecessary to consider.[37] Second, it is not necessary for a finding of inconsistency that the legislation *expressly* violates the international obligation. The character of legislation can be revealed simply by necessary implication from its terms.[38] Third, one should not give too much weight to the primacy of the legislative text. International tribunals should be willing to consider the effect of legislation in the context of its surrounding matrix of facts.[39] This is consistent with the rule of international law that domestic law is considered as a factual matter in international proceedings and is not given a special status apart from the other facts in a dispute.[40] Finally, a focus on characterization de jure or characterization de facto does not in principle indicate a greater or lesser degree of deference to the legislating State. As we will see in the discussion of factor characterization in Chapter 6, it may suit the interests of the legislating State to support characterization de jure in some cases, but characterization de facto in other cases.

However, different considerations apply to making inferences from such facts. We now turn to issues regarding such inferences.

4.3. INFERENCE DEFERENCE

The making of inferences is one of the most subtle tasks facing a tribunal that is hearing a challenge to legislation. Both tribunals and domestic legislatures have

---

37. As the Appellate Body put it:

> When a measure is challenged 'as such', the starting point for an analysis must be the measure on its face. If the meaning and content of the measure are clear on its face, then the consistency of the measure as such can be assessed on that basis alone. If, however, the meaning or content of the measure is not evident on its face, further examination is required.

US – Corrosion-Resistant Steel Sunset Review, Appellate Body Report, para. 168.

38. Appellate Body Report, *Canada – Autos*, para. 100. However, the Appellate Body stressed (at para. 78) that the relevant provision in the case (Art. I.1 GATT) could apply to de facto discrimination.
39. See Section 6.2.
40. See above, text at n. 30.

legitimate claims to make such inferences. The critical question here is the degree of deference to be given to inferences by a legislature, or more concisely, the degree of *inference deference*.

Domestic legislatures have particular expertise in evaluating local conditions and making predictions about how legislation will affect those conditions. In other words, they are well placed to make inferences through forming opinions and making prognoses.[41] Such inferences may include assessments of existing and future local situations, and assessments of how particular measures will affect local situations (i.e., assessments of causation). Domestic legislatures have a claim to be given considerable deference in making inferences regarding such issues.

One such issue is causation. Answering causal questions in concrete situations is a familiar task, but doing so in the context of justifying legislation may exceed judicial capacities. Thus, the causal connections inherent in a legislative prognosis pose problems for courts and tribunals. The Appellate Body recognized this in *US – Gasoline*, noting that 'the problem of determining causation, well-known in both domestic and international law, is always a difficult one'.[42]

An even more difficult issue for international tribunals is the effect of domestic sentiment. A domestic legislature has a very good claim to be the best judge of inferences concerning domestic sentiment. This is especially the case for an inference relating to local popular perceptions, or other social, cultural, and economic matters. Domestic legislatures may also be best placed to judge

---

41. Domestic constitutional courts have long recognized the need to defer to legislative opinions and prognoses. German public law provides a useful background here. The Federal Constitutional Court recognizes three levels of *Kontrolldichte* (intensity of judicial control) according to which a legislative prognosis can be tested. These levels are, in increasing degree of intensity:

    - *bloße Evidenzkontrolle* (bare review of evidence underlying a prognosis);
    - *Vertretbarkeitskontrolle* (review of the defensibility of a legislative position); and
    - *Inhaltskontrolle* (review of the justice of legislation, or merits review).

    See also W. Zeidler, 'Landesbericht Bundesrepublik Deutschland: Die Verfassungsrechtssprechung im Rahmen der Staatliche Funktion', 15 *EuGRZ* (1988): 207, at 217; N. Stedler, *Gesetzgeber und Bundesverfassungsgericht* (Hamburg: Dr Kovač, 1998), 75–76. The three levels of intensity was first developed in the context of the constitutional right to freedom of occupation, where the intensity of review was seen as increasing from intrusions into: first, exercise of occupation,; second, subjective requirements of registration; and third, objective requirements of registration (also known as the 'three step theory' or *Dreistufenlehre*): Schlaich & Korioth, above n. 40, 293–296; C. Gusy, *Parlamentarische Gesetzgeber und Bundesverfassungsgericht* (Berlin: Duncker & Humblot, 1985), 174; B. Pieroth & B. Schlink, *Grundrechte*, 19th edn (Heidelberg: CF Müller, 2003), 212, para. 846. German lawyers recognize that these three levels of intensity are the result of a strict application of the principle of proportionality: BVerfGE 13, 97 (104) – *Handwerksordnung*.
42. Appellate Body Report, *US – Gasoline*, Art. III(C). Domestic constitutional courts rarely challenge the causal inferences made by the legislature. For example, in Germany, Sachs, Art. 20, in M. Sachs (ed.), *Grundgesetz*, 4th edn (München: CH Beck, 2007), para. 150, at 816 lists only a handful of examples (BVerfGE 17, 306 (315 et seq.), BVerfGE 19, 330 (338 et seq.), BVerfGE 55, 159 (165 et seq.)).

local sentiment as to risk, effectiveness, and causation. This has led domestic constitutional courts to defer to the legislature's opinion in such matters.[43] Special deference is given to the legislature in making assessments of facts and making prognoses about the future effects of a law.[44] As we will see later, these concepts are reflected in WTO law on deference, concerning the standard of review of characterization of facts.[45]

Issues of domestic sentiment are most acute if the relevant inference concerns a conflict of values. We can see this in the WTO: conflicts of values such as free trade and environmental protection provoke intense controversy about the relative responsibilities of WTO tribunals and domestic authorities. Here, Oesch argues for considerable deference to domestic authorities:

> [F]actual conclusions and ultimate decisions to adopt trade-restrictive policies and measures may well involve political, economic, ethical, and other societal considerations. Therefore, there might be circumstances in which more than only one factual conclusion drawn from the 'raw' evidence, and thus more than only one 'truth', to use Mavroidis' words, can legitimately coexist. In such cases, panels and the Appellate Body are well advised not to decide on the prioritisation of diverse political and societal values and priorities. They could leave room for domestic regulatory decision-making by establishing an 'institutional sensitivity' to the superior credentials which other institutions of

---

43. For example, German constitutional law takes account of the legislature's *Spielraum* (room to move), or the *gesetzgeberische Einschätzungsprärogative* (legislative opinion-making prerogative). See Pieroth & Schlink, above n. 41, 66, para. 287.
44. In Germany, there is large body of jurisprudence and commentary about the concepts of *Tatsachenfeststellung* (legislative fact finding) and *Prognosefeststellung* (legislative forecasting): Schlaich & Korioth, above n. 40, 293–296; E. Benda, & E. Klein, *Verfassungsprozeßrecht*, 2nd edn (Heidelberg: C.F. Müller, 2001), 114–116. Legislative fact-finding concerns existing or past matters. Legislative forecasting concerns future matters. The legislature enjoys some freedom of movement in legislative fact-finding and forecasting. It enjoys a certain freedom in assessing these matters (*gesetzgeberische Einschätzungsprärogative*): Pieroth & Schlink, above n. 41, 66, para. 287. For example, in legislative forecasting, the Federal Constitutional Court has 'observed, in consistent case law, the legislature's *Spielraum* for assessment in decisions with the character of a prognosis': BVerfGE 62, 1 (50). Nevertheless, this freedom is not absolute: BVerfGE 50, 290 (332). Gusy, above n. 41, 165 suggests:

    > However, facts and prognoses are not norms . . . A norm is not unconstitutional simply because it 'contradicts' reality: this means that facts and prognoses can be critical to a decision only to the extent that constitutional law norms regard them as yardsticks. *Tatsachen und Prognosen sind jedoch keine Normen . . . Da eine Norm nicht deshalb verfassungswidrig ist, weil sie Realitäten 'widerspricht', können Tatsachen und Prognosen nur insoweit entscheidungserheblich sein, als Normen des Verfassungsrechts sie als Maßstab einbeziehen.*

    However, a constitutional court should avoid replacing an uncertain opinion of the legislature with its own uncertain opinion: K. Hesse, *Grundzüge des Verfassungsrechts der Bundesrepublik Deutschland*, 20th edn (Heidelberg: CF Müller, 1995), 270.
45. See Section 4.6.1.2.

> governance potentially have in deciding substantive trade-offs between various policy preferences.[46] [footnotes omitted]

Perhaps the most controversial conflicts here deal with rights, whether fundamental or otherwise. Legislatures have a lesser claim to deference when they intrude on basic human rights. For example, domestic authorities can expect close scrutiny in a determination of whether a particular kind of conduct constitutes 'torture' – especially if those authorities claim that local customs and standards are relevant – as this is a matter of universal interest. However, outside such core areas of human rights, the picture is less clear. For example, to the extent that WTO obligations can be said to create trade rights, such rights could be seen as absolute or relative, depending on one's perspective. The extent to which such rights should be subject to international standards is still a matter of political and legal debate.[47]

Nevertheless, international tribunals have particular expertise in interpreting the content of international obligations. When the crux of a dispute is the abstract general meaning of an international obligation (rather than the characterization of a particular situation), the tribunal has particular expertise in resolving the dispute. In such cases, the tribunal may refuse to defer to the opinion of the legislature, as the issue relates to the interpretation of the international obligation. To do otherwise would risk the international obligation taking on a 'patchwork quilt' of meanings, depending on the preferences of each individual State.[48]

---

46. Oesch, above n. 21, 641. See also S. Zleptnig, 'The Standard of Review in WTO Law – An Analysis of Law, Legitimacy and the Distribution of Legal and Political Authority', *EIoP* 6 (2002), <http://eiop.or.at/eiop/texte/2002-017a.htm> (visited 21 Mar. 2007), 16, who applies a 'deliberation test':

> [W]henever national authorities engage in a balancing act between competing interests, they are required to take into account the interests of (foreign and domestic) stakeholders in a transparent, deliberate manner.

47. Ehlermann & Lockhart, above n. 32, 520, suggest that there will be more deference to administrative decision-making where there is an independent and dedicated decision-maker with a particular decision-making process. They suggest that there will be less deference in cases where the decision-maker is simply a general part of government. However, this suggestion does not translate easily to legislative decision-making. The decision-maker here is the legislature, which is a general part of government. Yet the legislature, by its nature, demands deference from the courts, domestic and international. It is nevertheless arguable that more deference should be given where the legislator has followed a decision-making process specially tailored to the issue in question: for example, where the legislature has based legislation on the findings of a special parliamentary committee.
48. See Section 4.6, text at n. 134. These issues are not unique to challenges to legislation. Similar questions about the relative competences of domestic authorities and international tribunals also arise in international challenges to administrative action. However, challenges to legislation pose these questions from a different perspective. Domestic administrators and domestic legislatures themselves have differing competences, and thus have differing grounds for their claims for inference deference. In particular, domestic parliaments with a popular mandate have special claims to making inferences about public sentiment, while administrators may have special claims for deference based on their technical expertise.

The distinction between the expertise of domestic legislatures and that of international tribunals reflects an ancient distinction in legal theory between questions of fact and questions of law.[49] For example, the Appellate Body has said:

> [P]anels routinely draw inferences from the facts placed on the record. The inferences drawn may be inferences of fact: that is, from fact A and fact B, it is reasonable to infer the existence of fact C. Or the inferences derived may be inferences of law: for example the ensemble of facts found to exist warrants the characterization of a 'subsidy'.[50]

An inference of fact (which does not result in automatic characterization within a legal category) should attract deference. By contrast, an inference of law (which does result in such automatic characterization) is purely a matter for the tribunal. For example, an inference that consumers prefer one kind of product over another kind (an inference of fact) should attract deference from a tribunal that has limited expertise in making such findings. However, an inference that the two products are 'like' (an inference of law) would attract less deference from the same tribunal, on the basis that it has considerable expertise in findings of law.

While the fact or law distinction is easy to discuss in this theoretical way, in practice, it has limited use in determining inference deference. The process of inference takes place in a grey zone between the interpretation of international obligations (a legal task entrusted to courts) and the forming of opinions about the meaning of facts (a task that the legislature may claim to be better equipped for than the courts). The problem here is that there is no clear border between an opinion or prognosis on the one hand, and a legal interpretation on the other hand. The fact or law distinction is really a matter of judicial policy:

> Matters of law grow downward into roots of fact, and matters of fact reach upward, without a break, into matters of law. The knife of policy alone effects an artificial cleavage at the point where the court chooses to draw the line.[51]

Indeed, the fact or law distinction is a troubled one when used as a legal decision-making criterion. Courts deal with questions of fact every day,[52] just as legislatures and administrators deal with questions of law. It is the 'knife of policy' – as determined by the tribunal – that draws the line between the two.

---

49. A. Stuart, ' "I tell ya I don't get no respect!": The Policies Underlying Standards of Review in U.S. Courts as a Basis for Deference to Municipal Determinations in GATT Panel Appeals', *Law & Pol'y Int'l. Bus.* 23, no. 49 (1992): 760.
50. *Canada – Aircraft*, Appellate Body Report, para. 198.
51. Dickinson, *Administrative Justice and the Supremacy of Law in the United States* (Cambridge: Cambridge University Press, 1927), 55.
52. According to an authoritative common law commentary (J. Wigmore, *Wigmore on Evidence*, 3rd edn (Boston: Little Brown, 1940), vol. 4, at § 1353):

    > The judicial function under the constitution is to apply the law in controverted cases; to apply the law necessarily involves the determination of the facts; to determine the facts necessarily involves the investigation of evidence as a basis for that determination. To forbid investigation is to forbid the exercise of an indestructible judicial function.

The problem for international tribunals here is that there are few yardsticks by which matters of law (attracting low deference) can be separated from matters of fact (attracting higher deference). Rarely, the relevant international obligation may expressly set such a standard.[53] In most cases, however, international tribunals are left on their own to discover the relevant standard.

One common yardstick here is rationality. If an inference is rational, it is said to be beyond the capacity of a court to review it. Clear irrationality will justify judicial review. This is a measure of deference often used in the review of administrative decisions. This is unsurprising, given that administrators *must* act rationally, and often must often demonstrate that they have done so. No administrator claims the right to act based on emotion or feelings alone. Of course, the difficulty here is to set an objective measure for rationality. In some cases, this may be done by reference to the opinions of outside experts[54] or to internationally recognized standards.[55] In other cases, the rationality criterion may focus on matters of procedure rather than substance; that is, the focus will be on the procedures by which domestic actors make decisions, rather than the substance of those decisions.

Arguably, the rationality criterion can also be extended to challenges to legislative inferences. Yet, there are difficulties in doing so. Legislative decision-making, particularly in pluralistic legislatures, is done in ways that are different from administrative decision-making. Administrative inferences are made by one or a few people, but legislative inferences may be made by a large group. Administrative decisions are made on the basis of fixed criteria, but legislative decisions are not. This creates difficulties for courts, which can make decisions only according to legal criteria to review legislative inferences. Legislative decisions are made on a polycentric basis,[56] involving an unlimited number of actors, inputs, and criteria. Courts are ill-equipped to analyse polycentric decision-making. Furthermore, the limits on legislative action are political in nature (and in democracies, are subject to the periodic judgment of the people). Thus, legislative decision-making must often be based on popular perceptions, at least in part. This explains the Appellate Body's famous and cryptic remark that health issues must be assessed 'in human societies as they actually exist', that is, 'in the real world where people live and work and die'.[57] Human societies as they actually exist are not entirely rational, but also involve traditions, perceptions, and instincts.

---

53. For example, Art. 17 Anti-Dumping Agreement.
54. There are numerous examples of international tribunals commissioning expert's reports as to inferences that can be drawn from the raw facts. See Kazazi, above n. 23, 170.
55. See Section 6.3, text at n. 22.
56. L. Fuller, 'The Forms and Limits of Adjudication', *Harvard Law Review* 92 (1978): 353, at 394.
57. Appellate Body Report, *EC – Hormones*, para. 187:

> It is essential to bear in mind that the risk that is to be evaluated in a risk assessment under Article 5.1 [SPS Agreement] is not only risk ascertainable in a science laboratory operating under strictly controlled conditions, but also risk in human societies as they actually exist, in other words, the actual potential for adverse effects on human health in the real world where people live and work and die.

These matters make it even harder for international tribunals to set a yardstick of deference to legislative inferences. Obvious irrationality or bad faith in decision-making will not attract deference, but it is quite difficult to prove this in the case of legislative decision-making. In any case, some leeway should be given to domestic traditions and popular perceptions – the best judge of which is a representative domestic legislature.[58]

An example is helpful here to illustrate these points. In WTO cases concerning the national treatment obligation in Article III of the GATT, the crucial issue is often whether imported and local products are 'like' products. WTO jurisprudence sets out a list of factors that should be taken into account in deciding this question, including consumer sentiment.[59] But who is the best judge of consumer sentiment? The raw facts – consumption statistics, responses to surveys, etc. – may be agreed upon, but the inferences that can be made from these facts are likely to be highly controversial. A domestic legislature may claim that it can best judge popular perception. Yet the scope of the 'like product' concept is a matter of law, and a tribunal may be best placed to apply legal methods in determining that scope. The degree of deference here cannot be defined by a bright line. According to Ehlermann and Lockhart:

> Panels make findings that: (a) are purely legal in nature; (b) are purely factual; and (c) involve the application of the facts to the law. This last activity is the most difficult to pin down. It involves the weighing and appreciation of the facts and their characterisation in terms of the legal rules.[60]

---

58. Here, admittedly, difficult questions arise as to whether the democratic basis of a legislature can be a relevant factor in international challenges to legislation. There is no easy answer to this question for a global community of States that includes a mixture of autocratic and democratic legislatures. However, regional communities of States sharing a common commitment to democracy may have no difficulties in translating this commitment into a legal norm affecting the measure of deference (as is the case in Europe, see n. 106).
59. In *Japan – Alcoholic Beverages II*, 113, the Appellate Body noted with approval the 1970 Report of the Working Party on Border Tax Adjustments (BISD 18S/97, para. 18):

    > [T]he interpretation of the term ['like or similar products'] should be examined on a case-by-case basis. This would allow a fair assessment in each case of the different elements that constitute a 'similar' product. Some criteria were suggested for determining, on a case-by-case basis, whether a product is 'similar': the product's end-uses in a given market; consumers' tastes and habits, which change from country to country; the product's properties, nature and quality.

    In the case of Art. I GATT, P. Mavroidis, *The General Agreement on Tariffs and Trade* (Oxford: Oxford University Press, 2005), 147–148, notes also the relevance of products' tariff classifications.
60. Ehlermann & Lockhart, above n. 32, 496. At 504, they say (in the context of Art. 17.6 Anti-Dumping Agreement):

    > [T]he panel must make a judgement that combines, inseparably, an appreciation of the facts with an interpretation of legal norms. It is, perhaps, *the interpretation of legal rules in*

It is this process of 'characterization in terms of the legal rules' that lies at the heart of most challenges to legislation. As we will see in Chapters 6–8, legislation must be characterized in terms of WTO obligations to determine its WTO-consistency. As Ehlermann and Lockhart suggest, one cannot see this characterization process as simply a matter of law (implying lesser deference) or a matter of fact (implying more deference). It is a complex mixture of both.[61]

In sum, legislating States make strong claims for deference about their own inferences drawn from the raw facts, and international tribunals face a difficult task in finding a yardstick to evaluate these claims. Inferences are often not susceptible to legal methods of analysis. In many case, particularly in challenges to legislation, inferences concern matters of subjective impression, judgment of popular perceptions, and balancing of values. Inferences are also often closely connected to domestic conditions. Domestic legislatures have a good claim to be the best judge of such matters. They can, and do, make legitimate claims for deference here.

We now briefly explore some established concepts of deference in public international law, namely, the reserved domain of domestic jurisdiction and the margin of appreciation. We will then go on to look at the WTO concept of substantive deference, that is, the standard of review.

> *concreto rather than in abstracto*. As this characterisation process is very much a mixed question of fact and law, it is difficult to decide which of the two 'boxes' in Article 17.6 applies because, in a sense, both do. [emphasis added]

61. The Appellate Body may sometimes treat findings of a kind involving 'the application of the facts to the law' as a legal matter, e.g., in *EC – Hormones*, para. 132:

> The determination of whether or not a certain event did occur in time and space is typically a question of fact . . . Determination of the credibility and weight properly to be ascribed to (that is, the appreciation of) a given piece of evidence is part and parcel of the fact finding process and is, in principle, left to the discretion of a panel as the trier of facts. The consistency or inconsistency of a given fact or set of facts with the requirements of a given treaty provision is, however, a legal characterization issue.

See also Appellate Body Report, *Argentina – Footwear (EC)*, para. 120. However, this approach is arguably driven by the need to allow appellate review of Panel decisions about such matters. The Appellate Body has made this quite clear in relation to challenges to legislation:

> [T]he municipal law of WTO Members may serve not only as evidence of facts, but also as evidence of compliance or non-compliance with international obligations. Under the DSU, a panel may examine the municipal law of a WTO Member for the purpose of determining whether that Member has complied with its obligations under the WTO Agreement. Such an assessment is a legal characterization by a panel. And, therefore, a panel's assessment of municipal law as to its consistency with WTO obligations is subject to appellate review under Article 17.6 of the DSU.

Appellate Body Report, *US – Section 211 Appropriations Act*, para. 105. See also Appellate Body Report, *Chile – Price Band System*, para. 273.

4.4. INTERNATIONAL OBLIGATIONS PROVIDING A STANDARD OF DEFERENCE

Determining the degree of deference inherent in a particular international obligation is generally a matter of applying principles of treaty interpretation.[62] In most cases, these principles are applied on a textual and contextual basis in light of the object and purpose of the treaty. That is, the degree of deference depends in each case on the unique features of the treaty in question.

However, some general questions can be asked here:

- First, can treaty rules allow States discretion in interpreting those rules?
- Second, can the content of a particular obligation be determined by domestic law?

These questions are discussed below.

4.4.1. Allowing States Discretion in Applying an International Obligation

Commonly, a legislating State claims that it should be allowed some discretion in applying an international obligation. But what is the legal basis of such a claim?

Some commentators have tried to identify general patterns in the extent to which international obligations give discretions to legislating States. Perhaps the most ambitious attempt was that of Ago, drawing on the distinction between obligations of conduct and obligations of result.[63] An obligation of conduct attracts less deference, as States are obliged to adopt certain means to achieve an end. An obligation of result attracts more deference, as States are free to choose their own means to achieve an end. However, Ago's theory suffers from indeterminacy. In particular, the degree to which an obligation requires particular conduct to achieve an end depends on the way in which one characterizes that end.[64] As discussed earlier, Ago's general theory was not commonly accepted by States as a legal concept.[65]

---

62. Except in the rarer case where the international obligation is based in customary law. In these cases, the degree of deference inherent in the obligation is determined by the methods of determining customary international law, that is, by an examination of State practice and *opinio iuris*.
63. See Section 4.2.1.
64. Take, for example, an international obligation to provide a period of patent protection of twenty years. The purpose of the obligation can be characterized in two ways. On the one hand, the purpose can be seen as ensuring a *suitable* length of patent protection. Characterized in this way, the obligation is, in Ago's terms, an obligation of conduct: the obligation sets out the means by which a suitable length of protection can be provided, namely by providing twenty years of protection. On the other hand, the purpose can be seen as ensuring *twenty years* of patent protection. Characterized in this way, the obligation is one of result: the obligation sets out the result of twenty years of protection, and leaves it to the State to determine the means by which this period of protection will be provided.
65. See Prelude, text at n. 38.

Some years after Ago's attempt, Shany suggested that deference be given in a number of recognized categories of international obligation. These are 'standard-type norms, discretionary norms and result-oriented norms'.[66] Standard-type norms are norms that set broad standards rather than provide detailed rules. Discretionary norms are norms that expressly allow States some discretion (e.g., when a rule is conditioned upon a State 'considering' that a certain situation exists).[67] Result-oriented norms are obligations of result (Shany is a supporter of Ago's theory in this regard). However, Shany is careful not to make these categories too rigid:

> [T]he degree of judicial deference in the context of application of the doctrine [of margin of appreciation] is not fixed. It should vary in the light of a variety of considerations. The practice of the ECtHR, the most experienced of the international courts applying the doctrine, as well as the policy considerations developed above suggest that these considerations should include: (a) importance of the interests implicated by the relevant norms; (b) the degree of normative uncertainty; and (c) the comparative decision-making facilities of international courts and domestic institutions relating to the specific matter at hand.[68]

As stressed many times in this book, the particular features of the relevant obligation will be the decisive factor in each case.

It is worth examining more closely the three factors identified by Shany. The importance of the relevant interests is a problematic criterion in deciding whether an international obligation allows more or less deference. International tribunals are badly placed to judge the relative importance of interests, unless the international obligation makes this clear. Nevertheless, if the obligation implies a proportionality-type analysis, it may force a tribunal to account for the importance of the relevant interests.[69] The degree of normative uncertainty is perhaps a more useful criterion for an international tribunal. Lawyers are well suited to discovering uncertainties in legal norms; when international tribunals do so, this will be an indication that the international obligation in question grants a high degree of

66. Shany, above n. 14, 939.
67. A good example is Art. XXI GATT, discussed in text at n. 125.
68. Shany, above n. 14, 939. He also notes (again at 939) that:

> [T]he doctrine is particularly suitable only for certain types of international law norms, which are intrinsically uncertain or consciously sacrifice legal certainty for pluralism (standard-type norms, discretionary norms and result-oriented norms). It should not be used to obfuscate areas of the law where legal precision has been or is in the process of being attained. Second, the scope of the margin of appreciation could change over time, in the light of emerging specific norms, the development of value choices which place a higher premium on legal certainty (or uniformity) and shifts in the respective institutional capacities of national and international courts.

69. See Ch. 7 on proportionality characterization.

deference. By contrast, the balance between international and domestic decision-making abilities, as a legal criterion, is inadequate when the international tribunal has no yardstick for judging those abilities. This criterion brings us back to the issues discussed in the previous section about inference deference.

In the WTO, the Appellate Body has expressly adopted the interpretive principle known as *in dubio mitius*.[70] According to this principle, if there is any ambiguity in the meaning of an international obligation, the ambiguity should be resolved in favour of the sovereignty of the State. The principle therefore reflects Shany's criterion of normative uncertainty mentioned above. However, the Appellate Body's adoption of the *in dubio mitius* principle has been criticized.[71] In any case, the *in dubio mitius* principle does not give States total discretion: there must be an ambiguity in an international obligation before it applies.[72] Nevertheless, legislating States have often claimed a right to this deference.[73]

It seems likely that there are no clear general principles for determining the degree of deference from the content of international obligations. As is the case dealing with inferences, the appropriate degree of deference depends on a range of factors, the relative importance of which will depend on the circumstances of the case.

A particular feature of some international obligations is considered next. These are the obligations that attract deference because they incorporate the content of domestic law.

4.4.2. Determining the Content of an International Obligation via Domestic Law

It may be surprising to suggest that domestic law can determine (part) of the content of international law. However, it is clear that this is correct. According

70. Appellate Body Report, *EC – Hormones*, para. 165 and fn. 154, citing R. Jennings & A. Watts (eds), *Oppenheim's International Law*, 9th edn (Essex: Longman's, 1992), 1278:

> The principle of *in dubio mitius* applies in interpreting treaties, in deference to the sovereignty of states. If the meaning of a term is ambiguous, that meaning is to be preferred which is less onerous to the party assuming an obligation, or which interferes less with the territorial and personal supremacy of a party, or involves less general restrictions upon the parties.

71. See, for example, M. Lennard, 'Navigating by the Stars: Interpreting the WTO Agreements', JIEL 5 (2002): 17, at 62–65.
72. See the US and EC insistence on there being an ambiguity for the principle to apply, Appellate Body Report, *Korea – Alcoholic Beverages*, paras 47 and 78.
73. For example, see the US claim in Panel Report, *US – Section 301 Trade Act*, para. 4.388; the EC claim in Panel Report, *EC – Export Subsidies on Sugar (Australia)*, para. 4.208; Chile's claim in Panel Report, *Chile – Price Band System*, para. 4.45; Korea's claim in Appellate Body Report, *Korea – Alcoholic Beverages*, para. 5.

to general theories on the sources in international law,[74] there are basically three[75] ways in which domestic legislation can affect international law:

- Domestic legislation can form State practice, and/or *opinio iuris* as to the content of a rule of customary international law.[76]
- Rules of treaty interpretation allow the 'subsequent practice'[77] of the parties to be treated as context to treaty text. Such subsequent practice could include the ongoing existence of old domestic legislation, or the passage of new domestic legislation.
- The content of international obligations (treaty or customary law) may refer expressly or impliedly to the content of domestic legislation.[78]

The second factor has been expressly recognized in WTO litigation. In two cases, the Appellate Body has held that a WTO member's legislation on customs classification is relevant to the interpretation of that member's tariff schedule to the GATT.[79]

However, the third factor here is by far the most important for challenges to legislation. Such challenges often involve a claim by the legislating State that a particular treaty obligation was drafted with particular domestic legislation in mind. A typical example is a reference in a treaty to 'nationality'. Normally, such a reference is read in light of domestic legislation defining nationality for a particular State.[80]

A few international tribunals have mentioned this issue, and several commentators have dealt with it in detail.[81] One example is the judgment of ad hoc Judge Kreca in the *Bosnia* case:

> One can think of a long list of rules of positive international law that rest on the symbiosis of an international norm containing both implicit and explicit references to the internal law and the respective norms of that internal law . . . [a number of examples are given]. Thus, in the present case, this is not a

74. For theoretical debates over the general doctrines of sources of international law, see M. Koskenniemi (ed.), *Sources of International Law* (Aldershot: Ashgate Publishing Company, 2000).
75. A possible fourth way is that of the domestic Statute as a *unilateral act* with significance in international law: see generally, International Law Commission, *Report of the International Law Commission*, 58th session, A/61/10 (2006), Ch. IX.
76. Jennings & Watts, above n. 70, 26: I. Brownlie, *Principles of Public International Law*, 6th edn (Oxford: Oxford University Press, 2003), 6, fn. 16.
77. Vienna Convention on the Law of Treaties (23 May 1969, 1155 UNTS 331; 8 ILM 679), Art. 31.3(b) allows 'any subsequent practice in the application of the treaty which establishes the agreement of the parties regarding its interpretation' to be treated as context to treaty text.
78. Jennings & Watts, above n. 70, 83–84.
79. Appellate Body Report, *EC – Computer Equipment*, para. 94; Appellate Body Report, *EC – Chicken Cuts*, para. 308.
80. For example, BVerfGE 16, 27 – *Iranian Embassy*, 62.
81. See the references quoted in Jennings & Watts, above n. 70, 83–84, fn. 4. This point has also been made by domestic constitutional courts. For example, in *Hamdan v. Rumsfeld* 548 US 557

> matter of a conflict between a norm of international and a norm of internal law, a type of case adjudicated by several international courts . . . but rather of the application of an international norm of a complex structure, namely a norm that incorporates relevant norms of internal law.[82]

This issue was also raised in the PCIJ in the *Exchange of Greek and Turkish Populations* case.[83] It may be referred to as the 'incorporation of domestic law in international law'.

(2006), Justice Alito noted in relation to the reference to 'a regularly constituted court' in common Art. 3 of the Geneva Conventions as follows:

> In order to determine whether a court has been properly appointed, set up, or established, it is necessary to refer to a body of law that governs such matters. I interpret Common Article 3 as looking to the domestic law of the appointing country because I am not aware of any international law standard regarding the way in which such a court must be appointed, set up, or established, and because different countries with different government structures handle this matter differently. Accordingly, 'a regularly constituted court' is a court that has been appointed, set up, or established in accordance with the domestic law of the appointing country.

82. *Application of the Convention on the Prevention and Punishment of the Crime of Genocide* (*Bosnia and Herzegovina v. Yugoslavia*), Preliminary Objections 1996 (II) ICJ Reports 595); see <www.icj-cij.org/icjwww/idocket/ibhy/ibhyjudgment/ibhy_ijudgment_960711_dissentingopinionkreca.htm> (visited 22 Feb. 2007).
83. *Exchange of Greek and Turkish Populations* (1925) PCIJ, Series B, No. 10, at 20. The treaty obligation concerned all Greeks who were 'established' in a certain area before a certain date. The PCIJ rejected a Turkish argument that the meaning of the word 'established' had to be given by domestic legislation. It said:

> [I]f an expression, not in itself of a legal nature, is used in a convention which derives legal consequences from it, it does not in the least follow that this criterion must be sought in the legislation of the respective contracting States.

Nevertheless, the Court appeared to acknowledge that particular international obligations could incorporate domestic law in this way, acknowledging that the question before it was whether the particular obligation in that case made 'implicit reference to national legislation' (at 19). In *US – Softwood Lumber IV*, the Appellate Body noted that 'an examination of municipal law or particular transactions governed by it might be relevant, as evidence, in ascertaining whether a financial contribution exists' (at para. 56). However, it noted (again at para. 56):

> [M]unicipal laws – in particular those relating to property – vary amongst WTO Members. Clearly, it would be inappropriate to characterize, for purposes of applying any provisions of the WTO covered agreements, the same thing or transaction differently, depending on its legal categorization within the jurisdictions of different Members.

See also Appellate Body Report, *US – Corrosion-Resistant Steel Sunset Review*, fn. 87.

These issues are discussed in more detail in the dissenting opinion of Judge Cassese in *Prosecutor v. Drazen Erdemovic*, International Criminal Tribunal for the former Yugoslavia, Appeals Chamber, 7 Oct. 1997, <www.un.org/icty/erdemovic/appeal/judgement/erd-adojcas971007e.htm> (visited 11 Apr. 2008). Judge Cassese suggests a strict approach to incorporation, allowing it only if '[domestic] notions or terms are given a totally autonomous significance in the international context, i.e., whether, once transposed onto the international level, they have acquired a new lease of life, absolutely independent of their original meaning' (at para. 6).

The incorporation of domestic law in international law has obvious implications for the degree of deference shown in challenges to legislation. If the relevant international obligation incorporates rules contained in domestic legislation, the international tribunal should show total deference to those rules because they represent the international law applicable in the case.

However, total deference to incorporated rules of domestic legislation is not always appropriate. For example, reduced deference is appropriate if the international obligation merely requires a comparison between the challenged legislation and other domestic legislation. This is a familiar concept in international human rights law dealing with discrimination. For example, legislation may 'discriminate' against a particular group only in the sense that it does not protect the group in the ways in which other groups are protected by other legislation. It is the existence of the other legislation that creates the relevant discrimination. That is, the yardstick against which the international prohibition of 'discrimination' is to be applied is that given by domestic legislation. To that extent, the rules set by domestic legislation are incorporated into the international obligation. However, those standards are determined by a process of characterization: they are not set out on the face of the legislation. As will be discussed in Chapters 5–8, the process of characterization need not be deferential in nature.

This situation is fairly common in WTO litigation. It occurs, for example, in subsidy cases involving the element of forgoing revenue 'that is otherwise due'. The Appellate Body has made clear that the concept of 'otherwise due' needs to be applied in light of the general standards of the respondent State, which in many cases is set by domestic legislation. For example, in the *US – FSC* dispute, the question of whether a tax exemption created forgone revenue 'otherwise due' was judged in light of the general tax base, set by domestic tax law.[84]

In summary, the amount of deference given to a legislature by an international tribunal varies according to the nature of the international obligation concerned. It is difficult to give any general yardstick for the appropriate amount of deference; this will be determined by the exact content of the international obligation. In the case of a treaty, this content is determined using the general principles of treaty interpretation.

4.5. GENERAL CONCEPTS OF DEFERENCE IN GENERAL PUBLIC INTERNATIONAL LAW

We now move on to consider two doctrines developed by international lawyers to express deference to domestic decision-making: the reserved domain of domestic jurisdiction and the margin of appreciation. This will set the context for our discussion of the WTO standard of review later in this chapter.

---

84. See Section 6.3, text at n. 25. Compare also the EU jurisprudence on State aids, for example, in C-217/03 *Belgium and Forum 187 v. Commission* [2006] ECR I-5479, para. 120.

4.5.1. THE RESERVED DOMAIN OF DOMESTIC JURISDICTION

International law has traditionally recognized a doctrine of the reserved domain of domestic jurisdiction.[85] According to this doctrine, certain matters are solely within the domestic concerns of States. Thus, States sometimes argue that international courts lack jurisdiction to consider matters that are within the 'reserved domain of domestic jurisdiction'.[86] However, in today's environment of increasingly ambitious international regimes, the concept of the reserved domain of domestic jurisdiction is becoming less and less useful as a measure of deference.[87] Nevertheless, the concept is still a general principle of international law,[88] and it can sometimes affect the degree of deference shown in a particular dispute.

The reserved domain of domestic jurisdiction has obvious implications for deference in international challenges to legislation. If domestic legislation deals with a matter within this domain, it is arguably unchallengeable *ratione materiae*: the degree of deference is total. Arguably, legislative activity has traditionally been within the reserved domain of domestic jurisdiction. This is because until fairly recently, international law and international relations have been governed mainly by the executive branch. In the past, legislatures were not often involved in international legal processes (although there were notable exceptions, such as the US Congress). Now, however, international law intrudes deeply into the legislative field, particularly concerning subjects such as human rights and trade.

Nevertheless, the reserved domain of domestic jurisdiction is perhaps not the most useful measure of deference to apply to modern challenges to legislation. While it may have been useful in earlier disputes, involving much less-detailed international obligations, the doctrine is not suited to modern disputes involving international obligations that delve deeply into the workings of a State (such as human rights and international trade obligations). The doctrine is simply too blunt an instrument to be of use in today's complex disputes.

---

85. G. Fitzmaurice, 'Law and Procedure of the International Court of Justice, 1951-4: International Organizations and Tribunals', BYIL 1, no. 29 (1952): 34–39; H. Waldock, 'Plea of Domestic Jurisdiction before International Legal Tribunals', BYIL 31 (1954): 96; G. Fitzmaurice, 'Law and Procedure of the International Court of Justice, 1954-9: General Principles and Sources of International Law', BYIL 1, no. 34 (1959): 197–207.
86. For example, some States have included reservations to their acceptance of ICJ jurisdiction based on this doctrine: J. Combacau & S. Sur, *Droit International Publique* (Paris: Montchrestien, 2001), 591.
87. Thus Brownlie, above n. 76, 290–291, argues that the doctrine is a 'tautology', 'not very fruitful' and 'a source of confusion'. He rejects the view that lists of categories of subject-matters (such as nationality and immigration) within the reserved domain can be drawn up, as 'everything depends on the precise facts and legal issues arising therefrom'.
88. Relevant literature is cited by Brownlie, above n. 76, 290.

Inroads into 'domestic jurisdiction' were foreseen by the PCIJ in the *Nationality Decrees in Tunis and Morocco* case:[89]

> The question whether a certain matter is or is not solely within the jurisdiction of a State is an essentially relative question; it depends upon the development of international relations. Thus, in the present state of international law, questions of nationality are, in the opinion of the Court, in principle within this reserved domain.
>
> For the purposes of the present opinion, it is enough to observe that it may well happen that, *in a matter which, like that of nationality, is not, in principle, regulated by international law*, the right of the State to use its discretion is nevertheless restricted by obligations which it may have undertaken towards other States. In such a case, jurisdiction, which in principle, belongs solely to the State, is limited by rules of International Law.[90] [emphasis added]

Therefore, it is possible to mount an international challenge to legislation that is 'not in principle regulated by international law'. This is true if special international rules affect matters within the general reserved domestic domain, as can be seen in the *Nationality Decrees* case itself. There, decrees were issued in Tunis, Morocco, and France conferring French nationality (and liability to military service) on a class of persons (including some British nationals). In reply to a British complaint, France claimed that nationality rules were within the reserved domain of domestic jurisdiction and that the decrees were therefore outside the jurisdiction of the PCIJ (in other words, claiming total deference from the PCIJ). The PCIJ disagreed. On the basis of the reasoning cited above, it allowed the British claim to proceed.[91]

The PCIJ's argument that specific international rules can intrude into the reserved domain implies that this domain will contract as the scope of international obligations expand. There is no doctrine of international law that forbids the development of treaty obligations with respect to a particular subject matter. The rapid expansion of treaty regimes in recent days means that there is little scope for the reserved domain principle to restrict the jurisdiction of international tribunals. In the case of the WTO, we have already seen that basic jurisdictional limitations to challenges to legislation have receded dramatically.

However, the concept of 'domestic jurisdiction' still appears in particular incarnations. One common example occurs in reservations to a jurisdictional declaration under Article 36(2) of the Statute of the ICJ.[92] Here, it is not clear whether

89. PCIJ Ser. B, No. 4 (1923).
90. PCIJ Ser. B, No. 4 (1923), 24.
91. The case was eventually resolved by negotiation, with France altering the decrees to exempt British subjects: see W. Benedek, 'Nationality Decrees in Tunis and Morocco (Advisory Opinion)', in *Encyclopedia of Public International Law*, ed. R. Bernhardt, vol. 3 (Elsevier, 1997), 510.
92. *Statute of the International Court of Justice*, 26 Jun. 1945, UKTS 1946 No. 67 (Cmd. 7015). See for example the Canadian reservation discussed in *Fisheries Jurisdiction* (*Spain v. Canada*), Jurisdiction, Judgment, ICJ Reports (1998) 432, 439: 'disputes with regard to questions which by international law fall exclusively within the jurisdiction of Canada'.

the concept can have a major impact on the Court's jurisdiction to hear a case.[93] However, the mention of a reserved domain in a particular substantive rule may have some impact on the outcome of a case. For example, in *US – Section 211 Appropriations Act*, the Appellate Body noted that the 'conditions for the filing and registration of trademarks' had been reserved to domestic jurisdiction by WTO rules.[94] This led the Appellate Body to interpret specific WTO rules related to those conditions in a stricter way than it might have done in the absence of the reservation.[95] One might therefore conclude that an express mention in a treaty of a matter reserved to domestic jurisdiction may have a general restrictive effect on related obligations in that treaty. However, the extent of such a restrictive effect is unclear; in any case, it is likely to be subject to the text and context of particular treaty obligations.

We now turn to a more modern and more flexible measure of deference in public international law: the margin of appreciation.

4.5.2. The Margin of Appreciation

The margin of appreciation is a measure of judicial deference that originated in European regional law. Applied by the ECtHR and the ECJ, it has spread into the discourse of global courts such as the International Tribunal on the Law of the Sea, international arbitral tribunals, and international commissions. Shany argues that the margin of appreciation should be considered a general principle of international law and points to its (albeit inconsistent) use by the ICJ.[96] The doctrine has also gained the attention of domestic constitutional courts in both civil law[97] and common law jurisdictions.[98]

One reason for the growing popularity of the margin of appreciation doctrine is its flexibility: it holds that international courts should 'leave States a certain margin of appreciation with regard to the fulfilment of their obligation' and 'up to a

93. In modern times, the ICJ has generally joined a plea of the reserved domain of domestic jurisdiction to the merits phase of a dispute (Brownlie, above n. 76, 294, quoting *Losinger*, PCIJ Ser. A/B, No. 67, 23–25; *Rights of Passage*, ICJ Reports (1957) 125, 149–150), although the form of the plea is a preliminary objection (again Brownlie, above n. 76, 294, quoting *Electricity Company of Sofia and Bulgaria*, 1939, PCIJ, Series A/B, No. 77, 64, at 82–83).
94. Appellate Body Report, *US – Section 211 Appropriations Act*, para. 131, noting Art. 6(1) *Paris Convention for the Protection of Industrial Property* (1967) as incorporated into TRIPS.
95. Appellate Body Report, *US – Section 211* Appropriations *Act*, para. 139. See also R. Howse & D. Neven, 'US – Section 211 Omnibus Appropriations Act of 1998 – A Comment', *The American Law Institute Reporters' Studies on WTO Case Law*, <www.ali.org/doc/wto/wto2002/HavanaClub.pdf> (visited 10 Oct. 2007).
96. Shany, above n. 14, 931 et seq.
97. Y. Arai-Takahashi, *The Margin of Appreciation Doctrine and the Principle of Proportionality in the Jurisprudence of the ECHR* (Antwerp: Intersentia, 2002), 3.
98. See for example, *de Freitas v. Permanent Secretary of Ministry of Agriculture, Fisheries, Lands and Housing* [1999] 1 AC 69 at 80; *Cunliffe v. Commonwealth of Australia* (1994) 182 CLR 272, Mason CJ at para. 38, Brennan J at para. 28.

point leave it to the States to choose the appropriate means to guarantee a right'.[99] However, this flexibility means that the exact amount of deference to be applied may be hard to define.

Commentators on the margin of appreciation have generally defined the limits of deference that it requires in terms of a list of factors to be weighed and balanced; that is, the nature of the international obligation needs to be assessed.[100] Some factors said to indicate a greater degree of deference include the following:

- when the international obligation expressly gives weight to the opinion of the State (e.g., 'if the State considers that a [relevant circumstance] exists';[101]
- when the international obligation concerns national security or internal government operations;[102]
- when the international obligation concerns factual matters that a domestic authority is best placed to evaluate;[103]
- when the international obligation is phrased in terms of a broad standard or a result to be achieved, rather than requiring specific action;[104]
- when the community of States has not reached consensus in the means of implementing the obligation;[105] and
- when the challenged measure is legislation of a democratically elected legislature.[106]

The last-mentioned factor arises because the law of the European Union and the European Convention on Human Rights (ECHR)[107] expressly recognizes the value of democracy, and legislative democracy at that.[108] Thus, the ECtHR and the ECJ tend to give an extra margin for decisions made by directly elected representatives of the people:[109] in contrast, in challenges to administrative action under those regimes, the margin of appreciation is reduced.

However, when one moves beyond those regional regimes to a global level, the legal commitment to democracy is less than universal. In a global system such as the WTO, which covers democracies and authoritarian States alike, applying deference in this way raises very difficult issues. Democratically elected legislatures may claim, as in Europe, a right to deference because of their special status as directly elected representatives of the people. But does this mean that

99. *Belgian Linguistics Case (No. 2)* (1968) 1 EHRR 252.
100. Arai-Takahashi, above n. 97, 206–216; Shany, above n. 14, Part 1.C.
101. C. Grabenwarter, *Europäische Menschenrechtskonvention*, 2nd edn (München: CH Beck, 2005), 113. For an example of such a provision, see Art. XXI GATT, discussed below at n. 125.
102. Arai-Takahashi, above n. 97, 43, 83, 105, 139.
103. Shany, above n. 14, 919.
104. Arai-Takahashi, above n. 97, 238; Shany, above n. 14, 921.
105. Shany, above n. 14, 927.
106. Arai-Takahashi, above n. 97, 244–248; Shany, above n. 14, 910.
107. European Convention on Human Rights, 4 Nov. 1950.
108. Arai-Takahashi, above n. 97, 244–248.
109. *Ibid.*

autocratically appointed legislatures are not entitled to this deference? The text of the WTO Agreements makes no distinction between democracies and authoritarian States (although one can find support for a concept of the rule of law).[110]

Furthermore, European law draws strength from the shared history, culture, and location of the States that it binds. This is apparent in the way the ECtHR draws on State practices in applying the margin of appreciation. In some cases, it has pointed to a European consensus on an issue and reduced the margin of appreciation to the extent of the consensus. Such consensus is much harder for a WTO tribunal to identify. The shared history, culture, and location of the European States simply does not exist in a global system such as the WTO.

One can take a contrary view here. Some would argue that the margin of appreciation in Europe is diminishing, as European States move closer to harmonized systems of laws; that is, the margin of appreciation is applicable to a diversity of State legislation, and it is less relevant to a system of harmonized legislation. The concept of the margin of appreciation may therefore be better suited to a diversity of legal systems, as is the case in the WTO. There may be some strength in this argument. However, the margin of appreciation, as currently applied in Europe, is unlikely to become a yardstick for WTO law in the foreseeable future.

The margin of appreciation has a special relationship to concepts of proportionality and legal certainty. As these latter concepts are central to our later discussion of substantive issues in challenges to legislation, some preliminary discussion of this relationship is worthwhile here.

Proportionality and the margin of appreciation can be seen as two sides of the same coin. When international law imposes an obligation to act proportionately to a legitimate purpose,[111] the relevant international tribunal must decide on the intensity with which it will measure this proportionality. The intensity of proportionality indicates the margin of appreciation:

> The more intense the standard of proportionality becomes, the narrower the margin allowed to national authorities. If a reasonable or fair balance is found, the national authorities are considered to remain within the bounds of appreciation.[112]

Similarly, the principle of legal certainty[113] and the margin of appreciation have an interdependent relationship. When a dispute concerns the certainty with which legislation operates consistently with international law, the international tribunal must decide on the intensity with which it will measure the required certainty.

110. For example, see the recitals to the Agreement On Rules Of Origin ('clear and predictable rules of origin and their application facilitate the flow of international trade'), the recitals to the Licensing Agreement ('that import licensing, particularly non-automatic import licensing, should be implemented in a transparent and predictable manner'), and Art. 3.2 DSU ('The dispute settlement system of the WTO is a central element in providing security and predictability to the multilateral trading system').
111. See Ch. 7 on proportionality characterization.
112. Arai-Takahashi, above n. 97, 14.
113. See Section 8.2.

The intensity with which certainty is examined indicates the margin of appreciation in these cases.[114]

Thus, the required measure of proportionality or certainty can determine the margin of appreciation in a particular dispute. As we will see in Chapters 7 and 8, these measures are critical in determining the deference applied in challenges to legislation in the WTO as well. As always, however, the exact degree of deference to be applied in a particular dispute will depend on the content of the international obligation in question. In WTO cases, this content will depend on the formal measure of deference in the WTO, namely, the standard of review.

4.6. THE WTO STANDARD OF REVIEW

4.6.1. Introduction to the Standard of Review

The WTO legal system has its own concept of deference, known as the standard of review – a concept originally developed under US administrative law.[115] The standard of review should be distinguished from other concepts of judicial deference in the WTO. It does not cover other ways in which WTO tribunals avoid making controversial decisions, such as the doctrines of ripeness for decision, mootness and similar procedural rules.[116] Nor does the standard of review cover the deference that WTO tribunals give to other WTO organs, such as the WTO Ministerial Council. One should also exclude the deference given by the Appellate Body to WTO Panels' findings of factual matters.[117] Strictly speaking, the standard of review covers only the degree of deference that WTO tribunals give to domestic decision-makers.

The phrase *standard of review* does not appear in the main body of the WTO Agreements, although it appears in a Ministerial Decision attached to those Agreements.[118] That Decision makes clear that the Uruguay Round negotiators saw the standard of review as a major issue, to be discussed and revised in future negotiations. Nevertheless, its absence from the text of the WTO Agreements gives little express basis for its existence in WTO law.[119] The Appellate

---

114. See Section 8.4.
115. S. Croley & J. Jackson, 'WTO Dispute Procedures, Standard of Review, and Deference to National Governments', AJIL 90 (1996): 193.
116. W. Davey, 'The Authority of the WTO dispute Settlement System', JIEL 4 (2001): 79.
117. As to this deference, see Appellate Body Report, *EC – Asbestos*, para. 161.
118. A reference is made to the concept in the Ministerial Decision concerning revisions to Art. 17.6 Anti-Dumping Agreement: see Decision on Review Of Art. 17.6 of the Agreement on Implementation of Art. VI of the General Agreement On Tariffs And Trade 1994.
119. On one view, the legal basis of the standard of review is Art. 3.2 DSU:

> Recommendations and rulings of the DSB cannot add to or diminish the rights and obligations provided in the covered agreements.

Clearly this Article is aimed at preventing judicial activism. However, beyond encouraging a focus on the actual wording of WTO obligations, the Article gives little clue of the measure of deference to be applied.

Body sees this basis in Article 11 of the DSU,[120] which obliges WTO tribunals to make an 'objective assessment' of matters before them. Therefore, WTO tribunals are obliged to assess measures, and to do so in an objective way. Particular provisions, such as Article 17.6, of the Anti-Dumping Agreement, can alter the content of this basic standard.

In considering the standard of review, one also should keep in mind the concept of stable rights and obligations. Article 19.2 of the DSU provides as follows:

> In accordance with paragraph 2 of Article 3, in their findings and recommendations, the panel and Appellate Body cannot add to or diminish the rights and obligations provided in the covered agreements.

This rather loose concept can be seen as an attempt by WTO members to discourage judicial activism in WTO tribunals. In practice however, if a WTO tribunal uses justifiable methods to interpret WTO rules (particularly the methods described in the Vienna Convention on the Law of Treaties[121]), it is unlikely to add to the rights and obligations of WTO members. In the *Chile – Alcohol* case, the Appellate Body said:

> [W]e have difficulty in envisaging circumstances in which a panel could add to the rights and obligations of a Member of the WTO if its conclusions reflected a correct interpretation and application of provisions of the covered agreements.[122]

Therefore, Articles 3.2 and 19.2 of the DSU can be seen as promoting legally supportable methods for interpreting WTO rules. WTO members invoke it to encourage WTO tribunals to be cautious in their reasoning.

The standard of review provided by Article 11 of the DSU is a general principle, which is applied in different ways in different WTO provisions. The exact content of the standard of review for any given provision will depend on the text, context, and purpose of that provision, in accordance with general principles of treaty interpretation.[123] Therefore, the standard will vary according to the exact wording of the obligation concerned. In one provision, Article 17.6, of the Anti-Dumping Agreement, there are express rules relating to the standard of review. However, these rules merely supplement the general standard in Article 11 of the DSU but do not replace that standard.[124]

---

120. See *EC – Hormones*, Appellate Body Report, para. 116. Art. 11 DSU provides (in part):

> [A] panel should make an objective assessment of the matter before it, including an objective assessment of the facts of the case and the applicability of and conformity with the relevant covered agreements, and make such other findings as will assist the DSB in making the recommendations or in giving the rulings provided in the covered agreements.

121. Lennard, above n. 71; K. Schollendorf, *Die Auslegung völkerrechtlicher Verträge in der Spruchpraxis des Appellate Body der Welthandelsorganisation* (Berlin: Duncker & Humblot, 2005).
122. Appellate Body Report, *Chile – Alcohol*, para. 79.
123. Appellate Body Report, *US – Countervailing Duty Investigation on DRAMS*, para. 184.
124. Appellate Body Report, *US – Hot-Rolled Steel*, para. 62.

This can be seen from some examples. Some WTO obligations require fact-finding and evaluation to be done in a certain way. For example, Article 5.1 of the Sanitary and Phytosanitary Measures (SPS) Agreement provides that the only appropriate measures will be those that are based on a scientific risk assessment. Little deference will be given here to a domestic legislature that designs its legislation based on factors other than such a risk assessment. Other WTO obligations use phrases that indicate lowered deference in general. For example, Article 3.2 of the Licensing Agreement requires that non-automatic licensing be no more administratively burdensome than 'absolutely necessary' to administer measures that they are used to implement. The reference here to 'absolutely' necessary indicates a very thorough testing of the appropriateness of non-automatic licensing legislation.

Other phrases in WTO rules may indicate increased deference. An obvious example is Article XXI of the GATT, which provides an exception for measures that a WTO member 'considers necessary for the protection of its essential security interests'. The level of deference set by Article XXI is very high, as all measures that the WTO member 'considers necessary' will be covered.[125] This may be compared with other exceptions, which merely allow matters that are actually 'necessary'.[126] Other WTO rules might have an analogous operation to Article XXI of the GATT.[127]

---

125. H. Schloemann & S. Ohlhoff, 'Constitutionalization and Dispute Settlement in the WTO: National Security as an Issue of Competence', AJIL 93 (1999): 424; W. Cann, 'Creating Standards and Accountability for the Use of the WTO Security Exception: Reducing the Role of Power-Based Relations and Establishing a New Balance Between Sovereignty and Multilateralism', *Yale JIL* 26 (2001): 413; P. Lindsay, 'The Ambiguity of GATT Article XXI: Subtle Success or Rampant Failure?', *Duke LJ* 52 (2003): 1277.

126. Lindsay, above n. 125, 1285, points here to the ICJ's ruling in *Military and Paramilitary Activities in and against Nicaragua (Nicaragua v. United States of America)*, Merits, Judgment, ICJ Reports (1986) 14, at 116. Here the Court ruled that a reference in a bilateral treaty to measures 'necessary to protect... essential security interests' did not exclude the Court's jurisdiction to review such measures:

> That the Court has jurisdiction to determine whether measures taken by one of the Parties fall within such an exception, is also clear *a contrario* from the fact that the text of Article XXI of the Treaty does not employ the wording which was already to be found in Article XXI of the General Agreement on Tariffs and Trade. This provision of GATT, contemplating exceptions to the normal implementation of the General Agreement, stipulates that the Agreement is not to be construed to prevent any contracting party from taking any action which it 'considers necessary for the protection of its essential security interests', in such fields as nuclear fission, arms, etc. The 1956 treaty, on the contrary, speaks simply of 'necessary' measures, not of those considered by a party to be such.

127. Lindsay, above n. 125, 1283–1285 adds the example of the *Declaration on the TRIPS Agreement and Public Health*, WT/MIN(01)/DEC/2 (2001), para. 5(c). Art. 31 TRIPS allows abrogation of intellectual property rights 'in the case of a national emergency or other circumstances of extreme urgency'. The Declaration, para. 5(c), confirms the right of Members to 'determine what constitutes a national emergency or other circumstances of extreme urgency'. Lindsay notes controversy about whether this gives an unfettered right to domestic authorities to determine *any kind* of emergency.

The WTO standard of review is divided into two basic areas: the standard of review for facts and for law. The standard of review for law deals with the degree of deference given to domestic interpretations of WTO law. The standard of review for facts deals with the degree of deference given to domestic fact finding. According to the Appellate Body, the 'objective assessment' standard covers both of these areas.[128] Nevertheless, as a matter of practice, far more deference is given to domestic fact finding than to domestic interpretations of WTO law, as will now be described.

4.6.1.1. The Standard of Review of WTO Law

The WTO standard of review of law (i.e., of reviewing the meaning of WTO law) is close to de novo review. This standard is subject to an overriding duty of WTO tribunals to apply the customary rules of interpretation of public international law.[129] Thus, WTO tribunals give little deference to domestic authorities' views on the meaning of WTO obligations.[130] This lack of deference has also extended to international rules existing outside the WTO that have been incorporated into the WTO legal system.[131] This is consistent with the general principle of international law that an international court has judicial knowledge of the rules of international law.[132] However, one must also keep in mind the principle of *in dubio mitius* if there is an ambiguity in the obligation. Special considerations apply to the standard of review in the circumstances set out in Article 17.6 of the Anti-Dumping Agreement.[133]

---

128. Appellate Body Report, *EC – Hormones*, para. 116.
129. Appellate Body Report, *EC – Hormones*, para. 118, Art. 3.2 DSU.
130. Ehlermann & Lockhart, above n. 32, 497.
131. In *EC – Bananas III*, the European Communities tried to claim deference as to the meaning of the *Lome Convention* – negotiated by the European Communities outside the WTO – but failed, as the Appellate Body considered that the *Lome Convention* had been incorporated into WTO law to the extent of the Lome Waiver: Appellate Body Report, *EC – Bananas III*, para. 167.
132. According to the Appellate Body in *EC – Tariff Preferences*, para. 105, fn. 220:

    > The principle of *jura novit curia* has been articulated by the International Court of Justice as follows:
    >
    >> It being the duty of the Court itself to ascertain and apply the relevant law in the given circumstances of the case, the burden of establishing or proving rules of international law cannot be imposed upon any of the parties, for the law lies within the judicial knowledge of the Court.
    >>
    >> (International Court of Justice, Merits, Case Concerning Military and Paramilitary Activities in and against Nicaragua *(Nicaragua v. United States of America)*, 1986 ICJ Reports, p. 14, para. 29 (quoting International Court of Justice, Merits, Fisheries Jurisdiction Case *(United Kingdom of Great Britain and Northern Ireland v. Iceland)*, 1974 ICJ Reports, p. 9, para. 17)).

133. This provides that Panels should defer to a national authority's interpretation of WTO law, so long as that interpretation is 'permissible'. Theoretically, this could allow domestic legislatures some latitude in setting a 'permissible' level of deference for anti-dumping legislation. In practice, however, this has not been the case. It may be that standard principles of

The near de novo standard of review of WTO law springs from at least two considerations. The first is the need to have a uniform interpretation of WTO obligations. Deferring to national authorities' interpretations could create a patchwork of different applications of WTO law in different domestic jurisdictions.[134] The second consideration is the particular expertise of WTO tribunals in interpreting international obligations. One can reasonably expect that specialized international tribunals have greater expertise in interpreting their own 'rule books' than do domestic tribunals.[135] Thus, little deference is given to domestic interpretations of WTO law.

The near de novo standard of review of law does not deny freedom of action for domestic legislatures in framing WTO-related legislation. WTO rules are often broadly drafted, result-oriented, or expressly based on domestic decision-making. These features allow domestic authorities freedom of action within the parameters set by WTO rules – reminiscent of the way in which such features allow a margin of appreciation in European law.[136] Although WTO tribunals enjoy a privileged position in interpreting WTO rules, the rules themselves delegate much detailed decision-making to the domestic level. Thus, one needs to consider (as discussed earlier)[137] the questions of whether some WTO rules allow States discretion in interpretation, and whether the content of a particular rule can be determined by domestic legislation.

For these reasons, the standard of review of law has a limited (though important) role to play in challenges to legislation. WTO tribunals exercise near de novo review in interpreting WTO rules and are thus able to identity the limits within which deference is set by those rules. Domestic legislatures are able to act within those limits but are not themselves able to define those limits. Of course, the ultimate power to set the limits of deference is held by WTO members in drafting the content of WTO rules. However, given the practical problems in creating and altering those rules, considerable power is held by WTO tribunals in resolving ambiguities as to deference.

Of more practical importance in challenges to legislation is the standard of review of facts.

---

interpretation of treaties do not allow more than one permissible interpretation. Croley & Jackson, above n. 115, 200, therefore suggest that the standard of review in Art. 17.6 Anti-Dumping Agreement would have little effect once accepted principles of interpretation have been applied.

134. Oesch, above n. 21, 644 (citing numerous supporting sources at fn. 34); Ehlermann & Lockhart, above n. 32, 498.
135. According to G. Schwarzenberger, *A Manual of International Law*, 5th edn (London: Steven and Sons, 1967), 36, the authority of a body's statement of international law should be judged solely on the merits of the body, and in particular its international outlook, the degree of independence enjoyed by its members, and the technical expertise of those members. The Appellate Body of the WTO scores well on all of these indicators.
136. See Section 4.5.2.
137. See Section 4.4.

4.6.1.2. The Standard of Review of Facts

The standard of review of facts is based on the 'objective assessment' principle, which requires some – but not total – deference. As the Appellate Body stated in *EC – Hormones*:

> [T]he applicable standard is neither *de novo* review as such, nor 'total deference', but rather the 'objective assessment of the facts'. Many panels have in the past refused to undertake *de novo* review, wisely, since under current practice and systems, they are in any case poorly suited to engage in such a review. On the other hand, 'total deference to the findings of the national authorities', it has been well said, 'could not ensure an "objective assessment" as foreseen by Article 11 of the DSU'.[138] [footnotes omitted]

Thus, it is often said that the standard of review of facts lies somewhere between de novo review and total deference.[139] The same broad standard applies to both the review of raw facts and the review of inferences.[140]

However, the exact content of the standard is still a matter for debate. Ehlermann and Lockhart argue that the 'objective assessment' standard here is too vague: '[a]ny assessment of the facts, whether it is highly deferential, marginally deferential, or not deferential at all, can be "objective" '.[141] They suggest that the standard of review of facts can depend on whether the relevant WTO obligation requires a formal investigative process at the national level; where such a process is envisaged in the obligation, WTO tribunals should show deference to that process.[142] Oesch argues for a certain degree of deference to domestic authorities in reviewing the raw facts. He argues that Panels should refrain from de novo review of factual records and interfere only when summary examination of the record discloses proof of 'egregious error'.[143] Zleptnig argues for a 'deliberation test', under which WTO tribunals should 'be sensitive to institutional strengths and weaknesses of other actors' and 'determine how much weight (or credibility) should be accorded to the determinations of these actors'.[144] Becroft emphasizes the different application of the standard of review under different WTO agreements

138. Appellate Body Report, *EC – Hormones*, para. 117. See also *Dominican Republic – Import and Sale of Cigarettes*, para. 84, where the Appellate Body said that 'a mere divergence of views between a party and a panel on the inferences to be drawn from pieces of evidence is not a sufficient ground to conclude that the Panel failed to "make . . . an objective assessment of the facts of the case" '.
139. Appellate Body Report, *EC – Hormones*, para. 117.
140. Article 11 obliges Panels not only to make 'an objective assessment of the facts of the case', but also 'an objective assessment of the matter before it': Appellate Body Report, *Chile – Price Band System*, para. 172.
141. Ehlermann & Lockhart, above n. 32, 501.
142. *Ibid.*, 520.
143. Oesch, above n. 21, 641.
144. Zleptnig (2002), above n. 46, 33. In this respect, S. Bhuiyan, *National Law in WTO Law* (Cambridge: Cambridge University Press, 2007), 198, suggests that less deference will be given in respect of economic data as opposed to (uncertain) scientific evidence. This would

and argues that the content of the standard is far from settled. He suggests that the Appellate Body needs to issue a clear restatement of its application in certain cases,[145] particularly because it is requiring Panels to scrutinize domestic fact finding in increasingly strict ways.[146]

Even less clear is the exact content of the standard as applied to challenges to legislation. Most WTO jurisprudence on the standard of review concerns challenges to administrative actions (mainly relating to trade remedies). If one takes a quick look at the principles developed in this jurisprudence, one sees that they fit awkwardly with the nature of challenges to legislative action.

Cases concerning challenges to administrative actions appear to adopt a standard similar to the rationality concept discussed earlier.[147] While it is outside the scope of this book to make a full survey of the jurisprudence on trade remedies, one can see an indication of it in the Appellate Body's comments in *US – Softwood Lumber VI* (*Article 21.5 – Canada*). (One should keep in mind that the following discussion does not take into account the subtle differences between the standard of review for particular WTO obligations, but rather makes some broad observations for the point of illustration and contrast.)

According to the Appellate Body, Panels should test whether domestic authorities have given a 'reasoned and adequate' explanation of their factual conclusions.[148] This will depend on the facts and circumstances of the case and the particular claims made.[149] Nevertheless, the Appellate Body has required quite a high standard of domestic administrative authorities here. The reasoning of such authorities should be 'coherent and internally consistent', and their inferences must be based on 'positive evidence'.[150] A Panel should examine whether domestic authorities 'took proper account of the complexities of the data before [them]' and 'explained why [they] rejected or discounted alternative explanations and interpretations of the record evidence'.[151] Furthermore, a Panel should 'be open to the possibility that the explanations given by the authority are not reasoned or adequate in the light of other plausible alternative explanations'.[152] A Panel's

accord with Zleptnig's argument, if one accepts that WTO Panels have more expertise (or have more access to expertise) in economics than in the physical sciences.

145. R. Becroft, 'The Standard of Review Strikes Back: The US – Korea DRAMS Appeal', JIEL 9 (2006): 207, at 217.

146. *Ibid.*, 216.

147. See Section 4.3, text at n. 54.

148. Appellate Body Report, *US – Softwood Lumber VI* (*Article 21.5 – Canada*), para. 93, citing as follows: Appellate Body Report, *Argentina – Footwear* (*EC*), paras 119–121; Appellate Body Report, *US – Cotton Yarn*, paras 74–78; Appellate Body Report, *US – Countervailing Duty Investigation on DRAMS*, paras 183, and 186–188; Appellate Body Report, *US – Hot-Rolled Steel*, para. 55; Appellate Body Report, *US – Lamb*, paras 101 and 105–108; Appellate Body Report, *US – Steel Safeguards*, para. 299; and Appellate Body Report, *US – Wheat Gluten*, paras 160–161.

149. Appellate Body Report, *US – Softwood Lumber VI (Article 21.5 – Canada)*, para. 93.

150. *Ibid.*

151. *Ibid.*

152. *Ibid.*

overall approach will be 'critical and searching', and a Panel will not 'simply accept the conclusions of the competent authorities'.[153] The overall thrust of this approach seems to be a fairly rigorous substantive review of a domestic authority's decision-making processes.

It seems doubtful that this approach can be transplanted into WTO challenges to legislation, at least in cases where the legislature is a parliamentary body. Legislative decision-making is generally more polycentric than is administrative decision-making, involving a wider range of evidence and more-complex interactions between decision-makers. As discussed earlier,[154] legislative decision-making can also involve (legitimately) evaluations of subjective matters and popular perceptions. One cannot expect that WTO tribunals will examine whether legislative inferences are 'coherent and internally consistent' or based on 'positive evidence'. The degree of subjectivity in legislative decision-making is much greater than in administrative decision-making. Nor can one expect that WTO tribunals will always examine whether the legislature 'took proper account of the complexities of the data' before it or whether it gave explanations that are 'not reasoned or adequate in the light of other plausible alternative explanations'. WTO tribunals, using legal methods, are simply not in a position to evaluate the complexities of data before legislatures or to thoroughly evaluate the adequacy of legislative inferences.

One can see hints of a looser standard of review of legislative action in decisions on whether legislation is 'necessary' to achieve a particular goal. In *US – Gambling*, the Appellate Body reiterated the need for an 'independent' and 'objective' review of legislation inferences[155] but held back from the kind of 'critical and searching' review described earlier. Indeed, the Panel in that case showed considerable respect for the legislature's view of evidence before it. The Panel held that the challenged legislation was effective in achieving its legislative purpose, based in large part on evidence given to Congressional committees.[156] There was no suggestion that the Panel should have examined whether the legislature 'took proper account of the complexities of the data' before it or whether it gave explanations that were 'not reasoned or adequate in the light of other plausible alternative explanations'. One can also see hints of a less-intrusive standard of

---

153. Appellate Body Report, *US – Lamb*, para. 106, quoted in Appellate Body Report, *US – Softwood Lumber VI (Article 21.5 – Canada)*, para. 93.

154. See Section 4.3, text at n. 43.

155. Appellate Body Report, *US – Gambling*, para. 304:

> [A] Member's characterization of a measure's objectives and of the effectiveness of its regulatory approach – as evidenced, for example, by texts of statutes, legislative history, and pronouncements of government agencies or officials – will be relevant in determining whether the measure is, objectively, 'necessary'. A panel is not bound by these characterizations, however, and may also find guidance in the structure and operation of the measure and in contrary evidence proffered by the complaining party. In any event, a panel must, on the basis of the evidence in the record, independently and objectively assess the 'necessity' of the measure before it.

156. Panel Report, *US – Gambling*, paras 6.499–6.521.

review of facts in *US – Section 301 Trade Act*. There, the Panel said that although it would not accept the legislating State's views unquestioningly, that State 'can reasonably expect that considerable deference be given to its views on the meaning of its own law'.[157] This issue is discussed in detail in the analysis of certainty characterization in Chapter 8.

In sum, the standard of review as applied to challenges to legislation is still quite an underdeveloped concept. WTO tribunals need to make an 'objective assessment' of both legislative inferences and the raw facts that underlie them, but the intensity of that assessment is yet to be described in detail by the Appellate Body. This is an unsatisfactory situation, given the importance of WTO challenges to legislation and the need for domestic legislatures to have an idea of how closely their decisions will be scrutinized in WTO litigation. As commentators have already pointed out in relation to the standard of review generally, more clarity is needed in relation to the standard here as well.

4.7. CONCLUDING REMARKS

In this chapter, we have seen the characteristics of deference in the substantive aspects of challenges to legislation. These characteristics lie in ascertaining raw facts and making inferences from such facts, in interpreting international obligations deferentially or by reference to domestic law, and in applying general international law concepts of deference.

In WTO challenges to legislation, the relevant measure of deference is the so-called standard of review of facts. This measure has been developed to some extent in WTO challenges to administrative actions, but it is noticeably underdeveloped in relation to challenges to legislation. WTO tribunals have little guidance as to how to apply substantive deference to legislative challenges. The standard of review of facts as applied to challenges to legislation is still too abstract to be of major practical use in any particular challenge. To some extent, therefore, WTO tribunals are left to their own devices in determining how much deference to give to domestic legislatures.

It is the aim of the following chapters to describe ways in which WTO tribunals have actually applied substantive deference in particular cases – and to identify benchmarks of deference, where they exist. This is done through viewing WTO jurisprudence through the lens of legislative characterization. The next chapter provides a brief introduction to this concept. Chapters 6–8 then examine substantive deference by WTO tribunals in relation to three particular kinds of characterization, namely, factor characterization, proportionality characterization, and certainty characterization. We will see that the aspects of deference discussed in this chapter appear in different guises with respect to each of these kinds of characterization.

---

157. Panel Report, *US – Section 301 Trade Act*, para. 7.19.

Chapter 5

Introduction to the Concept of Legislative Characterization

5.1. WHAT IS CHARACTERIZATION?

An Australian judge once described the word *characterization* as 'uncouth for grammarians and those who care for English undefiled'.[1] Nevertheless, characterization lies at the heart of substantive issues in challenges to legislation. It describes the process of extracting the character of legislation from its purpose, its legal structure, and its other effects. In any challenge to legislation, the legislation must be characterized in light of the relevant constitutional or international obligation.

Characterization is a concept inherent in the application of legal rules.[2] Once relevant constitutional or international rules have been interpreted in the abstract, they must be applied to the evidence. To do so, one must extract the character, in light of those rules, of the situation described by the evidence. The process of doing so is characterization. This process can be applied to concrete situations (e.g., in determining whether a particular loan to a particular undertaking is a 'subsidy').

---

1. Windeyer J, *Worthing v. Rowell and Muston Pty Ltd* (1970) 123 CLR 89 at 130. The difficulties inherent in the concept were summarized by Kirby J in *Attorney-General (Vic) v. Andrews* (2007) 233 ALR 389, paras 146–148:

> [V]erbal explanations of the requirements for characterisation are not themselves part of the Constitution or immutable formulae. They represent judicial attempts to explain a complex process involving ultimately matters of assessment and judgment . . . Characterisation notoriously involves classification and assignment of legislation by reference to considerations that are inherently disputable and upon which informed and reasonable observers can quite often reach different conclusions. Those who think otherwise deceive themselves. Nowadays, they are unlikely to mislead others.

2. For another discussion of characterization, see S. Bhuiyan, *National Law in WTO Law* (Cambridge: Cambridge University Press, 2007), Ch. 5.

It can also be applied to abstract rules (e.g., in determining whether a statutory scheme for giving loans is in itself a 'subsidy'). It is the latter kind of characterization that is relevant to the abstract rules at issue in a challenge to legislation.

Characterization has obvious parallels in domestic constitutional law.[3] In common law jurisdictions, in Australia and Canada in particular, constitutional judicial review of legislation is consciously based upon characterization.[4] Various models of characterization have been proposed by common law courts, and similar concepts can be seen in civil law jurisdictions.[5]

Characterization also has its place in international challenges to legislation. Here, one must characterize the legislation in light of the relevant international obligation. This involves extracting a character from the bundle of abstract rules embodied in the legislation, and then comparing that character to pre-existing conceptual categories provided by the international obligation.

Characterization is related to, but separate from, treaty interpretation. The process of treaty interpretation is abstract in nature. It fills out the broad structures provided by treaty texts, providing more details to the treaty norms by processes of textual, contextual, and purposive interpretation. Yet, the details provided by treaty interpretation are often themselves broad in nature, and they do not always lead automatically to particular results in particular challenges to legislation. In contrast, the process of characterization is concrete.[6] It applies treaty text and the details provided by treaty interpretation to the complex fact situations of a challenge to legislation. Characterization provides the results of a particular dispute – and for this reason it is often the matter of most interest to litigators.

Of course, in many cases, there is no clear borderline between interpretation and characterization. Detailed interpretation of a treaty fades into broad characterization of challenged legislation. Treaty interpretation guides the characterization process, and a developed body of case law on characterization will begin to influence treaty interpretation.

Characterization also has its place in the WTO system. As the Appellate Body pointed out in *EC – Hormones*, the 'consistency or inconsistency of a given fact or set of facts with the requirements of a given treaty provision is . . . a legal characterization issue'.[7] To date, the Appellate Body has made its most detailed

3. The concept of characterization has also long been shared by areas of private law, such as in the conflict of laws: for example, see J. Morse, 'Characterization: Shadow or Substance', *Colum. L Rev* 49 (1949): 1027; Bhuiyan, above n. 2, 125.
4. L. Zines, *The High Court and the Constitution*, 4th edn (Sydney: Butterworths, 1997), 17–54 (Australia); Hogg, P., *Constitutional Law of Canada*, 3rd edn (Ontario: Carswell, 1992), 377–390 (Canada).
5. G. Taylor, *Characterisation in Federations: Six Countries Compared* (Berlin: Springer, 2006).
6. Admittedly, this could be described as 'the interpretation of legal rules *in concreto* rather than *in abstracto*': C. Ehlermann & N. Lockhart, 'Standard of Review in WTO Law', JIEL 7 (2004): 491, at 504.
7. Appellate Body Report, *EC – Hormones*, para. 132 (in the context of the scope of appellate review).

comments on characterization in dealing with the national treatment rule.[8] In *Japan – Alcoholic Beverages II*, the Appellate Body discussed whether legislation applied taxation 'so as to afford protection' within the meaning of Article III(2) Sentence 2 of the GATT:

> [W]e believe that an examination in any case of whether dissimilar taxation has been applied so as to afford protection requires a *comprehensive and objective analysis of the structure and application of the measure* in question on domestic as compared to imported products. We believe it is possible to examine objectively *the underlying criteria* used in a particular tax measure, *its structure, and its overall application* to ascertain whether it is applied in a way that affords protection to domestic products.
>
> Although it is true that the aim of a measure may not be easily ascertained, nevertheless, its protective application can most often be discerned from the design, the architecture, and the revealing structure of a measure. The very magnitude of the dissimilar taxation in a particular case may be evidence of such a protective application, as the Panel rightly concluded in this case. Most often, there will be other factors to be considered as well. In conducting this inquiry, panels should give full consideration to all the relevant facts and all the relevant circumstances in any given case.[9] [emphasis added]

Thus, WTO tribunals make a complete and objective analysis of the design, architecture, structure, and application of the legislation (at least, under Article III(2) Sentence 2 of the GATT). If one can generalize this to most WTO challenges to legislation, WTO characterization has the following features:

- It is comprehensive.
- It is objective (especially in relation to the underlying criteria of a measure).
- It relates to the structure and overall application of the measure, and the overall application is mostly found from the design, architecture, and revealing structure of the measure.

---

8. See also, in other contexts Appellate Body Report, *US – Corrosion-Resistant Steel Sunset Review*, para. 168. See also Appellate Body Report, *US – Oil Country Tubular Goods Sunset Reviews*, para. 187. Also of interest is the Panel's statement in *EC – Approval and Marketing of Biotech Products*, para. 7.1334, that the issue of whether a law is an SPS measure 'is to be determined . . . by reference to such criteria as the objective of the measure, its form and its nature'. In *China – Auto Parts*, the Appellate Body considered whether a specific charge fell under Art. II(1)(b) or Art. III(2) GATT. It stated (at para. 171 of its Report) that:

   > A panel must thoroughly scrutinize the measure before it, both in its design and in its operation, and identify its principal characteristics. Having done so, the panel must then seek to identify the leading or core features of the measure at issue, those that define its 'centre of gravity' for purposes of characterizing the charge that it imposes as an ordinary customs duty or an internal charge.

9. Appellate Body Report, *Japan – Alcoholic Beverages II*, 120. See also Appellate Body Report, *Chile – Alcoholic Beverages*, para. 72.

– It gives full consideration to all relevant facts and relevant circumstances in the given case.

These general principles are uncontroversial, but their practical application can be highly controversial. Intense disputes arise over the nature of the underlying criteria, the design, architecture, and revealing structure of the legislation, or over what facts and circumstances are relevant. What is vital to one State might be irrelevant to another: every society has sacred cows incomprehensible to societies elsewhere. This makes it difficult to say which matters should be relevant in characterization, and in what perspective they should be viewed.

Thus, it is important to understand the characterization process if one wants to understand the nature of substantive deference in international challenges to legislation. This issue is highly complex and will occupy much of the rest of this book. In setting the context for this discussion, it is useful to have a conceptual structure with which to analyse the various aspects of characterization.

Different kinds of characterization give rise to different kinds of deference. I suggest that characterization can be classified into three types:[10] certainty characterization, proportionality characterization and factor characterization. These are idealized types, and they often overlap in real-world disputes. However, it is useful analytically to separate these various types because each type of review highlights a particular kind of deference to the domestic legislature by international tribunals. This issue of deference is usually the central aspect of a challenge to legislation.

The remainder of this chapter discusses these types in brief, before they are discussed in detail in the following three chapters.

5.2. THREE TYPES OF CHARACTERIZATION

The first type of characterization occurs when the legal operation of the legislation is uncertain. The characterization process thus involves an intense scrutiny of the legislative environment, that is, various elements of the legal system surrounding the challenged legislation, which may give some certainty to its operation. I call the characterization process in these cases *certainty characterization*. The next two

10. Clearly, there are other ways of classifying the characterization of legislation. For example, Bhuiyan, above n. 2, 131–140, divides characterization into 'extra/intra-regime characterization', 'intra-regime characterization' and 'provision-specific characterization'. These categories are based on the effect of the applicable international rule. Thus 'extra/intra-regime characterization' occurs where the international rule determines whether a particular international regime is applicable at all to particular legislation. 'Intra-regime characterization' occurs where the international rule determines which aspect of an international regime is applicable to particular legislation (e.g., whether the GATT or the GATS is applicable). 'Provision-specific characterization' occurs where the question is whether a particular international rule is applicable. Unlike Bhuiyan's categorization, the categorization used in this book is based on the ways in which particular features of legislation (such as legislative purpose, legal and practical operation and the legislative environment) are dealt with in the characterization process.

types of cases occur when the legal operation of the legislation is relatively clear. In these cases, the characterization process focuses less on the legislative environment and more on the legal and practical operation of the legislation. The purpose of the legislation is also a prominent indicator of its character. In *proportionality characterization*, purpose is all-important, because the character of the legislation depends on the extent to which it achieves its purpose in a proportionate manner. The characterization process focuses on the effectiveness of the legislation in achieving its purpose and on the extent to which it affects other protected values. In contrast, in *factor characterization*, purpose becomes less important, as it is only one of a number of factors relevant to legislative character. The most important of these factors usually concern the legal operation of the legislation, its practical operation, and its underlying purpose, as well as external standards. Here, the characterization process focuses on the choice and balancing of these relevant factors.

One can see the differences among these three classes in the ways in which they balance matters. In proportionality characterization, there is some explicit weighing and balancing of policy goals, namely, the policy goals underlying the legislation and the policy goals that the legislation may impinge upon. For example, the question of whether an import ban on a toxic substance is legally 'necessary' to protect human health involves some explicit weighing of the goals of health and of free trade. In contrast, factor characterization involves the weighing and balancing of features of the legislation that do not necessarily correspond to particular policy goals. For example, the question of whether a toxic substance is legally 'like' another substance involves the weighing of various features of both substances as regards their physical properties, uses, tariff classifications, and the way in which they are viewed by consumers.[11] These matters, although of policy significance, are not in themselves policy goals. Factor characterization thus balances matters that may or may not be policy goals in themselves. Similarly, in certainty characterization, the balancing exercise is not of explicit policy goals, but rather of the features of the domestic legal system. For example, the question of whether legislation treats an imported toxic substance 'less favourably' than its domestic counterpart might depend on domestic administrative and judicial practices. In characterizing such legislation, one needs to weigh and balance the various features of the domestic legal system.

The distinction can be further illustrated through the following examples from WTO jurisprudence.

A WTO example of certainty characterization is *India – Patents* (*US*). In this case, the Indian government argued that administrative guidelines created a mailbox system for patent applications in India, as required under transitional rules in the TRIPS Agreement. In essence, India argued that the guidelines, combined with the legislative environment of its legal culture, ensured consistency with the TRIPS Agreement. The Appellate Body rejected India's argument, stating that the legal basis for India's mailbox system was not adequate because it did not provide the

11. See Section 6.3.

required degree of certainty. The Appellate Body rejected the judgment of the Indian government that its administrative guidelines could provide that certainty.[12] In contrast, in *US – Export Restraints*, the legislative environment did provide the required certainty. In this case, the United States argued that regulations and administrative statements narrowed the operation of the relevant legislation so as to ensure that it operated in a WTO-consistent way. The Panel accepted this argument.[13]

An example of proportionality characterization can be seen in *Korea – Various Measures on Beef*.[14] In this case, Korean legislation set up a dual retail system for beef, under which foreign beef had to be sold in special shops set apart from other beef retailers. Korea claimed that this system was needed to enforce its competition laws by preventing fraudulent misrepresentation about the origin of beef. Enforcement of such laws was clearly a worthwhile goal. However, the system conflicted with another worthwhile goal, namely, the free trade aims of the GATT. The task of WTO tribunals was to balance the conflict according to the content of the relevant GATT rule.[15] The Panel found that the dual retail system was 'a disproportionate measure not necessary to secure compliance with the Korean law against deceptive practices', [16] mainly because alternative measures were available that were more consistent with the relevant GATT rule.

An example of factor characterization is the treatment of the legislation in *Argentina – Hides and Leather*. In this case, Argentine legislation measured duties on certain goods by multiplying the applicable tariff rate against a standardized 'representative international price' of the goods. Article II of the GATT bound Argentina to apply tariff rates at a rate no less favourable to the rate specified in Argentina's Schedule to the GATT. Those rates were to be applied to the *actual* value of goods. Clearly, the legislation operated consistently with Article II where the actual value was higher than the standardized price, but it operated inconsistently where the actual value was lower than the standardized price. Thus, the Appellate Body characterized the legislation as providing 'less favourable' treatment in breach of Article II.[17] No issues of the proportionality or certainty of the legislation were involved expressly in the characterization process. The sole issue was the character of the legislation determined by reference to its practical and legal operations.

It is apparent that factor characterization covers a wider range of issues than do proportionality characterization and certainty characterization. The latter kinds of characterization are tightly focused on two issues, namely, the extent to which

---

12. Appellate Body Report, *India – Patents (US)*, paras 69–70.
13. Panel Report, *US – Export Restraints*, para. 8.131.
14. Appellate Body Report, *Korea – Various Measures on Beef*. The challenged 'legislation' was a system of 'Management Guidelines'.
15. Article XX(d) GATT provides an exception from GATT disciplines for measures 'necessary to secure compliance with laws or regulations which are not inconsistent with the provisions of this Agreement'.
16. Panel Report, *Korea – Various Measures on Beef*, para. 675.
17. Appellate Body Report, *Argentina – Hides and Leather*, para. 53.

legislation achieves its purpose and the extent to which the legislative environment affects legislative operation.[18] In contrast, factor characterization is an umbrella term that covers a multitude of possible characterization exercises: it may be seen as a default category, covering all kinds of legislative characterization that do not focus on examining proportionality or legislative certainty. Yet, it would be wrong to see factor characterization as *merely* a default category. There is a loose theme that ties together all examples of factor characterization: this is the identification of certain characteristics of legislation as relevant factors, and the weighing and balancing of those factors. Of course, the loose nature of the concept of factor characterization makes it a harder subject of generalization than the other two kinds of characterization. Yet, as we will see in Chapter 6, some useful observations can be made about WTO factor characterization cases.

The three types of review correspond to three different kinds of deference. In all cases, some, but not total, deference is shown. However, the matter to which the deference relates varies. In certainty characterization, the matter to which the deference relates is the operation of the domestic legal system. Clearly, some degree of deference will be given here. However, it is rare in modern disputes for such deference to be total. In proportionality characterization, the matter to which the deference relates is the relationship between the legislation and the legislative purpose (in particular, the effectiveness, optimality, and appropriateness of the legislation in achieving that purpose). Here again, some deference to domestic views about this matter – but not total deference – is apparent in practice. In factor characterization, the matter to which the deference relates is the weighting of various factors (in particular, factors concerning objective standards, legal operation, practical operation, and legislative purpose). Yet again, international tribunals show some, but not total, deference to domestic preferences about this relative weight. However, this deference is not about the operation of the domestic legal system, or the effectiveness and appropriateness of legislation, but rather about the degree of emphasis to be given to particular aspects of the legislation at issue.

The remainder of this book discusses the application of the three types of characterization in WTO challenges to legislation and how issues of deference arise in different ways for each type. We will see that WTO tribunals have often developed rough benchmarks for deference to domestic legislatures, although these benchmarks are not applied consistently in all cases.

---

18. Factor characterization also has a special relationship to the other two kinds of characterization. First, before one examines the proportionality of legislation, one must determine what the legislation is, what it does, and why it uses particular means to achieve its purposes. These are factors relevant to the process of factor characterization. Proportionality characterization nevertheless goes a step further, and asks whether those means are appropriate for a given purpose. Thus, factor characterization precedes proportionality characterization. Furthermore, examining the certainty of legislation involves determining what the legislation is and what it does – and these things are often vital factors in the process of factor characterization. Certainty characterization thus precedes factor characterization in some cases (although in most case resolving the certainty question makes the character of the legislation obvious).

Chapter 6

Substantive Deference: Factor Characterization

6.1. INTRODUCTION

Is a product that is dealt with by legislation *like* another product that is not dealt with by that legislation? Is predatory pricing legislation an action *against* dumping? Does legislation confer a *financial benefit*? Does legislation that places conditions on the ownership of a trademark allow for the filing and protection *as is* of the trademark? These are all questions that have arisen in WTO challenges to legislation involving a particular kind of characterization. This characterization does not concern the proportionality or certainty of the legislation as such. Rather, in such cases, the character of the legislation is determined by examining and balancing its various features, or factors. These factors may include such matters as legal operation, practical operation, legislative purpose, and external standards. In this book, I call this kind of characterization *factor characterization*.

In factor characterization, international tribunals undertake a weighing and balancing of factors to determine whether legislation corresponds with international agreements. This is not a weighing and balancing of policies and alternative measures (as takes place under proportionality characterization). Rather, it is a weighing and balancing of a broad range of features of the legislation that may or may not be linked directly to a particular policy. Sometimes, the international obligation is fairly clear, resulting in a bright-line rule that gives clear guidance as to the choice and weight of relevant factors. However, in many cases, the international obligation merely disguises a failure to agree on the choice of factors to be balanced. In these cases, the tribunal must use legal methods to determine the choice and weight of relevant factors. The domestic legislature must also decide which factors are important and relevant in drafting its legislative rules.

Thus, as with all challenges to legislation, factor characterization is closely connected with the question of deference to the domestic legislature. Deference here concerns the domestic legislature's own view of which factors are important to the character of the legislation. The legislating State tends to prefer the factors that suggest compliance with the international obligation, while the challenging State naturally prefers other factors. For example, the legislating State may focus on the legal operation of the legislation (where it enjoys considerable deference) or on practical matters concerning the effects of the legislation in the real world (where, concerning prognoses of such effects, it again enjoys considerable deference). In contrast, the challenging State may focus on clear discriminatory factors on the face of the legislation or a discriminatory practical operation. The extent to which an international tribunal favours one or other of these factors has a major impact on the overall deference shown to the legislating State, and on the ultimate outcome of a case.

This chapter will examine the deference issues involved in the choice and weighting of factors in factor characterization. As an introduction, we will briefly examine the nature of factor characterization and its application in the WTO. Then, we will focus on the issue of deference in factor characterization. In particular, we will look at the weight given to specific kinds of factors, such as external standards, the legal operation and the practical operation of the legislation, and the legislative purpose.

6.2. THE CONCEPT OF FACTOR CHARACTERIZATION

Factor characterization is a process of identifying factors and giving them relative weight so as to characterize legislation. These factors may relate to the legal operation, practical operation, or purpose of the legislation, or to external standards. A tribunal looks at these kinds of factors, weighs them against each other, and from this weighing process distils the character of the legislation. In doing so, the tribunal can focus on one of these kinds of factors or a mixture of them.[1] The identification and weighing of the various factors are governed by the content and interpretation of the relevant international obligation.

Factor characterization can be seen as the default category of characterization; that is, as characterization that does not involve assessment of proportionality or certainty. Proportionality characterization focuses entirely on legislative purpose.

1. In determining *which* factors are relevant, courts often set out a list of relevant matters. Such a list can be inclusive or exclusive, compulsory or indicative. For example, the list may set out factors that *must* be taken into account in characterization, and that exclude all other factors: in this case the list is exclusive and compulsory. Alternatively, the list may set out examples of factors that may or may not be relevant, according to the circumstances: in this case the list is inclusive and indicative. Perhaps most commonly, the list may set out some factors that must be taken into account, some factors that may be taken into account, and some factors that must not be taken into account. The nature of factor characterization often results from the kind of 'list' that a court applies.

It requires an assessment of the effectiveness with which legislation achieves that purpose and of the appropriateness of the means by which it does so. Factor characterization requires neither of these assessments, but deals with legislative purpose as merely one among many potential factors. Certainty characterization focuses entirely on identifying the legal operation of the challenged legislation. It requires an assessment of the domestic legislative environment, with a view to establishing the legal operation of the challenged legislation. Factor characterization starts from an established legal operation of the legislation, and, again, deals with that legal operation as merely one among many potential factors.

There is considerable commentary on factor characterization in domestic constitutional law. An outstanding work on this issue is that of Taylor, who analysed the nature of constitutional characterization in several major federations. He suggests that there are several approaches to constitutional characterization. These include a 'pith and substance approach', giving great weight to legislative purpose; a 'historical approach', giving great weight to the characterization of analogous previous legislation; and a 'formal approach', emphasizing the legal rights and duties created by the legislation.[2]

Surprisingly, there has been little analysis of the nature of factor characterization in public international law. Instead, international lawyers have generally concentrated on analysing the process of interpreting international obligations. Their sophisticated jurisprudence about treaty interpretation is helpful to tribunals in characterizing legislation, but it does not cover the entirety of the characterization exercise. Treaty interpretation often yields a broad overview of which factors are relevant in characterizing legislation. However, it does not give a complete solution to a factor characterization problem. Even a very detailed interpretation of an international obligation will often not determine how a tribunal proceeds with factor characterization in a particular case. There is an unavoidable element of judicial discretion in factor characterization: international tribunals have much latitude in weighing and balancing factors.

This high degree of judicial freedom in factor characterization often does not sit well with the legal nature of the task assigned to courts and tribunals. Judges do not want to make decisions that could be seen as political rather than legal in nature. There is a point at which judicial freedom tends to undermine the nature of the judicial process: a decision is judicial only if it is governed by legal standards and legal methods. This has led some courts and tribunals to seek objective standards to guide them through the process of factor characterization. Such standards may be domestic or international in nature and include standards created by professional bodies, international organizations, and longstanding practice – as

2. G. Taylor, *Characterisation in Federations: Six Countries Compared* (Berlin: Springer, 2006), 137–138. The 'formal approach' is factor characterization with an emphasis on factors of legal operation. The 'historical approach' is factor characterization with an emphasis on historical factors. The 'pith and substance' approach is factor characterization with an emphasis on legislative purpose. Admittedly, the 'pith and substance' approach may, if one starts to examine the way in which legislation achieves its purpose, lead to proportionality characterization.

well as other matters that could provide objective measures with which to give weight to particular kinds of factors.

Thus, when the relevant constitutional or international rule allows the application of such standards, courts and tribunals are eager to focus on the factors that are relevant to these standards. This is indeed one of the features of international challenges to legislation. Many international obligations refer expressly or implicitly to international standards.

However, objective standards are not a universal panacea in international challenges to legislation. In many cases, there is no standard available, or the available standard is controversial. Indeed, most international factor characterization is carried out without reference to any such standard.

When such objective standards do not exist or are controversial, international tribunals look to other factors in the characterization process. These factors tend to fall into particular categories. The most important of these are the legal operation and practical operation of the challenged legislation and legislative purpose. We will consider these factors here briefly as background to a later discussion of deference in WTO factor characterization.

The relative weight to be given to the factors of legal operation and practical operation is an ever-present feature of factor characterization. In most cases, the legal operation of challenged legislation is given great weight because courts have an inherent expertise in understanding legal norms and feel comfortable making inferences about these norms. This is well illustrated by the views of some Australian judges who focus on 'the actual operation of the law in question in creating, changing, regulating or abolishing rights, duties, powers or privileges' when undertaking factor characterization.[3] According to this approach, the practical effects of legislation should not be given much weight, as these give rise to political questions rather than questions of law. Thus, Justice Dixon famously said that 'There is no other safe guide to judicial decisions in great conflicts than a strict and complete legalism.'[4]

The practical operation of legislation is more difficult for courts to deal with, as it involves the collection of raw facts and a complex process of inference from those facts. Many of these inferences can be highly controversial politically. Nevertheless, if practical operation were ignored, legislatures would be able to avoid constitutional and international norms merely by the clever design of the appearance of legislative rules. For example, it is well known that statutes that are non-discriminatory on their face often have very discriminatory effects in practice. Thus, the practical operation of legislation is usually taken into account in factor characterization in domestic constitutional law.[5] Depending on the circumstances

3. *Bank of NSW v. The Commonwealth* (1948) 76 CLR 1 at 187 per Latham CJ.
4. O. Dixon, 'Upon Taking the Oath of Office as Chief Justice' in *Jesting Pilate*, ed. S. Woinarski (Sydney: Law Book Co., 1965), 245, at 247.
5. For example, see *Grain Pool of Western Australia v. The Commonwealth* (2000) 202 CLR 479 at 492 (Australia); BVerfG, 2 BvF 4/03, 12.3.2008, para. 81 (Germany). See more generally Taylor, above n. 2.

of a dispute, practical operation can sometimes even outweigh legal operation as a factor in the characterization process.

In any case, the legal operation of legislation is sometimes unclear. This is the case when there is a dispute about the effect of the surrounding norms of the domestic legal system, that is, about the effect of the legislative environment.[6] In domestic law, constitutional courts have little difficulty in taking the legislative environment into account as a factor in characterization. This is because domestic constitutional courts are generally experts in the operation of the domestic legal system. In contrast, international tribunals face difficulties in assessing the effect of the legislative environment. We have already seen that public international lawyers attempt to resolve this difficulty by treating the legislative environment as a matter of fact to be proved in evidence before international tribunals.[7] We will see in Chapter 8 that this broad approach leads us to a different kind of characterization, namely, certainty characterization.

Perhaps the most controversial question in factor characterization is the weight to be given to legislative purpose.[8] In many cases, the crux of an international challenge to legislation is the question of whether the intent behind the legislation is contrary to the spirit of the relevant treaty. In the WTO, for example, the existence of an alleged protectionist legislative purpose is often the main motivation to begin litigation.

However, courts generally are reluctant to give much weight to legislative purpose in factor characterization. There are three main reasons for this reluctance. First, it is often difficult to determine an actual purpose,[9] because legislation is often the result of compromise between several competing interests. It is also often difficult to get reliable evidence as to the actual intentions of the legislature (although there are exceptional cases in which the legislature has expressly stated its purpose). Second, legislation may have several purposes simultaneously. For example, it may be designed both to protect the environment and to protect domestic industries. Third, it is difficult to give weight to legislative purpose in characterization without drawing attention to the suitability of the legislation to

---

6. This concept of the legislative environment is discussed in detail at 25.
7. See Section 4.2, text at n. 30.
8. Legal operation and practical operation are often directly linked to legislative purpose, but they are not the same thing. Legislative purpose may be in complete harmony with both legal and practical operation, or with only one or the other. Legislative purpose may also contradict legal and practical operation, as is the case where the legislation is badly drafted, or where the legislator was unaware of important facts. Therefore, a tribunal can often get additional insights into the character of legislation from its purpose (to the extent that this can be determined). Of course, the relative weight to be given to legislative purpose as a factor in factor characterization is a difficult question, particularly where such purpose contradicts the legislation's practical operation.
9. In *Japan – Alcoholic Beverages II*, the Appellate Body expressly avoided considering actual legislative purpose, stating that '[i]t is not necessary for a panel to sort through the many reasons legislators and regulators often have for what they do and weigh the relative significance of those reasons to establish legislative or regulatory intent': Appellate Body Report, *Japan – Alcoholic Beverages II*, 119.

achieve its purpose. This starts to look like an examination of proportionality. Thus, if one starts to give a lot of weight to legislative purpose in the course of factor characterization, one starts to shift the nature of the process away towards proportionality characterization. Indeed, the distinction between proportionality and factor characterization can be seen in terms of the weight given to legislative purpose in the characterization process.

Nevertheless, factor characterization often involves considering the ostensible (as opposed to the actual) purpose of legislation. This is sometimes described as considering the objective purpose of legislation (as determined through its legal and practical operation), rather than considering the legislation's actual purpose. This approach focuses on the more formal aspects of legislation and intentionally avoids examining policy questions. This formalism is often seen as a way for courts to avoid overt value judgments about policy.[10]

To sum up, factor characterization involves considering factors such as standards, legal and practical operations, and legislative purpose. These factors are given varying weight in the characterization process, with the actual legislative purpose tending to be a minor factor. As we will now see, these general remarks also apply to factor characterization in the WTO.

6.3. FACTOR CHARACTERIZATION IN THE WTO

The concept of factor characterization is not referred to in any WTO provision. Furthermore, factor characterization is a not a normative principle of WTO law. However, this type of characterization can be seen in many, if not most, WTO challenges to legislation. One can say that factor characterization is a good description of a method often used by WTO tribunals in characterizing challenged legislation.

The Appellate Body came close to describing factor characterization in *China – Auto Parts*. In this case, one issue was whether a particular charge fell under Article II(1)(b) of the GATT (customs duties) or Article III(2) of the GATT

---

10. Taylor, above n. 2, 138. Latham CJ (in *Bank of NSW v. The Commonwealth* (1948) 76 CLR 1 at 187) described the Australian approach as follows:

> It has often been decided that the motives of Parliament, and, as a general rule, the objects which a Parliament seeks to achieve, are not relevant to questions of constitutional validity . . . The operation and effect of a customs duty on certain goods is to make the importation of those goods subject to the duty imposed. That is what the law does. The motive of Parliament may have been to assist a particular industry or business. When validity is in question, that fact is irrelevant.
>
> [W]hen a question arises as to the validity of legislation it is the duty of the Court to determine what is the actual operation of the law in question in creating, changing, regulating or abolishing rights, duties, powers or privileges, and then to consider whether that which the enactment does falls in substance within the relevant authorized subject matter, or whether it touches it only incidentally, or whether it is really an endeavour, by purporting to use one power, to make a law upon a subject which is beyond power.

(internal charges). The Appellate Body noted that a Panel must scrutinize the design and operation of the measure and 'identify its principal characteristics'.[11] It continued:

> Having done so, the panel must then seek to identify the leading or core features of the measure at issue, those that define its 'centre of gravity' for purposes of characterizing the charge that it imposes as an ordinary customs duty or an internal charge. . . . [A] panel must identify all relevant characteristics of the measure, and recognize which features are the most central to that measure itself, and which are to be accorded the most significance for purposes of characterizing the relevant charge.[12]

The 'features' mentioned here are the factors in factor characterization. The identification of 'leading or core' features that 'are the most central to the measure itself' is the result of giving them particular weight compared with other features of the measure. The weighing process in factor characterization is vividly described by the Appellate Body as defining a measure's 'centre of gravity'.

A good example of factor characterization applied in WTO practice is the treatment of the 'likeness' of legislative product categories under Article III of the GATT. According to the Appellate Body, the purpose of Article III of the GATT is 'to prevent Members from applying internal taxes and regulations in a manner which affects the competitive relationship, in the marketplace, between the domestic and imported products involved, "so as to afford protection to domestic production"'.[13] Thus, the relevance of any particular matter in factor characterization about the likeness of products is determined by the extent to which the matter relates to the 'competitive relationship' between the products.[14]

Consistent with this broad principle, WTO tribunals look to a range of factors in determining the 'likeness' of products. These factors include the following:

- the properties, nature, and quality of the products;
- the end-uses of the products;

---

11. Appellate Body Report, *China – Auto Parts*, para. 171. Here, the issue was which WTO provision was applicable to the measure. However, the Appellate Body's comments could apply also to the issue of whether the measure had a mix of characteristics such that it breached a particular WTO provision.
12. *Ibid.*
13. Appellate Body Report, *EC – Asbestos*, para. 98.
14. *Ibid.*, para. 103:

> The kind of evidence to be examined in assessing the 'likeness' of products will, necessarily, depend upon the particular products and the legal provision at issue. When all the relevant evidence has been examined, panels must determine whether that evidence, as a whole, indicates that the products in question are 'like' in terms of the legal provision at issue . . . [W]hether the Border Tax Adjustments framework is adopted or not, it is important under Article III(4) to take account of evidence which indicates whether, and to what extent, the products involved are – or could be – in a competitive relationship in the marketplace.

- consumers' tastes and habits – more comprehensively termed *consumers' perceptions and behaviour* – in respect of the products; and
- the tariff classification of the products.[15]

The Appellate Body seems to have regarded this list of factors as compulsory, but not as exclusive. This can be seen, for example, in *EC – Asbestos*. In this case, the core of the dispute was whether a product's effects on health could determine its likeness to another product. The Appellate Body held that the listed matters were 'simply tools to assist in the task of sorting and examining the relevant evidence' and did not constitute a 'closed list of criteria that will determine the legal characterization of products'.[16] It added:

> More important, the adoption of a particular framework to aid in the examination of evidence does not dissolve the duty or the need to examine, in each case, all of the pertinent evidence.[17]

In any case, the Appellate Body decided that evidence relating to health risks fell within the standard categories (namely, physical properties and consumers' tastes and habits).[18] Furthermore, the standard categories were compulsory considerations in the context of the particular dispute, and the Panel fell into legal error by not considering all of them.[19]

There are many other examples of this kind of factor characterization in WTO challenges to legislation.[20] In all such cases, WTO tribunals identify a list of relevant factors and then weigh and balance those factors to determine the character of the legislation. The content of the relevant WTO obligation guides the tribunal in this process by providing clues about the relevance and importance of various factors.

Although the content of WTO obligations can guide a tribunal in factor characterization, there is an inescapable element of judicial discretion in the process. In finding the 'centre of gravity' of various measures, different weightings may be given to different factors. For example, the list of four factors set out above in relation to Article III of the GATT was not determined by the content of the Article itself, but was instead developed by GATT Panels through a process of treaty interpretation – a process almost inevitably involving a degree of judicial choice.

---

15. Appellate Body Report, *EC – Asbestos*, para. 101. See also Appellate Body Report, *Japan – Alcoholic Beverages II*, 113; Appellate Body Report, *Canada – Periodicals*, 21. This approach dates from the 1970 *Report of the Working Party on Border Tax Adjustments* (BISD 18S/97, para. 18).
16. Appellate Body Report, *EC – Asbestos*, para. 102.
17. *Ibid.*
18. *Ibid.*, para. 113.
19. *Ibid.*, para. 109.
20. For example, consider the jurisprudence about whether legislation is 'against' dumping or subsidies. The governing principle here is whether the legislation 'has an adverse bearing on, or, more specifically, has the effect of dissuading the practice of dumping or the practice of subsidization, or creates an incentive to terminate such practices': Appellate Body Report, *US – Offset Act (Byrd Amendment)*, para. 254.

This judicial discretion may cause problems for WTO tribunals, given that the WTO standard of review does not allow them to add to or detract from the content of WTO obligations.[21] It is therefore not surprising that they seek ways to limit their discretion.

Thus, one can see WTO tribunals attempting to seek objectivity in factor characterization by recourse to some kind of objective standard. Such a standard might be set out expressly in the relevant WTO obligation. The best known of these are probably the international health and safety standards referred to in the Sanitary and Phytosanitary (SPS) Agreement and the Technical Barriers to Trade (TBT) Agreement.[22] In cases under the purview of these agreements, international standards play a major role in characterizing the challenged legislation.

The Appellate Body has also referred to standards that are not expressly mentioned in the relevant WTO obligation. For example, it has held that an international system for classifying tariff nomenclatures could be a useful basis for confirming 'likeness' in products – although such standards are not mentioned in the relevant text of the GATT.[23] Similarly, the Appellate Body referred to an Organization for Economic Cooperation and Development (OECD) arrangement establishing minimum interest rate guidelines for export credits, in determining whether a scheme was 'used to secure a material advantage in the field of export credit terms' under the Subsidies and Countervailing Measures (SCM) Agreement.[24] The standards used here are not always international in nature. For example, in *US – FSC*, the Appellate Body determined whether an income tax exemption created forgone revenue 'otherwise due' under Article 1.1(a)(1)(ii) of the SCM Agreement in the light of the general tax base set by domestic tax law.[25]

---

21. See Section 4.6, text at n. 122.
22. Article 3.2 SPS Agreement presumes an SPS measure to be consistent with the Agreement if it conforms to 'international standards, guidelines or recommendations'. Article 2.4 TBT Agreement requires the use of such standards as a basis of domestic technical regulations, except where the standard itself fails a proportionality requirement in relation to the legislative purpose.
23. Appellate Body Report, *Japan – Alcoholic Beverages II*, 114. P. Mavroidis, *The General Agreement on Tariffs and Trade* (Oxford: Oxford University Press, 2005), 80 queries whether WTO tribunals should be deciding tariff classification questions at all. He suggests that such tribunals should instead seek, and act on, advice from the World Customs Organization.
24. Appellate Body Report, *Brazil – Aircraft*, para. 181. The relevant provision was item (k) of the Illustrative List of Export Subsidies in Annex I SCM Agreement.
25. Appellate Body Report, *US – FSC*, paras 90–91:

    > [T]he term 'otherwise due' implies some kind of comparison between the revenues due under the contested measure and revenues that would be due in some other situation . . . [T]he basis of comparison must be the tax rules applied by the Member in question . . . What is 'otherwise due', therefore, depends on the rules of taxation that each Member, by its own choice, establishes for itself.

    See also Appellate Body Report, *US – Softwood Lumber IV*, para. 56. M. Matsushita, T. Schoenbaum & P. Mavroidis, *The World Trade Organization: Law, Practice, and Policy* (Oxford: Oxford University Press, 2003), 271, refer this as the use of a 'local' element rather than an 'international' element as the decisive criterion for decision-making. As discussed

As a general proposition, the United States agreed with the use of this standard.[26]

Nevertheless, standards cannot resolve every controversy about the characterization of legislation in the WTO. An existing standard may be controversial,[27] or no standard may exist at all. In the majority of cases, WTO tribunals therefore have to fall back on general methods of factor characterization, weighing and balancing the inherent features of the legislation and their effects in the real world. Here they encounter the other types of factors: legal operation, practical operation, and legislative purpose.

The Appellate Body insists that the starting point for characterization must be the legal operation of legislation as evidenced by its text.[28] Indeed, WTO tribunals have sometimes found legal operation to be decisive in factor characterization. Thus, they have sometimes held that the *only* relevant factor in characterization is legal operation.

An example is the Appellate Body decision in *US – Offset Act* (*Byrd Amendment*). This case concerned Article 18.1 of the Anti-Dumping Agreement and Article 32.1 of the SCM Agreement, which in some situations prohibit 'specific action against' dumping and 'specific action against' subsidies.[29] The challenged legislation provided for distribution of anti-dumping and countervailing duties to domestic producers. The legislation was on its face clearly 'specific action' in relation to dumping and subsidies,[30] and the crux of the dispute was whether the legislation was 'against' dumping and subsidies. The United States argued that that practical operation – in the form of the economic effects of the legislation – was not relevant to this issue. The Appellate Body agreed, focusing more on the 'design and structure' of the legislation:

> In our view, in order to determine whether the [challenged legislation] is 'against' dumping or subsidization, it was not necessary, nor relevant, for the Panel to examine the conditions of competition under which domestic products and dumped/subsidized imports compete, and to assess the impact of the measure on the competitive relationship between them. An analysis of

---

earlier in the context of deference generally (see Section 4.4.2), this can be seen as a limited form of the incorporation of domestic law into the international obligation.

26. Appellate Body Report, *US – FSC*, para. 91. The United States nevertheless argued that this general proposition was subject to a special rule derived from another provision of the SCM Agreement. The Appellate Body rejected this argument via a process of treaty interpretation (see Appellate Body Report, paras 92–94).
27. For example, in *EC – Sardines*, Art. 2.4 TBT Agreement required labelling rules to be based on international standards that were 'adequate and effective' in achieving regulatory objectives. The EC objected strenuously to the use of particular international standards, as it considered them controversial and inadequate. On the circumstances of that particular case, the Appellate Body rejected this argument, and required the application of the standard.
28. Appellate Body Report, *US – Corrosion-Resistant Steel Sunset Review*, para. 168. See also Appellate Body Report, *US – Oil Country Tubular Goods Sunset Reviews*, para. 187.
29. Under both provisions, such action can be taken in 'accordance with the provisions of GATT 1994'.
30. Appellate Body Report, *US – Offset Act* (*Byrd Amendment*), para. 242.

> the term 'against', in our view, is more appropriately centred on the design and structure of the measure; such an analysis does not mandate an economic assessment of the implications of the measure on the conditions of competition under which domestic product and dumped/subsidized imports compete.[31]

To divine the 'design and structure' of the legislation, the Appellate Body focused predominantly on its text.[32] That is, the legal operation of the legislation was decisive in determining its character.

Despite decisions that focus on legal operation, it is clear that in other cases, WTO tribunals place great weight on the practical operation of legislation. We can take here as an example the cases on the national treatment obligation in Article III of the GATT. In deciding whether products are 'like'. WTO tribunals look to practical matters concerning the 'competitive relationship' between products, including product end-uses; consumers' tastes and habits; the product's properties, nature, and quality; and its tariff classification.[33] Furthermore, in deciding whether legislation provides 'less favourable' treatment of imports under Article III(4) of the GATT, the Appellate Body has held that discriminatory legal operation does not necessarily result in such treatment.[34] Instead, Panels should examine the practical operation of the legislation in the form of the conditions of competition existing in relation to the relevant product.[35] A similar emphasis on practical operation can be seen in relation to some other WTO rules.[36]

The relative weight of legal and practical operation in characterization depends on the content of the relevant WTO obligation. Sometimes, that content strongly suggests an examination of practical operation. An example of this is Article III of the GATT, with its express mention of measures as they are 'applied'.

---

31. *Ibid.*, para. 257.
32. Appellate Body Report, *US – Offset Act (Byrd Amendment)*, paras 255–259. The Appellate Body also gave legislative purpose some minor weight in the characterization process, see para. 259.
33. See n. 15.
34. Appellate Body Report, *Korea – Various Measures on Beef*, paras 135–137.
35. *Ibid.*, para. 136, quoting GATT Panel Report, *United States – Section 337 of the Tariff Act of 1930*, L/6439, adopted 7 Nov. 1989, BISD 36S/345, para. 5.11.
36. For example, see Appellate Body Report, *US – Upland Cotton*, which concerned Art. 13 Agreement on Agriculture (the 'peace clause'). This Article immunized certain agricultural subsidies from WTO challenges. These were subsidies that did 'not grant support to a specific commodity in excess of that decided during the 1992 marketing year'. The United States granted benefits to farmers, on the condition that they had previously planted upland cotton on certain acreages. As a matter of law, the farmers did not have to produce cotton on those acreages to gain the benefits. However, as a matter of fact, many farmers did produce cotton on those acreages. The Appellate Body said (para. 378):

    > [T]he absence of an express reference in the legislation to continued production of upland cotton does not mean that the payments do not grant support to upland cotton. This is because a link between the four measures at issue and the continued production of upland cotton is discernible from the characteristics, structure and operation of those measures.

    Here, it is clear that the characterization exercise goes beyond the legal operation of the legislation, and extends to the practical operation that gives legislation meaning in the real world.

This express reference to the application of a measure is a clear indication that practical operation is relevant. Even clearer in this respect is the definition of an export subsidy in Article 3.1(a) of the SCM Agreement; that is, as a 'subsidy, contingent in law or in fact...on export performance'.[37] Here, the obligation expresses the need for both de facto and de jure characterization. It is harder to find examples of WTO obligations that expressly require de jure characterization only. Perhaps the best candidates here are obligations setting forth a highly specific concrete requirement, such as a time period or amount.[38] If the legal operation of challenged legislation reflects the requirement (or not), this is likely to be the end of the matter, regardless of evidence of practical operation.

Beyond the content of the relevant WTO obligation, it is harder to discern a principle for distinguishing between preference for practical operation or preference for legal operation. One can speculate that there is a relevant distinction between obligations of non-discrimination and obligations of harmonization.[39] Traditionally, international trade law has been a law of non-discrimination (e.g., via the national treatment and most-favoured-nation (MFN) rules). More recently, we have seen the rise of obligations to harmonize trade rules (most obviously, in TRIPS). Obligations of non-discrimination lend themselves to de facto characterization because the nature of discrimination is a practical matter, and to focus on legal operation may obscure the substance of the international obligation – particularly if a legislature hides practical discrimination behind a cloak of legal equality. In contrast, obligations of harmonization tend to lend themselves to de jure characterization. The nature of harmonization assumes some equality in the external environment. Thus, the practical operation of harmonized legislation should, in principle, not create a basis for a challenge to the legislation. The focus instead should be on whether the legislation is properly harmonized – this is a matter of its legal operation. However, it is probably too early to say whether the distinction will be a guiding matter for WTO characterization of legislation.

Even if an appropriate balance can be found between legal and practical operations as factors in the characterization process, WTO tribunals have often

---

37. Article 3.1(a) SCM Agreement footnotes the text 'in law or in fact' as follows:

> This standard is met when the facts demonstrate that the granting of a subsidy, without having been made legally contingent upon export performance, is in fact tied to actual or anticipated exportation or export earnings. The mere fact that a subsidy is granted to enterprises which export shall not for that reason alone be considered to be an export subsidy within the meaning of this provision.

38. For example, Art. 33 TRIPS requires a minimum period of patent protection of twenty years from the date of filing the application for the patent. This was discussed in Appellate Body Report, *Canada – Patent Term*. It is hard to see how matters other than legal operation (and perhaps the linked factor of the legislative environment) could be relevant to characterization in relation to the time period expressed in this Article.
39. J. Jackson, *The World Trading System: Law and Policy of International Economic Relations*, 2nd edn (Cambridge: MIT Press, 1997), 345, distinguishes between obligations of 'harmonization', 'reciprocity' and 'interface'. The third type of obligation is that which ameliorates tension between fundamentally different kinds of domestic economic systems.

experienced problems when the legal operation is unclear because of the operation of the domestic legal system. In many cases, the dispute is not about the weight given to legal operation in the characterization process, but rather about what that legal operation actually is. These are the cases concerning certainty characterization. The weighing and balancing process in such cases is of a very particular nature, as it concerns the operation of the legislative environment. I discuss these cases in more detail in Chapter 8 of this book and do not consider them further here.

A similarly problematic issue is the weight to be given to legislative purpose in WTO factor characterization. The more weight one gives to legislative purpose in the characterization process, the more one is tempted to engage in a proportionality analysis. Perhaps for this reason, legislative purpose plays a secondary role to legal and practical operations in WTO factor characterization. In *Japan – Alcoholic Beverages II*, the Appellate Body considered whether directly competitive or substitutable products were taxed in a way that afforded protection (contrary to Article III(2) of the GATT). The Appellate Body expressly avoided considering actual legislative purpose here and focused on practical operation instead:

> This is not an issue of intent. It is not necessary for a panel to sort through the many reasons legislators and regulators often have for what they do and weigh the relative significance of those reasons to establish legislative or regulatory intent. If the measure is applied to imported or domestic products so as to afford protection to domestic production, then it does not matter that there may not have been any desire to engage in protectionism in the minds of the legislators or the regulators who imposed the measure. It is irrelevant that protectionism was not an intended objective if the particular tax measure in question is nevertheless, to echo Article III(1), '*applied* to imported or domestic products so as to afford protection to domestic production'.[40]

This sentiment has been confirmed in many decisions.[41] Its most notorious expression can be seen in the Appellate Body's rejection of an aim and effects test in determining the 'likeness' of products.[42] Some Panels under the old GATT system had used legislative purpose as a relevant factor together with practical operation in factor characterization. For example, one Panel held that US legislation taxing low-alcohol beer at a lower rate than high-alcohol beer did not discriminate between like products, as the purpose of discouraging high alcohol consumption

---

40. Appellate Body Report, *Japan – Alcoholic Beverages II*, 119.
41. Appellate Body Report, *US – Offset Act (Byrd Amendment)*, para. 259 (whether a measure is 'against' dumping or subsidies under Art. 18.1 of the Anti-Dumping Agreement or Art. 32.1 of the SCM Agreement); Appellate Body Report, *US – Section 211 Appropriations Act*, paras 110–114 (regarding TRIPS); Appellate Body Report, *EC – Bananas III*, para. 248 (regarding tariff preferences for the purpose of aiding hurricane damaged regions).
42. On the demise of the aim and effects test under the Art. III GATT, see R. Hudec, 'GATT/WTO Constraints on National Regulation: Requiem for an "Aim and Effects" Test', *International Lawyer* 32 (1998): 619; Matsushita, Schoenbaum & Mavroidis, above n. 25, 161–162.

indicated that no protectionism was involved.[43] Another Panel held that a tax on 'gas-guzzler' luxury cars (which were often imported) did not discriminate between like products, because the objective of encouraging fuel economy was a valid one.[44] This kind of reasoning became known as the 'aim and effects test'. However, in *Japan – Alcoholic Beverages II*, the Appellate Body rejected the aim and effects test, finding that it had no textual basis in the GATT.[45] Among other reasons, the aim and effects test would have made Article XX of the GATT (the general exceptions clause) redundant, for it is under this Article that legislative purpose is dealt with expressly under a proportionality-like test.

The Appellate Body has nevertheless stressed the relevance of the objective purpose of a measure. This is not the actual legislative purpose, but rather, the 'objectives or purposes as revealed or objectified in the measure itself', that is, as 'objectively manifested in the design, architecture and structure of the measure'.[46] This reflects a distinction, common in domestic constitutional law, between the subjective and objective purposes of legislation.[47] As discussed earlier, the Appellate Body describes its general approach to characterization as 'a comprehensive and objective analysis of the structure and application of the measure in question'.[48] It is this structure and application – i.e., the legislation's legal and practical operations – that determines objective purpose. The subjective purpose of the legislation is a matter that WTO tribunals prefer not to deal with in factor characterization.[49]

This quick survey of WTO practice indicates that factor characterization can be a useful way to gain an overview of WTO jurisprudence relating to many challenges to legislation. If this is so, the concept of factor characterization should also have close linkages with the degree of deference given by WTO tribunals in such challenges. It is to the subject of deference that we now turn.

---

43. GATT Panel Report, *US – Malt Beverages*, BISD 39S/206, para. 5.19 (adopted on 19 Jun. 1992).
44. GATT Panel Report, *United States – Taxes on Automobiles*, DS31/R, 11 Oct. 1994, unadopted. The controversy surrounding this reasoning led to its lack of adoption by the GATT Contracting Parties.
45. Appellate Body Report, *Japan – Alcoholic Beverages II*, 119, confirmed in Appellate Body Report, *EC – Bananas III*, para. 241. See also Hudec, above n. 42.
46. Appellate Body Report, *Chile – Alcoholic Beverages*, para. 71.
47. See above, text at n. 10.
48. Appellate Body Report, *Japan – Alcoholic Beverages II*, 120. See also Ch. 5, text at n. 9.
49. This is not to say that subjective legislative purpose is never given weight in WTO factor characterization. For example, in *Canada – Periodicals,* the Appellate Body cited statements by the Canadian government and the Minister of Canadian Heritage as supporting an inference that the challenged legislation imposed taxation 'so as to afford protection' in breach of Art. III(2) s. 2 GATT. The statements indicated that the purpose of the legislation was to encourage flows of advertising revenues to Canadian publications (Appellate Body Report, *Canada – Periodicals*, 30–31). The Panel in *Chile – Alcohol Beverages* took note of this approach, holding that 'the stated objectives by the government of the Member concerned may be relevant in evaluating the design of a measure' (Panel Report, *Chile – Alcoholic Beverages*, paras 7.118–7.119), although only 'as a factor confirming other evidence' (at para. 7.120). However, it cautioned that 'many views can be expressed in open parliamentary debates' (at para.

6.4. DEFERENCE AND FACTOR CHARACTERIZATION IN THE WTO

Domestic legislatures usually have their own opinions about which features of legislation are important. Deference in factor characterization is thus deference to a domestic legislature's own view on how to prioritize factors in characterization. Therefore, choosing and weighting factors always involves, whether expressly or implicitly, the issue of how much deference international tribunals should give to the views of domestic legislatures.

The process of factor characterization often disguises the implicit policy choices made by WTO tribunals and the weight that they give to domestic legislative preferences. Factor characterization appears, superficially, to be a legal, apolitical process of selecting and weighing particular features of legislation. However, the way in which those features are selected and weighed is a highly political process. Setting the 'rules of the game' here often involves the greatest of political struggles. For example, the list of factors relating to the likeness of legislative product categories has been the subject of major disputes. In particular, the question of whether the process of manufacture can be a relevant factor in characterizing products has been a very controversial issue: it has major implications for domestic legislative freedom in setting environmental and employment standards in relation to imported products.[50]

One is reminded here of the problem of deference in making judicial inferences.[51] A legislature makes its own legal inferences from various factors, and the question facing an international tribunal is how much deference to give to those inferences. Two extremes are possible here. On the one hand, the tribunal could make its own inferences and ignore those of the legislature. On the other hand, the tribunal could identify the inferences made by the legislature and simply accept them without further analysis. The actual degree of deference lies between these two extremes.

In the following discussion, we will see that the degree of deference shown by WTO tribunals in factor characterization has generally involved a fairly intrusive analysis of domestic legislative decision-making. This can be best seen in relation

---

7.118), noting again the Appellate Body's reluctance to examine individual legislators' intent, and holding that more weight could be given to *government* statements of legislative purpose (at para. 7.118). Furthermore, it held (at para. 7.119) that:

> Statements by a government against WTO interests (e.g., indicating a protective purpose or design) are most probative. Correspondingly, it is less likely that self-serving comments by a government attempting to justify its measure would be particularly probative.

See also Appellate Body Report, *US – Offset Act (Byrd Amendment)*, para. 259, where legislative purpose was allowed as a factor in characterization, but only to *confirm* a characterization achieved through other factors.

50. R. Howse & D. Regan, 'The Product/Process Distinction-An Illusory Basis for Disciplining Unilateralism in Trade Policy', EJIL 11 (2000): 249; J. Jackson, 'Comments on Shrimp/Turtle and the Product/Process Distinction', EJIL 11 (2000): 303.
51. See Section 4.3.

to the factors discussed earlier; namely, the use of standards and the relative weight given to the practical and legal operations of legislation and to legislative purpose.

6.4.1. Standards and Deference

WTO tribunals' use of standards can be a rather intrusive aspect of WTO factor characterization if those standards are not specified in WTO rules. Domestic legislatures may question whether the use of such standards is really required by WTO rules or is simply the result of judicial choice. Although judicial choice is an inevitable part of litigation, a tribunal should exercise that choice with a close eye on the applicable standard of review. Adopting a standard not mentioned in WTO rules as a benchmark for characterizing legislation undercuts legislative freedom in adopting alternative benchmarks. There is nothing exceptional in a tribunal adopting a benchmark to underpin its reasoning process. However, the tribunal shows a distinct lack of deference if it imposes this benchmark on the domestic legislature or if it creates evidentiary barriers to the domestic legislature adopting its own benchmark.

This can be illustrated by the Appellate Body's decision in *Brazil – Aircraft*. The issue in this case was whether loans provided under a Brazilian scheme were 'used to secure a material advantage in the field of export credit terms' contrary to the SCM Agreement.[52] The Appellate Body found that certain Organization for Economic Cooperation and Development (OECD) guidelines were a useful benchmark for measuring material advantage.[53] It later stressed that the domestic rule maker was free to use a different benchmark if it was 'based on evidence from relevant, comparable transactions in the marketplace'.[54] However, as was made clear in later compliance proceedings, the evidential onus for establishing such an alternative was on the legislating State. Brazil suggested such an alternative in the form of the ten-year US Treasury Bond rate (plus 20 basis points), but the Appellate Body rejected this suggestion.[55] The rejection was based on evidentiary grounds: Brazil had relied merely on evidence of a single transaction to support the relevance of its suggested benchmark, and that transaction differed in many ways from the kinds of payments that Brazil was defending.[56] Thus, the Appellate Body appears to have ruled that the OECD guidelines were the relevant benchmark unless proven otherwise. If so, the ruling has considerably restricted domestic legislative freedoms in adopting alternative benchmarks.

---

52. Paragraph (k) Annex I, Illustrative List of Export Subsidies SCM Agreement.
53. Appellate Body Report, *Brazil – Aircraft*, para. 181.
54. Appellate Body Report, *Brazil – Aircraft* (Article 21.5 – Canada), para. 74.
55. *Ibid.*, para. 76.
56. The Appellate Body pointed out that the suggested transaction related to large civil aircraft involving floating interest rate financing and a government loan guarantee, while the relevant Brazilian payments related to regional jet aircraft involving fixed interest rate financing and interest rate equalization payments: Appellate Body Report, *Brazil – Aircraft* (*Article 21.5 – Canada*), para. 75.

One should stress here that the OECD guidelines may well be a very good benchmark in terms of rational trade policy. What is striking here is that they may have been adopted as a legal presumption by the Appellate Body without express sanction from the WTO membership. One might expect that in these circumstances, the evidentiary onus on the legislating State in establishing an alternative benchmark should be quite light. Indeed, one could view the outcome in *Brazil – Aircraft* as exceptional, based on the Appellate Body's view that Brazil's evidence was demonstrably inadequate to support the inference that Brazil desired.

In any case, in the majority of WTO challenges to legislation, there is no clear international standard that could be applied as a legal yardstick for factor characterization. Thus, WTO tribunals most often fall back on factors relating to the legal and practical operations of legislation.

6.4.2. Legal and Practical Operations and Deference

The Appellate Body's preference for legal operation as a factor in characterization[57] tends, in a very general sense, to increase deference to the legislating State. This is because the legislating State has control over the text of its legislation, whereas it does not have the same control over the legislation's practical operation. A sporting analogy may be helpful here. The factor of legal operation is the legislating State's home turf. When WTO tribunals prefer legal operation in factor characterization, they give the legislating State a home-game advantage.

This can be seen in the Appellate Body's reasoning in *US – Section 211 Appropriations Act*. One issue in this case concerned Article 15.1 of TRIPS, which defines the signs or combinations of signs that are capable of constituting a trademark.[58] According to the Appellate Body, a measure that *relates to ownership* does not concern the issues addressed by Article 15.1. The critical question, therefore, was whether the challenged legislation related to ownership.[59] Based on a purely textual analysis of the legislation, the Appellate Body held that it did relate to ownership,[60] as the United States had argued.[61] It did not consider the practical operation of the legislation and disregarded the plea of the European Communities (EC) to consider legislative purpose.[62] The nature of the characterization exercise, favouring legal operation, thus favoured the legislating State.

One should not conclude that WTO tribunals will always defer to the legislating State's views about the nature of the legal operation of its legislation. The process of de jure characterization has resulted in several defeats for the legislating

57. See Section 6.3, text at n. 28.
58. Appellate Body Report, *US – Section 211 Appropriations Act*, para. 154.
59. *Ibid.*, para. 166. The case is unusual in that the Appellate Body began its analysis with the characterization of the legislation (i.e., as relating to ownership), without giving a textual basis in the WTO Agreements for why it chose this category.
60. Appellate Body Report, *US – Section 211 Appropriations Act*, paras 113–121.
61. *Ibid.*, para. 111.
62. *Ibid.*, para. 110.

State.[63] Yet, such a finding is often controversial, as it involves rejecting the legislating State's own view of the character of the legal operation of the legislation. *US – FSC* is an example of this, in which de jure characterization of certain US international taxation legislation has resulted in a somewhat frosty response from the US Congress, resulting in a series of awkward compliance proceedings.[64]

As a general proposition, focusing on the practical operation of legislation in factor characterization can involve a less-deferential approach than does de jure characterization. This is because WTO tribunals can examine a broad range of factual matters that a domestic legislature may prefer to discount or ignore.[65] De facto characterization can also open the door to independent fact finding by WTO tribunals. The standard of review involved is sometimes close to de novo in nature.[66]

An intensive standard of review in dealing with the practical operation of legislation can be seen in cases concerning the direct competitiveness and substitutability of products under Article III(2) of the GATT. Let us consider two such cases here.

The first case, *Chile – Alcoholic Beverages*, concerned differential taxes on alcohol. The Panel considered whether pisco (a Chilean alcoholic beverage) had a directly competitive or substitutable relationship with other alcoholic beverages (such as whisky). The Panel conducted a nearly de novo review of this matter, considering and balancing a variety of evidential sources supplied by Chile, as well as by the complainant (the European Communities). Most notably, one of these sources was a survey of the drinking habits of spirits consumers, conducted by a market research consultant at the request of the EC spirits industry.[67] Of course, the Panel was careful to give reasons as to why it gave weight to particular evidence.[68] In all, however, the Panel's approach in considering the practical effect of the taxation legislation showed little deference to the Chilean legislature.[69]

The second case, *Korea – Alcoholic Beverages*, dealt with the issue of whether imported liquor was directly competitive or substitutable with Korean soju. In this case, the Panel referred to evidence from the Japanese liquor market. Not surprisingly, Korea objected to this evidence. One may have some sympathy for this objection, as the text of the GATT does not refer to the use of evidence from foreign markets. The Appellate Body nevertheless approved the Panel's approach,

63. For example: Appellate Body Report, *US – FSC* (de jure export contingency of a subsidy under Art. 3 SCM Agreement); Appellate Body Report, *Argentina – Hides and Leather* (de jure consistency with Art. II GATT); Appellate Body Report, *US – Offset Act (Byrd Amendment)* (whether a measure is 'against' dumping or subsidies under Art. 18.1 of the Anti-Dumping Agreement or Art. 32.1 of the SCM Agreement).
64. See G. Luengo, *Regulation of Subsidies and State Aids in WTO and EC Law* (London: Kluwer, 2007), 270–279.
65. See Section 4.2.
66. See C. Ehlermann & N. Lockhart, 'Standard Of Review in WTO Law', JIEL 7 (2004): 491, at 520.
67. Panel Report, *Chile – Alcoholic Beverages*, para. 4.103, para. 7.39.
68. *Ibid.*, para. 4.103, Part VII.C.2.
69. This was also noted by Ehlermann & Lockhart, above n. 66, 518.

holding that the evidence of the Japanese market related to the competitive relationship between Korean liquor and imported liquor.[70] It is possible, but unlikely, that such evidence was considered by Korean lawmakers. The Panel's choice to emphasize this evidence showed a distinct lack of deference to Korea. Indeed, the Panel's finding – taken at its broadest – seemed to expand the range of evidence relevant to the practical operation of legislation into the realm of international comparisons.[71]

Of course, one should not draw too wide a conclusion from the lack of deference shown in WTO tribunal decisions concerning this aspect of Article III(2) of the GATT. In other areas of WTO jurisprudence, an emphasis on factors of practical operation in the characterization process can often lead to acceptance of the legislature's view. For example, in *EC – Asbestos*, the Appellate Body agreed with the European Communities in deciding that evidence about health risks was relevant to determining the likeness of products.[72] At a more systemic level, the Appellate Body's jurisprudence regarding Article 5.1 of the SPS Agreement encourages deference in the choice of relevant evidence. This article requires sanitary and phytosanitary measures (such as quarantine legislation) to be based on a scientific risk assessment.[73] The Appellate Body has held that a measure is based on a risk assessment if there is 'a rational relationship between the measure and the risk assessment'.[74] A domestic legislature may perceive such a rational relationship 'in good faith on the basis of what, at a given time, may be a divergent opinion coming from qualified and respected sources'.[75] Thus, the Appellate Body, as a matter of principle, mandates some deference to domestic legislatures in assessing the practical operation of legislation, to the extent that such operation could be seen as being supported rationally by a risk assessment.[76]

Indeed, a focus on practical operation in the process of factor characterization can sometimes enhance deference. In some cases, WTO tribunals show deference to the legislating State's findings of raw facts (and inferences from those facts).[77] An example of this can be seen in *Argentina – Hides and Leather*, in which the legislation was alleged to be a de facto restriction on exports in breach of Article XI

70. Appellate Body Report, *Korea – Alcoholic Beverages*, para. 137.
71. Thus, Ehlermann & Lockhart, above n. 66, 520, suggest that WTO tribunals engage in an 'original, open-ended, and contemporaneous' examination of domestic rules under Art. III GATT (as well as under Art. XX GATT and under the SPS Agreement and TBT Agreement).
72. Appellate Body Report, *EC – Asbestos*, para. 113.
73. M. Matsushita, T. Schoenbaum & P. Mavroidis, *The World Trade Organization: Law, Practice, and Policy*, 2nd edn (Oxford: Oxford University Press, 2006), 512–513; Stoll & Strack, 'Article 5 SPS', in *WTO – Technical Barriers and SPS Measures*, eds R. Wolfrum, P. Stoll & A. Seibert-Fohr (Netherlands: Brill Academic Publishers, 2007).
74. Appellate Body Report, *EC – Hormones*, para. 193.
75. *Ibid.*, para. 194.
76. However, as a matter of practice, the Appellate Body has often found the legislation to not be 'based on' a risk assessment: Appellate Body Report, *EC – Hormones*; Appellate Body Report, *Australia – Salmon*.
77. See Section 4.2.

of the GATT.[78] The Panel noted that the challenger had to establish a causal link between the measure and a low level of exports. It then continued:

> In our view, whatever else it may involve, a demonstration of causation must consist of a persuasive explanation of precisely how the measure at issue causes or contributes to the low level of exports.[79]

That is, the challenger had a heavy burden of proof in establishing the underlying raw facts (and inferences) supporting a finding that the measure at issue caused a low level of exports. A similar approach applies in cases in which the challenger alleges a de facto export subsidy.[80] In such cases, an emphasis on practical operation in factor characterization places a heavier than usual burden on the challenger to demonstrate the existence of the alleged facts and to justify the inferences that it draws from these facts.[81]

One may conclude that a preference for legal operation, or for practical operation, may increase or decrease the level of deference, depending on the nature of the WTO obligation and the challenged legislation. That is, it is difficult to identify trends in this area. For many WTO obligations, the Appellate Body states that it will characterize measures on a case-by-case basis, depending on the legal and factual matrices concerned.[82] This may simply be a function of the youth of the WTO system. When sufficient case law develops around each WTO obligation, one may see clearer rules developing about which factors are relevant in the characterization process. For the time being, it is useful to observe WTO tribunals' approach in each case to consider whether an emphasis on legal or practical operation is a greater intrusion on the role of domestic legislatures.

In contrast, the Appellate Body has consistently downplayed the factor of legislative purpose in factor characterization. It is to this issue that we now turn.

6.4.3. Legislative Purpose and Deference

The Appellate Body's downplaying of legislative purpose in factor characterization has significant effects on deference to domestic legislatures. A valid legislative purpose will probably be seen by a legislature as decisive for the characterization of legislation. That is, a legislature that enacts legislation in good faith for a valid purpose may consider that this is the end of the matter, and that legal and

78. The legislation allowed representatives of domestic tanners to participate in the inspection of raw bovine hide exports.
79. Panel Report, *Argentina – Hides and Leather*, para. 11.21.
80. Matsushita, Schoenbaum & Mavroidis, above n. 73, 361–363.
81. P. Mavroidis, *The General Agreement on Tariffs and Trade* (Oxford: Oxford University Press, 2005), 38–39.
82. For example: whether products are 'like' (Appellate Body Report, *EC – Asbestos*, para. 101); whether a measure is 'based on' an international SPS standard (Matsushita, Schoenbaum & Mavroidis, above n. 73, 506–507); whether a measure is 'based on' a risk assessment (Appellate Body Report, *EC – Hormones*, para. 194).

practical operation is of little relevance in the characterization process. Yet, as discussed earlier,[83] the Appellate Body will generally not respect such a view, but instead will search for the legislation's 'objective' purpose (as evidenced by legal and practical operations) rather than its 'subjective' purpose.

There is a good reason for this downplaying of actual legislative purpose. If legislative purpose could govern factor characterization, the scope of WTO obligations could be severely limited: 'a manifestly WTO-inconsistent measure cannot be justified by assertions of good intentions'.[84] This can be illustrated by an issue that arose in *US – FSC*. The US legislation expressly stated that it was enacted 'to comply with decisions of a World Trade Organization Dispute Panel and Appellate Body'.[85] If this purpose governed the inherent character of the legislation, there would be no dispute: the character of the legislation would be WTO-consistent. However, it would be close to total deference to allow the legislature to determine characterization via simple statements of purpose. Accordingly, the Appellate Body, while taking note of the ostensible legislative purpose, refused to let it govern the characterization of the legislation.[86]

This is not to say that purpose – and deference to a domestic legislature's view of legislative purpose – is irrelevant in WTO factor characterization. At the very least, one can say that a declared protectionist purpose is relevant in the characterization process.[87] As the Panel in *Mexico – Taxes on Soft Drinks* pointed out in the context of Article III Sentence 2 of the GATT:

> [T]he declared intention of legislators and regulators of the Member adopting the measure should not be totally disregarded, particularly when the explicit objective of the measure is that of affording protection to domestic production. Indeed, the Appellate Body has confirmed that statements made by government representatives of a Member, admitting to the protective intent of a measure, may be relevant as part of a number of considerations in reaching the conclusion that a measure is applied so as to afford protection to domestic production.[88]

Yet, legislative purpose is also relevant when it is *not* expressly protectionist. This is because of the close relationship between legislative purpose and the practical operation of legislation. Generally speaking, the operation of legislation should match the legislative purpose (unless the legislature has made a miscalculation in drafting its rules). This implies that legislative purpose may in some cases be an

---

83. See Section 6.3, text at n. 40 et seq.
84. Panel Report, *Argentina – Hides and Leather*, para. 11.90.
85. Appellate Body Report, *US – FSC (Article 21.5 – EC)*, para. 150.
86. *Ibid.*
87. See above, n. 49.
88. Panel Report, *Mexico – Taxes on Soft Drinks*, para. 8.91. The last sentence of the passages cites in a footnote 'Appellate Body Report on *Canada – Periodicals*, pp. 30–32, DSR 1997:1, 449, at pp. 475–476.' There, the Appellate Body noted a statement by the Government of Canada that it 'uses policy instruments that encourage the flow of advertising revenues to Canadian periodicals, since a viable Canadian periodical industry must have a secure financial base'.

indicator of the legal and practical operations of legislation. A good match between legislative purpose and legislative operation points to a characterization favourable to the legislating State, whereas a bad match points in the other direction.

Therefore, a mismatch between legislative purpose and practical operation is a warning sign for WTO tribunals in the factor characterization process. This was the view of the Panel in *Chile – Alcoholic Beverages* (again in the context of Article III Sentence 2 of the GATT):

> In our view, the failure of a measure to conform to its stated objectives may be indicative of certain aspects of its design structure and architecture. That is, while we will not examine the stated objective itself to determine its legitimacy, it is a relevant inquiry to examine the relationship between the stated objective and the measure in question. If a rational relationship between the stated objective and the measure is lacking, this may provide evidence of protective application, which we will take into consideration along with other factors.[89]

Thus, legislative purpose may provide evidence as to legal and practical operations. The Panel's reasoning mentions only a mismatch between the two. However, this reasoning applies equally where purpose matches operation. In such cases, a valid legislative purpose and matching legislative operation should be evidence (albeit weak evidence) that the legislation has no protective application.[90] However, no WTO tribunal has yet made such a finding.

One can conclude that legislative purpose is sometimes an important factor in characterization, but rarely so. In any case, this relevance does not extend to an examination of the effectiveness of legislation to achieve its purpose. The Panel in *Chile – Alcoholic Beverages* spoke merely of 'a rational relationship between the stated objective and the measure'. This would not involve a very searching analysis. In particular, it would not extend to examining the proportionality of the legislation to its stated purpose – as that would be to change the nature of the exercise from factor characterization to proportionality characterization. Proportionality characterization is available only where the relevant WTO obligation allows it. Accordingly, the Appellate Body in *Chile – Alcoholic Beverages* refused to allow an examination of the *necessity* of the legislation.[91]

All of this makes the boundary between factor characterization and proportionality characterization very important. Determining the side of the boundary on which a dispute falls can be crucial to a tribunal's reasoning, and to the ultimate result. This is illustrated by the treatment of Article 18.1 of the Anti-Dumping Agreement in the *US – 1916 Act* case.[92] In this case, the challenged US legislation

---

89. Panel Report, *Chile – Alcoholic Beverages*, para. 7.148.
90. A contrary view is noted in Hestermeyer, 'Article III GATT 1994', in eds Wolfrum, Stoll & Seibert-Fohr, above n. 73, 25.
91. Appellate Body Report, *Chile – Alcoholic Beverages*, para. 72.
92. For analysis of the case, see P. de Keyser, 'Exploring WTO Dispute Settlement in US Antidumping Act 1916: An Easy Case?', Jean Monnet working paper, No. 11/01, New York

allowed civil and criminal actions against importers selling foreign-produced goods at prices 'substantially less' than the prices for the same products in a relevant foreign market. Such actions were allowable only if the importer had an intention to destroy or injure a US industry, to prevent the establishment of a US industry, or to restrain or monopolize trade or commerce in the United States. Article 18.1 of the Anti-Dumping Agreement creates requirements for taking 'specific action against dumping'. The US legislation did not meet those requirements. Therefore, the main issue was whether the legislation should be characterized as a 'specific action against dumping'. The Appellate Body ruled that it should,[93] emphasizing legal operation rather than legislative purpose (thus engaging in factor characterization rather than proportionality characterization). It did not defer to US arguments that legislative purpose was the 'primary indicator' of the conduct targeted by the legislation.[94] The nature of the characterization exercise thus determined the outcome of the dispute.[95]

In sum, the factor of legislative purpose plays a secondary but important role in factor characterization. WTO tribunals refuse to give it a decisive role in characterization, as this would increase deference to domestic legislatures to unacceptable levels. If WTO obligations in a particular dispute require close attention to legislative purpose, the dispute has probably moved to the realm of proportionality characterization, which involves a different kind of analysis. In factor characterization, legislative purpose tends to play a supporting role to analysis based on legal and practical operations. In this way, the purpose proffered by a domestic legislature is recognized as relevant, but not as authoritative.

6.5. CONCLUDING REMARKS

Factor characterization is a common exercise in WTO challenges to legislation. The weight to be given to various factors is often not specified in WTO obligations, and principles of treaty interpretation leave much discretion to WTO tribunals. The overall impression here is of varying levels of deference, depending on the facts of each particular case.

We are thus reminded of the International Law Commission's warning to focus on the individual aspects of a challenge to legislation in each case.[96] Yet, the levels of deference in WTO challenges involving factor characterization are not

---

University School of Law (2001) available at <www.jeanmonnetprogram.org/papers/papers01.html> (visited 2 Apr. 2008).

93. Appellate Body Report, *US – 1916 Act*, para. 130.
94. *Ibid.*, para. 20, 128 and 131.
95. This example may be contrasted with characterization under Arts III and XX GATT. Here, legislative purpose has a reduced significance at the first stage of characterization under Art. III (factor characterization), but is nevertheless relevant at the second stage of characterization under the paragraphs of the general exception provision in Art. XX (proportionality characterization).
96. See Prelude, text at n. 41.

totally without structure or organization. We have seen that WTO tribunals have tried where possible to rely on external standards as a yardstick in factor characterization. This has occasionally involved an intrusive approach to domestic legislative judgments, even when it has not been entirely clear that the external standard was applicable to the legislation. Where such standards are clearly not applicable, WTO tribunals have preferred factors relating to legal operation. This type of factor will generally increase deference, as the text of legislation is clearly within the control of the domestic legislature. However, factors relating to practical operation are also often important in WTO factor characterization. These factors involve non-deferential processes of fact finding and inference making by the tribunals. Nevertheless, in some cases, WTO tribunals are consciously deferential in the process of fact finding and inference making. In any case, a legislature's desired legislative purpose tends to be a secondary matter in the WTO factor characterization process – despite any claims by a legislature that it has produced rules in good faith in pursuit of a legitimate goal.

The overall result has been a quite intense standard of review in some cases. Although WTO tribunals have tried to avoid outright interference in legislative decision-making, they have on rare occasions intruded deeply into the domestic legislative domain. For the most part, however, WTO tribunals have exerted some effort to be objective and deferential in factor characterization, and to avoid intrusive and subjective decision-making.

Different considerations apply when we move away from factor characterization and encounter issues of proportionality and legislative certainty. In these areas, the structure of deference in the characterization process is somewhat clearer. We will see in the next chapter, dealing with proportionality characterization, that WTO tribunals have established principles that allow an intrusive standard of review in theory, but, in most cases, they do not have this result in practice. Chapter 8, dealing with certainty characterization in the WTO, also indicates that WTO tribunals have established some yardsticks of deference in the characterization process. Here too, one can see occasional cases in which these yardsticks have allowed tribunals to show a clear lack of deference to domestic legislatures.

Chapter 7

Substantive Deference: Proportionality Characterization

7.1. INTRODUCTION

Legislatures sometimes overreact to problems, and even give favours to particular interest groups. In some legal systems, the courts can correct such legislative misjudgments. For obvious reasons, domestic courts and international tribunals hesitate to make such corrections. The legislature is usually the better judge of the appropriateness of legislation, and courts should intervene only in clear cases of legislative failure. Thus, very clear proof of error in legislative judgment is needed for courts to intervene.

Such cases often concern the proportionality of legislation. They arise when legislation intrudes into a protected legal right or concept, such as human rights or free trade. Such intrusions can be justified only if legislation is designed to achieve another worthy purpose, such as health or environmental protection. Thus, the proportionality concept is fundamentally based on a conflict of purposes. Some weighing and balancing of competing purposes is involved. This process is generally accomplished through an examination of the legislation's effectiveness and balance. If the legislation can be regarded as effective in achieving its purpose, and it can be regarded as a balanced means of doing so, it satisfies the test of proportionality. However, if reasonably available alternative measures can be identified that intrude less into a protected area than the challenged legislation and are still suited to the legislative purpose, then the legislation is in danger of failing the test of proportionality.

How can judges, and especially international judges, make rulings about effectiveness, reasonably available alternative measures, and – most controversially – balance? How can they weigh competing policy purposes by using legal methods? Legislatures are better suited to deal with these issues, especially in cases in which they have superior access to information and policy expertise. Judges are therefore reluctant to intervene in legislative assessments. Rarely can a judge say confidently that a legislature's opinions and prognoses are wrong.

However, judges must engage in proportionality characterization if required to do so by the relevant constitutional or international obligations. Many domestic and international rules contain proportionality-type tests. Where such rules apply, a judge would fail his or her professional duty by refusing to examine effectiveness, optimality, and balance. The crucial issue is how much deference a judge gives to a legislature's assessments of these matters.

The question of deference is particularly acute for international tribunals engaging in proportionality characterization. International tribunals are often worse equipped than are domestic constitutional courts for evaluating local conditions and making prognoses about how to deal with those conditions. They therefore show correspondingly greater deference to domestic legislatures in most cases.

In the WTO, therefore, one might expect considerable deference to domestic legislatures in the substantive aspects of a claim. We have already seen that procedural deference has dwindled dramatically in the WTO. WTO tribunals have responded to this by showing a thorough and careful approach to proportionality characterization. Generally speaking, where they have found a lack of proportionality in domestic legislation, they have done so by pointing to inconsistencies in domestic practices. However, their methodology theoretically allows for intrusive review of domestic legislation, particularly in relation to the relative value of alternative measures. In some cases, WTO tribunals have not hesitated to find a domestic legislature's own judgments to be defective.

This chapter examines how WTO tribunals deal with deference when characterizing legislation using the proportionality concept. First, it briefly examines the concept of proportionality. Next, it examines the ways in which this concept has been applied in the WTO system, in particular, in WTO challenges to legislation. This will lead to a discussion of how WTO proportionality characterization affects deference to domestic legislatures.

7.2. THE CONCEPT OF PROPORTIONALITY CHARACTERIZATION

Proportionality has a long history. It appears to have its source in civil law, particularly from the administrative law of Germany.[1] It has since flowed into the legal systems of the European Union (EU) and of regional human rights systems, as well as into the public law of the world of common law. It has also made considerable inroads into international law, for example, in the law of self-defence, humanitarian law, international human rights law, and the law of reprisals and

1. See G. Nolte, 'General Principles of German and European Administrative Law – A Comparison in Historical Perspective', MLR 57 (1994): 191.

remedies.[2] The International Court of Justice (ICJ) used the proportionality concept in the *North Sea Continental Shelf* case as a matter to take into account in applying equitable principles in maritime delimitation.[3] It is arguable that the proportionality principle is now a 'general principle of law' within the meaning of Article 38(c) of the Statute of the ICJ,[4] or alternatively, a general principle of international law.[5]

However, in each of the domestic, regional, and global legal systems that have adopted the proportionality concept, it is applied in a different way. The concept of proportionality must be applied according to the characteristics of the particular legal system in which it operates.[6] Further, proportionality can be applied in different ways, depending on whether a challenged measure is an administrative action or legislation.

Despite this diversity, commentators have generally found three common themes within the proportionality concept: effectiveness, optimality, and balance:[7]

- Effectiveness deals with causation, that is, the extent to which the legislation causes its purpose to be achieved.
- Optimality concerns comparisons, that is, the extent to which reasonably available alternative measures could achieve the legislative purpose at a lesser cost to protected values.

2. J. Delbrück, 'Proportionality', in *Encyclopedia of Public International Law*, vol. 3, ed. R. Bernhardt (Amsterdam: Elsevier, 1997), 1140. See also D. Grieg, 'Reciprocity, Proportionality, and the Law of Treaties', *Virginia J. Int Law* 34 (1994): 295.
3. *North Sea Continental Shelf*, Judgment (1969) ICJ Reports 3, at 52, para. 98.
4. *Statute of the International Court of Justice*, 26 Jun. 1945, UKTS 1946 No. 67 (Cmd. 7015).
5. Delbrück, above n. 2, 1144. But see Grieg (1994), above n. 2, 322.
6. Thus Delbrück, above n. 2, 1140, suggests:

   > [Proportionality] primarily fulfils a guiding function for the law-applying authorities rather than in itself being a substantive, concrete legal norm. It may be compared with other open constitutional principles, the concrete legal meaning of which must be ascertained in their application to individual cases.

   See also G. Desmedt, 'Proportionality in WTO Law', JIEL 4 (2001): 441.
7. The terminology for these themes varies widely between authors, for example see J. Kirk, 'Rights, Review and Reasons for Restraint', *Sydney Law Rev* 23 (2001): 19 (suitability, necessity, balancing); Desmedt, above n. 6 (suitability, means least restrictive, balancing test); J. Neumann, & E. Türk, 'Necessity Revisited: Proportionality in World Trade Organization Law After Korea – Beef, EC – Asbestos and EC – Sardines', JWT 37 (2003): 199 (effectiveness, necessity, proportionality *strictu sensu*); A. Stone Sweet, 'Proportionality Balancing and Global Constitutionalism' (2007), <www.law.columbia.edu/null/Stone-Sweet+-+Proportionality+Balancing?exclusive=filemgr.download&file_id=101159&showthumb=0> (visited 27 Nov. 2007) (suitability, necessity, balancing in the strict sense).

   I have chosen the labels of 'effectiveness, optimality and balance' for two reasons: firstly, because they offer useful adjectives (effective, optimal and balanced), and secondly, because they avoid awkward ambiguities (most notably, between 'necessity' in the sense of optimality and 'necessity' in the sense used in Art. XX GATT). This terminological variety is a matter of form: in substance the labels used are unimportant.

– Balance deals with proportionality in a strict sense, that is, the extent to which the legislation strikes a balance between competing purposes. This is the most controversial aspect of proportionality characterization, as it involves direct review of a legislature's opinions and prognoses.

Even if legislation is held to be effective in achieving its purpose, it is not necessarily balanced. Effective legislation causes its purpose to be achieved. Balanced legislation does this in a cost-effective way, that is, with relatively proportionate costs to a protected value (such as free trade). Balance in proportionality characterization is therefore a balancing of various policy considerations. A legislature promotes a particular purpose using particular means; an international tribunal must balance that purpose and those means against other policy considerations.

There are considerable overlaps among these three themes. Most obviously, optimality can be seen as a particular application of the balance concept. These overlaps suggest that one cannot apply the proportionality concept as a simple three-point checklist. Each of the three aspects of the concept expresses part of each of the other aspects.

It is apparent that the three aspects of the proportionality concept have a direct relevance to deference in challenges to legislation. Deference in determining effectiveness concerns the extent to which a judge defers to legislative views about causation. Deference in determining optimality is deference to legislative views about the effectiveness, practicability, and cost of alternative measures. Deference in determining balance is about deference to a legislature's decisions about how to balance various policies. However, it would be a mistake to assume that the proportionality concept implies a particular level of deference. It is possible to have low or high levels of deference in proportionality characterization, depending on the legal norms and system concerned. Deference is closely linked to the proportionality concept, but the extent of deference is an independent factor that is set outside the proportionality concept itself.

It is useful here to contrast the nature of deference in proportionality characterization with the nature of deference in factor characterization. Generally speaking, the issue of deference can be more visible in the former than in the latter. In factor characterization, issues of deference are often disguised in the process of weighing and balancing different factors. In contrast, in proportionality characterization, deference becomes quite an open issue in the process of weighing and balancing different policies. Proportionality characterization strips away the veneer of formalism that is an attribute of factor characterization.

In the following discussion, we will examine the role of proportionality in WTO challenges to legislation with these points in mind. The three aspects of proportionality are useful ways of classifying cases, but they should not be taken as expressing strict rules of WTO law. Furthermore, one cannot assume that the proportionality concept will be applied in the same way in each legal system. In particular, one cannot assume that the degree of proportionality deference in one system will be the same in another system. Thus, one should bear in mind the risk in applying the term *proportionality* to the WTO environment.

The characteristics of the proportionality principle as applied in a particular legal system cannot be transplanted carelessly into WTO law. The nature of proportionality analysis applied by WTO tribunals is dependent on the legal structure of the WTO agreements, and on the nature of the particular WTO obligations. It is only the broadest of outlines that WTO proportionality shares with the proportionality principle applied in other legal systems. Even within the WTO system, proportionality operates in different ways for different WTO rules.

7.3. PROPORTIONALITY IN THE WTO

Proportionality is a very useful concept for dealing with WTO jurisprudence. The WTO Director-General has written of 'WTO exceptions [that] are subject to . . . a "necessity test", a test having features of a "proportionality" requirement'.[8] The term *proportionality* suggests analogies with existing jurisprudence in a range of other jurisdictions, which, if used cautiously, provide a valuable tool for analyzing WTO jurisprudence.

Proportionality as a concept appears expressly in very few WTO obligations.[9] Indeed, the proportionality principle is entirely inapplicable in relation to many WTO obligations, an example of which was discussed in the case of *EC – Poultry*.[10] An EC Commission Regulation provided for measuring the price of imports for the purposes of special safeguards allowed under Article 5.1 of the Agreement on Agriculture. The Regulation measured the price by reference to a 'representative price' of the imports, which was an average of three price elements over a period of time. The EC argued that the representative price was a means of reducing bureaucracy and paperwork and of avoiding fraud.[11] However, Article 5.5 of the Agreement on Agriculture requires that price be measured by the cost, insurance and freight price of the shipment of the imports. The Appellate Body therefore held that the European Communities' justification (however meritorious and proportionate) was irrelevant, and that the regulation was inconsistent with Article 5.5 regardless of its underlying justification.[12] Under Article 5.5 of the Agreement on Agriculture, the existence of a proportionate means of achieving a good legislative purpose is simply not relevant. With these kinds of rules, the WTO membership has itself determined the appropriate parameters for legislation and set them out in bright-line rules. In drafting such rules, the WTO community has withheld the role of reviewing proportionality from WTO tribunals. Thus, WTO tribunals deal with such rules according to factor characterization rather than

8. P. Lamy, 'The Place of the WTO and Its Law in the International Legal Order', EJIL 17 (2006): 969, at 979.
9. Examples include: Art. 8.2(c)(iv) SCM Agreement; Art. 4.10 footnote SCM Agreement; Arts 46 and 47 TRIPS.
10. See also Appellate Body Report, *Chile – Price Band System*, para. 227.
11. Appellate Body Report, *EC – Poultry*, para. 170.
12. *Ibid.*, paras 170–171.

proportionality characterization. Probably, the majority of WTO rules fall within this class.

Studies show that proportionality is not a universal binding legal principle in the WTO legal system in the way that it is in European law.[13] Nevertheless, the concept of proportionality reaches deeply into many fundamental WTO rules. The most notable of these are the general exception provisions, such as Article XX of the GATT, Article XIV of the General Agreement on Trade in Services (GATS), and Article 8 of TRIPS, which permit restrictive trade measures that are necessary for (or related to) achieving a particular purpose. Legislation promoting non-trade ideals is generally WTO-consistent if it is covered under such exception provisions. These provisions can therefore be seen as the general intermediary between trade policy and other policy concerns. Not surprisingly, much of our discussion here will concern these provisions. Nevertheless, proportionality-like norms also appear in other provisions, such as those forbidding arbitrary or discriminatory measures[14] and in WTO rules on remedies.[15] The latter rules reflect the general principle of international law that a response to a breach of an international

13. Trachtman reviewed the proportionality principle as applied in several domestic and international systems (J. Trachtman, 'Trade and . . . Problems, Cost-Benefit Analysis and Subsidiarity' (1997) Jean Monnet working paper, No. 1/97, New York Univ. School of Law (1997), available at <www.jeanmonnetprogram.org/papers/97/97-01.html> (visited 6 Sep. 2007)). However, his study was written before much WTO jurisprudence was available, and he therefore was unable to conclude much about the principle's application in practice. Hilf briefly examined the proportionality principle, suggesting that it was one of the basis principles underlying the world trading system (M. Hilf, 'Power, Rules and Principles – Which Orientation for WTO/GATT Law?', JIEL 4 (2001): 111). Desmedt reviewed the jurisprudence on WTO remedies, the SPS Agreement, the TBT Agreement and Art. XX GATT. He concluded that WTO tribunals have not expressly recognized the principle of proportionality, although the principle was growing in importance in the WTO (Desmedt, above n. 6, 443). Desmedt did not appear to mean that WTO tribunals have never spoken of proportionality – because they have on occasion (e.g., Appellate Body Report, *US – Shrimp*, para. 141; Panel Report, *Korea – Various Measures on Beef*, para. 675) – but rather that they have never recognized proportionality as an overarching principle applying with binding force in all situations. He noted that proportionality as a principle is applied as a general principle in mature legal systems, and noted its absence in WTO law as a signal of the youth of the WTO legal system (at 443). Neumann & Türk, above n. 7, 233, suggest that 'the WTO is not ready for classical proportionality from an institutional perspective'), Mitchell appears to confirm this (A. Mitchell, 'Proportionality and Remedies in WTO Disputes', EJIL 17 (2007): 985). However, Mitchell appears to go further here and confines the use of the proportionality principle mainly to WTO remedies (at 1008). See also S. Bhuiyan, *National Law in WTO Law* (Cambridge: Cambridge University Press, 2007), Part 3.2.
14. Examples include Art. XX chapeau GATT, Art. 5.6 SPS Agreement and Art. 2.2 TBT Agreement.
15. Article 22.4 DSU (equivalence of level of the suspension of concessions etc. to level of nullification or impairment); Art. 5.1 Agreement on Safeguards (see Appellate Body Report, *US – Line Pipe*, paras 252–260); Art. 7.1 Agreement on Safeguards (duration of remedial measures); Art. 7.1(iii) Anti-Dumping Agreement (provisional measures); Art. 8.1 Anti-Dumping Agreement (extent of price increases under voluntary undertakings); Art. 11.1 Anti-Dumping Agreement (duration of anti-dumping measures); Art. 21.1 Anti-Dumping Agreement (duration of remedial measures); Art. 17.1(c) SCM Agreement (measures necessary to prevent injury) and Art. 18.1(b) SCM Agreement (extent of price increases under voluntary undertakings).

obligation should be in proportion to the breach.[16] The Appellate Body has recognized this general principle and expressly noted that it is an application of the 'principle of proportionality'.[17] There is also a range of miscellaneous provisions that involve the proportionality concept.[18]

It is fair to say that the structural complexity of some WTO rules has made it difficult for WTO tribunals to apply a coherent proportionality analysis. This is most evident in the structure of the general exception provisions and related rules. In national treatment cases under the GATT, for example, the issue of proportionality arises in three separate overlapping stages, with no clear division among the tasks performed at each stage. The first stage is the determination of breach of Article III of the GATT. As we have seen,[19] this is mainly a question of factor characterization, but it nevertheless can touch on the proportionality-related issue of the extent to which the legislation achieves its purpose. The second stage is characterization under one or more of the paragraphs of Article XX of the GATT, which provides for exceptions to GATT disciplines. This involves clear questions of proportionality, such as the extent to which legislation is 'necessary to protect human, animal or plant life or health'.[20] The third stage is characterization under the chapeau to Article XX of the GATT,[21] which is a restriction on the general exceptions in Article XX. This also arguably[22] concerns issues of proportionality,

---

16. International Law Commission, 'Draft Articles and Commentaries on Responsibility of States for Internationally Wrongful Acts', *Report of the International Law Commission*, 53rd session (A/56/10) (2001), Commentary to Art. 51.
17. In *US – Cotton Yarn*, para. 120, the Appellate Body said:

    > It would be absurd if the breach of an international obligation were sanctioned by proportionate countermeasures, while, in the absence of such breach, a WTO Member would be subject to a disproportionate and, hence, 'punitive', attribution of serious damage not wholly caused by its exports. In our view, such an exorbitant derogation from the principle of proportionality in respect of the attribution of serious damage could be justified only if the drafters of the ATC had expressly provided for it, which is not the case.

18. In *Turkey – Textiles*, the Appellate Body dealt with a balancing of the purposes of allowing regional trade agreements and of discouraging trade diversion under such agreements (Appellate Body Report, *Turkey – Textiles*, paras 61–62). The structure of Art. XXIV GATT requires such a balancing exercise. In *EC – Tariff Preferences*, the Appellate Body balanced the purpose of allowing trade preferences to developing countries against the purpose of discouraging discrimination between developing countries. The structure of the *Enabling Clause* requires such an analysis (Appellate Body Report, *EC – Tariff Preferences*, paras 133, 162–165).
19. See Section 6.3, text at n. 14.
20. Article XX(b) GATT.
21. This provides:

    > Subject to the requirement that such measures are not applied in a manner which would constitute a means of arbitrary or unjustifiable discrimination between countries where the same conditions prevail, or a disguised restriction on international trade, nothing in this Agreement shall be construed to prevent the adoption or enforcement by any Member of measures: [the list of allowable policies follows].

22. Neumann & Türk, above n. 7, 227–228, point to an ongoing debate as to whether the chapeau contains a proportionality test, or whether it merely relates to discrimination and disguised trade

here relating to whether the application of legislation amounts to 'arbitrary or unjustifiable discrimination' or a 'disguised restriction on international trade'. WTO tribunals are still wrestling with the problem of how to locate the various aspects of proportionality within this three-stage structure.[23] There is probably no complete, logical, and coherent legal solution here: the division between the three stages will remain a matter of judgment for WTO tribunals on the facts of each case. The application of proportionality characterization to other WTO rules is comparatively simpler.[24]

A common theme running through WTO proportionality characterization is the concept of the appropriate level of protection (ALOP). In applying a proportionality analysis, WTO tribunals always emphasize the rights of WTO members to set the level of protection (or level of risk) that they wish to have in achieving legitimate legislative purposes. An ALOP is not identical to the rules contained in legislation. Rather, it is a legislative goal set at a higher level of abstraction.[25] The process of stating an ALOP can be seen as a way of making legislative purpose more explicit. Indeed, some WTO rules imply that the legislating State must state an ALOP, to at least some degree of precision.[26] Failure to do so will allow WTO tribunals to determine the relevant ALOP by inference from the content of the challenged legislation.[27] This approach is set forth expressly in some WTO obligations,[28] or has been found by the tribunal to be implied by the obligation.[29]

---

restrictions. For present purposes, we can view the chapeau as exhibiting at least some of the features of a proportionality test, such as the consideration of alternative measures (e.g., in Appellate Body Report, *US – Gasoline*).

23. See generally Neumann & Türk, above n. 7.
24. For example, the rules dealt with in the Appellate Body Reports in *Turkey – Textiles* and *EC – Tariff Preferences* implied a proportionality analysis at only one stage (see above n. 18). Nevertheless, there may be some issues in locating proportionality analysis across Arts 2.2 and 5.6 SPS Agreement: M. Matsushita, T. Schoenbaum & P. Mavroidis, *The World Trade Organization: Law, Practice, and Policy*, 2nd edn (Oxford: Oxford University Press, 2006), 519–521.
25. Appellate Body Report, *Australia – Salmon*, para. 203: 'The determination of the level of protection is an element in the decision-making process which logically precedes and is separate from the establishment or maintenance of the SPS measure.'
26. Appellate Body Report, *Australia – Salmon*, para. 203:

> [T]he SPS Agreement contains an implicit obligation to determine the appropriate level of protection. We do not believe that there is an obligation to determine the appropriate level of protection in quantitative terms. This does not mean, however, that an importing Member is free to determine its level of protection with such vagueness or equivocation that the application of the relevant provisions of the SPS Agreement, such as Article 5.6, becomes impossible.

27. Appellate Body Report, *Australia – Salmon*, para. 203:

> [I]n cases where a Member does not determine its appropriate level of protection, or does so with insufficient precision, the appropriate level of protection may be established by panels on the basis of the level of protection reflected in the SPS measure actually applied.

See also Appellate Body Report, *Korea – Various Measures on Beef*, para. 178.

28. Most notably Art. 5 SPS Agreement.
29. For example, Appellate Body Report, *Korea – Various Measures on Beef*, para. 176.

The ALOP allows legislating States some power to affect the degree of deference shown by WTO tribunals in proportionality characterization. If the ALOP is set quite high, the tribunal is more constrained in seeking out possible alternative measures in the characterization process.[30] Thus, the ALOP is a restraint, set at the level that the legislating State prefers, on the 'optimality' aspect of proportionality characterization described above, that is, the process of searching for reasonably available alternative measures. We will come back to the ALOP concept in more detail later.[31]

Overall, one can see a rather complex partial application of proportionality to the WTO system. Some WTO rules do not involve proportionality at all. Other WTO rules clearly do adopt proportionality-like concepts in a variety of ways. The kind of proportionality involved is likely to vary between these rules, depending on the exact text and context concerned. Of these rules, the general exceptions provisions are probably the most significant, and they provide much of the WTO jurisprudence concerning proportionality characterization. However, this jurisprudence is also affected by many other WTO obligations that adopt proportionality-type concepts. This jurisprudence is also complicated by the awkward drafting structures of many WTO rules.

Thus, one must be careful in generalizing about the application of proportionality to WTO rules. WTO tribunals have not developed a binding, unitary proportionality jurisprudence across a multitude of obligations. However, the concepts and ideas applicable to one WTO obligation are often useful guides in analyzing other obligations. In particular, the existing jurisprudence about the general exception provisions provides a useful framework – but not a binding precedent – for looking at WTO proportionality characterization in general.

In describing this jurisprudence, it is convenient to refer to the three aspects of proportionality described earlier (effectiveness, optimality, and balance). As we will see, the optimality aspect is dominant in a practical sense in WTO proportionality characterization.

7.3.1. Balance Analysis: The Right Policy Mix

For several important WTO obligations, WTO tribunals have confirmed that the concept of balance is at the core of proportionality characterization. This is most obvious in relation to the various general exception provisions, and it is thus convenient to start with the paragraphs of these provisions. Although they are worded in subtly different ways, the Appellate Body has stated a common approach

30. For example, quarantine legislation may set an acceptable level of quarantine risk at very low levels, and set out measures to achieve this strict ALOP. In determining whether the legislation is 'necessary' in the sense of being the least trade-restrictive measure reasonably available, a WTO tribunal will have to consider whether proposed alternative measures also achieve this strict ALOP. See, for example, Panel Report, *Australia – Salmon* (*Article 21.5 – Canada*), where Australia set its ALOP at 'a high or very conservative level of protection aimed at reducing risk to very low levels, while not based on a zero-risk approach'.
31. See Section 7.4.3.3.

to all of them. In *US – Gambling*, it set out this approach in the context of the public morals exception under Article XIV(a) of the GATS:

> The process begins with an assessment of the 'relative importance' of the interests or values furthered by the challenged measure.[32] Having ascertained the importance of the particular interests at stake, a panel should then turn to the other factors that are to be 'weighed and balanced'.[33]

This idea of balancing the relative importance of values promoted by legislation is also reflected in the jurisprudence about the chapeaus to the various general exception provisions. These chapeaus contain rules that cut back the scope of the paragraphs of the general exception provisions.[34] Although the chapeaus relate to the application of legislation rather than the legislation as such, they provide a useful context for the application of proportionality in WTO law generally. According to the Appellate Body, the chapeaus are governed by a general balancing concept. The Appellate Body has expressed this as 'location of the line of equilibrium', which 'is not fixed and unchanging; the line moves as the kind and the shape of the measures at stake vary and as the facts making up specific cases differ'.[35] Opinions differ as to whether this equilibrium reflects a proportionality concept or not.[36]

The Appellate Body has also confirmed that the concepts of effectiveness and optimality are factors to be considered in the balancing exercise. In *US – Gambling*, after stating the balancing process, the Appellate Body pointed to these two factors as being usually concerned in the balancing exercise:

> The Appellate Body has pointed to two factors that, in most cases, will be relevant to a panel's determination of the 'necessity' of a measure ['necessity' referred to by the Appellate Body here has a broader denotation than mere effectiveness], although not necessarily exhaustive of factors that might be considered.[37] One factor is the contribution of the measure to the realization of the ends pursued by it; the other factor is the restrictive impact of the measure on international commerce.[38]

In *Brazil – Retreaded Tyres*, the Appellate Body confirmed that the analysis of balance is linked to both the analysis of effectiveness and of optimality, as part of 'a holistic operation' involving 'putting all the variables of the equation together and evaluating them in relation to each other after having examined them individually, in order to reach an overall judgment'.[39]

---

32. [original footnote] [*Korea – Various Measures on Beef*], para. 162. See also Appellate Body Report, *EC – Asbestos*, para. 172.
33. Appellate Body Report, *US – Gambling*, para. 305.
34. See Art. III GATT and Art. XIV GATS. See also Art. 8 TRIPS.
35. Appellate Body Report on *US – Shrimp*, para. 159.
36. Neumann & Türk, above n. 7, 227–228.
37. [original footnote] Appellate Body Report, *Korea – Various Measures on Beef*, para. 164.
38. Appellate Body Report, *US – Gambling*, para. 305.
39. Appellate Body Report, *Brazil – Retreaded Tyres*, para. 182. At para. 178, the Appellate Body suggested that this 'holistic operation' could be carried out by first examining effectiveness

Optimality tends to be a much more important factor than effectiveness in WTO proportionality characterization. As we will see later, much of the Appellate Body's attention in the balancing process is placed on finding reasonably available alternative measures to the legislation under challenge. For the moment, however, we turn to the role of effectiveness in WTO proportionality characterization.

7.3.2. Effectiveness Analysis: Causation

As the Appellate Body noted in *EC – Sardines*, the question of the effectiveness of a measure is based upon the results of the means employed; an ineffective means does not have the function of accomplishing the legitimate objective pursued.[40] This confirms that effectiveness relates to causation between legislation and legislative purpose.[41]

The Appellate Body has given a number of guides for testing legislative effectiveness, each adapted to the wording of particular WTO obligations. Different wording produces subtly different tests of effectiveness. For example, Article XX(g) of the GATT (covering measures 'relating to' relevant goals) produces the test of an 'observably close and genuine relationship of ends and means', while Article XX(d) of the GATT (covering measures 'necessary' for relevant goals) produces a test of 'the contribution made' by the measure.[42] While the most-developed jurisprudence here concerns Article XX of the GATT,[43] other WTO provisions exhibit analogous patterns.[44]

(together with balance) in order to reach a 'preliminary conclusion'. Second, this conclusion should be confirmed (or refuted) by examining optimality, again together with balance.

40. Appellate Body Report, *EC – Sardines*, para. 285. Admittedly, this case did not concern the proportionality of *legislation* to its purpose, but rather the proportionality of an *international standard* to a goal specified in the TBT Agreement.
41. Appellate Body Report, *EC – Sardines*, para. 285.
42. Appellate Body Report, *Korea – Various Measures on Beef*, para. 164.
43. In relation to Art. XX(g) (which has been interpreted to require a measure to be 'primarily aimed at' its professed purpose), the Appellate Body suggested that the measure could not be 'merely incidentally or inadvertently aimed' at that purpose (Appellate Body Report, *US – Gasoline*, 17). Again in the context of Art. XX(g), it noted that an observably close and genuine relationship of ends and means would be sufficient (Appellate Body Report, *US – Shrimp*, paras 141 and 136) as would a direct connection between the measure and the purpose (Appellate Body Report, *US – Shrimp*, para. 140). The measure should not be 'disproportionately wide in its scope and reach in relation to the policy objective' (Appellate Body Report, *US – Shrimp*, para. 141). In the context of one Art. XX(b) case, it noted that the measure at issue was 'clearly designed and apt to achieve' its desired purpose (Appellate Body Report, *EC – Asbestos*, para. 168). For Art. XX(d), the Appellate Body requires an assessment of 'the contribution made by the compliance measure to the enforcement of the law or regulation at issue' (Appellate Body Report, *Korea – Various Measures on Beef*, para. 164). However, there is no need to guarantee this result with absolute certainty (Appellate Body Report, *Mexico – Taxes on Soft Drinks*, para. 74).
44. For example, a measure is effective for the purposes of Art. 2.4 TBT Agreement if it has a 'capacity to accomplish' the relevant purpose (Appellate Body Report, *EC – Sardines*, para. 288). Concerning the exception in Art. XIV(a) GATS, the Appellate Body has said that the measure 'must contribute' to addressing the relevant concerns (Appellate Body Report, *US – Gambling*, para. 313).

While different wording in different WTO provisions appears to require different standards of effectiveness,[45] one should not make too much of these differences. Given the difficulties for legal tribunals in examining causation, fine differences in the form of the applicable legal test are unlikely to make much difference in practice. Thus, in *Dominican Republic – Import and Sale of Cigarettes*, the Appellate Body appeared to merge its various previous statements about effectiveness under particular provisions into a general test that WTO tribunals must assess 'the contribution of the measure to the realization of the end pursued'.[46]

7.3.3. Optimality Analysis: Reasonably Available Alternatives

Identifying reasonably available alternative measures is an important aspect of the overall balancing process in assessing proportionality in WTO challenges to legislation. If reasonably available alternative measures achieve the legislative purpose with less cost than the legislation, this is a strong indication that the legislation is not proportionate to its purpose. Optimality analysis is therefore a central part of the analysis of proportionality.

The general exceptions provisions again provide a useful overview of the Appellate Body's approach to optimality analysis. In *US – Gambling*, it described this approach as follows:

> A comparison between the challenged measure and possible alternatives should . . . be undertaken, and the results of such comparison should be considered in the light of the importance of the interests at issue. It is on the basis of this 'weighing and balancing' and comparison of measures, taking into account the interests or values at stake, that a panel determines whether a measure is 'necessary' or, alternatively, whether another, WTO-consistent measure is 'reasonably available'.[47]

In practice, the availability of alternative measures has been treated as the predominant criterion in proportionality characterization. In *Korea – Various Measures on Beef*, the Appellate Body stated that the general balancing process is, in practice, expressed through an analysis of optimality:

> [T]he weighing and balancing process we have outlined is comprehended in the determination of whether a WTO-consistent alternative measure which the

45. Appellate Body Report, *US – Gasoline*, 16. See also Appellate Body Report, *Korea – Various Measures on Beef*, para. 161, fn. 141, where the Appellate Body expressly distinguished between different intensities of effectiveness set by various WTO provisions.
46. Appellate Body Report, *Dominican Republic – Import and Sale of Cigarettes*, paras 69–70. Nevertheless, the degree of required contribution may increase if the measure has a severe impact on international trade: Appellate Body Report, *Brazil – Retreaded Tyres*, para. 150.
47. Appellate Body Report, *US – Gambling*, paras 307–308. See also Appellate Body Report, *Dominican Republic – Import and Sale of Cigarettes*, para. 70; Appellate Body Report. *Brazil – Retreaded Tyres*, para. 178.

> Member concerned could 'reasonably be expected to employ' is available, or whether a less WTO-inconsistent measure is 'reasonably available'.[48]

The predominance of an optimality analysis is confirmed by the nature of proportionality analysis under other WTO provisions. For example, the Appellate Body's application of Article 5.6 of the SPS Agreement has generally been a search for alternative measures that meet the legislating State's ALOP.[49] One can also see this approach under Article XXIV of the GATT and the Enabling Clause.[50]

Given the importance of the optimality analysis, the Appellate Body has gone to some effort to describe the parameters of the analysis. In *US – Gambling*, it said:

> An alternative measure may be found not to be 'reasonably available', however, where it is merely theoretical in nature, for instance, where the responding Member is not capable of taking it, or where the measure imposes an undue burden on that Member, such as prohibitive costs or substantial technical difficulties. Moreover, a 'reasonably available' alternative measure must be a measure that would preserve for the responding Member its right to achieve its desired level of protection with respect to the objective pursued.[51]

One can take from this passage three factors that would prevent an alternative measure from being 'reasonably available':

- if the measure 'is merely theoretical in nature, for instance, where the responding Member is not capable of taking it';
- if the measure 'imposes an undue burden on that Member, such as prohibitive costs or substantial technical difficulties'; or
- if the measure would not 'preserve for the responding Member its right to achieve its desired level of protection with respect to the objective pursued'.

I suggest that these three factors are likely to apply in optimality analysis generally across most relevant WTO obligations. It is true that the Appellate Body's comments were directed at the general exceptions provisions (more particularly, at Article XIV of the GATS). However, the logic behind these three factors is universal,[52] and WTO tribunals are likely to take account of them in all kinds of proportionality characterization.

---

48. Appellate Body Report, *Korea – Various Measures on Beef*, para. 166. Similarly, the Appellate Body in *EC – Asbestos*, para. 172, said that the question was 'whether there is an alternative measure that would achieve the same end and that is less restrictive of trade'.
49. Appellate Body Report, *Australia – Salmon*, paras 181–210; Panel Report, *Japan – Apples (Article 21.5 – US)*, paras 8.169–8.196.
50. Appellate Body Report, *EC – Tariff Preferences*, paras 182–186; Appellate Body Report, *Turkey – Textiles*, para. 62.
51. Appellate Body Report, *US – Gambling*, para. 308. See also Appellate Body Report, *Dominican Republic – Import and Sale of Cigarettes*, para. 70.
52. The third factor (the need for a proposed alternative measure to achieve a desired level of protection) is expressly recognized in several provisions of the SPS Agreement (such as

We now turn to deference in WTO proportionality characterization. The three factors mentioned by the Appellate Body in *US – Gambling* relating to optimality analysis play a major role here, as we will see.

7.4. DEFERENCE AND PROPORTIONALITY CHARACTERIZATION IN THE WTO

The nature of deference in proportionality characterization is based on deference to legislative inferences. In proportionality characterization, those inferences concern the causal effectiveness of the legislation, its optimality in the light of economic and political realities, and its overall appropriateness. The domestic legislature chooses what it considers to be a balanced policy measure, based on the inferences it makes from available information. WTO tribunals need to give significant weight to these inferences, for reasons discussed earlier.[53]

I suggest that the practice of WTO tribunals has generally been careful here. Nevertheless, there has been a striking lack of deference in several cases. We will look at this practice in light of the three aspects of proportionality discussed earlier: balance, effectiveness, and optimality. Of these three aspects, WTO tribunals have been most careful to show deference in assessing balance. They have also shown considerable deference in assessing effectiveness, although there are some exceptional cases regarding this issue. In any case, we have already seen that most of the work in WTO proportionality characterization is loaded into the optimality aspect. Here, WTO tribunals have applied sophisticated and clever techniques to achieve substantial yet limited deference to domestic legislatures. Again, there are some exceptional cases, in which WTO tribunals have ventured out some way into the territory of raw policy balancing.

Art. 5.6). The second factor (technical capacity) is also recognized in the footnote to Art. 5.6 SPS Agreement:

> For purposes of paragraph 6 of Article 5, a measure is not more trade-restrictive than required unless there is another measure, reasonably available taking into account technical and economic feasibility, that achieves the appropriate level of sanitary or phytosanitary protection and is significantly less restrictive to trade.

Scott, *The WTO Agreement on Sanitary and Phytosanitary Measures* (Oxford: Oxford University Press, 2007), 160–161 argues that the Art. XX GATT jurisprudence cannot be transferred carelessly to Art. 5.6 SPS Agreement cases. Nevertheless, she notes that 'the more developed case law in that area [Art. XX GATT] is at least useful in identifying the kind of key questions which remain unsolved . . . [T]he Article XX case law is also undeveloped on this point [i.e., the concept of feasibility in respect of alternative measures], but close attention should be paid to its development in contemplating the parameters of Art. 5.6 SPS'.

53. See Section 4.3.

7.4.1. Deference and Balance

As we have already seen, some WTO jurisprudence acknowledges the balance aspect of proportionality, most notably in characterizing legislation under the general exceptions provisions. At the same time, WTO tribunals have pulled back from actually balancing competing policies in a direct and open fashion. This is not surprising, given that it is the primary function of the legislature, not of the judiciary, to balance policy considerations.[54] Much of the substantial decision-making in WTO proportionality characterization is instead made in a more indirect way under the optimality aspect of proportionality. Nevertheless, in some cases, one can occasionally see minor intrusions into raw policy balancing.

The potential scope for policy balancing in WTO litigation is great, because there are a multitude of purposes competing with free trade. Nevertheless, there is only a minimal textual basis for judicial activity here. The WTO agreements give only minimal clues as to the balance between the importance of free trade and the importance of those competing purposes. Furthermore, not all possible purposes are mentioned expressly in WTO texts. The Preamble to the WTO Agreement at least mentions some important alternative purposes, such as development and environmental protection.[55] Yet, there are obvious gaps in these listed purposes (perhaps the most important of which is the lack of mention of protection of human rights).

WTO tribunals are on thin ice if they try to balance the policy of free trade against competing policies not expressly mentioned in the WTO agreements. To provide some support here, some commentators have referred to non-WTO international law as a context for the interpretation of WTO obligations. Encouraged by the apparent willingness of the Appellate Body to abandon the 'clinical isolation' of WTO law from general public international law,[56] those commentators have attempted to use international human rights law and international environmental law to overcome what they see as gaps in the general structure of WTO

54. See Section 4.1, text at n. 1.
55. The text to the Preamble mentions the following purposes:

  - raising standards of living;
  - ensuring full employment;
  - ensuring a large and steadily growing volume of real income and effective demand;
  - allowing for the optimal use of the world's resources in accordance with the objective of sustainable development;
  - seeking both to protect and preserve the environment and to enhance the means for doing so in a manner consistent with WTO members' respective needs and concerns at different levels of economic development; and
  - ensuring that developing countries, and especially the least developed among them, secure a share in the growth in international trade commensurate with the needs of their economic development.

  Interestingly, the Preamble to the GATS gives a much wider scope for balancing, as it provides generally for the achievement of 'national policy objectives'.
56. Appellate Body Report, *US – Gasoline*, para. 3.B.

law.[57] In cases involving proportionality characterization, they have suggested that these 'non-WTO' purposes must be given considerable weight in any balancing process.

Unfortunately, these arguments do not give the Appellate Body a clear answer as to how to balance 'WTO' purposes with 'non-WTO' purposes in a particular dispute. Basic concepts of treaty interpretation, such as those set out in Article 31 of the Vienna Convention on the Law of Treaties (VCLT), and 'tiebreaker' rules about timing,[58] generality,[59] and participation[60] are not determinative. On the positive side, these principles of treaty interpretation at least lend a voice to 'non-WTO' purposes, rather than silencing them entirely. In the end, however, such principles give WTO tribunals little hard juristic guidance in balancing policy goals.

Thus WTO tribunals generally avoid too much emphasis on the balance aspect of proportionality characterization. They purport to examine balance – particularly in the context of general exception provisions – but they do not actually do so to any great degree.[61] As discussed earlier,[62] the Appellate Body has ruled that the proportionality analysis for such provisions should begin with an assessment of the relative importance of the legislative purpose, and then turn to other factors to be weighed and balanced. Despite this, outright policy balancing makes only a very minor appearance in decisions about the relative importance of policy goals. For the most part, WTO tribunals have simply acknowledged the importance of the legislative purpose without detailed analysis. For example, in *US – Gambling*, the Panel found it relevant that the United States measures protected 'very important societal interests'.[63] In *EC – Asbestos*, the Appellate Body stressed the vital nature of the goal of protecting human health.[64] Other 'important' purposes have included protection of animal and plant life and health,[65] environmental protection,[66] protection of tax revenue,[67] prevention of money laundering,[68] prevention of fraud,[69]

57. For an analysis of the possible influences of non-WTO international law on WTO law, see J. Pauwelyn, *Conflict of Laws in Public International Law* (Cambridge: Cambridge University Press, 2003).
58. Article 83(2), 3 VCLT.
59. Part IV VCLT.
60. Article 83(4) VCLT.
61. An example here is Appellate Body Report, *Korea – Various Measures on Beef*. There, the Appellate Body expressly noted the need for a balancing process (at para. 164), yet did not engage in any direct balancing of the relevant goals (which in that case were free trade, and the enforcement of trade practices laws).
62. See Section 7.3, text at n. 47.
63. Panel Report, *US – Gambling*, paras 6.492 and 6.533.
64. Appellate Body Report, *EC – Asbestos*, para. 172. See also Panel Report, *Brazil – Retreaded Tyres*, para. 7.210.
65. Panel Report, *Brazil – Retreaded Tyres*, para. 7.151.
66. Appellate Body Report, *US – Gasoline*; Appellate Body Report, *US – Shrimp*.
67. Appellate Body Report, *Dominican Republic – Import and Sale of Cigarettes*, para. 59.
68. Appellate Body Report, *US – Gambling*, para. 313.
69. *Ibid.*

and prevention of compulsive and under-aged gambling.[70] Unsurprisingly, no WTO tribunal has yet assessed a legislative purpose as unimportant.[71] Instead, the substance of the proportionality analysis has been in assessing possible alternatives, that is, relating to the optimality of legislation. The practical primacy of optimality over balancing was recognized by the Appellate Body in *Korea – Various Measures on Beef*, when it said that the balancing process is 'comprehended' by an optimality analysis.[72]

The balancing aspect of proportionality characterization nevertheless raises some practical issues in WTO litigation. Perhaps the most controversial issue here is whether a particular legislative purpose is legitimate in the first place. In pre-WTO days, Panels under the GATT system decided that certain environmental protection purposes did not fall within the relevant general exceptions provisions of the GATT.[73] These decisions appear to have been reversed in the WTO.[74]

---

70. *Ibid.*
71. In *Canada – Wheat Exports and Grain Imports*, the Panel ranked policy goals. Nevertheless, this was an entirely uncontroversial finding; the Panel found that need to 'ensure the quality of Canadian grain, maintain the integrity of the Canadian grading system, protect consumers against misrepresentation and preserve and enforce the CWB monopoly' was not as important as protecting human health: Panel Report, *Canada – Wheat Exports and Grain Imports*, paras 6.224 and 6.303.
72. Appellate Body Report, *Korea – Various Measures on Beef*, para. 166:

 > [T]he weighing and balancing process we have outlined is comprehended in the determination of whether a WTO-consistent alternative measure which the Member concerned could 'reasonably be expected to employ' is available, or whether a less WTO-inconsistent measure is 'reasonably available'.

73. In *US – Tuna/Dolphin I*, the Panel held that 'exhaustible natural resources' mentioned in Art. XX(g) GATT referred only to natural resources within the territorial jurisdiction of the WTO member concerned (GATT Panel Report, *United States – Restrictions on Imports of Tuna*, DS21/R, DS21/R, 3 Sep. 1991, unadopted, BISD 39S/155, paras 5.26, 5.31). That is to say, it was *not* a legitimate purpose for a WTO member to legislate to protect natural resources outside its own territorial jurisdiction. This kind of reasoning was exceptional even under the old GATT system. In other cases, GATT panels recognized the legitimacy of legislative purpose without demur (although they were not so deferential in measuring optimality). For example, the GATT Panel in *Thailand – Cigarettes* recognized that 'smoking constituted a serious risk to human health and that consequently measures designed to reduce the consumption of cigarettes fell within the scope of Article XX(b)' (GATT Panel Report, *Thailand – Restrictions on Importation of and Internal Taxes on Cigarettes*, DS10/R, adopted 7 Nov. 1990, BISD 37S/200, para. 73). In the second *US – Tuna/Dolphin* case, the Panel took a wider view of the acceptability of extraterritorial purposes. It saw 'no valid reason supporting the conclusion that the provisions of Article XX(g) apply only to . . . the conservation of exhaustible natural resources located within the territory of the contracting party invoking the provision'. However, it still restricted choice of legislative purpose by ruling that measures justified under Art. XX(g) GATT should only be enforced against the nationals and vessels of the legislating member (GATT Panel Report, *United States – Restrictions on Imports of Tuna*, DS29/R, 16 Jun. 1994, unadopted, para. 5.20; see also Matsushita, Schoenbaum & Mavroidis, above n. 24, 796).
74. WTO tribunals have, in general, not followed the *US – Tuna/Dolphin I* approach (see previous footnote). This is illustrated by cases dealing with general exceptions provisions of Art. XX GATT and Art. XIV GATS. In *US – Gasoline*, the Appellate Body saw no problem in

However, the architecture of WTO obligations leaves some doubts here about non-trade purposes, because several WTO obligations refer to restricted lists of purposes,[75] while others refer to open-ended ranges of purposes.[76] This rule structure is bound to create tricky practical issues for WTO tribunals in determining the legitimacy of particular legislative purposes.[77]

For the most part, WTO tribunals have been very deferential to legislatures in judging the legitimacy of legislative purposes. An example can be seen in the *EC – Tariff Preferences* case. The measure in dispute in this case was an EC tariff preference directed towards certain developing countries. The measure clearly breached the general MFN principle. The EC nevertheless tried to justify it via the Enabling Clause,[78] which allows 'generalized, non-reciprocal and non-discriminatory preferences beneficial to the developing countries'.[79] The Appellate Body held that this meant that 'preference-granting countries must make available identical tariff preferences to all similarly-situated beneficiaries',[80] that is, developing countries 'that have the "development, financial and trade needs" to which the treatment in question is intended to respond'.[81] But did the Enabling Clause limit the range of purposes for the relevant treatment? The EC claimed that its legislative purpose was to combat illicit drug production and trafficking in certain developing countries,[82] through providing 'alternative licit activities' (and thereby discouraging illegal activities).[83] The Appellate Body accepted the validity of this purpose without hesitation or analysis.

There is a series of cases in which WTO tribunals have regarded the legislative purpose as not legitimate. However, these cases should be regarded as exceptional. They generally occur under Article XX(d) of the GATT, which is a general exception provision regarding measures 'necessary to secure compliance with laws or

recognizing 'the US objective of improving air quality in the United States' (Panel Report, *US – Gasoline*, para. 6.40; Appellate Body Report, text at fn. 31). In *US – Shrimp* it distanced itself from the restrictive readings in the *US – Tuna/Dolphin* cases (Appellate Body Report, para. 133). Instead, the Appellate Body directed the issue of extraterritoriality towards Art. XX chapeau GATT, involving more of a balancing test than a bright line rule (Matsushita, Schoenbaum & Mavroidis, above n. 24, 799, 803).

75. For example, Art. III GATT, Art. XIV GATS and Art. 8 TRIPS.
76. For example, Art. 2.2 TBT Agreement.
77. A particularly tricky issue is whether it is legitimate to encourage other States to adopt a domestic legislative purpose. The Appellate Body in *US – Shrimp*, para. 133, refused to rule on whether Art. XX(g) GATT contains an implied jurisdictional limitation in this respect. However, it was critical of such 'encouragement' so far as the chapeau to Art. XX was concerned (see paras 161–165).
78. Decision on Differential and More Favourable Treatment, Reciprocity, and Fuller Participation of Developing Countries, GATT Document L/4903, 28 Nov. 1979, BISD 26S/203.
79. Paragraph 2(a) footnote Enabling Clause.
80. Appellate Body Report, *EC – Tariff Preferences*, para. 154. See also para. 173.
81. Appellate Body Report, *EC – Tariff Preferences*, para. 173.
82. *Ibid.*, para. 180.
83. *Ibid.*, para. 29.

regulations which are not inconsistent with the [GATT]'.[84] It is possible that the 'laws or regulations' protected by the challenged legislation are themselves GATT-inconsistent. An analogous issue arose in *Mexico – Taxes on Soft Drinks*. In this case, Mexico attempted to justify its legislation on the basis that it was designed to encourage the United States to comply with certain rules under the North American Free Trade Agreement (NAFTA).[85] In other words, the purpose of the legislation was to secure compliance with Mexico's treaty rights. The Appellate Body did not find this purpose to be adequate under Article XX(d) of the GATT. The text and context of Article XX(d) clearly suggests that international laws are not relevant 'laws and regulations'.[86] Furthermore, allowing the purpose of securing compliance with international law would have required the Appellate Body to consider the exact effect of such international law. Inevitably, this would have involved making decisions about disputes under non-WTO international regimes[87] – a function to which WTO tribunals are clearly unsuited. For these reasons, this decision should be seen as an exceptional case.

We can conclude that the balancing aspect of proportionality characterization is, in itself, not the decisive measure of deference for WTO tribunals. Of much more importance is the aspect of optimality. However, the aspect of effectiveness also has some significance here. It is to this aspect that we now turn.

7.4.2. Deference and Effectiveness

As noted earlier,[88] the effectiveness aspect of proportionality relates to causation. WTO tribunals have tended towards deference in assessing domestic legislative inferences about causation, and they have generally held that legislation is effective. They have done this by reference to legislative texts,[89] agreed positions between the litigants,[90] findings of expert witnesses,[91] and statements of

---

84. One might also see such cases emerging under the 'arbitrary or unjustifiable discrimination' aspect of the chapeaus to the general exception provisions (such as Art. XX GATT). In *Brazil – Retreaded Tyres*, the Appellate Body held that the discriminatory application of a measure is 'arbitrary or unjustifiable' if the reasons for the discrimination 'bear no rational connection' to the objective allowing the measure to be provisionally justified under a paragraph of Art. XX GATT (Appellate Body Report, *Brazil – Retreaded Tyres*, para. 227). In that case, the reason for the discriminatory application of Brazil's import ban was Brazil's need to comply with its MERCOSUR obligations. The Appellate Body held that this purpose was not sufficient for the chapeau, because it bore no relationship to the underlying purpose of the import ban, that is, health protection (see para. 228).
85. NAFTA 32 ILM 605 (1993).
86. Appellate Body Report, *Mexico – Taxes on Soft Drinks*, paras 69–71.
87. *Ibid.*, para. 56. This might also be an explanation of the result in Appellate Body Report, *Brazil – Retreaded Tyres* described at n. 84 above.
88. See Section 7.3.2.
89. For example, Appellate Body Report, *US – Gasoline*, Art. III(B).
90. Appellate Body Report, *US – Shrimp*, para. 140.
91. *Ibid.*, para. 140.

international bodies.[92] Significantly, the Appellate Body has held that inferences about causation can only be tested over a period of time.[93] This suggests that domestic legislatures may be given the benefit of the doubt in making prognoses about the effectiveness of their measures. In some cases, the Appellate Body has avoided the question of effectiveness entirely.[94]

One can nevertheless see less deference in examining effectiveness when the measure has a severe effect on trade. In *Brazil – Retreaded Tyres*, the Appellate Body said:

> [W]hen a measure produces restrictive effects on international trade as severe as those resulting from an import ban, it appears to us that it would be difficult for a panel to find that measure necessary unless it is satisfied that the measure is apt to make a material contribution to the achievement of its objective.[95]

The yardstick of 'material contribution' could, in theory, result in WTO tribunals rejecting the domestic legislative view that particular legislation is effective in meeting its objectives.[96] However, there is no need for legislation to actually 'make' such a contribution; rather, it need only be 'apt' to do so. The degree of deference shown by WTO tribunals here corresponds to the degree to which they examine aptness.

In practice, the Appellate Body has been willing to accept that legislation is effective if there are signs of a genuine attempt to achieve the legislative purpose. This is so even in the case of import bans. In *US – Shrimp*, the Appellate Body found that an import ban on shrimp was effective in protecting turtles, given that there were a number of exceptions to the ban directed at such protection (e.g., an exception for shrimp harvested 'under conditions that do not adversely affect sea

---

92. For example, Appellate Body Report, *EC – Asbestos*, para. 182, noting the Panel's observation that 'the carcinogenic nature of chrysotile asbestos fibres has been acknowledged since 1977 by international bodies, such as the International Agency for Research on Cancer and the World Health Organization' – an observation that led to the finding that the EC ban on such fibres was clearly designed and apt to achieve its desired level of health protection (para. 168). See also the finding in GATT Panel Report, *Thailand – Restrictions on Importation of and Internal Taxes on Cigarettes*, DS10/R, adopted 7 Nov. 1990, BISD 37S/200.
93. Appellate Body Report, *Brazil – Retreaded Tyres*, para. 151.
94. In *US – Gasoline*, the Appellate Body avoided examining causal issues completely. The case concerned Art. XX(g) GATT, which requires that measures for the conservation of exhaustible natural resources be 'made effective' in conjunction with restrictions on domestic production or consumption. The reference to 'made effective' might be interpreted as requiring some kind of causation of the desired result – but the Appellate Body held otherwise. It decided that 'made effective' here only meant coming into operation, force or effect, and that this aspect of Art. XX(g) GATT was simply a requirement of 'even-handedness'. The Appellate Body thus avoided an examination of causation in that case: Appellate Body Report, *US – Gasoline*, III(C).
95. Appellate Body Report, *Brazil – Retreaded Tyres*, para. 150.
96. In *US – Shrimp*, the Appellate Body appeared to consider that a *blanket* import ban on shrimp would not have had an observably close and genuine relation to the purpose of protecting turtles: Appellate Body Report, *US – Shrimp*, para. 141.

turtles').[97] In *Brazil – Retreaded Tyres*, the Appellate Body held that an import ban was 'likely to bring a material contribution' to reducing volumes of tyre waste, in combination with other parallel measures directed at this goal (such as collection and disposal rules).[98] These cases suggest a fairly deferential approach in effectiveness analysis, even in the case of severely trade-restrictive measures. However, a mere assertion of effectiveness will not suffice;[99] WTO tribunals will test such an assertion to see if it is at least plausible.

One rare example of challenged legislation failing proportionality characterization because of ineffectiveness is *EC – Tariff Preferences*.[100] The legislation in this case created tariff preferences directed towards certain developing countries, in breach of the MFN principle. However, the Enabling Clause allows 'generalized, non-reciprocal and non-discriminatory preferences beneficial to the developing countries'.[101] The Appellate Body held that tariff preferences could be 'non-discriminatory' if they were 'addressed to a particular "development, financial [or] trade need" ' of developing countries generally.[102] The particular need claimed here was the prevention of illicit drug production and trafficking. The Appellate Body concluded that the legislation was not effective in meeting that need on a non-discriminatory basis,[103] because it did not set forth clear criteria to developing countries as to how to become beneficiaries under the scheme.[104] More importantly, it did not give any indication of how its arrangements would provide 'an adequate and proportionate response' to the drug problem.[105] This is an unusual finding. In most WTO cases, the tribunal does not question the factual inferences supporting the effectiveness of the legislation. In *EC – Tariff Preferences*, the Appellate Body appeared to require some support of those inferences on the face of the legislation as a condition of consistency with the relevant WTO rules. For this reason, the case should be seen as exceptional, resting on the unusual nature of the Enabling Clause itself.[106]

Although legislation is unlikely to fail entirely a test of effectiveness, causal issues are still important in WTO proportionality characterization. The Appellate Body views a weak causal link between the legislation and its alleged purpose as an

---

97. Appellate Body Report, *US – Shrimp*, para. 141. The *application* of the measure was nevertheless found to be in breach of Art. XX chapeau GATT.
98. Appellate Body Report, *Brazil – Retreaded Tyres*, paras 154–155.
99. Furthermore, it appears that WTO tribunals need not accept the *method* by which the legislator supports its view on effectiveness. In *Brazil – Retreaded Tyres*, Brazil attempted to prove the effectiveness of its legislation by *qualitative* analysis. The Appellate Body held that it was open to the Panel to engage in a separate *quantitative* analysis if it wanted to (Appellate Body Report, *Brazil – Retreaded Tyres*, paras 147, 151). The issue was not critical in the case, however, as the Panel proceeded by qualitative methods anyway.
100. Appellate Body Report, *EC – Tariff Preferences*. See also n. 42.
101. Paragraph 2(a) footnote Enabling Clause.
102. Appellate Body Report, *EC – Tariff Preferences*, para. 165.
103. *Ibid.*, para. 180.
104. *Ibid.*, para. 183.
105. *Ibid.*
106. See also Panel Report, *Canada – Periodicals*, para. 5.10.

indication that the legislative purpose is a sham.[107] However, a direct finding of sham purpose is unlikely in practice, because this would impute bad faith to a domestic legislature. Instead, WTO tribunals may emphasize weak effectiveness in the overall proportionality analysis. This can be seen in *Dominican Republic – Import and Sale of Cigarettes*. In this case, the challenged measure required tax stamps to be fixed to cigarette packages in the Dominican Republic, ostensibly to combat tax fraud and smuggling. The Panel found that the measure was 'a useful instrument to monitor tax collection on cigarettes and, conversely, to avoid tax evasion' – a finding undisturbed by the Appellate Body.[108] The legislation was nevertheless ineffective: 'the tax stamp requirement was of limited effectiveness in preventing tax evasion and cigarette smuggling'.[109] However, this finding of ineffectiveness was not the decisive criterion in the Panel's proportionality analysis. Rather, the finding was only one element in a wider finding that the measure was not optimal.[110] This indicates that low effectiveness is merely a useful indicator that special care needs to be taken in testing the overall optimality of legislation.[111]

---

107. Appellate Body Report, *US – Gasoline*, Art. III(C):

> We are not, however, suggesting that consideration of the predictable effects of a measure is never relevant. In a particular case, should it become clear that realistically, a specific measure cannot in any possible situation have any positive effect on conservation goals, it would very probably be because that measure was not designed as a conservation regulation to begin with. In other words, it would not have been 'primarily aimed at' conservation of natural resources at all.

Compare the Panel's view in *Japan – Alcoholic Beverages II*, para. 6.31, that a Japanese econometric study purporting to show no elasticity of substitution between certain domestic and imported spirits was of little evidential weight due to errors in the statistical methods used in the study. (The elasticity of substitution of products is a causal issue, relating to the extent to which one product can be substituted for another in a market.) Compare also the Panel's view in *Japan – Alcoholic Beverages II*, para. 6.25, that the purported purpose of the challenged legislation to 'maintain a "roughly constant" tax/price ratio' was 'an ex post facto rationalization'.

108. *Dominican Republic – Import and Sale of Cigarettes*, Appellate Body Report, para. 71.
109. *Ibid.*
110. *Ibid.*:

> According to the Panel, requiring that tax stamps be affixed in the Dominican Republic under the supervision of the tax authorities 'in and of itself, would not prevent the forgery of tax stamps, nor smuggling and tax evasion'. In this respect, the Panel indicated that other factors, such as security features incorporated into the tax stamps, or police controls on roads and at different commercial levels, would play a more important role in preventing forgery of tax stamps, tax evasion and smuggling of tobacco products. [footnotes omitted]

111. In *EC – Sardines*, the Appellate Body suggested that ineffective legislation can be appropriate, and that inappropriate legislation can be effective. This suggestion should be taken with some caution. It is difficult to imagine appropriate legislation that is ineffective in achieving its purpose (B. Pieroth & B. Schlink, *Grundrechte*, 19th edn (Heidelberg: CF Müller, 2003), 66–67). If legislation is ineffective, there will almost certainly be reasonably available alternative measures, and some of those alternative measures will be better able to achieve the desired purpose. One could read nevertheless read the Appellate Body's comment as meaning that

Thus, effectiveness, like pure policy balancing, is a fairly minor aspect of WTO proportionality characterization. Both effectiveness and balancing are factors that feed into the heart of the analysis – optimality. It is here that WTO tribunals are confronted with the most complex problems of deference.

7.4.3. Deference and Optimality

As in all aspects of proportionality characterization, WTO tribunals give considerable deference to the judgments of domestic legislatures. This is evident in the optimality aspect of a proportionality analysis. A domestic legislature must be presumed to have considered various ways to achieve its desired purpose: an international tribunal is generally slow to conclude that there are other, better, ways.

For the most part, WTO tribunals have indeed shown substantial respect for legislative decisions about optimality. Where they have disagreed with such decisions, they have used sophisticated techniques to avoid direct conflict with legislatures. It is only in some exceptional cases that WTO tribunals have shifted into the controversial area of openly contradicting a legislature. Given the critical importance of optimality analysis in proportionality characterization, we will now look at their jurisprudence in some detail.

One aspect of WTO jurisprudence, at first glance, suggests a generally intrusive optimality analysis. This is the 'least degree of inconsistency' doctrine laid down by the GATT Panel in *US – Section 337*:

> [I]n cases where a measure consistent with other GATT provisions is not reasonably available, a contracting party is bound to use, among the measures reasonably available to it, that which entails the least degree of inconsistency with other GATT provisions.[112]

On its face, the least degree of inconsistency doctrine compels a domestic legislature to search all available ways of achieving its goals and choose the one that is most consistent with WTO rules. Furthermore, it may imply that a WTO tribunal has the power to undertake the same search and to come up with a different answer. This would be a striking result if the doctrine were to be taken at face value,

---

measures that are considered by the legislature as effective *when enacted* may after some time be found to actually be ineffective. Such legislation may well be appropriate *at the time of its enactment*. A legislature must be allowed some scope to make prognoses as to future effectiveness. Nevertheless, once ineffectiveness becomes apparent, there is a good argument that the legislation ceases to be appropriate. This type of argument is seen in domestic constitutional law, particularly in Germany (Sachs, Art. 20, in M. Sachs (ed.), *Grundgesetz*, 4th edn (München: CH Beck, 2007), para. 151, 816). The argument is also consistent with the inter-temporal principle of international law (see Section 2.4.1).

112. GATT Panel Report, *United States Section 337 of the Tariff Act of 1930*, L/6439, adopted 7 Nov. 1989, BISD 36S/345, para. 5.26. This statement was approved in Appellate Body Report, *Korea – Various Measures on Beef*, para. 166.

because it would give WTO tribunals the power to undertake nearly de novo review. Thus, there is some degree of deference to legislative fact finding and inference making to moderate the least degree of inconsistency rule. The least degree of inconsistency doctrine is not applied literally and to its full extent in a dispute.[113]

In practice, the theoretical intrusiveness of the 'least degree of inconsistency' doctrine has been tempered by a number of limitations. Some WTO rules modify the rule expressly.[114] The least degree of inconsistency doctrine has also been limited by general WTO jurisprudence. A good starting point here is the Appellate Body's statement on optimality analysis in *US – Gambling*.[115] According to the Appellate Body, a measure is not 'reasonably available' if:

- it 'is merely theoretical in nature, for instance, where the responding Member is not capable of taking it';
- it 'imposes an undue burden on that Member, such as prohibitive costs or substantial technical difficulties'; or
- it would not 'preserve for the responding Member its right to achieve its desired level of protection with respect to the objective pursued'.[116]

These three limitations to the least degree of inconsistency doctrine provide us with a useful framework for examining deference in WTO optimality analysis. As we will see, it is the third limitation that is of most practical significance.

7.4.3.1. Incapacity

The first limitation is of somewhat restricted use, as it states the obvious: a measure is not available if the legislating State cannot take it. Legislation cannot be characterized as disproportionate merely because there is an alternative that a State is not able to take. Such an alternative would be ineffective and thus itself fail an analysis of proportionality. The obviousness of this principle makes it an uncommon argument in WTO challenges to legislation.

7.4.3.2. Costs and Resources

The second limitation is of more practical importance. It requires WTO tribunals to account for the relative costs of measures and the availability of resources to implement them.[117] A very expensive proposed alternative measure, or one not suited to the resources of the legislating State, should not be seen as reasonable. However, the task of assessing the costs of proposed alternatives and the resources

113. In Panel Report, *Argentina – Hides and Leather*, para. 11.304, the Panel noted that the European Communities had argued for a strict application of the doctrine but that Argentina saw this as overly restrictive. The Panel saw no need to resolve this issue in the case before it.
114. For example, the note to Art. 5.6 SPS Agreement.
115. See Section 7.3, text at n. 51.
116. Appellate Body Report, *US – Gambling*, para. 306.
117. Appellate Body Report, *Korea – Various Measures on Beef*, paras 180–181.

available to meet those costs will be difficult for WTO tribunals. Such tribunals are not well qualified to make detailed financial analyses. In principle, one therefore could expect some deference to domestic legislative fact finding and inference making as to such financial matters. Thus, the costs and resources limitation could be an important source of deference in optimality analysis, particularly for smaller States with modest financial resources.

The application of the costs and resources limitation can be seen in *Brazil – Retreaded Tyres*. In this case, Brazil legislated an import ban on retreaded and used tyres, for the purpose of protecting human, animal, and plant life and health by reducing tyre waste to the maximum extent possible. The EC claimed that there were alternative (less-trade restrictive) measures available to achieve the same purpose, including recycling schemes. The Panel held that various recycling schemes would not achieve Brazil's purpose because of their high costs.[118] This finding was not overturned on appeal.[119]

Nevertheless, the costs and resources limitation has sometime failed to attract deference in WTO optimality analysis. In *Korea – Various Measures on Beef*, the challenged measure created a dual retail system for beef, separating sales of domestic and imported products. Korea claimed that this was justified under Article XX(d) of the GATT for the purpose of combating misrepresentation in the retail market as to the origin of beef. One of the several proposed alternative measures considered by the Panel was the application of 'basic measures' – investigations, policing, fines, and record keeping – to enforce its trade practices laws. Korea pleaded a lack of resources, with little success before the Panel.[120] The Appellate Body agreed with the Panel, even giving some suggestions about how to reduce costs:

> Korea's argument about the lack of resources to police thousands of shops on a round-the-clock basis is, in the end, not sufficiently persuasive. Violations of laws and regulations like the Korean Unfair Competition Act can be expected to be routinely investigated and detected through selective, but well-targeted, controls of potential wrongdoers. The control of records will assist in selecting the shops to which the police could pay particular attention.[121]

At first glance, one is struck by the Appellate Body's lack of deference here to Korea's own inferences about costs and resources. Nevertheless, the result here is not so surprising, given the familiar and routine nature of the alternative measure proposed. Basic measures of law enforcement are unlikely to be too expensive for

118. Panel Report, *Brazil – Retreaded Tyres*, para. 7.208. Admittedly, the Panel also disqualified the proposed alternatives on the basis of safety concerns: Panel Report, *Brazil – Retreaded Tyres*, para. 7.208.
119. Nevertheless, the Appellate Body stressed that the Panel disqualified the recycling alternatives not because of high costs as such, but rather because high costs would limit their disposal capacity: Appellate Body Report, *Brazil – Retreaded Tyres*, para. 207.
120. Panel Report, *Korea – Various Measures on Beef*, para. 673.
121. Appellate Body Report, *Korea – Various Measures on Beef*, para. 180.

developed States such as Korea, except in unusual problematic cases. Similar rejections of a costs and resources argument can be found in other WTO cases.[122]

An interesting aspect of *Korea – Various Measures on Beef* was the Appellate Body's view that removing trade barriers could actually reduce costs for a legislating State. These costs would otherwise be borne by consumers. According to this view, the costs and resources argument could be overcome by pointing to net economic gains from making legislation WTO-compliant:

> It is pertinent to observe that, through its dual retail system, Korea has in effect shifted all, or the great bulk, of these potential costs of enforcement (translated into a drastic reduction of competitive access to consumers) to imported goods and retailers of imported goods, instead of evenly distributing such costs between the domestic and imported products. In contrast, the more conventional, WTO-consistent measures of enforcement do not involve such onerous shifting of enforcement costs which ordinarily are borne by the Member's public purse.[123]

This view may provide some clue as to why the costs and resources limitation is difficult to apply in practice. WTO tribunals start from the position that WTO-inconsistent measures have an intrinsic economic cost: this position automatically discounts, to an extent, the influence of a costs and resources argument in their optimality analysis.[124]

---

122. Compare here Panel Report, *Argentina – Hides and Leather*, para. 11.327. The Panel was concerned there with laws establishing advance tax payments that created a higher burden on imports as opposed to domestic products, due to interest costs on tax on imports. The Panel considered a proposed alternative measure that would involve Argentina paying compensation for those interest costs. Argentina argued that such a compensation scheme would involve unacceptable administrative costs. The Panel disagreed, holding that administrative costs could be contained by placing some of the burden of paperwork on importers (at para. 11.327). Furthermore, the Panel held that the tax collected would far exceed any administrative costs (at para. 11.327).

    An indirect example of the non-application of the costs and resources limitation can be seen in *US – Gasoline*. There, the challenged legislation restricted the sale of low quality gasoline, with the aim of protecting air quality. Gasoline could not be sold at a quality less than 'baseline' gasoline quality levels for the year 1990. Domestic refiners, blenders and importers were able to use individual baselines tailored to their circumstances, but foreign competitors had to use generalized statutory baselines. These statutory baselines were challenged by Brazil and Venezuela in WTO proceedings. They argued that individual baselines for foreign competitors, with suitable verification procedures, would be a less-discriminatory, reasonably available alternative measure. The US Congress had denied funding for such an alternative. It is not clear from the face of the Appellate Body report whether Congress denied funding to save costs or for other reasons. However, the Appellate Body simply did not deal with the possibility that the suggested alternative appeared to be unreasonably expensive to Congress (Appellate Body Report, *US – Gasoline*, 25).
123. Appellate Body Report, *Korea – Various Measures on Beef*, para. 181.
124. See also Panel Report, *Argentina – Hides and Leather*, para. 11.327. One should keep in mind here that most challenges to legislation have been directed at large defendants, such as the European Communities and the United States. WTO tribunals are reluctant to analyse such legislators' ability to pay for alternative measures, probably because of their enormous

However, there is considerable potential for a legislating State to benefit from the costs and resources argument, if it is willing to produce hard evidence to support the argument. If there is specific and compelling evidence about the unacceptable costs of a proposed alternative, or the lack of resources for it, it will be difficult for a WTO tribunal to resist the argument. Challenging the validity of such evidence would stretch the boundaries of judicial capacity. As with many aspects of challenges to legislation, the issue comes down to the application of the burden of proof. Although this burden often rests on the legislating State in optimality analysis,[125] it should be relatively easily to establish in relation to financial matters, provided that the evidence extends beyond a mere assertion of an inability to pay. However, there is no clear case law to support this speculation.[126] For the time being, the main efforts of legislating States have related to the third limitation to the least degree of inconsistency doctrine – the ALOP.

7.4.3.3. The ALOP

The third limitation to the least degree of inconsistency doctrine concerns the ALOP concept discussed earlier.[127] The ALOP provides a clear conceptual brake on optimality analysis, and it thus increases deference to legislatures. If a domestic legislature has set a strict ALOP, WTO tribunals will be more constrained in seeking out possible alternative measures during optimality analysis.[128] The

---

resources, and their complex and polycentric financing arrangements. An interesting question is whether a small State could argue that it simply cannot afford alternative measures available to larger States. To my knowledge, such an argument has not yet arisen in the WTO.

125. Panel Report, *Korea – Various Measures on Beef*, para. 665:

> The Panel considers that in the presence of an alternative measure consistent with WTO rules, it is for Korea to demonstrate that such an alternative measure is not reasonably available or is unreasonably burdensome, financially or technically, taking into account a variety of factors including the domestic costs of such alternative measure, to ensure that consumers are not misled as to the origin of beef.

126. The Panel Report in *Brazil – Retreaded Tyres* may provide some support here. The evidence before the Panel on the costs of tyre recycling schemes (as an alternative to Brazil's import ban) was not mere assertion, but included statements from recognized authorities such as the OECD (Panel Report, *Brazil – Retreaded Tyres*, para. 7.201 (fn. 1358); para. 7.205 (fn. 1357); para. 7.207 (fn. 1371).
127. See Section 7.3, text at n. 25.
128. For example, quarantine legislation may set an acceptable level of quarantine risk at very low levels, and set out measures to achieve this strict ALOP. In determining whether the legislation is 'necessary' in the sense of being the least trade-restrictive measure reasonably available, a WTO tribunal will have to consider whether proposed alternative measures also achieve this strict ALOP.

Nevertheless, the legislating State must be careful in setting a very strict ALOP for some products, while relaxing the ALOP for other products. It is clear that the legislating State is able to do so (Appellate Body Report, *Korea – Various Measures on Beef*, para. 177). However, this may be an indication that alternative measures are available (Appellate Body Report, *Korea – Various Measures on Beef*, para. 172). It may also be a factor indicating

complex fact situations involved and the abstractness of the ALOP may also constrain WTO tribunals.[129] Furthermore, although a Panel may explore any alternative measures that it sees fit, it is not compelled to examine any alternatives beyond those raised by the challenging State.[130]

The deference created by the ALOP limitation is increased by the prerogative of the legislating State to choose the intensity of its ALOP.[131] In *Australia – Salmon*, the legislation at issue was a prohibition on the importation of fresh, chilled, or frozen salmon unless heat-treated as prescribed.[132] Australia determined that its ALOP was 'a high or "very conservative" level of sanitary protection aimed at reducing risk to "very low levels", "while not based on a zero-risk approach" '.[133]

The Panel focused on the 'level of protection currently achieved by the measure at issue',[134] which it found to be the heat-treatment requirement. It also held that it could not defer completely to Australia as to the choice of the measure to achieve its desired level of protection.[135] Australia objected, arguing that its ALOP was to be measured by the content of the import prohibition.[136] The

---

a breach of a separate non-discrimination obligation (such as Art. 5.5 SPS Agreement). In *EC – Hormones*, para. 215, the Appellate Body said:

> [T]he arbitrary or unjustifiable character of differences in levels of protection . . . may in practical effect operate as a 'warning' signal that the implementing measure in its application might be a discriminatory measure or might be a restriction on international trade disguised as an SPS measure for the protection of human life or health.

See also Appellate Body Report, *Australia – Salmon*, paras 161–164; Panel Report, *Australia – Salmon (Article 21.5 – Canada)*, para. 158).

129. Scott, above n. 52, 36.
130. Appellate Body Report, *US – Gambling*, paras 309, 310, 320.
131. Appellate Body Report, *Australia – Salmon*, para. 199; Appellate Body Report, *EC – Asbestos*, para. 168; Appellate Body Report, *Brazil – Retreaded Tyres*, para. 140. Scott, above n. 52, 160 argues to the contrary, suggesting that the prerogative 'is sacrosanct only in the case of particularly important or vital interests, such as human life or health'. If so, this raises the difficult question for WTO tribunals of distinguishing between important and less-important interests.

    A related question here is the operation of Art. 5.5 SPS Agreement, which forbids 'arbitrary or unjustifiable distinctions' in the ALOP that lead to 'discrimination or a disguised restriction on international trade'. The Article is thus a safeguard against the use of a strict ALOP to discriminate against international trade. This Article raises different issues of deference for a WTO tribunal, namely, the extent to which it should defer to domestic opinions about what are 'arbitrary or unjustifiable distinctions'. Matsushita, Schoenbaum & Mavroidis, above n. 24, 531, point out that in *EC – Asbestos*, the strict French health protection ALOP for asbestos was much higher than that for cigarettes. Article 5.5 SPS Agreement was not an issue for the Appellate Body in that case. However, it seems likely that a WTO tribunal would defer to the domestic judgment that asbestos and cigarettes were not comparable, and would hold the distinction between the respective ALOPs as not being 'arbitrary or unjustifiable'.
132. Appellate Body Report, *Australia – Salmon*, para. 102, quoting Panel Report, para. 8.18.
133. *Ibid.*, para. 197, quoting Panel Report, para. 8.107.
134. Panel Report, *Australia – Salmon*, paras 8.173 and 8.175.
135. Appellate Body Report, *Australia – Salmon*, para. 198, quoting Panel Report, para. 8.172.
136. *Ibid.*, para. 190.

Appellate Body held that Australia had a prerogative to choose its desired level of protection and refused to allow the Panel to substitute its own reasoning about the level of protection implied in an impugned measure.[137] However, if Australia had failed to state an ALOP, the Panel could have worked out an ALOP by itself through inference from the content of the challenged legislation.[138]

One can find several examples of cases where the ALOP limitation has increased deference during a WTO tribunal's optimality analysis. The most obvious examples occur under Article 5.6 of the SPS Agreement, which expressly requires a proposed alternative measure to achieve the legislating State's 'desired level of protection'. Generally speaking, WTO tribunals have required clear evidence that an alternative measure will achieve a desired level of SPS protection.[139] One can also see this under general exceptions provisions. For example, in *EC – Asbestos*, France set a very high level of health protection with respect to asbestos exposure, namely, to 'halt' the spread of asbestos-related health risks.[140] Its challenged legislation banned certain forms of asbestos but allowed the use of certain other fibres that might also pose health risks. Canada argued that a reasonable alternative measure would be the controlled use of asbestos. The Panel disagreed, noting unclear scientific evidence as to the health effects of such controlled use, with particular doubts about health effects on do-it-yourself enthusiasts and in the building industry.[141] This conclusion was not affected by the permitted use of alternative fibres. The Appellate Body took a deferential approach to the European Communities' ALOP, holding that it was 'perfectly legitimate for a Member to seek to halt the spread of a highly risky product while allowing the use of a less risky product in its place'.[142]

The need for a proposed alternative measure to be effective in achieving the ALOP also protects the legislating State from vague or uncertain alternatives. In *US – Gambling*, the United States restricted access to its gambling markets for online betting providers, with a view to preventing crime and underage and pathological gambling. The Panel found that a reasonable alternative measure would have been for the United States to engage in international consultations to achieve

137. *Ibid.*, para. 199; see also Appellate Body Report, *EC – Asbestos*, para. 168. In the final result in *Australia – Salmon*, the Appellate Body held that the level of protection inherent in the import prohibition was higher than Australia's chosen level of protection, and was therefore inconsistent with Art. 5.6 SPS Agreement.
138. Appellate Body Report, *Australia – Salmon*, para. 203; see also Appellate Body Report, *Korea – Various Measures on Beef*, para. 178. In theory, there is some incentive for legislating States to not state the ALOP, as an inferred ALOP from the contents of the challenged legislation will reinforce the optimality of those contents. However, more pragmatically, legislating States may prefer to prevent WTO tribunals from any kind of decision-making about the ALOP: Scott, above n. 52, 38–39.
139. Appellate Body Report, *Australia – Salmon*, paras 210, 242; Panel Report, *Japan – Agricultural Products II*, para. 8.83, 8.84.
140. Appellate Body Report, *EC – Asbestos*, para. 168.
141. *Ibid.*, para. 174, quoting Panel Report, *EC – Asbestos*, para. 8.209.
142. *Ibid.*, para. 168.

these goals.[143] However, the Appellate Body disagreed, holding that such consultations 'are by definition a process, the results of which are uncertain and therefore not capable of comparison with the measures at issue in this case'.[144] Thus, a proposed alternative measure cannot be supported on the basis of a try-it-and-see approach; rather, an alternative must be demonstrably effective in achieving the ALOP.[145]

When WTO tribunals have found that a proposed alternative measure achieves the ALOP, they have been very cautious in doing so. They often prefer not to contradict the legislating State directly, but rather base their findings on evidence provided by the legislating State itself. For example, in identifying alternatives to the dual retailing system challenged in *Korea – Various Measures on Beef*, the Panel pointed out that 'Korea, in the past, had been able to distinguish imported beef from domestic beef, and had, in fact, published figures on the amount of imported beef fraudulently sold as domestic beef'.[146] Furthermore, Korea did not apply a dual retail system to related product areas or to sale through restaurants (which accounted for about 45% of all beef imports).[147] Similarly, in *Turkey – Textiles*, the Appellate Body found an alternative to Turkey's quantitative restrictions, in the form of rules of origin, noting that Turkey had recognized the ability of such rules to deal with undesirable trade diversion.[148] Relying on domestic admissions and inconsistencies in this way is a useful method of avoiding direct conflict with domestic legislative inferences.

Nevertheless, one can find examples of direct conflict with domestic legislative inferences, leading to a striking lack of deference. In *Japan – Apples (Article 21.5 – US)*, Japan had created a number of restrictions on imports of apples, with a view to preventing the entry of the fire blight disease and damage to its apple industry. It set a strict ALOP, namely, the level of protection equivalent

143. Panel Report, *US – Gambling*, para. 6.531.
144. Appellate Body Report, *US – Gambling*, para. 317.
145. Rather different results appeared in analogous cases concerning the *chapeau* to a general exception provision. In *US – Gasoline*, the Appellate Body found a breach of Art. XX chapeau GATT, in part because the United States could have been able to verify foreign data through cooperative arrangements with foreign governments. The Appellate Body said that the United States 'had not pursued the possibility of entering into cooperative arrangements with the governments of Venezuela and Brazil or, if it had, not to the point where it encountered governments that were unwilling to cooperate' (Appellate Body Report, *US – Gasoline*, text at fn. 51). In *US – Shrimp*, the Appellate Body again found a breach of this chapeau, in part because the United States had failed to engage in sufficient international negotiations to achieve its goal of turtle protection. These two decisions did not discuss the ALOP concept. This may indicate that optimality analysis is more intense under such a chapeau. Alternatively, it may indicate that a chapeau to a general exception provision does not require a proportionality analysis (see above, n. 22).
146. This was the Appellate Body's summary of the Panel's finding here: Appellate Body Report, *Korea – Various Measures on Beef*, para. 179, noting Panel Report, *Korea – Various Measures on Beef*, para. 668.
147. Appellate Body Report, *Korea – Various Measures on Beef*, para. 168, noting Panel Report, *Korea – Various Measures on Beef*, paras 659–663.
148. Appellate Body Report, *Turkey – Textiles*, para. 62.

to a ban on importation of commercial apples.[149] However, according to the Panel, scientific evidence suggested that mature, symptom-free apples would not spread fire blight.[150] The United States argued that its domestic procedures to export only mature and symptom-free apples would achieve Japan's ALOP.[151] Japan nevertheless had concerns about regulatory failures in US procedures that would allow imports of other, riskier, apples. The Panel held Japan's measure to be in breach of Article 5.6 of the SPS Agreement. It refused to defer to Japan's concerns about US regulatory failure, pointing out that there was no relevant evidence of such failure in the past.[152] Furthermore, the Panel held that the chance of such failure, if it did occur, would be 'unlikely' to spread fire blight.[153] The Panel conceded that if Japan failed to receive sufficient guarantees as to compliance with US procedures, the US proposal would not achieve Japan's ALOP. However, the Panel played this down, saying that this was merely a matter of 'controls necessary to enforce the requirement'.[154] Presumably, Japan was free to legislate ways to achieve sufficient control, but it could not ban imports of any class of US mature, symptom-free apples. This finding is rather striking, as the Panel effectively placed the burden of proof on Japan to produce hard evidence about the likelihood of US regulatory failure.

Also striking is the result in *Australia – Salmon (Article 21.5 – Canada)*.[155] There, Australian laws prevented salmon products from being released from quarantine unless they were 'consumer-ready'. For particular classes of fish to be 'consumer-ready', certain parts of the fish (such as the skin, fins, belly flap or certain bones) needed to be removed. Australia said that this was needed to deal with 'the pest/disease risk presented by the creation of substantial concentrations of waste material (skin, fins, flaps, bones, etc.) from commercial processing of imported salmon'.[156] Australia set its ALOP at 'a high or very conservative level of protection aimed at reducing risk to very low levels, while not based on a zero-risk approach'.[157] The Panel held the laws to be inconsistent with Article 5.6 of the SPS Agreement. It noted that the experts advising it could not find a justification for the 'consumer-ready' requirement in Australia's risk assessment for the measure.[158] Thus, the Panel held that 'it may be that not imposing consumer-ready requirements at all would also meet Australia's ALOP'.[159] The Panel found two alternative measures to be attractive: individually wrapping the fish to deter

149. Panel Report, *Japan – Apples (Article 21.5 – US)*, para. 8.193.
150. *Ibid.*, para. 8.194.
151. *Ibid.*
152. *Ibid.*, para. 8.178. Although there was evidence of US regulatory failures in allowing coddling moth in shipments into Taiwan, the Panel found that this was not persuasive because of the greater obviousness of symptoms of infection of fire blight as opposed to coddling moth.
153. Panel Report, *Japan – Apples (Article 21.5 – US)*, para. 8.179.
154. *Ibid.*, para. 8.195.
155. Panel Report, *Australia – Salmon (Article 21.5 – Canada)*.
156. *Ibid.*, para. 7.133.
157. *Ibid.*, para. 7.129.
158. *Ibid.*, para. 7.135.
159. *Ibid.*, para. 7.137.

commercial processing (as was done in New Zealand), and issuing import permits with specific end-use requirements to prevent such processing. A curious conclusion followed:

> We referred above to several options without deciding that one of these would necessarily meet Australia's ALOP. We have been convinced, however, that there are other measures available, be it the options discussed above taken separately or a combination thereof, that would meet Australia's ALOP. We leave it up to Australia, preferably in close cooperation with Canada and other trading partners, to select and identify the details of such other measure(s).[160]

It is not clear here whether the Panel actually made a finding that the two proposed alternative measures would actually achieve Australia's ALOP. If no such finding had been made, the Panel would be in error, as inconsistency with Article 5.6 of the SPS Agreement is predicated on such a finding. The Panel did note as follows in relation to the proposal for end-use requirements:

> [T]o avoid the imposition of costly and technically difficult control measures to fully ensure appropriate end-use, this alternative could be combined with other measures that, in combination, would meet Australia's ALOP.[161]

Even here, the Panel did not specify which exact alternative measure would achieve Australia's ALOP. As such, the Panel's reasoning is unsatisfactory. If a WTO tribunal does not defer to a legislative view on how to achieve the ALOP, it must state exactly its reasons for doing so.

Australia – Salmon (*Article 21.5 – Canada*) may nevertheless be seen as a clear but gentle prod at the domestic legislature. The Panel did not require a fundamental recasting of the quarantine restrictions, but rather pointed out ways in which they could be made more WTO-consistent – expressly leaving it to Australia to work out the details of doing so.[162] Such encouragement for incremental improvement rather than radical change is a feature of many WTO cases. For example, in *US – Shrimp*, the implied alternative measures were not an overturning of the import prohibitions, but rather a refining of the exceptions to those prohibitions (in the form of more flexible and transparent administrative procedures).[163] Similarly, in *EC – Tariff Preferences*, the Appellate Body did not criticize the challenged

---

160. *Ibid.*, para. 7.144.
161. *Ibid.*, para. 7.148.
162. One might view *Japan – Apples* (*Article 21.5 – US*) and *Australia – Salmon* (*Article 21.5 – Canada*) as examples of *procedural* rather than *substantive* deference. As discussed earlier (see Section 3.3.2), WTO tribunals can express deference in the *remedy* they provide, by building in considerable domestic discretion as to the details of any resulting legislative amendments. From this standpoint, the Panel in *Japan – Apples* (*Article 21.5 – US*) may have allowed Japan considerable discretion in designing measures to guarantee US regulatory compliance, and the Panel in *Australia – Salmon* (*Article 21.5 – Canada*) may have allowed Australia considerable discretion in combining aspects of the various alternative measures proposed in the case.
163. Appellate Body Report, *US – Shrimp*, paras 180–183.

preferences as a whole, but merely pointed out that qualifications for such preferences should be subject to objective criteria.[164] In all of these cases, such gentle refinements were unlikely to affect the ability of the challenged legislation to achieve the relevant ALOP. In the case of *Australia – Salmon (Article 21.5)*, however, the Panel's admirable tact was not backed up by a rigorous statement of its optimality analysis.

7.5. CONCLUDING REMARKS

WTO tribunals are generally respectful of domestic legislative decisions about proportionality. They are very unlikely to find a lack of balance in legislative purpose (although there are exceptional cases in which they will find that a legislative purpose itself is not appropriate). Similarly, they are unlikely to find that legislation is ineffective. The real battlefield of any WTO proportionality dispute is in the analysis of optimality. Here, WTO tribunals also show considerable deference to the legislature and avoid direct conflict wherever possible. In identifying reasonable alternative measures, they prefer to point out domestic contradictions rather than rely on their own independent judgment (or even the judgment of independent experts). Such alternative measures may be modest adjustments to legislation, rather than radical changes.

Nevertheless, there are some striking examples of Panel decisions that take on a domestic legislature directly, showing a striking lack of substantive deference to domestic inferences. The Panel decisions in *Japan – Apples (Article 21.5 – US)* and *Australia – Salmon (Article 21.5 – Canada)* indicate that the WTO system sometimes deviates from its usual moderate approach to deference in proportionality characterization.[165]

Before concluding this chapter, let us consider one more Appellate Body decision, which raises characterization issues of a very special character. In *US – Gambling*, various US statutes prohibited the provision of certain gambling services to the US market, in breach of Articles XVI(2)(a) and XVI(2)(c) of the GATS.[166] However, the Appellate Body held that they fell within the public morality exception in Article XIV(a) of the GATS, on the basis that they were necessary to prevent money laundering, fraud, and compulsive and under-aged

---

164. Appellate Body Report, *EC – Tariff Preferences*, para. 183.

165. Both cases must be seen in the context of declining procedural deference in WTO challenges to legislation. WTO tribunals are careful to make allowances for their impressive – and recently won – procedural advantages, both in terms of jurisdiction and remedy. In my view, in the current state of WTO development, deference in the substantive aspects of challenges to legislation needs to correspond to such procedural advantages – and particularly so in the case of proportionality characterization, where legislative inferences come under direct judicial scrutiny. Combining low procedural deference with low substantive deference may create systemic tensions that are dangerous in the early stages of the WTO system. Admittedly, such policy views lie outside the descriptive nature of this book.

166. Appellate Body Report, *US – Gambling*, para. 265.

gambling.[167] The case then turned on whether the United States could establish that the statutes were consistent with the chapeau to Article XIV, that is, that they did not create arbitrary and unjustifiable discrimination between US and foreign service suppliers. Antigua argued, with partial success, that the statutes were applied in the US legal system in a way that allowed some US service suppliers access to the US market.[168] It said that an alternative measure was available (i.e., the prohibition of market access for both foreign and domestic suppliers). As an example of proportionality review, this was an unremarkable example of the application of the optimality concept.[169] What is striking here is the nature of the evidence raised by Antigua, namely, the operation of the US legal system. Evidence about the operation of the domestic legal system raises special issues of deference for WTO tribunals. How intensively do they review the operation of a domestic legislative environment?

US – Gambling raises particular issues that cannot be dealt with by pure factor characterization or proportionality characterization. The question of the operation of a domestic legislative environment in relation to challenged legislation deserves special consideration. This is the focus of the next chapter.

167. *Ibid.*, para. 327.
168. *Ibid.*, para. 357, 364. See also Panel Report, *Brazil – Retreaded Tyres*, para. 7.243, where the Panel held that domestic court injunctions allowing domestic tyre retreaders to import used tyres for retreading discriminated against imported retreaded tyres in favour of domestic retreaded tyres.
169. However, there is some debate about whether the chapeaus to general exception provisions such as Art. XIV GATS truly involve a proportionality analysis: see above n. 22.

Chapter 8
Substantive Deference: Certainty Characterization

8.1. INTRODUCTION

This chapter deals with challenges to the certainty of legislation. Legislation often has uncertain effects, either because it is inherently ambiguous, or because it confers wide administrative discretion. In certainty characterization, the challenging State claims that this uncertainty is in itself a breach of an international obligation. The legislating State usually claims that the legislation will be administered consistently with international law. The challenging State replies that the likelihood of this happening is low, or that the lack of clarity is in itself deterring its nationals from taking advantage of benefits conferred by the international obligation. In the WTO, this argument has been called the 'chilling effect' of uncertain legislation on international trade.[1]

Certainty characterization arises from the nature of legislation. Unlike administrative action, legislation is generalized and abstract in nature; it need not have identifiable consequences in particular cases. Legislation sets up broad rules that may allow for some flexibility in implementation, and it may have an unpredictable operation. Certainty characterization is a challenge to this lack of predictability. Thus, certainty characterization is peculiar to challenges to legislation, so there are few, if any, examples of certainty characterization of administrative action.

Certainty characterization often has a particular political background. It often occurs when a domestic interest group has lost a debate at the international level but tries to regain ground through the drafting of domestic legislation. The result is unclear legislation that tries to reconcile the international obligation with the desires of the interest group. The interest group then lobbies to exploit the

1. Panel Report, *US – Section 301 Trade Act*, paras 7.81–7.92.

uncertainty in its favour. Naturally, this meets resistance from the 'winners' at the international level, who may encourage an international challenge to the legislation because of its uncertain effects.

The central issue in certainty characterization is the degree of deference given to the legislating State's assessment of how the legislation works. As noted earlier,[2] international tribunals treat domestic legislation as fact, rather than as law. In other words, domestic legislation is generally characterized de facto in its legislative environment and surrounding factual matrix, rather than de jure on its face alone. International courts try to avoid the appearance of making binding interpretations of domestic law.[3] Nevertheless, they need to do so with appropriate deference to local legal expertise. The deference issue involves a cluster of sub-questions. How can international tribunals make an independent review of the effect of domestic legislation? Should such tribunals accept domestic assurances that unclear legislation will be applied in a particular way? Does it matter whether those assurances come from the judiciary, the legislature, or the executive?

In previous times, these questions were suppressed by a high degree of jurisdictional deference on the part of international tribunals. Such tribunals often simply refused to entertain challenges to uncertain legislation. Instead, they deferred consideration of the challenge until the legislation had been actually implemented (hoping, perhaps, that the underlying political conflict would have dissipated by this stage). This approach was reflected in the old GATT system via the procedural device known as the 'mandatory/discretionary distinction'. Only mandatory legislation could be challenged before a GATT Panel; legislation that contained discretionary elements could not. The degree of procedural deference to domestic administrative decision-making was therefore total.

Yet, as we have already seen in previous chapters, this jurisdictional deference is waning in international challenges to legislation. We have also seen that there has been considerable substantive deference in factor characterization and proportionality characterization in WTO challenges to legislation (although there are also several 'outrider' cases involving a more intrusive approach). So far as the WTO is concerned, the mandatory/discretionary distinction has now been abandoned as a procedural rule; it is now considered to be merely an *analytical tool*. Thus, WTO tribunals are not allowed to adopt a wait-and-see approach to uncertain legislation. They must consider whether such legislation is, in the abstract, consistent with WTO obligations. This has led to a surge in cases of certainty characterization before WTO tribunals.

2. See Section 4.2, text at n. 30.
3. Appellate Body Report, *India – Patents (US)*, para. 66; Appellate Body Report, *US – Section 211 Appropriations Act*, para. 105. See also for the ECtHR, *Malone v. The United Kingdom*, 2 Aug. 1984, Series A, No. 82, para. 79.

8.2. THE CONCEPT OF CERTAINTY

The concept of certainty is shared by many legal systems. It can be seen in private and public law settings in both common law and civil law jurisdictions.[4] In particular, public law in many countries requires legislation to reach minimum standards of certainty in its operation.[5] The concept of certainty can be seen as an element of the rule of law.

Yet, the concept of certainty is a complex one, comprised of several elements and operating interdependently with several other basic legal principles. Keeping in mind the risk of oversimplification, these can be set out as follows:

- Law must be published.
- Law must be stable and not changed too frequently.
- Law must be clear enough to be comprehensible.
- The operation of law must be foreseeable.
- Retrospective law is to be discouraged.
- Some matters must be regulated by law, rather than by practice.[6]

These principles can apply both in domestic constitutional law and in international law, as can be demonstrated by a brief description of the operation of the certainty

---

4. For example, the common law prohibits overly vague terms of contracts and trusts: N. Seddon & M. Ellinghaus, *Cheshire & Fifoot's Law of Contract*, 7th Australian edn (Sydney: Butterworths, 1997), Ch. 6.
5. E. Hammer-Strnad, *Das Bestimmtheitsgebot als allgemeiner Rechtsgrundsatz des Europäischen Gemeinschaftsrechts* (Hamburg: Verlag Dr. Kovač, 1999). Hammer-Strnad has made a comparative study of the requirement for certainty in legislation in Germany, Austria, France, the United Kingdom and in the European human rights system. She identified Germany as the jurisdiction with the most-developed requirement here (see Ch. 4 of her book).
6. This list can be seen in various guises in legal literature. Most notably in the common law world, see L. Fuller, *The Morality of Law* (New Haven: Yale University Press, 1973), 262. More recent discussions in English can be found in J. Maxeiner, 'Legal Certainty: A European Alternative to American Legal Indeterminacy', *Tul. J. Int'l. & Comp. Law* 15 (2006–2007): 541 and P. Popelier, 'Legal Certainty and Principles of Proper Law Making', *EU Journal of Law Reform* 2 (2000): 321.

   The matters in this list also appear in civil law literature in Germany. The German requirement for legal certainty (*Bestimmtheitsgebot*) is supported by principles such as clarity of law (*Rechtsklarheit*), dependability (*Beständigkeit*) and the matters reserved to law (*Vorbehalt des Gesetzes*) (Sachs, Art. 20, in M. Sachs (ed.), *Grundgesetz*, 3rd edn (München: CH Beck, 2003), 848, para. 122; C. Münch, 'Rechtssicherheit als Standortfaktor', *NJW* 50 (1996): 3320, 3321). The first two principles require, respectively, availability and comprehensibility of law and the stability of law (Sachs, 848–857, paras 122–144). They discourage retrospective laws (*BVerfGE* 45, 142 (167) – *Rückwirkende Verordnungen*; P. Kunig, *Das Rechtsstaatsprinzip* (Tübingen: Mohr, 1986), 193 et seq.; K. Sobota, *Das Prinzip Rechtsstaat* (Jena: Mohr, 1997), 130) and impose a requirement of forseeability of operation (e.g., *BVerfGE* 45, 142 (167) – *Rückwirkende Verordnungen*; *BVerfGE* 83, 130 (145) – *Josephine Mutzenbacher*; Sachs, 850, para. 126). The third principle, the *Vorbehalt des Gesetzes*, requires that certain important matters – in particular the restriction of human rights – be regulated by law, rather than by executive action (*BVerfGE* 49, 89 (133) – *Kalkar I*).

principle in the constitutional law of Germany and in the jurisprudence of the European Court of Human Rights (ECtHR).

8.2.1. The German *Bestimmtheitsgebot*

The German requirement for legal certainty in legislation is known as the *Bestimmtheitsgebot*.[7] German legislation is required to be expressed as exactly as possible according to the particular qualities of the area of life being regulated and with regard to the purpose of the legislative norm.[8] The *Bestimmtheitsgebot* does not prevent the use of very broadly phrased rules (*Generalklausel*),[9] or unclear legal concepts.[10] Nor does it forbid the conferral of administrative discretions, if such discretions can be reviewed judicially.[11] The German Federal Constitutional Court has said that 'The certainty requirement is met if problems with interpretation can be overcome with conventional juristic methods.'[12]

The Federal Constitutional Court views its own and other courts' jurisprudence as a method for improving the certainty of legislation, especially in cases in which a low degree of certainty is required.[13]

The requirements of the *Bestimmtheitsgebot* vary from case to case. The Federal Constitutional Court described these requirements as follows:

> Concerning the question of which requirements for certainty have to be met in the particular case, one needs to take account of the particularities of the relevant area of regulation as well as the intensity of regulation.... There

7. The German federal constitution (*Grundgesetz*) provides a limited express basis for the *Bestimmtheitsgebot*. Article 80 I *Grundgesetz* requires subordinate legislation to attain a degree of certainty; its enabling statute must state its content, purpose, and scope. Article 103 II *Grundgesetz* requires certainty in the criminal law; it prevents people from being punished for actions done at a time before the criminality of the action was determined by statute. Furthermore, many of the basic human rights (*Grundrechte*, or basic rights) set out in the *Grundgesetz* can only be limited as determined by law. For example, the content and limits to the rights to property are to be determined by law: Art. 14 I *Grundgesetz*. This express constitutional basis of the *Bestimmtheitsgebot* needs to be supported by fundamental constitutional doctrine (H. Papier & J. Möller, 'Das Bestimmtheitsgebot und seine Durchsetzung', *AöR* 122 (1997): 177, 178).
8. Hammer-Strnad, above n. 5, 93. This is my broad translation of a phrase from *BVerfGE* 48, 210 (222).
9. For example, *BVerfGE* 90, 1 (16).
10. Hammer-Strnad, above n. 5, 93.
11. *Ibid.*, quoting *BVerfGE* 6, 32 (42); 8, 274 (327); 21, 73 (78); 22, 330 (345); 34, 165 (193); 46, 120 (157); 49, 89 (145).
12. *BVerfGE* 90, 1 (16) – *Jugendgefährdende Schriften*:

    > Dem Bestimmtheitserfordernis ist genügt, wenn Auslegungsprobleme mit herkömmlichen juristischen Methoden bewältigt werden können.

13. Hammer-Strnad, above n. 5, 106, quoting *BVerfGE* 49, 168 (180).

> are lesser requirements for complex situations . . . or when one expects that the factual conditions will change quickly.[14]

For example, the regulation of technical, scientific, and economic matters may require a flexible approach.[15] In areas that are relatively simple and easy to oversee, the requirement for certainty increases.[16] The *Bestimmtheitsgebot* also becomes more intense when complexity can obviously be avoided, for example, when a law is internally inconsistent or absurd.[17] This intensity also increases for significant areas of regulation, in particular, interferences with basic rights.[18]

8.2.2. The Requirement for Certainty Applied by the ECtHR

The requirement for legal certainty is now part of the settled jurisprudence of the ECtHR.[19] This requirement is part of the more general rule that limitations of certain rights are to be in accordance with 'law'. The European Convention on Human Rights (ECHR) provides that some rights can be limited by national legislation, but only if this is done 'in accordance with the law'.[20] From this textual basis in the ECHR, the ECtHR has built up a sophisticated definition of *law*,

---

14. *BVerfGE* 49, 89 (133) – *Kalkar I*:

    > Bei der Frage, welche Bestimmtheitsanforderungen im einzelnen erfüllt sein müssen, sind die Besonderheiten des jeweiligen Regelungsgegenstandes sowie die Regelungsintensität zu berücksichtigen . . . Geringere Anforderungen sind vor allem bei vielgestaltigen Sachverhalten zu stellen . . . oder wenn zu erwarten ist, daß sich die tatsächlichen Verhältnisse rasch ändern werden.

15. For example, *BVerfGE* 58, 257 (277) – *Schulentlassung*. See also Sobota, above n. 6, 135 (critical view); Hammer-Strnad, above n. 5, 94. In the taxation area, the *Bestimmtheitsgebot* merely requires that the taxpayer be able to calculate his liability in advance; Hammer-Strnad, above n. 5, 95, quoting *BVerfGE* 19, 253 (267); 34, 358 (366).
16. Hammer-Strnad, above n. 5, 94–95.
17. *BVerfGE* 1, 14 – *Südweststaat* (head note 14):

    > Wenn die Fassung eines Gesetzes seinen wirklichen Gehalt nicht zum Ausdruch bringt, wenn sie missverständlich oder irreführend ist, oder wenn das Gesetz in sich widerspruchsvoll ist, kann es wegen Widerspruchs mit den Grundsätzen des Rechtsstaates nichtig sein.

    > If the wording of legislation does not express its actual content, if it is apt to lead to misunderstandings or is misleading, or if the legislation is internally inconsistent, it can be void because of inconsistency with the principles of the rule of law.

18. For example, *BVerfGE* 83, 130 (145) – *Josephine Mutzenbacher*.
19. See especially Hammer-Strnad, above n. 5. Also, see J. Meyer-Ladewig, *Konvention zum Schutz der Menschenrechte und Grundfreiheiten* (Baden-Baden: Nomos, 2003), 149 et seq.; A. Peters, *Einführung in die Europäische Menschenrechtskonvention* (München: CH Beck, 2003), 22.
20. See Arts 8–11 ECHR. Sometimes this phrase is slightly different, that is 'prescribed by law', but this difference is insignificant.

involving a requirement for legal certainty, stated in *Sunday Times v. The United Kingdom:*

> In the Court's opinion, the following are two of the requirements that flow from the expression 'prescribed by law'. Firstly, the law must be adequately accessible: the citizen must be able to have an indication that is adequate in the circumstances of the legal rules applicable to a given case. Secondly, a norm cannot be regarded as a 'law' unless it is formulated with sufficient precision to enable the citizen to regulate his conduct: he must be able – if need be with appropriate advice – to foresee, to a degree that is reasonable in the circumstances, the consequences which a given action may entail.[21]

The dual requirements for accessibility and sufficient precision, therefore, are the basic content of the requirement for legal certainty under the ECHR. The requirement of precision can also be expressed as the requirement for forseeability. The ECtHR and many commentators[22] have tended to focus on the concept of forseeability as the cornerstone of the ECHR requirement for legal certainty.

The *Sunday Times v. The United Kingdom* statement of the requirement for legal certainty was applied in a dramatic way in the 1984 case of *Malone v. The United Kingdom.*[23] This case dealt with UK rules on surveillance. At the time, those rules had a rather fuzzy legal basis, being sourced in a mix of pure executive power, widely phrased statutory rules, and statements of administrative principles. The ECtHR ruled that the requirement for 'law' related to the quality of the relevant law and that the system of surveillance had to be 'compatible with the rule of law'.[24] The ECtHR also argued that arbitrariness in such a system would be incompatible with the rule of law: 'there must be a measure of legal protection in domestic law against arbitrary interferences by public authorities with the rights safeguarded by paragraph 1 (Article 8-1)'.[25]

The ECtHR concluded that the UK system of surveillance was not in accordance with 'law', and that, therefore, the UK had breached the ECHR.[26]

The passage quoted above from *Sunday Times v. The United Kingdom* also highlights some limits to the ECHR requirement for legal certainty; forseeability only has to be 'reasonable in the circumstances', and might require a citizen to get 'appropriate advice'. Absolute certainty in law is not required. In *Sunday Times v. The United Kingdom*, the ECtHR said:

> Those consequences [of a measure] need not be foreseeable with absolute certainty: experience shows this to be unattainable. Again, whilst certainty

21. *Sunday Times v. The United Kingdom,* 25 Mar. 1983, Series A, No. 30, para. 49; *Silver v. The United Kingdom*, 25 Mar. 1983, Series A No. 61, paras 87 and 88.
22. For example, Meyer-Ladewig, above n. 19, 149; Peters above n. 19, 22.
23. *Malone v. The United Kingdom*, 2 Aug. 1984, Series A, No. 82.
24. *Ibid.*, para. 67.
25. *Ibid.*
26. *Ibid.*, para. 80.

> is highly desirable, it may bring in its train excessive rigidity and the law must be able to keep pace with changing circumstances. Accordingly, many laws are inevitably couched in terms which, to a greater or lesser extent, are vague and whose interpretation and application are questions of practice.[27]

The Court's recognition that 'absolute certainty' in legislation is unattainable has led it into an analysis of the appropriate degree of flexibility in legislation.

The ECtHR has given some useful guidelines as to the degree of flexibility allowed by the ECHR requirement for legal certainty. In *Malone v. The United Kingdom*, the ECtHR held that '[t]he degree of precision required of the "law" in this connection will depend upon the particular subject-matter'.[28] In *Klass v. Germany*, the ECtHR set forth a list of relevant factors:

> The Court must be satisfied that, whatever system of surveillance is adopted, there exist adequate and effective guarantees against abuse. This assessment has only a relative character: it depends on all the circumstances of the case, such as the nature, scope and duration of the possible measures, the grounds required for ordering such measures, the authorities competent to permit, carry out and supervise such measures, and the kind of remedy provided by the national law.[29]

The Court added to these factors in *Vogt v. Germany*:

> [T]he level of precision required of domestic legislation – which cannot in any case provide for every eventuality – depends to a considerable degree on the content of the instrument in question, the field it is designed to cover and the number and status of those to whom it is addressed.[30]

The factor of the place of particular rules in a domestic legal hierarchy was addressed in *Rekvényi v. Hungary*.[31] In this case, provisions of the Hungarian Constitution were at issue. The provisions prevented members of the police from joining any political party or from engaging in any political activity. However, Hungarian legislation allowed some political activities by police in limited circumstances. The claimant, a policeman and a member of a police trade union, alleged that the constitutional provisions infringed upon his rights of freedom of expression and freedom of association. Hungary argued in the following way:

> [I]n the Hungarian legal system it was the practice that certain provisions of the Constitution could properly be interpreted only if read together with legislation of a lower level completing and explaining their precise content. Contemporary legislative techniques often left it to laws lower in the hierarchy

27. *Sunday Times v. The United Kingdom*, 25 Mar. 1983, Series A, No. 30, para. 49.
28. *Malone v. The United Kingdom*, 2 Aug. 1984, Series A, No. 82, para. 68.
29. *Klass v. Germany*, 6 Sep. 1978, Series A, No. 28, para. 50.
30. *Vogt v. Germany*, 26 Sep. 1995, Series A, No. 323, para. 48.
31. *Rekvényi v. Hungary*, GC, No. 25390/94, ECHR 1999-III.

> to define general notions used in higher laws – a law-making method not uncommon at least in continental legal systems and never in principle disapproved by the Convention organs.[32]

Perhaps unsurprisingly, the ECtHR refused to find the lack of detail in the Hungarian Constitution to be inconsistent with the ECHR: 'Because of the general nature of constitutional provisions, the level of precision required of them may be lower than for other legislation.'[33]

This may indicate that the Court more or less accepted the Hungarian argument and, by implication, that it accepted a principle that the higher the level a law occupies in a legal hierarchy, the less there is of a need for it to have a precise content.[34]

Another aspect of the 'appropriate flexibility' issue is how the ECtHR views the role of domestic courts in providing forseeability in the operation of domestic legislation. In *Rekvényi v. Hungary*, the ECtHR expressly acknowledged the role of domestic courts in providing such forseeability:

> [M]any laws are inevitably couched in terms which, to a greater or lesser extent, are vague and whose interpretation and application are questions of practice . . . The role of adjudication vested in the courts is precisely to dissipate such interpretational doubts as remain.[35]

An example of the ability of domestic courts to provide legal certainty to vague legislation arose in *Kokkinakis v. Greece*.[36] Kokkinakis, a Jehovah's Witness, was convicted under Greek legislation that created the crime of 'proselytizing'. This legislation was aimed at protecting Greek Orthodox believers from the missionary attempts of other religions. The ECtHR refused to find the legislation inconsistent with the ECHR, holding that the general practice built up around the legislative provision provided the necessary degree of forseeability.[37]

It is worth summarizing here the factors mentioned by the ECtHR in *Malone v. The United Kingdom*, *Klass v. Germany*, *Vogt v. Germany*, *Rekvényi v. Hungary*, and *Kokkinakis v. Greece*. The following list sets forth the factors that the ECtHR will take into account in applying the ECHR requirement for legal certainty in relation to domestic legislation:

- the nature and scope of the legislation and its content;
- the field the legislation is designed to cover;
- the duration of the legislation;
- the number of those to whom the legislation is addressed;
- the status of those to whom the legislation is addressed;

---

32. *Ibid.*, para. 29.
33. *Ibid.*, para. 34.
34. Meyer-Ladewig, above n. 19, 150, para. 38.
35. *Rekvényi v. Hungary*, GC, No. 25390/94, ECHR 1999-III, para. 34.
36. *Kokkinakis v. Greece*, 25 May 1993, ECHR, Series A, No. 260-A.
37. *Ibid*, para. 40. Nevertheless, on the facts of the case, Kokkinakis' conviction did violate the ECHR.

- the grounds for the legislation;
- the nature of the authorities competent to permit, carry out, and supervise the implementation of the legislation;
- the kind of relevant remedies provided for under national law;
- the level that the legislation occupies in the domestic legal hierarchy; and
- the degree to which domestic courts have created jurisprudence giving clearer meaning to broadly cast legislative rules.

Many of the themes developed in the previous discussion of the *Bestimmtheitsgebot* and the ECtHR's application of a certainty requirement also arise in WTO challenges to legislation. Of course, these themes have a particular character in the WTO, influenced by the nature and character of WTO rules. We now return to this subject.

8.3. CERTAINTY IN THE WTO

The concept of legal certainty has a strong basis in both the text of WTO rules and the jurisprudence of WTO tribunals. The textual basis for the concept is particularly visible in Article 3.2 of the Dispute Settlement Understanding (DSU), with its references to the need for 'security and predictability' in multilateral trade: 'The dispute settlement system of the WTO is a central element in providing security and predictability to the multilateral trading system.'

In *US – Corrosion-Resistant Steel Sunset Review*, the Appellate Body clarified that 'security and predictability' are concerns that extend beyond dispute settlement to the entirety of WTO rules, in the interests of future trade.[38]

Other WTO provisions draw on the concept of legal certainty in specific regulatory areas.[39] For example, Article X of the GATT provides guarantees against arbitrariness in the administration of legislation, through requirements

---

38. Appellate Body Report, *US – Corrosion-Resistant Steel Sunset Review*, para. 182:

 > [T]he disciplines of the GATT and the WTO, as well as the dispute settlement system, are intended to protect not only existing trade but also the security and predictability needed to conduct future trade.

39. For example, the reference in Art. VII(5) GATT to customs values being determined 'with a reasonable degree of certainty', echoed by the reference to 'certainty' in the Preamble to the WTO Customs Valuations Agreement. Other examples may include the following:

 > Article XIII(3)(b) GATT requires the publication of certain details of quantitative restrictions. In *US – Cotton Underwear*, Costa Rica argued that Article XIII(3)(b) GATT aims at achieving 'legal certainty and predictability' (Appellate Body Report, text at footnote 15). The Appellate Body did not comment on this argument.
 >
 > Article 13 TRIPS requires limitations or exceptions to exclusive rights to be confined to 'certain' special cases. The Panel in *US – Section 110 Copyright Act* thought that the word 'certain' meant that 'an exception or limitation in national legislation must be clearly defined', although 'there is no need to identify explicitly each and every possible situation to which the exception could apply, provided that the scope of the exception is known and particularised' (Panel Report, *US – Section 110 Copyright Act*, para. 6.108).

for publication and impartiality, as well as for independent processes for review of decisions.[40]

The need for security and predictability has also been a theme in several WTO cases dealing with matters such as tariff bindings,[41] the application of the Agreement on Agriculture,[42] risk assessments under the SPS Agreement[43] and trade remedies.[44] Many WTO members, including the United States,[45] the European Communities,[46] China,[47] Brazil[48] and Canada,[49] have used certainty-related arguments in WTO litigation. The security and predictability criterion has also been used as a requirement for certainty, for example, in *EC – Chicken Cuts*. In this case, the European Communities was bound by heading 02.10 of its GATT Schedule to provide a maximum 15.4% *ad valorem* tariff on salted meat. However, heading 02.07 allowed a heavier tariff of EUR 102.4/100 kg/net for fresh, chilled, or frozen poultry meat. EC legislation imposed the heavier tariff unless the meat was salted so as to ensure 'long-term preservation'.

In the course of its reasoning, the Appellate Body dealt with an argument that the criterion of 'preservation' was inherently uncertain. The Panel had found that this uncertainty could undermine the 'security and predictability' underlying the WTO system. The Appellate Body agreed:[50]

> [T]he security and predictability of 'the reciprocal and mutually advantageous arrangements directed to the substantial reduction of tariffs and other barriers

---

40. However, Art. X appears to have a limited operation, as the Appellate Body has held it to apply only to the *administration* of legislation, and not legislation *as such*: Appellate Body Report, *EC – Poultry*, para. 115; Appellate Body Report, *EC – Bananas III*, para. 200. In *EC – Selected Customs Matters*, para. 200, the Appellate Body noted that legislation could be challenged under Art. X(3)(a) GATT if it 'regulates the application or implementation' of another legal instrument. Presumably the other legal instrument should be of a higher level in the domestic legal hierarchy than the legislation under challenge.
41. Panel Report, *Argentina – Textiles and Apparel*, para. 6.68. In *EC – Computer Equipment*, the Panel used a similar principle to conclude that legitimate expectations were a vital element of tariff bindings: Panel Report, *EC – Computer Equipment*, paras 8.24–8.25. On appeal, the Appellate Body reversed the Panel's conclusion on legitimate expectations – but did not reject the underlying principle (see Appellate Body Report, *EC – Computer Equipment*, para. 82).
42. Appellate Body Report, *Chile – Price Band System*, para. 234; Panel Report, *Turkey – Rice*, para. 7.120.
43. In *Japan – Apples*, the Panel mentioned the possibility that the need under the SPS Agreement to consider alternative options under a risk assessment might create 'a problem of legal certainty for a Member performing risk assessments': Panel Report, *Japan – Apples*, para. 7.19. However, the Panel did not consider this issue further.
44. Appellate Body Report, *US – Corrosion-Resistant Steel Sunset Review*, para. 182.
45. Appellate Body Report, *India – Patents (US)*, para. 15.
46. GATT Panel Report, *EEC – Regulation on Imports of Parts and Components*, L/6657, adopted 16 May 1990, BISD 37S/132, para. 3.83; Panel Report, *US – Section 301 Trade Act*, para. 4.372; Panel Report, *US – 1916 Act (EC)*, para. 3.368.
47. Panel Report, *US – Steel Safeguards*, para. 7.1863.
48. Appellate Body Report, *EC – Poultry*, para. 16; Panel Report, *Mexico – Telecoms*, para. 5.16.
49. Appellate Body Report, *Canada – Patent Term*, para. 88.
50. Appellate Body Report, *EC – Chicken Cuts*, paras 249 and 347(b)(iii).

to trade' is an object and purpose of the WTO Agreement, generally, as well as of the GATT 1994.[51]

The uncertainty of the criterion of preservation arose because of the treatment of meat that was both frozen and salted. The EC assured the Appellate Body that frozen salted meat could take advantage of the lower tariff for salted meat.[52] However, the Appellate Body was not satisfied as to the legal certainty provided by this assurance.[53]

Despite these examples, one cannot conclude at this time that there is a general requirement for legal certainty in WTO members' domestic measures. Such requirements exist under particular WTO rules, but one cannot thereby infer a general WTO requirement for such certainty. The need for certainty must be examined on a provision-by-provision basis.

The earlier GATT system did not use this provision-by-provision approach. Instead, GATT tribunals traditionally used a bright-line rule based on a distinction between mandatory and discretionary legislation. Discretionary legislation was supposed not to be subject to challenge. However, the importance of the mandatory/discretionary rule has declined in recent Appellate Body decisions. It is unlikely to be applied as a rule in the future, but rather as merely an analytical tool.[54] We now discuss these matters in more detail.

8.3.1. The Mandatory/Discretionary Distinction and Its Recent Decline

The mandatory/discretionary distinction has its roots in the jurisprudence of Panels under the old GATT system. The history of the distinction in the GATT and the early days of the WTO have been described in detail by Bhuiyan, Kwan Kiat Sim and Naiki.[55] The distinction appears to have been grounded more in the practice of GATT Panels than on the text of the GATT itself. It is nevertheless related to a (now obsolete) grandfathering rule relating to mandatory legislation in existence before the GATT was established.[56]

---

51. *Ibid.*, para. 243, citing the Panel Report in that case at para. 7.318, which in turn quoted Appellate Body Report, *EC – Computer Equipment*, para. 82.
52. Appellate Body Report, *EC – Chicken Cuts*, para. 247.
53. *Ibid.*, para. 248. In the end, the Appellate Body, found (at para. 346) that this criterion for the lighter tariff was too strict, as 'salted' meat need not be 'preserved' meat – an example of de jure factor characterization.
54. See later in this section, text at n. 71.
55. See S. Bhuiyan, 'Mandatory and Discretionary Legislation: The Continued Relevance of the Distinction under the WTO', JIEL 5 (2002): 571; Kwan Kiat Sim, 'Rethinking the Mandatory/ Discretionary Legislation Distinction in WTO Jurisprudence', *World Trade Review* 2 (2003): 33; Y. Naiki, 'The Mandatory Discretionary Doctrine in WTO Law: The *US – Section 301* Case and Its Aftermath', JIEL 7 (2004): 23; S. Bhuiyan, *National Law in WTO Law* (Cambridge: Cambridge University Press, 2007), Ch. 8.
56. See Bhuiyan (2002), above n. 55; Kwan Kiat Sim, above n. 55; Naiki, above n. 55.

The GATT Panel in *US – Tobacco* described the mandatory/discretionary distinction as follows:

> [P]anels had consistently ruled that legislation which mandated action inconsistent with the General Agreement [i.e., the GATT] could be challenged as such, whereas legislation which merely gave the discretion to the executive authority of a contracting party to act inconsistently with the General Agreement could not be challenged as such; only the actual application of such legislation inconsistent with the General Agreement could be subject to challenge.[57] [footnotes omitted]

Thus, legislation was said to be challengeable only if it mandated a GATT-inconsistent outcome. Discretionary legislation was presumed to be implemented in a GATT-consistent way and was therefore unchallengeable.

One undoubted advantage of the mandatory/discretionary distinction was that it gave GATT Panels clear guidelines to as to the degree of deference to apply. Deference was virtually total if legislation was discretionary. Panels presumed that discretionary legislation would be applied consistently with the GATT.[58] This meant that if a Panel felt uncomfortable about holding that legislation was in itself GATT-inconsistent, it could instead focus on the application of the legislation. If the legislation had not yet been applied, the Panel could hold that it was discretionary in nature and therefore unjusticiable. The rule thus was a handy method for GATT Panels to express procedural deference.

A focus on the application of challenged legislation rather than the legislation itself meant that implementation of Panel decisions was often left to the executive branch of a GATT member. The legislature was not necessarily involved in the implementation process, provided that the relevant legislation contained suitable executive discretions. The mandatory/discretionary distinction was therefore a device for shifting the domestic pressure of GATT disputes from the legislature to the executive. The executive, it was felt, was often better able to negotiate the treacherous paths of a trade dispute than was the legislature.

Nevertheless, the mandatory/discretionary distinction has one fatal flaw as a rule. It is not mentioned in the text of the WTO Agreements.[59] Nevertheless, there are a number of provisions relevant to this distinction. Annex 1.1 to the Technical Barriers to Trade (TBT) Agreement, for example, defines a *technical regulation* to be a document 'with which compliance is mandatory'. This suggests that discretionary-type rules will not be regulated as technical regulations under the

---

57. GATT Panel Report, *United States – Measures Affecting the Importation, Internal Sale and Use of Tobacco*, DS44/R, adopted 4 Oct. 1994, BISD 41S/131, para. 88, quoted in Appellate Body Report, *US – 1916 Act*, para. 88.
58. See the GATT Panel Reports quoted in Appellate Body Report, *US – 1916 Act*, para. 88.
59. A provision of central importance to the mandatory/discretionary distinction is Art. XVI(4) WTO Agreement:

    > Each Member shall ensure the conformity of its *laws, regulations and administrative procedures* with its obligations as provided in the annexed Agreements [emphasis added].

TBT Agreement.[60] In general, however, the text of the WTO Agreements does not provide a clear basis for the mandatory/discretionary distinction to apply as a rule.

This lack of a textual basis has led to a decline of the distinction as a rule in the WTO dispute resolution system. The watershed decision was the Panel report in *US – Section 301 Trade Act*. In this case, the Panel found that it was possible in principle for discretionary legislation to breach WTO rules.[61] It held that this would be the case if the WTO rules in question prohibited the type of discretion contained in the legislation.[62] To discover whether this is the case, the WTO rules in question need to be considered closely, and individually, to see whether they prohibit some or all kinds of legislative discretions.[63]

Appellate Body comment has been sparse on this Article. In *US – 1916 Act*, the Appellate Body was given the opportunity to comment on the operation of Art. XVI(4), but declined. It did, however, uphold Panel findings in that case that US legislation was inconsistent with the Article (at para. 155). Similarly, in *India – Patents (US)*, the Appellate Body mentioned the Article, but did not give any guidance as to its meaning (at para. 79). In *US – Hot-Rolled Steel*, the Appellate Body confirmed that US legislation was not in conformity with the article, although it gave no analysis of the effect of Art. XVI(4) as such (Appellate Body Report, para. 240(c)). In Appellate Body Report, *EC – Sardines*, para. 213, the Appellate Body said that the Article provides 'general context for all the covered agreements [in WTO law]'.

60. The Appellate Body has found in two cases that measures were 'mandatory' and therefore able to be regulated as a technical regulation under the TBT Agreement (Appellate Body Report, *EC – Asbestos*, para. 73; Appellate Body Report, *EC – Sardines*, para 194).

Another relevant provision is Item 1 Illustrative List in the Agreement on Trade-Related Investment Measures (TRIMs):

> TRIMs that are inconsistent with the obligation of national treatment provided for in paragraph 4 of Article III of GATT 1994 include those which are *mandatory or enforceable under domestic law* or under administrative rulings, or compliance with which is necessary to obtain an advantage. [emphasis added].

The text of this provision clearly implies a distinction between 'mandatory' measures and 'enforceable' measures. Arguably, this distinction is similar to the mandatory/discretionary distinction. An 'enforceable' measure could be one that can be enforced at executive discretion. This conclusion gains some support from the reasoning of the Panel in *India – Autos*:

> It is notable in this respect that the more specific terms of [GATT] Article III(4) ('laws, regulations or requirements'), as noted in our analysis of the indigenization, has been broadly interpreted to cover measures which are not mandatory but are either binding and enforceable or necessary in order to obtain an advantage.

Panel Report, *India – Autos*, para. 7.250. See also the Panel's remarks at para. 7.192.

61. Panel Report, *US – Section 301 Trade Act*, paras 7.53–7.54.
62. *Ibid.*, para. 7.54.
63. *Ibid.*, para. 7.53:

> Despite the centrality of this issue in the submissions of both parties, we believe that resolving the dispute as to which type of legislation, in abstract, is capable of violating WTO obligations is not germane to the resolution of the type of claims before us. In our view the appropriate method in cases such as this is to examine with care the nature of the WTO obligation at issue and to evaluate the Measure in question in the light of such examination. The question is then whether, on the correct interpretation of the specific WTO obligation at issue, only mandatory or also discretionary national laws are

It is true that the Panel in *US – Section 301 Trade Act* expressly refrained from overturning the 'the classical test in the pre-existing jurisprudence that only legislation mandating a WTO inconsistency or precluding WTO consistency, can, as such, violate WTO provisions'.[64] This statement was added at the suggestion of the United States, which supported the continued existence of the distinction.[65] In a clever piece of legal reasoning, the Panel said that the 'classical' mandatory/discretionary distinction allows discretionary legislation to be challenged in WTO litigation. If the WTO obligation in question forbids the enactment of legislation containing certain kinds of discretions, then such legislation will actually mandate a breach of the WTO obligation.[66] In other words, the Panel was able to re-characterize (what was previously thought to be) discretionary legislation as actually mandatory in nature.

The Appellate Body has neither clearly rejected nor supported the Panel's reasoning in *US – Section 301 Trade Act*. Indeed, it has often pointed out that it has never ruled on the ongoing validity of the distinction between mandatory and discretionary legislation.[67]

Nevertheless, the Appellate Body clearly does not support the mandatory/discretionary distinction in the form of an absolute rule. In *US – Corrosion-Resistant Steel Sunset Review*, the Appellate Body found 'no reason for concluding that, in principle, non-mandatory measures cannot be challenged "as such" '.[68] Furthermore, there is no general rule that that Panels are obliged 'as a preliminary jurisdictional matter, to examine whether the challenged measure is mandatory'.[69] Echoing the case-by-case approach of the *US – Section 301 Trade Act* Panel, the Appellate Body appeared to favour a focus on the content of the particular WTO rules at issue:

> This issue [of whether a measure is mandatory or not] is relevant, if at all, only as part of the panel's assessment of whether the measure is, as such, inconsistent with particular obligations.[70]

Tellingly, the Appellate Body described the mandatory/discretionary distinction as an analytical tool or technique, rather than as a rule.[71] As an analytical tool, it

---

> prohibited. We do not accept the legal logic that there has to be one fast and hard rule covering all domestic legislation. After all, is it so implausible that the framers of the WTO Agreement, in their wisdom, would have crafted some obligations which would render illegal even discretionary legislation and crafted other obligations prohibiting only mandatory legislation?

64. Panel Report, *US – Section 301 Trade Act*, para. 6.9.
65. *Ibid.*
66. *Ibid.*, para. 7.54.
67. See Appellate Body Report, *US – Corrosion-Resistant Steel Sunset Review*, para. 93, and the cases cited in that paragraph at fn. 94.
68. Appellate Body Report, *US – Corrosion-Resistant Steel Sunset Review*, para. 88.
69. *Ibid.*, para. 89.
70. *Ibid.*
71. *Ibid.*, para. 93.

should not be applied in a 'mechanistic fashion'.[72] Emphasizing the focus on the particular WTO rules at issue, the Appellate Body said that 'the import of the "mandatory/discretionary distinction" may vary from case to case'.[73]

It is clear that the Appellate Body's comments in *US – Corrosion-Resistant Steel Sunset Review* have altered the perceptions of the mandatory/discretionary distinction in the WTO. Only a few years ago, Panels appeared to see the distinction as a rule rather than as a technique.[74] After *US – Corrosion-Resistant Steel Sunset Review*, such statements run the risk of being seen by the Appellate Body as applying the mandatory/discretionary distinction in a mechanistic fashion. Today, Panels would consider more carefully the context of the particular WTO obligations in question before applying the distinction as an analytical tool (and would avoid applying it as a rule).[75] Still, some Panels seem attracted to the mandatory/

---

72. *Ibid.*
73. *Ibid.*
74. In 1999, the Panel in *India – Quantitative Restrictions* was able to say (at para. 5.60) that:

    > [A] measure can only be reviewed by a panel if it is applied (a measure that is not applied can only be reviewed if it is mandatory legislation, i.e., it is certain that it will be applied).

    Even in 2002, some Panels were still applying the mandatory/discretionary distinction quite strictly. The Panel in *US – Steel Plate* considered (at para. 7.89) that:

    > [T]he question before us is whether the US statutory provisions in question require USDOC to take action which contravenes the US obligations under the WTO AD Agreement. Indeed, the parties do not disagree with this formulation of the issue.

    Again in 2002, the Panel in *US – Countervailing Measures on Certain EC Products* thought that (at para. 7.122):

    > [A] piece of legislation would not violate the WTO if it can be applied by the executive authority of the WTO Member in a manner consistent with the WTO Agreement; WTO Members are presumed to administer their national laws in conformity with their WTO obligations.

    The Appellate Body itself in that case seemed to adopt a similar approach, see Appellate Body Report, *US – Countervailing Measures on Certain EC Products*, para. 159.
75. The decline of the mandatory/discretionary distinction signalled in *US – Corrosion-Resistant Steel Sunset Review* was recognized by the Panel in *US – Oil Country Tubular Goods Sunset Reviews*, para. 7.140, finding that the distinction is in a state of 'uncertainty':

    > We note that the Appellate Body's findings [in *US – Corrosion-Resistant Steel Sunset Review*] and its underlying reasoning appear to represent a significant shift from the mandatory/discretionary distinction previously applied by a number of GATT/WTO panels. The Appellate Body did not, however, clearly state whether this decision meant that the mandatory/discretionary test has from now on to be applied in a different manner. We are therefore left with a certain degree of uncertainty regarding the content and the applicability of this test in WTO dispute settlement proceedings.

    The Panel then appeared to adopt the approach of the Panel in *US – Section 301 Trade Act*, that is, to interpret the particular WTO obligation in question rather than to apply the mandatory/discretionary distinction as a blanket rule:

    > It is, however, clear to us from Section VI.E of the Appellate Body's Report that we must analyse the substance of Argentina's claim on the basis of the provisions of the SPB cited

discretionary distinction as a rule.[76] However, in 2006, the Appellate Body expressly rejected an appeal grounded 'simply on the basis that [the Panel] did not apply the mandatory/discretionary distinction in analyzing and finding a violation' of the relevant WTO obligation.[77] Other WTO tribunals have already started to take a more nuanced view on discretionary legislation. In *US – Zeroing (EC)*, the Panel drew away from the strict rule that only mandatory legislation could be WTO-inconsistent and moved towards a looser rule that WTO-inconsistent legislation had to be inconsistent 'with a certain degree of specificity'.[78]

Thus, the mandatory/discretionary distinction is in decline as a rule.[79] WTO tribunals will increasingly use the approach of the Panel in *US – Section 301 Trade Act*; that is, by interpreting individual WTO obligations in their own particular context and in the circumstances of the dispute. A number of WTO tribunals have considered domestic legislation without feeling the need to refer to the distinction.[80] This is likely to continue.[81]

Having described the decline of the mandatory/discretionary distinction, I believe that the concept retains some practical importance in WTO law, for two reasons.

First, the mandatory/discretionary distinction retains a symbolic status as part of WTO jurisprudence. The Appellate Body has refused expressly to overturn the distinction because of its long heritage in the GATT, and in the early days of the WTO. In a young legal system such as the WTO, the judiciary will be loath to upset

---

> by Argentina. It is only as part of our substantive analysis of the SPB that we may decide whether it mandates WTO-inconsistent behaviour or precludes WTO-consistent behaviour. We shall refrain from applying the mandatory/discretionary test in the abstract to determine whether the SPB can give rise to a WTO violation or not. In the words of the Appellate Body, this would amount to applying the mentioned test in a 'mechanistic fashion' and would not be acceptable. [footnote omitted]

76. One Panel saw the mandatory/discretionary distinction as basically still in force (Panel Report, *Korea – Commercial Vessels*, paras 7.60–7.67) and another saw it as a 'relatively consistent approach' (Panel Report, *US – Upland Cotton*, para. 7.333).
77. Appellate Body Report, *US – Zeroing (EC)*, para. 214. The Appellate Body nevertheless distanced itself from the question in that case (at para. 213), holding that the Panel's decision that the challenged legislation was mandatory was a finding of fact, and thus unchallengeable on appeal (except in the case of clear Panel error).
78. Panel Report, *US – Zeroing (EC)*, para. 7.67:

> [W]hile we are cognizant of the need for caution with respect to the application of what after all is nothing more than an 'analytical tool', we cannot see any support in GATT and WTO dispute settlement practice, including recent Appellate Body decisions, for the proposition that a law can be found to be WTO-inconsistent as such with respect to an issue that it does not specifically address. In our view, the very notion of a law as being WTO-inconsistent necessarily entails that the law must address that issue with a certain degree of specificity.

79. For a contrary view, see Naiki, above n. 55, 60–70.
80. See Bhuiyan (2002), above n. 55, 598, fn. 95.
81. This point is brought out by the Appellate Body's decision in *US – Shrimp* concerning chapeau Art. XX GATT. The chapeau prevents measures from being applied in a manner constituting 'arbitrary discrimination between countries where the same conditions prevail'. The Appellate Body considered that a lack of certainty in the US administration of its legislation pointed to 'arbitrary discrimination' here (Appellate Body Report, para. 181).

expectations by overturning established principles.[82] Thus, the Appellate Body has been cautious. It rarely rules that discretionary legislation, as such, breaches WTO rules.[83] Instead, it has been careful to characterize legislation as mandatory before ruling on the issue of a breach.[84] This makes it advisable for WTO members to at least consider the mandatory/discretionary distinction when presenting their cases before WTO tribunals.

The second reason for the ongoing relevance of the mandatory/discretionary distinction is its use as an 'analytical tool'. The fact that legislation is mandatory or discretionary in nature is still relevant to the reasoning of WTO tribunals (although not necessarily determinative). In particular, the distinction may have continuing effects in relation to particular WTO obligations. According to the reasoning of the Panel in *US – Section 301 Trade Act*, each WTO obligation must be interpreted on its own terms. Such interpretation could reveal that some WTO provisions apply only to mandatory legislation.[85]

---

82. Perhaps paradoxically, this approach is recommended by the principle of legal certainty advocated in this book. Occasionally, the principle of legal certainty (in the sense of a constant jurisprudence) will indicate against the adoption of novel, but more certain, legal ideas.
83. *US – Section 211 Appropriations Act* may be an exception here. In *US – Corrosion-Resistant Steel Sunset Review,* the Appellate Body said (at fn. 94):

    > [T]he appeal in *US – Section 211 Appropriations Act* presented a unique set of circumstances. In that case, in defending the measure challenged by the European Communities, the United States unsuccessfully argued that discretionary regulations, issued under a separate law, cured the discriminatory aspects of the measure at issue.

    For an example of when a Panel found that a WTO obligation was applicable to both mandatory and discretionary measures, see Panel Report, *China – Intellectual Property Rights*, para. 7.253.
84. For example, Appellate Body Report, *US – Corrosion-Resistant Steel Sunset Review*, para. 100.
85. A possible example of this is the second sentence of fn. 1 to the Understanding on Balance-of-Payments Provisions of GATT 1994:

    > The provisions of Articles XXII and XXIII of GATT 1994 as elaborated and applied by the Dispute Settlement Understanding may be invoked with respect to any matters arising from the application of restrictive import measures taken for balance-of-payments purposes.

    In considering this provision, the Appellate Body in Appellate Body Report, *India – Quantitative Restrictions*, para. 93, held that the words 'matters arising from the application of':

    > reflect the traditional GATT doctrine that, with the exception of mandatory rules, only measures that are effectively applied can be the subject of dispute settlement proceedings.

    While the issue before the Panel in that case did not concern the mandatory/discretionary distinction directly, there seems to be an implication here that the second sentence of fn. 1 to the Understanding on Balance-of-Payments Provisions of GATT 1994 is directed at measures *actually applied*. If this is the case (detailed consideration of the provision and its context and purpose would be required for a firm conclusion here), there is a good argument that legislation that mandates the application of such measures would also be covered by the sentence. However, the same argument may not apply for discretionary legislation. Thus, there is a chance that the mandatory/discretionary distinction applies in relation to such measures.

    See also para. 1(a) Annex TRIMs, which refers to measures 'which are mandatory or enforceable under domestic law or under administrative rulings'.

8.3.2. Certainty in WTO Law Today: The Importance of the Legislative Environment and the Two-Stage Approach

The decline of the mandatory/discretionary distinction leaves unclear the kind of certainty requirements to be applied in the future. As described earlier, there is no general requirement for certainty in WTO law. However, one can start to see patterns in recent WTO jurisprudence in the area of certainty characterization. These patterns have a common theme: the role of the legislative environment. Here we will look at the effects of the legislative environment in general; this will set the scene for a discussion of deference in certainty characterization.

If there is some doubt as to whether legislation achieves a particular result with certainty, its legislative environment becomes crucial. Thus, if the character of legislation is not obvious on its face, WTO tribunals also look to 'evidence of the consistent application of such laws, the pronouncements of domestic courts on the meaning of such laws, the opinions of legal experts and the writings of recognized scholars'.[86]

Sometimes the legislation on its face is consistent with the international rule, but the challenging State argues that the legislative environment makes it inconsistent. Alternatively, the legislation on its face may be inconsistent with the international rule, but the legislative environment may cure the inconsistency.

The distinction between that legislation and its legislative environment can clearly be seen in the case of *US – Section 301 Trade Act.* Here, the legislation on its face breached WTO obligations but was saved by its legislative environment (in the form of a promise by the US executive government). The legislation under challenge mandated the US Trade Representative (USTR) to determine whether a foreign measure was consistent with WTO provisions. Article 23.2(a) of the DSU prohibits WTO members from making determinations of WTO-inconsistency, except through recourse to WTO dispute settlement. The United States argued that the USTR could exercise discretion under the legislation to ensure that its actions complied with Article 23.2(a) of the DSU. However, the Panel found that the USTR's determination was in some circumstances to be made before the adoption of Dispute Settlement Body (DSB) findings. The Panel's finding that 'mandating a determination *before* the adoption of DSB findings and statutorily reserving the right for this determination to be one of inconsistency' meant that the legislation was prima facie inconsistent with Article 23.2(a) of DSU.[87] However, it found this prima facie inconsistency to be cured by a combination of two factors:

- evidence that the USTR could exercise its discretion in a way consistent with Article 23.2(a) of the DSU; and
- a promise by the United States that the USTR would do so.[88]

86. Appellate Body Report, *US – Carbon Steel*, para. 157. See also Appellate Body Report, *US – Corrosion-Resistant Steel Sunset Review*, para. 168; Appellate Body Report, *US – Oil Country Tubular Goods Sunset Reviews*, para. 201. See also Bhuiyan (2007), above n. 55, Ch. 7.
87. Panel Report, *US – Section 301 Trade Act*, para. 7.96.
88. *Ibid.*, para. 7.126.

Thus, the Panel took a two-stage approach to the legislation. First, it made a prima facie finding of the effect of the legislation on its face. Second, it allowed evidence of the legislative environment in rebuttal to the prima facie finding. This two-stage approach has important consequences for deference in certainty characterization, as we will see later. For present purposes, however, it is enough to observe that the two-stage approach draws a clear distinction between the challenged legislation and its legislative environment. The Appellate Body has taken a similar two-stage approach in subsequent cases.[89]

This two-stage approach has important consequences for deference in certainty characterization, when considered together with the burden of proof. As noted earlier,[90] the burden of proof is an important practical factor in setting levels of deference in challenges to legislation. The two-stage approach provides a balanced approach to deference. It gives some deference by requiring the complaining State to prove the character of the legislation on its face. However, it reduces deference by requiring the legislating State to provide rebuttal evidence of the legislative environment.

The distinction between legislation and legislative environment – and the two-stage approach – indicates that there are two main issues in certainty characterization. First, one must determine whether legislation on its face is inconsistent with international obligations. Second, one must determine whether the legislative environment can change one's conclusion about the first issue, that is, about the operation of the legislation on its face. The legislative environment can support arguments for inconsistency or for consistency; whether it does so depends on the facts of the case. We will now examine these issues in more detail.

8.3.2.1. Consistency of Legislation on Its Face

In examining legislation on its face, three conclusions are possible:

(a) The text of the legislation is clearly consistent with the relevant international obligation.
(b) The text of the legislation is clearly inconsistent with the relevant international obligation.
(c) It is unclear whether the text of the legislation is consistent or inconsistent with the international obligation. For example, the legislation may use a broad concept, or confer an administrative discretion, which could be applied consistently or inconsistently with the international obligation.

89. Appellate Body Report, *US – 1916 Act*, para. 97. See also Appellate Body Report, *US – Section 211 Appropriations Act*, paras 232, 281–295. See also Panel Report, *US – Section 129(c)(1) URAA*, para. 6.29.
90. See Section 4.2.1.

One reaches these conclusions using a process of factor characterization, based on the legal operation of the text of the legislation.[91] The tribunal examines the text of the legislation and characterizes it against the content of the relevant WTO obligation.

The vital question in certainty characterization is the role (if any) of the legislative environment in altering these conclusions. There is a threshold issue here, namely, whether the legislative environment is a relevant matter to take into account. In some cases it is not; this is where the relevant WTO obligation simply prohibits ambiguity on the face of domestic legislation. In most cases, however, the legislative environment can be used to convert a prima facie finding of ambiguity into a final finding of inconsistency or to convert a prima facie finding of inconsistency into a final finding of consistency. We will now look at each of these possibilities.

8.3.2.2. WTO Obligations That Prohibit Ambiguity

An example of a WTO obligation that prohibits ambiguity is the *Canada – Patent Term* case (the facts of which were described earlier).[92] Article 33 of TRIPS requires that 'the term of protection available' for patents must not end before twenty years from date of filing. The Appellate Body held that *available* means 'available, as a matter of right', that is, 'available as a matter of legal right and certainty'.[93] Canada claimed that it provided a 'sound legal basis' for this term through administrative procedures.[94] However, the Appellate Body disagreed that the legislative environment was relevant here:

> The opportunity to obtain a twenty-year patent term must not be 'available' only to those who are somehow able to meander successfully through a maze of administrative procedures. The opportunity to obtain a twenty-year term must be a readily discernible and specific right, and it must be clearly seen as such by the patent applicant when a patent application is filed. The grant of the patent must be sufficient *in itself* to obtain the minimum term mandated by Article 33.[95]

The requirement here for 'a readily discernible and specific right' made the text of the legislation the crucial factor in the dispute. In such cases, it is not enough to

91. In theory, one could also imagine proportionality characterization being relevant to determining the WTO-consistency of legislation on its face. That is, the WTO tribunal could examine the proportionality of the legislation, judged by its text, against its legislative purpose. However, this is unlikely to occur. In judging proportionality, it is risky to focus merely on text and to defer consideration of the legislative environment to a later stage. Proportionality needs to be determined against the entire matrix of evidence, namely, legislative text, legislative environment and surrounding facts.
92. See Section 2.4.2.
93. Appellate Body Report, *Canada – Patent Term*, para. 90.
94. *Ibid.*, para. 89.
95. *Ibid.*, para. 92.

point to the legislative environment as supplying the necessary certainty. Once the tribunal concludes that the text of the legislation is inconsistent with the obligation or is ambiguous in this respect, it will make a finding of inconsistency.

Perhaps the most important examples of this kind of provision in the WTO are those that forbid arbitrariness in decision-making procedures. The most prominent example is the chapeau to Article XX of the GATT, as interpreted by the Appellate Body in *US – Shrimp*.

In *US – Shrimp*, the United States prohibited the import of commercially harvested shrimp, except in relation to certified harvesting countries. The challenged 'legislation' in the case was a set of administrative guidelines that provided detailed rules for certification. The Appellate Body held that the guidelines fell generally within the scope of Article XX of the GATT. The issue then arose as to whether the guidelines complied with the chapeau to Article XX, which does not allow 'arbitrary discrimination' in certain situations.

The Appellate Body found that the guidelines did not comply with the chapeau because, among other things, they amounted to 'arbitrary discrimination'. This was mainly because the certification guidelines were too rigid and inflexible, and failed to account for the conditions prevailing in exporting countries.[96] However, the Appellate Body added that the guidelines were also problematic for procedural reasons. The procedural flaws in the guidelines went to their failure to prevent arbitrary decision-making, leading to a loss of certainty. The Appellate Body said:

> There appears to be no way that exporting Members can be certain whether the terms of Section 609, in particular, the 1996 Guidelines, are being applied in a fair and just manner by the appropriate governmental agencies of the United States. It appears to us that, effectively, exporting Members applying for certification whose applications are rejected are denied basic fairness and due process, and are discriminated against, vis-à-vis those Members which are granted certification.[97]

The Appellate Body identified a number of particular flaws in the guidelines, amounting to a denial of 'basic fairness and due process':

- There was 'no formal opportunity for an applicant country to be heard, or to respond to any arguments that may be made against it, in the course of the certification process before a decision to grant or to deny certification is made'.[98]
- '[N]o formal written, reasoned decision, whether of acceptance or rejection, is rendered on applications for . . . certification.'[99]

96. Appellate Body Report, *US – Shrimp*, para. 177. This is an example of proportionality review, as the possibility of more flexibility indicated a problem in the optimality of the measure.
97. Appellate Body Report, *US – Shrimp*, para. 181.
98. *Ibid.*, para. 180.
99. *Ibid.*

- 'Countries which are granted certification are included in a list of approved applications published in the Federal Register; however, they are not notified specifically.'[100]
- 'Countries whose applications are denied also do not receive notice of such denial (other than by omission from the list of approved applications) or of the reasons for the denial.'[101] [footnote omitted]
- 'No procedure for review of, or appeal from, a denial of an application is provided.'[102] [footnote omitted]

To emphasize its concern over arbitrary decision-making, the Appellate Body referred to the context of Article X of the GATT, which provides guarantees against arbitrariness in the administration of legislation through requirements for publication and impartiality, as well as for independent processes for review of decisions. The Appellate Body emphasized the concept of procedural fairness in Article X, holding that 'Article X(3) of the GATT 1994 establishes certain minimum standards for transparency and procedural fairness in the administration of trade regulations.'[103]

It is not clear how many WTO provisions are affected by the Appellate Body's reasoning in *US – Shrimp*. Arguably, the reasoning applies only to the chapeau to Article XX of the GATT and its equivalents in other covered agreements. However, the Appellate Body made a comment suggesting that this standard can apply more widely to exceptions to WTO rules. It said:

> Inasmuch as there are due process requirements generally for measures that are otherwise imposed in compliance with WTO obligations, it is only reasonable that rigorous compliance with the fundamental requirements of due process should be required in the application and administration of a measure which purports to be an exception to the treaty obligations of the Member imposing the measure and which effectively results in a suspension pro hac vice of the treaty rights of other Members.[104]

The qualifier 'inasmuch' makes it unclear as to whether the Appellate Body intended to impose a general due process/procedural fairness standard of certainty

---

100. *Ibid.*
101. *Ibid.*
102. *Ibid.*
103. *Ibid.*, para. 183. It went on to hold that the relevant legislation failed these standards:

> The non-transparent and ex parte nature of the internal governmental procedures applied by the competent officials in the Office of Marine Conservation, the Department of State, and the United States National Marine Fisheries Service throughout the certification processes under Section 609, as well as the fact that countries whose applications are denied do not receive formal notice of such denial, nor of the reasons for the denial, and the fact, too, that there is no formal legal procedure for review of, or appeal from, a denial of an application, are all contrary to the spirit, if not the letter, of Article X(3) of the GATT 1994.

104. Appellate Body Report, *US – Shrimp*, para. 182.

for all WTO rules that create exceptions from general obligations. Nevertheless, this passage confirms at least a willingness of the Appellate Body to interpret such a requirement into particular WTO provisions.[105]

Leaving aside this kind of speculation, WTO obligations that prohibit ambiguity – and thus reduce the importance of the legislative environment – are rare. They are typically found in TRIPS, which goes beyond mere trade liberalization and extends to setting minimum standards for intellectual property protection.[106] Yet, even in TRIPS, one finds disputes in which the mere ambiguity of a legislative provision was not enough to establish inconsistency.

This can be illustrated by the *US – Section 110 Copyright Act* case. The challenged legislation allowed transmissions of copyrighted work on 'homestyle equipment', that is, 'on a single receiving apparatus of a kind commonly used in private homes'. According to the Panel, Article 13 of TRIPS requires that such derogations from copyright be 'clearly defined'.[107] Arguably, the 'homestyle equipment' concept was too vague in this respect. Nevertheless, the Panel held that Article 13 of TRIPS allows some degree of generalization:

> [T]here is no need to identify explicitly each and every possible situation to which the exception could apply, provided that the scope of the exception is known and particularised. This guarantees a sufficient degree of legal certainty.[108]

The Panel pointed out the potential of the broad concept of homestyle equipment to breach Article 13 of TRIPS in the future (e.g., in relation to equipment for Internet transmission).[109] However, it found that the homestyle equipment concept satisfied the certainty requirement today.[110] Any uncertainties here were not enough to establish a current breach.

Thus, most WTO obligations do not prohibit ambiguity on the face of legislation.[111] Broad drafting, ambiguity, or wide administrative discretion on the face

---

105. See also Appellate Body Report, *US – Cotton Yarn*, para. 74, in relation to due process/procedural fairness requirements for domestic authorities' fact-finding.
106. Another possible example is the provision discussed in Appellate Body Report, *EC – Chicken Cuts*, described above, text at n. 50.
107. Panel Report, *US – Section 110 Copyright Act*, para. 6.108.
108. *Ibid.*
109. Panel Report, *US – Section 110 Copyright Act*, para. 6.153.
110. *Ibid.*, para. 6.145:

> [A] Member is not required to identify homestyle equipment in terms of exceedingly detailed technical specifications in order to meet the [required] standard of clarity . . . While we recognize that homestyle equipment may become technologically more sophisticated over time, we see no need to enter into speculations about potential future developments in the homestyle equipment market. At any rate, we recall that our factual determinations are invariably limited to what currently is being perceived as homestyle equipment in the US market.

111. See also GATT Panel Report, *United States – Measures Affecting the Importation, Internal Sale and Use of Tobacco*, DS44/R, adopted 4 Oct. 1994, BISD 41S/131. There, US legislation

of the legislation are often only a starting point in the analysis. The substance of the dispute often concerns whether the legislative environment can cure or confirm such ambiguity (or can cure prima facie inconsistency). We now turn to these cases, in which the WTO obligation does not prohibit ambiguity completely. Here the crucial issue is the second step in the *US – Section 301 Trade Act* analysis: the effect of the legislative environment on a prima facie finding about the text of the legislation.

8.3.2.3. WTO Obligations That Allow Ambiguity: The Legislative Environment in Curing Prima Facie Inconsistency or Making Prima Facie Ambiguity into Inconsistency

Once legislation is found to be WTO-consistent or WTO-inconsistent on its face, the legislative environment often takes a central place in the analysis. The nature of the legislative environment varies widely among cases. Sometimes the focus will be on executive statements. These may be statements made during the passage of legislation (such as an explanatory memorandum).[112] In other cases, there may be subordinate rules or policy statements[113] published by the executive about the manner of exercise of the discretion. In yet other cases, the statement may be made as part of the proceedings before the international tribunal.[114] In contrast, sometimes the focus will be on domestic jurisprudence; for example, sometimes the relevant international obligation is said to be incorporated into domestic law, thus forming a part of the legislative environment.[115]

In many cases, these aspects of the legislative environment are sufficient to cure legislation that is WTO-inconsistent on its face. Perhaps the best known of these cases is the Panel decision in *US – Section 301 Trade Act*, as described earlier,[116] in which an undertaking made by the United States during WTO litigation saved the legislation from inconsistency.

In contrast, there are fewer cases in which the legislative environment has defeated prima facie consistency of legislative text and has been the basis of a finding of inconsistency. These are almost always cases in which legislation is not clearly consistent on its face and is somewhat ambiguous. Here, the legislative

---

required fees to be charged in relation to imported tobacco to be 'comparable' to equivalent fees to be charged in relation to domestic tobacco. Article XIII GATT requires that such fees be related to the costs of inspection of goods. The United States argued, successfully, that the broadness of the concept of 'comparable' allowed it to satisfy Art. XIII GATT (see Panel Report, para. 121).

112. For example, the US Statement of Administrative Action (H.R. 5110, H.R. Doc. 316, Vol. 1, 103d Congress, 2nd Session, 656, at 925–926 (1994)) considered in various disputes, such as Panel Report, *US – Export Restraints*, paras 8.93–8.100.
113. For an example, see Appellate Body Report, *US – Oil Country Tubular Goods Sunset Reviews*, para. 187.
114. See Section 8.4, text at n. 139.
115. See Section 8.4, text at n. 128.
116. See Section 8.3.2.1.

environment can convert this ambiguity into inconsistency with the relevant international obligation.

This can be illustrated by the dispute in *US – Oil Country Tubular Goods Sunset Reviews*. The relevant aspect of the dispute dealt with Article 11.3 of the Anti-Dumping Agreement. This article requires definitive anti-dumping duties to be sunsetted after five years, unless the investigating authority determines that there is a likelihood of continuation or recurrence of dumping and injury. According to the Appellate Body, in making such a determination, the investigating authority must weigh the evidence in each case.[117] Argentina challenged a US policy statement known as the Sunset Policy Bulletin[118] (SPB) on the basis that in some situations it allegedly required the investigating authority to treat certain factors as proving a likelihood of continuation or recurrence of dumping. It was unclear on the face of the SPB whether it actually required any particular action by the authority. Argentina then called on the legislative environment to prove inconsistency, in the form of documents relating to 297 actual determinations, together with a spreadsheet showing the results of those determinations.[119] The Appellate Body accepted that the legislative environment could be used in this way. Ultimately, however, it held that Argentina's evidence was not sufficient for this purpose.[120] We will look at the Appellate Body's reasoning in more detail shortly.[121] However, for present purposes, we can see the decision as confirming the possibility that the legislative environment can bring legislation, on its face consistent with a WTO obligation, into conflict with that obligation.

Whether the legislative environment is used to attack or defend legislation, the underlying issue is the same: to what extent will the tribunal defer to the legislating State's views on the meaning of the legislative environment? It is to this issue that we now turn.

8.4. DEFERENCE AND CERTAINTY CHARACTERIZATION IN THE WTO

Deference in certainty characterization is deference about the operation of the domestic legal system. Domestic authorities, including domestic legislatures, are generally experts in this area, and they certainly have more relevant expertise

---

117. Appellate Body Report, *US – Oil Country Tubular Goods Sunset Reviews*, para. 179. This is a paraphrase of the actual requirements laid down by the Appellate Body, which related to the need for positive evidence and a sufficient factual basis, leading to a reasoned and adequate conclusion: Appellate Body Report, *US – Oil Country Tubular Goods Sunset Reviews*, para. 179, quoting Appellate Body Report, *US – Corrosion-Resistant Steel Sunset Review*, para. 114 (in turn quoting Panel Report, *US – Corrosion-Resistant Steel Sunset Review*, para. 7.271).
118. Policies Regarding the Conduct of Five-Year ('Sunset') Reviews of Anti-dumping and Countervailing Duty Orders, *United States Federal Register*, vol. 63, No. 73 (16 Apr. 1998), 18871.
119. Appellate Body Report, *US – Oil Country Tubular Goods Sunset Reviews*, para. 203.
120. *Ibid.*, paras 209–210.
121. See later in this chapter, text at n. 147.

than do international tribunals. In general, therefore, one can expect the degree of deference here to be high (but not total).

Deference here links back to fundamental questions about the nature of breaches of international law and the jurisdiction of international tribunals to deal with such breaches.[122] There are basic conceptual issues about the nature of an 'act' comprised in domestic legislation: is the simple act of legislating the main way to ground a breach of international law, or is the focus more on the complex act comprised of the legislation and later executive actions? In earlier times, international tribunals tended to wait for the 'completing' executive action before they would be willing to declare a breach: mere uncertainty about this action was not sufficient.[123] More recently, international tribunals such as those in the WTO system have been given jurisdiction to consider legislation in the abstract.[124]

Relying on general international law doctrine that municipal legislation is treated evidentially as fact,[125] WTO tribunals scrutinize the meaning of domestic legislation within the framework of the standard of review of facts.[126] As the Appellate Body stated in one case:

> The United States has explained that, within the domestic legal system of the United States, the SPB does not bind the USDOC and that the USDOC 'is entirely free to depart from [the] SPB at any time'. However, it is not for us to opine on matters of United States domestic law. Our mandate is confined to clarifying the provisions of the WTO Agreement and to determining whether the challenged measures are consistent with those provisions.[127] [footnote omitted]

---

122. See Section 2.4, text at n. 20.
123. See the *Mariposa* case mentioned above, Preamble, text at n 22. An echo of this view can be seen in the following comment in Panel Report, *US – Section 301 Trade Act*, para. 7.80:

> [U]nder traditional public international law, legislation under which an eventual violation could, or even would, subsequently take place, does not normally in and of itself engage State responsibility. If, say, a State undertakes not to expropriate property of foreign nationals without appropriate compensation, its State responsibility would normally be engaged only at the moment foreign property had actually been expropriated in a given instance.

124. See Ch. 3.
125. See, for example, Appellate Body Report, *US – Section 211 Appropriations Act*, para. 105. Note that here the Appellate Body also noted that the legal characterization arising from such fact-finding is, unlike fact-finding in general, subject to appellate review.
126. The exact extent of that review for challenges to legislation has yet to be clarified by WTO tribunals: see Section 4.6.1.2.
127. Appellate Body Report, *US – Oil Country Tubular Goods Sunset Reviews*, para. 187. The jurisprudence here stretches back to the old GATT system, in particular the GATT Panel Report, *United States – Section 337 of the Tariff Act of 1930*, L/6439, adopted 7 Nov. 1989, BISD 36S/345 (quoted in Appellate Body Report, *India – Patents (US)*, para. 67). See also Panel Report, *EC – Trademarks and Geographical Indications (Australia)*, para. 7.106.

Thus, as is the case with all fact-finding, WTO tribunals give considerable (but not conclusive) weight to statements by domestic authorities as to the meaning of challenged legislation.

Deference in WTO certainty characterization depends on the way in which the legislative environment is used, in particular, whether it is used to create consistency or transform ambiguity into inconsistency. Accordingly, such deference depends on whether the legislative environment is being used as a defence by the legislating State or as a weapon by the complaining State. We will consider these scenarios separately.

8.4.1. Deference When the Legislative Environment Is Used to Defend against Inconsistency

Generally speaking, WTO tribunals do not give much deference to claims by the legislating State that the legislative environment removes prima facie inconsistency. Once the legislation, on its face, is found to be inconsistent with the relevant WTO obligation, there is a fairly heavy burden on the legislating State to show a specific and certain element of the legislative environment that cures the inconsistency. Even if this burden is satisfied, there is the risk that the legislative environment may itself create an extra hurdle that is inconsistent with WTO law.

The strictness of the legislating State's burden here is illustrated by WTO tribunals' fairly easy dismissal of claims that general doctrines of domestic law can cure prima facie inconsistency. For example, a legislating State has often claimed that under general domestic law, domestic legislation must be interpreted consistently with international law whenever possible. Thus, it is claimed, any ambiguity in legislation will be resolved in favour of WTO law, thus curing any prima facie inconsistency. This argument has been usually rejected when it has been raised.[128] Thus, in *Argentina – Textiles and Apparel*, the Panel said that the claimed doctrine did not provide enough legal certainty as to the outcome.[129] It is

128. See also Appellate Body Report, *Mexico – Anti-Dumping Measures on Rice*, para. 171; Panel Report, *India – Patents (EC)*, para. 7.49. Similar arguments were made in the following cases, but not addressed: Panel Report, *US – Export Restraints*, para. 442; Panel Report, *US – Section 129(c)(1) URAA*, para. 3.74.

129. Panel Report, *Argentina – Textiles and Apparel*, para. 6.68. The Panel justified this through reference to the PCIJ's statement in *Free Zones of Upper Savoy and the District of Gex* (1932, PCIJ, Series A/B, case No. 46, 167) that France could not rely on its own legislation to limit the scope of its international obligations. However, this statement may have been taken rather out of context. The PCIJ was there referring to a bald claim that action compelled by domestic legislation could not be inconsistent with international law. A better basis for the Panel's decision is simply that general Argentine law did not provide sufficient certainty. On the US domestic application of the argument, see A. Davies, 'Connecting or Compartmentalizing the WTO and United States Legal Systems? The Role of the Charming Betsy Canon', JIEL 10 (2007): 117.

true that such a doctrine has sometimes found success before WTO tribunals, but only as a way of confirming an outcome already achieved by other means.[130]

Similar considerations have applied when the 'curing' aspect of the legislative environment is claimed to be a general administrative or judicial discretion to decline to apply legislation in a particular way.[131] Little deference is given to such claims. For example, in *US – 1916 Act*, the United States argued that:

- the US Department of Justice had discretion under the legislation not to start criminal proceedings; and
- the US courts would not apply the legislation inconsistently with WTO law.[132]

The Appellate Body rejected both arguments. Using the language of the mandatory/discretionary rule (as this case was decided early in WTO history),

130. Panel Report, *US – Section 301 Trade Act*, paras 7.108 (fn. 681) and 7.113; Panel Report, *US – 1916 Act (Japan)*, para. 6.250.

131. In proceedings in *India – Patents (EC)* (which concerned time-frames for lodging certain patent applications), India stressed the following points (Panel Report, paras 7.46–7.68):

  - Indian patent legislation required patent applications to be referred to an examiner, but did not specify the time-frame within which this must be done.
  - According to a principle of Indian statutory interpretation, 'even where a statutory provision specifies a time for performing a statutory duty, the time specified is only directory and not mandatory'.
  - According to a principle of Indian statutory interpretation, Indian patent legislation must be read in accordance with India's international obligations, including its WTO obligations.

  India was effectively suggesting that there was a discretion, rather than an obligation, to refer patent applications to an examiner. This discretion could be exercised so as to delay such referrals (and accordingly, delaying the refusal of the application) for a long period. The discretion to delay would allegedly allow the patents legislation to operate in harmony with administrative instructions.

  The Panel rejected all of these arguments. It was not persuaded that the text of the patents legislation gave complete discretion regarding the timing of referrals of patent applications (para. 7.48). As to the first argument on principles of statutory interpretation, it held that the 'directory nature of a time-bound provision does not necessarily provide a legal basis for positive actions not stipulated in a statute' (para. 7.49). It rejected the second statutory interpretation argument on the basis that the interpretative principle only applied in cases of ambiguity, and the patents legislation here was not ambiguous (para. 7.49).

  India then raised a second argument, based on the practices of Indian courts. According to India, the referral procedure in its patent legislation would not be enforced in private proceedings. It suggested that:

  > [A]n Indian court will never examine a request by a competitor to force the Controller to refer a mailbox application to an examiner for examination because basic principles of standing and ripeness dictate the rejection of challenges to contingent, future rights such as are represented by mailbox applications [at para. 7.53].

  The Panel rejected this argument as well. It suggested that a competitor might be able to demonstrate *actual* damage before an Indian court, on the basis of future prospects that the patent will be granted (i.e., when full patent protection is created for relevant inventions) (para. 7.54). There was therefore a possibility of private proceedings to enforce the patent legislation.

132. Appellate Body Report, *US – 1916 Act*, para. 100.

the Appellate Body noted that the protection of discretionary legislation did not cover discretion as to whether or not to prosecute offences.[133] Nor did this protection extend to discretions vested in the courts: it covered only discretion vested in the executive branch of government.[134] This reasoning should still apply following the decline of the mandatory/discretionary rule. If it were otherwise, executive discretion not to prosecute would be an all-purpose WTO defence for legislation creating criminal offences.[135]

These examples of claims based on general legal doctrine should be contrasted with claims based on specific legal rules. The latter kind of claim usually attracts a high degree of deference. Such claims are nevertheless quite rare. If a specific legal rule exists that can rescue other legislation from WTO-inconsistency, it is unlikely that that the legislation itself will be challenged.[136]

However, there are a number of cases in which specific obligations in the legislative environment – in the form of executive promises – have rescued legislation from WTO-inconsistency. These obligations exist outside the domestic legal sphere and are made during WTO litigation. The best-known example occurred in the *US – Section 301 Trade Act* case. As described earlier,[137] the challenged legislation was prima facie WTO-inconsistent, but it was saved by a US promise during Panel proceedings that the USTR could exercise its legislative discretion in a WTO-consistent way. Similar arguments have been made in other disputes.[138]

These cases provide a fascinating example of the interaction of the international and domestic legal systems in challenges to legislation. Here, an executive promise at the international level – possibly binding in international law under the *Nuclear Tests* principle[139] – becomes critical to the operation of

133. *Ibid.*, para. 91.
134. *Ibid.*, para. 100.
135. An analogous point was made in GATT Panel Report, *EC – Anti-Dumping Duties on Audio Tapes in Cassettes Originating in Japan*, ADP/136, 28 Apr. 1995, unadopted, para. 362. See Naiki, above n. 55, 34.
136. A possible example of this is in the Panel Report, *US – DRAMS*, paras 6.52–6.53. There, US Department of Commerce regulations allowed the revocation of an anti-dumping order on various grounds, including when the Secretary of Commerce made particular certifications. Korea argued that the certification requirement was inconsistent with Art. 11.2 Anti-Dumping Agreement (which imposes requirements to 'review the need for the continued imposition of the duty'). The Panel refused to hold the certification regulation to be inconsistent with Art. 11.2, as there was other US legislation that allowed revocation of an anti-dumping order without a requirement for certification. This might be seen as a finding that the legislative environment contained specific legal rules that cured any possible inconsistency. (The Panel applied the mandatory/discretionary rule here – now in decline – but this does not alter the essential argument here.)
137. See Section 8.3.2.
138. GATT Panel Report, *United States – Taxes on Petroleum and Certain Imported Substances*, L/6175, adopted 17 Jun. 1987, BISD 34S/136, para. 5.2.9; Appellate Body Report, *US – Section 211 Appropriations Act*, para. 249.
139. *Nuclear Tests (Australia v. France; New Zealand v. France)*, Judgment, 20 Dec. 1974, ICJ Reports (1974) 253, 267, para. 43:

> It is well recognized that declarations made by way of unilateral acts, concerning legal or factual situations, may have the effect of creating legal obligations. Declarations of this

domestic legislation. The Panel in *US – Section 301 Trade Act* made clear that its ultimate finding of consistency was conditional upon the ongoing performance of that promise.[140] Therefore, the content of WTO litigation was itself an element in the operation of the US legislation. This suggests that it is not only the domestic legal system that provides certainty for the WTO-consistent administration of discretionary legislation. Promises made at the international level during WTO litigation can also help to provide that certainty. In other words, certainty that is lacking in elements of the domestic legal order is provided by elements of the international legal order. To the extent (if any) that such provisions could be enforced by a domestic court, the result is that international law has contributed to the certainty or operation of the domestic legal order. Of course, it is unclear what status these executive promises have in domestic law.[141]

Of course, for an executive promise to have the desired effect, it must be clear and specific. In some cases, executive promises have failed this criterion. In *EC – ACP-EC Partnership Agreement*, the European Communities asserted at a WTO arbitration hearing that it would implement a tariff quota on bananas from some countries to comply with WTO obligations to maintain market access for bananas from other countries.[142] The WTO Arbitrator rejected this promise as a means of curing WTO-inconsistency, holding that the operation of the promised quota was not clear enough.[143]

> kind may be, and often are, very specific. When it is the intention of the State making the declaration that it should become bound according to its terms, that intention confers on the declaration the character of a legal undertaking, the State being thenceforth legally required to follow a course of conduct consistent with the declaration. An undertaking of this kind, if given publicly, and with an intent to be bound, even though not made within the context of international negotiations, is binding. In these circumstances, nothing in the nature of a quid pro quo nor any subsequent acceptance of the declaration, nor even any reply or reaction from other States, is required for the declaration to take effect, since such a requirement would be inconsistent with the strictly unilateral nature of the juridical act by which the pronouncement by the state was made.

140. Panel Report, *US – Section 301 Trade Act*, para. 8.1:

> Significantly, all these conclusions are based in full or in part on the US Administration's undertakings mentioned above. It thus follows that should they be repudiated or in any other way removed by the US Administration or another branch of the US Government, the findings of conformity contained in these conclusions would no longer be warranted.

141. What is clear is that an *unlawful* executive promise is insufficient. In its Report in *US – Section 301 Trade Act*, para. 7.103, the Panel said:

> [T]he offending discretionary element has to be lawfully curtailed since, as found in WTO case law, conformity with WTO obligations cannot be obtained by an administrative promise to disregard its own binding internal legislation, i.e., by an administrative undertaking to act illegally.

142. Report of the Arbitrator, *EC – ACP-EC Partnership Agreement*, para. 72.
143. *Ibid.*, para. 74:

> The Arbitrator is not convinced that a simple cap in the volume of preferential imports would necessarily address the concern of ensuring that the envisaged rebinding would

Thus, there is a fairly heavy onus on the legislating State to prove clarity and specificity in any element of the legislative environment that is claimed to cure prima facie legislative inconsistency. Yet, even when this onus is satisfied, the legislating State needs to be aware of one more argument. This can be called the extra hurdle argument. Here, the element of the legislative environment called on as a defence is said to be an extra hurdle for foreign traders to jump: to take advantage of the benefits available to domestic traders, they must take the extra step of proving the application of that element. The need to take this extra step is said to be discrimination that in itself is WTO-inconsistent.

The phrase *extra hurdle* stems from the leading case in this area, *US – Section 211 Appropriations Act*. In this case, a provision of the challenged legislation prevented a US court from enforcing certain intellectual property rights that had been previously confiscated (most relevantly, by the Cuban government). The provision applied only to rights held by foreign nationals, and thus, on its face, it did not apply to US nationals who were successors-in-interest to the holders of confiscated rights. Such discrimination between foreign and US nationals could be a breach of the national treatment rule. However, the United States relied on an element of the legislative environment to cure this discrimination. This element was a combination of two factors: a rule that persons could not become successors-in-interest without licenses granted by an agency of the US Treasury, and the practice of that agency in never issuing such licenses in relation to confiscated rights. If such a license were granted to a US national, US courts were said to apply the 'longstanding principle against the recognition of foreign confiscations', which presumably prevented enforcement of the relevant rights.[144]

The Appellate Body nevertheless held that the legislative environment was not sufficient to cure the discrimination. It viewed the challenged legislation from the perspective of procedural hurdles. It noted that holders of rights had to jump a number of such hurdles to have their rights enforced. US nationals faced only one real hurdle: the practice of the US Treasury agency in not issuing licenses. By contrast, foreign nationals faced that hurdle as well as an extra one: the provisions of the challenged legislation. This extra hurdle itself constituted impermissible discrimination.[145] Thus, even specific and clear US administrative practice could not save the challenged legislation from WTO-inconsistency.

The extra hurdle argument represents a substantive reduction in deference by WTO tribunals to the legislating State. Even in the face of uncontradicted evidence of a legislative environment that ensures WTO-consistent outcomes, the mere structure of that environment can lead to WTO-inconsistency. Normally, States can choose how they structure their legal orders to achieve consistency with the

---

> result in at least maintaining total market access for MFN banana suppliers. Indeed, in the absence of any information as to how such a tariff quota might be administered, it is impossible to assess the effects that would be created by the new system

144. Appellate Body Report, *US – Section 211 Appropriations Act*, para. 257.
145. *Ibid.*, para. 265.

international legal order.[146] They can also claim deference as to this choice. However, the extra hurdle argument removes some of this deference and restricts that choice. For this reason, the extra hurdle argument represents a very intrusive standard of review in the process of certainty characterization. Clearly, it is a concept that is likely to be applied with great care in the future. Perhaps not surprisingly, *US – Section 211 Appropriations Act* remains the only case in which the concept has played a crucial role in the outcome of a dispute.

8.4.2. Deference When Legislative Environment Is Used to Convert Ambiguity into Inconsistency

Similar issues of deference apply when the meaning of legislation on its face is flexible enough to avoid a prima facie finding of inconsistency. The Appellate Body has placed a heavy onus on a challenging State that seeks to rely on the legislative environment to convert any uncertainty into WTO-inconsistency. Indeed, this onus is so heavy that it will be satisfied only in exceptional cases.

This heavy onus can be demonstrated by claims based on a legislative environment of published administrative decisions. An example of such a claim occurred in *US – Oil Country Tubular Goods Sunset Reviews*. As discussed earlier,[147] Argentina relied on compilation documents relating to 297 actual decisions under the challenged US legislation, alleging that these documents showed particular trends in decision-making. However, the Appellate Body was not satisfied with a mere trend based on statistics: rather, it required a qualitative assessment of individual decisions so as to determine whether any underlying determinative or conclusive decision-making principle was part of the legislative environment.[148] The Panel in that case failed to make such an assessment; thus, the Appellate Body had insufficient evidence to make a finding of inconsistency.[149]

The Appellate Body subsequently reaffirmed this heavy onus in *US – Anti-Dumping Measures on Oil Country Tubular Goods*. Like the previously mentioned case, this case involved a challenge to the US SPB,[150] on the basis that it allegedly treated certain factors as conclusive proof of a likelihood of continuation or recurrence of dumping. However, if the SPB had this effect, it would be inconsistent with Article 11.3 of the Anti-Dumping Agreement. This article requires that the likelihood of continuation or recurrence of dumping and injury be considered in the particular facts of each case. Mexico's challenge to the SPB relied on a legislative environment of 232 administrative decisions under the SPB. The Panel considered samples from these decisions in various ways and concluded that the decisions

146. *Ibid.*, para. 216.
147. See Section 8.3, text at n. 117.
148. Appellate Body Report, *US – Oil Country Tubular Goods Sunset Reviews,* paras 209–215.
149. *Ibid.*, para. 215.
150. Policies Regarding the Conduct of Five-year ('Sunset') Reviews of Anti-dumping and Countervailing Duty Orders, *United States Federal Register*, vol. 63, No. 73 (16 Apr. 1998), 18871.

were based exclusively on the factors set forth in the SPB and disregarded other factors.[151] However, the Appellate Body reversed this finding, holding that it had not been made according to a qualitative assessment of the administrative decisions and pointing to the Panel's failure to express its analysis of why the decisions were made.[152]

It will generally be very hard for a complainant to establish a qualitative assessment of the operation of the legislative environment. If the legislative environment consists of a number of administrative or judicial decisions, a qualitative assessment will require some analysis of the decision-making process. Here, the legislating State has a very strong natural advantage in fact-finding and inference making. Indeed, a complainant would probably be forced to engage local lawyers to provide the expertise necessary to understand the qualitative nature of local decision-making. It may be somewhat easier if the legislative environment consists of regulations and written practices, as these are more susceptible to abstract analysis. However, even so, local idiosyncrasies in legislative drafting may require local expertise to bolster a challenge. Again, in this situation the legislating State will enjoy considerable advantages in litigation.

These difficulties make it likely that a complainant will focus on the wording of ambiguous legislation instead. The difficulty here is illustrated in the case of *US – Gambling*. In this case, legislation regulating gambling was accused of being inconsistent with the chapeau to Article XIV of the GATS, because it allegedly discriminated between domestic and foreign gambling service providers. The United States argued that the legislation applied in practice against both kinds of providers and produced statistical and anecdotal evidence to show that domestic service providers had been prosecuted under the legislation.[153] However, Antigua itself raised the legislative environment issue in the form of a number of US firms that it claimed had supplied relevant gambling services but had not been prosecuted. The Appellate Body found that the evidence of the legislative environment was unsatisfactory,[154] and that, as a result, the Panel should instead have focused on the wording of the legislation.[155]

---

151. Panel Report, *US – Anti-Dumping Measures on Oil Country Tubular Goods*, para. 7.63.
152. Appellate Body Report, *US – Anti-Dumping Measures on Oil Country Tubular Goods*, paras 203–209.
153. Appellate Body Report, *US – Gambling*, paras 352–354.
154. *Ibid.*, para. 356:

> In our view, the proper significance to be attached to isolated instances of enforcement, or lack thereof, cannot be determined in the absence of evidence allowing such instances to be placed in their proper context. Such evidence might include evidence on the overall number of suppliers, and on patterns of enforcement, and on the reasons for particular instances of non-enforcement. Indeed, enforcement agencies may refrain from prosecution in many instances for reasons unrelated to discriminatory intent and without discriminatory effect.

155. Appellate Body Report, *US – Gambling*, para. 357.

8.5. CONCLUDING REMARKS

We have seen in previous chapters that deference in challenges to legislation has moved from procedural to substantive in nature. Furthermore, substantive deference, when viewed through the lens of factor characterization and proportionality characterization, has generally been applied by WTO tribunals in a measured way – although there are some unusual cases of intrusiveness. We have seen in this chapter that WTO tribunals are perhaps a little more adventurous in applying substantive deference in certainty characterization. They are willing to actively explore the legislative environment and its effects on challenged legislation, and they do not accept blindly domestic legal opinions about those effects. Nevertheless, this willingness to explore the legislative environment is tempered by a focus on the text of legislation. It seems that the legislative environment, whether used as a sword or as a shield in certainty characterization, has to meet very demanding criteria before it can determine the outcome of a dispute. WTO tribunals tend to place much greater weight on the wording of legislation than on its legislative environment.

The heavy onus applicable here means that in most cases of legislative ambiguity, the decisive factor will be the nature of the relevant WTO obligation. Ambiguous legislation will be WTO-inconsistent if the obligation requires domestic legislation to provide rules that are 'available as a matter of legal right and certainty'.[156]

However, most WTO obligations do not prohibit ambiguity in this way. In most cases, a degree of ambiguity is acceptable. Indeed, it is possible to convert a suspicious ambiguity on the face of challenged legislation into clear WTO-consistency by calling on the legislative environment. However, using the legislative environment in this way requires that environment to be fairly specific. Calls on general domestic legal doctrines, such as the incorporation of international law into domestic law, are likely to be rejected by WTO tribunals. They are far more likely to accept clear and specific aspects of the legislative environment, such as executive promises during WTO litigation, as providing the sufficient certainty. This focus on clarity can nevertheless also operate to the benefit of the legislating State. If the challenger attempts to use the legislative environment to make ambiguous legislation WTO-inconsistent, it will need very good evidence about the qualitative nature of that environment. Again, the text of the challenged legislation will be predominant.

It would therefore seem that WTO tribunals do not show a great deal of deference to domestic assertions about the effects of a legislative environment. Broad generalizations about such effects do not suffice: WTO tribunals prefer evidence of the clear and qualitative effects of a domestic legal system. They do not apply domestic law with the confidence of a domestic court, but they nevertheless take an active role in characterizing the operation of legislation in the context of its legislative environment.

---

156. Appellate Body Report, *Canada – Patent Term*, para. 90.

Chapter 9

Concluding Comments

I begin with a provocation: Is the international legal system incapable of dealing with challenges to domestic legislation? In other words, will matters of pure politics, rather than matters of law, always determine the result of such challenges? Some may argue that the answer to these questions is 'yes'. I take a more positive view. International legal proceedings will always be heavily political in nature – but they cannot become purely political, for in doing so they would cease to be 'legal' proceedings. International tribunals must persuade states to comply with their rulings. In the long run, their most effective tools of persuasion are neutrality, objectivity, and the use of a recognizably legal doctrine.

There is much to be said for political analyses of international challenges to legislation. Indeed, this kind of analysis has often been done in the past. However, there is far less analysis of the use of a legal doctrine in such challenges. This is a shame, because international tribunals need a more coherent legal doctrine to increase their effectiveness in dealing with the rapidly growing number of such challenges.

A coherent legal doctrine for dealing with international challenges to legislation has yet to be developed, and such development may take some time. However, a necessary pre-condition for developing a coherent legal doctrine is a coherent description of legal practice. This kind of description has been the focus of this book. Furthermore, this book has taken a legalistic perspective, consciously focusing on how legal doctrine is applied in challenges to legislation.

This legalistic approach inevitably leads back to domestic constitutional law, with its treasury of highly developed and sophisticated legal doctrines about challenges to legislation. An international legal doctrine about such challenges needs to draw on this treasury. International lawyers cannot develop a doctrine from nothing, but instead gain inspiration, consciously or unconsciously, from their domestic legal training. The trick here is to draw on doctrines from several domestic legal systems, without falling into the trap of careless use of comparative law. One way to avoid this trap is to test such doctrines against the background of published international tribunal reports. In this book, I have described the practice of WTO tribunals in dealing with challenges to legislation, often using concepts, doctrines, and perspectives developed by domestic lawyers, but modified to take into account the particular characteristics of the international legal system and the WTO.

Thus, we have seen that challenges to legislation involve the interaction of several points of legal doctrine, of both a procedural and substantive nature. At the procedural level, these include the nature of tribunal jurisdiction (including restrictions on jurisdiction by reason of person, subject matter, and time), justiciability, and the nature of the available remedy. At the substantive level, these doctrines include the measure of deference (such as standard of review, margin of appreciation, etc.) and the nature of characterization (de facto, de jure, etc.).

The interaction of these legal doctrines produces particular results in international challenges to legislation. The nature of tribunal jurisdiction was quite restricted in previous times, resulting in few challenges reaching a hearing on their merits. This meant that there was little need to develop a doctrine of deference as to the substance of disputes. However, now that WTO tribunal jurisdiction has few restrictions, much effort has gone into clarifying the meaning of that deference. One can also see other interactions of these legal doctrines. The temporal limits on jurisdiction can affect the type of remedy that can be granted. The specificity of a remedy affects the content of deference on the merits. The nature of characterization also affects the content of this deference.

Indeed, the legal doctrines that appear in international challenges to legislation all deal with the concept of deference, which appears to be a principle around which all other legal doctrines may be structured within such challenges. Deference appears in procedural and substantive issues in various ways, and with various results, depending on the circumstances. The WTO variant of this concept – the standard of review of facts – has at times resulted in low levels of deference.

The varying intensities of deference and the standard of review are evident in the three types of legislative characterization discussed in this book. The first two types are very familiar to domestic constitutional lawyers. Factor characterization concerns the characterization of legislation according to its legal operation and its practical operation and purpose, as well as to external standards. As such, there is no express weighing of policy considerations in this kind of review. The degree of deference here depends on the relative weight given to each of the elements mentioned. In contrast, proportionality characterization involves an international legal tribunal openly weighing policy considerations. Here, great deference is given to domestic assessments of what is a valid purpose and what is an effective means of achieving such a purpose. However, WTO tribunals show less deference in assessing whether such means are appropriate in light of the purposes of the WTO and the availability of alternative means. At times, the lack of deference to national legislatures in this respect is startling.

The third kind of legislative review is less familiar and involves delicate issues of deference. Certainty characterization concerns the certainty with which legislation operates consistently with international obligations in light of its legislative environment. This environment includes the entirety of the domestic legal system, such as binding norms both superior and inferior to the challenged legislation in the domestic legal hierarchy, as well as domestic administrative practices. Certainty characterization is a relatively minor feature of domestic legal systems. In contrast, in international challenges to legislation, it is gaining greater prominence. This is because international tribunals, unlike domestic courts, cannot assess the operation of domestic legislation in an authoritative way: they must instead assess that operation as a matter of fact inferred from the evidence. In earlier days, international tribunals simply avoided the issue by refusing to accept jurisdiction over abstract challenges to legislation (although they did accept jurisdiction over challenges to particular applications of legislation). Today, with a greatly expanded jurisdiction, WTO tribunals have been forced to make assessments of legislative environments. They have accepted as a matter of principle that substantial deference should be shown to domestic assessments of such environments. However, in practice, they have undertaken fairly intensive reviews of those assessments.

What can we conclude from all of this? I think that two general points can be made. First, challenges to legislation in international tribunals are a worthy and necessary subject of study for international lawyers, particularly those interested in the very early signs of constitutionalization of international law. The focus of such study will be in areas with a high volume of published cases; these will be in international trade law (in particular, the WTO) and in international human rights law (in particular, the ECtHR). Second, the study of international challenges to legislation provides a new perspective on the familiar theme of the interface between domestic law and international law. International challenges to legislation require international tribunals to 'look inside' the domestic legal sphere in a far more intensive way than they have done in the past. Certainty characterization in particular requires them to take a close look at domestic jurisprudence and administrative practices. Furthermore, in some cases – such as the executive promises made in *US – Section 301 Trade Act* – actions taken at the international level may begin to affect the domestic implementation of domestic legislation. This in turn may draw the interest of domestic constitutional lawyers. International challenges to legislation are likely to become an area of major interest to both international and domestic lawyers of the future.

Bibliography

Abraham, H. *The Judicial Process*. 5th edn. Oxford: Oxford University Press, 1986.

Ago, R. 'Le delit international'. *Recueil des Cours* 68 (1939): 508.

Ago, R. 'Fifth Report on State Responsibility', Doc. A/CN.4/291, in *Yearbook of the International Law Commission*, vol. 2, Part 1, 1976.

Ago, R., 'Sixth Report on State Responsibility', Doc. A/CN.4/302, in *Yearbook of the International Law Commission*, vol. 2, Part 1, 1977.

Allott, P. 'The Concept of International Law'. EJIL 10 (1999): 31.

Amerasinghe, C. *Principles of the Institutional Law of International Organizations*. Cambridge: Cambridge University Press, 1996.

Arai-Takahashi, Y. *The Margin of Appreciation Doctrine and the Principle of Proportionality in the Jurisprudence of the ECHR*. Antwerp: Intersentia, 2002.

Arup, C. 'The State of Play of Dispute Settlement the World Trade Organization'. JWT 37 (2003): 897.

Bakshi, P.M. 'Concurrent Powers of Legislation under List III of the Constitution', background paper prepared for the National Commission to Review the Working of the Constitution (2002); <http://lawmin.nic.in/ncrwc/finalreport/v2b3-3.htm> (visited 24 March 2007).

Baxter, R. 'The Quest for Certainty and Simplicity in International Law'. 1 *U. Brit. Colum. Law Rev.* 1 (1959–1963): 321.

Becroft, R. 'The Standard of Review Strikes Back: The *US – Korea DRAMS* Appeal'. JIEL 9 (2006): 207.

Behboodi, R. 'Legal Reasoning and the International Law of Trade'. JWT 32 (1998): 55.

Behboodi, R. ' "Should" means "Shall" ': A Critical Analysis of the Obligation to Submit Information Under Article 13.1 of the DSU in the *Canada – Aircraft* Case'. JIEL 3 (1998): 563.

Bello, J. 'The WTO Dispute Settlement Understanding: Less Is More'. AJIL 90 (1996): 416.

Benda, E. & Klein, E. *Verfassungsprozeßrecht*. 2nd edn. Heidelberg: C.F. Müller, 2001.

Benedek, W. 'Nationality Decrees in Tunis and Morocco (Advisory Opinion)'. In *Encyclopedia of Public International Law*, vol. 3, edited by Bernhardt, R. Amsterdam: Elsevier, 1997, 510.

Bhuiyan, S. 'Mandatory and Discretionary Legislation: The Continued Relevance of the Distinction under the WTO'. JIEL 5 (2002): 571.

Bhuiyan, S. *National Law in WTO Law*. Cambridge: Cambridge University Press, 2007.

Bilge, A. *La responsabiliti internationale des Etats et son application en matiere d'actes legislatifs*. Thesis No. 471. Istanbul: Tsitouris, 1950.

Bin Cheng. *General Principles of International Law as Applied by International Courts and Tribunals*. London: Stevens, 1953.

Braithwaite, J. & Drahos, P. *Global Business Regulation*. Cambridge: Cambridge University Press, 2000.

Brownlie, I. *State Responsibility – Part I*. Oxford: Oxford University Press, 1983.

Brownlie, I. *Principles of Public International Law*. 6th edn. Oxford: Oxford University Press, 2003.

Byers, M. 'Custom, Power, and the Power of Rules: Customary International Law from an Interdisciplinary Perspective'. *Mich, St. J, Int'l. L.* 17 (1995): 109.

Byers, M. 'Taking the Law out of International Law: A Critique of the Iterative Perspective'. *Har. v Int'l. L.J.* 38 (1997): 201.

Cann, W. 'Creating Standards and Accountability for the Use of the WTO Security Exception: Reducing the Role of Power-Based Relations and Establishing a New Balance Between Sovereignty and Multilateralism'. *Yale J. Int'l L.* 26 (2001): 413.

Cao Jianming. 'WTO and the Rule of Law in China'. *Temp. Int'l & Comp. L.J.* 16 (2002): 379.

Cappelletti, M. *The Judicial Process in Comparative Perspective*. Oxford: Oxford University Press, 1989.

Cass, D. 'The Constitutionalization of International Trade Law: Judical Norm-Generation as the Engine of Constitutional Development in International Trade'. EJIL 12 (2001): 39.

Cass, D. *The Constitutionalization of the World Trade Organization: Legitimacy, Democracy, and Community in the International Trading System*. Oxford: Oxford University Press, 2005.

Cho, Sungjoon. 'The Nature of Remedies in International Trade Law'. *U. Pitt. L. Rev.* 65 (2004): 763.

Clayton, R. & Tomlinson, H. *The Law of Human Rights*. Oxford: Oxford University Press, 2000.

Combacau J. & Sur, S. *Droit International Publique*. Paris: Montchrestien, 2001.

Cottier, S. & Schefer, K. 'The Relationship between World Trade Organization Law, National and Regional Law'. JIEL 1 (1998): 83.

Crawford, J. 'Marbury v. Madison at the International Level'. *Geo. Wash. Int'l. L. Rev.* 36 (2004): 505.

Crawford, J. 'Second Report on State Responsibility', Doc. A/CN.4/498, in *Yearbook of the International Law Commission*, vol. 2, Part 1, 1999 II.

Croley, S. & Jackson, J. 'WTO Dispute Procedures, Standard of Review and Deference to National Governments'. AJIL 90 (1996): 193; also in Jackson, J. *The Jurisprudence of GATT and the WTO*. Cambridge: Cambridge University Press, 2000, 133.

Daillier, P., Nguyen Q.D., & Pellet, A. *Droit International Public*. Paris: *Libairie. générale de droit et de jurisprudence*, 1986.

D'Amato, A. 'The Inductive Approach Revisited'. *Indian J. Int'l. L.* 6 (1966): 509.

Davey, W. 'The Authority of the WTO Dispute Settlement System'. JIEL 4 (2001): 79.

Davies, A. 'Connecting or Compartmentalizing the WTO and United States Legal Systems? The Role of the Charming Betsy Canon'. JIEL 10 (2007): 117.

de Keyser, P. 'Exploring WTO Dispute Settlement in US Anti-Dumping Act 1916: An Easy Case?' Jean Monnet Working Paper, No. 11/01, New York University School of Law (2001), available at <www.jeanmonnetprogram.org/papers/papers01.html> (visited 2 April 2008).

de Visscher, C. '*La responsibilité des Etats*' *Bibliotheca Visseriania*. Leyden: Brill, 1924.

de Visscher, C. *Theory and Reality in Public International Law*. Princeton: Princeton University Press, 1957.

Delbrück, J. 'Proportionality'. In *Encyclopedia of Public International Law*, vol. 3, edited by Bernhardt, R. Amsterdam: Elsevier, 1997, 1140.

Desmedt, G. 'Proportionality in WTO Law'. JIEL 4 (2001): 441.

Dixon, O. 'Upon Taking the Oath of Office as Chief Justice'. In *Jesting Pilate*, edited by Woinarski, S. Sydney: Law Book Co., 1965, 245.

Ehlermann, C. 'Six Years on the Bench of the "World Trade Court" – Some Personal Experiences as Member of the Appellate Body of the WTO'. JWT 36 (2002): 605.

Ehlermann, C. & Lockhart, N. 'Standard Of Review in WTO Law'. JIEL 7 (2004): 491.

Ehring, L. 'De facto Discrimination in WTO Law: National and Most-Favored-Nation Treatment or Equal Treatment?', Jean Monnet Working Paper, No.12/01, New York Uniersity. School of Law (2001), available at <www.jeanmonnetprogram.org/papers/papers01.html> (visited 2 April 2008).

Elias, T. 'The Doctrine of Intertemporal Law'. AJIL 74 (1980): 285.

Estella, A. *The EU Principle of Subsidiarity and Its Critique*. Oxford: Oxford University Press, 2003.

Fabre, A. *Principes du droit des gens*. Paris: *Librairie de droit et de jurisprudence*, 1974.

Feldman, D. & Birks, P. *English Public Law*. Oxford: Oxford University Press, 2004.

Fitzmaurice, G. 'Law and Procedure of the International Court of Justice, 1951-4: International Organizations and Tribunals'. BYIL 29 (1952): 1.

Fitzmaurice, G. 'Law and Procedure of the International Court of Justice, 1951-4: General Principles and Sources of Law'. BYIL 30 (1953): 1.

Fitzmaurice, G. 'Law and Procedure of the International Court of Justice, 1951-4: Points of Substantive Law, Part II'. BYIL 32 (1955–1956): 20.

Fitzmaurice, G., 'Law and Procedure of the International Court of Justice 1951-4: Treaty Interpretation and Other Treaty Points'. BYIL 33 (1957): 203.

Fitzmaurice, G. 'The General Principles of International Law Considered from the Standpoint of the Rule of Law'. *Recueil des Cours* 92 (1957): 1.

Fitzmaurice, G. 'Law and Procedure of the International Court of Justice, 1951-4: Questions of Jurisdiction, Competence and Procedure'. BYIL 34 (1958): 1.

Fitzmaurice, G. 'Law and Procedure of the International Court of Justice, 1954-9: General Principles and Sources of International Law'. BYIL 34 (1959): 1.

Fitzmaurice, G. 'Some Problems Regarding the Formal Sources of International Law' *Symbolae Verzijl* (1958): 153, reproduced in Koskenniemi, M. (ed.), *Sources of International Law*. Aldershot: Ashgate Publishing Company, 2000.

Friedman, B. 'Attacks on Judges: Why They Fail'. *Judicature* 81 (1998): 150 (reproduced at <www.ajs.org/cji/cji_attacks.asp> (visited 9 April 2008)).

Fuller, L. *The Morality of Law*. New Haven: Yale University Press, 1973.

Fuller, L. 'The Forms and Limits of Adjudication'. *Harvard Law Review* 92 (1978): 353.

Gallus, N. 'Recent BIT Decisions and Composite Acts Straddling the Date a Treaty Comes into Force'. ICLQ 56 (2007): 491.

Gassner, U. *Heinrich Triepel. Leben und Werk*. Berlin: Duncker & Humblot, *Tübinger Schriften zum Staats-und Verwaltungsrecht*, 1999.

Geiger, R. *Grundgesetz und Völkerrecht*. 3rd edn. München: CH Beck, 2002.

Glenn, P. *Legal Traditions of the World*. 2nd edn. Oxford: Oxford University Press, 2004.

Goh, G. & Witbreuk, T. 'An Introduction to the WTO Dispute Settlement System'. UWALR 30 (2001): 51.

Grabenwarter, C. *Europäische Menschenrechtskonvention*. 2nd edn. München: CH Beck, 2005.

Grane, P. 'Remedies Under WTO Law'. JIEL 4 (2001): 755.

Gray, C. *Judicial Remedies in International Law*. Oxford: Oxford University Press, 1987.

Green, L. *International Law through the Cases*. Toronto: Carswell, 1978.

Grewe, W. *The Epochs of International Law*. Translated by Byers, M. Berlin & New York: Walter de Gruyter, 2000.

Grieg, D. 'Reciprocity, Proportionality, and the Law of Treaties'. *Virginia J. Int'l. L.* 34 (1994): 295.

Guggenheim, P. *Traité de droit international public*. Geneva: 1954.

Gusy, C. *Parlamentarische Gesetzgeber und Bundesverfassungsgericht*. Berlin: Duncker & Humblot, 1985.

Halberstam, D. 'Desperately Seeking Europe: On Comparative Methodology and the Conception of Rights'. ICON 5 (2007): 166.

Hammer-Strnad, E. *Das Bestimmtheitsgebot als allgemeiner Rechtsgrundsatz des Europäischen Gemeinschaftsrechts*. Hamburg: Verlag Dr. Kovač, 1999.

Harrison, J. 'The Constitutional Origins and Implications of Judicial Review'. *Va. L. Rev.* 84 (1998): 333, at 347–349.

Hartmann, B. 'The Arrival of Judicial Review in Germany Under the Weimar Constitution of 1919'. *BYU J. Pub. L.* 18 (2003): 107.

Hein, P. *Die Unvereinbarkeitserklärung verfassungswidriger Gesetze durch das Bundesverfassungsgericht*. Baden-Baden: *Studien und Materialien zur Verfassungsgerichtsbarkeit,* 1988.

Helfer, L. & Slaughter, A.M. 'Towards a Theory of Effective Supranational Adjudication'. *Yale Law Rev.* 107 (1997): 273.

Hesse, Konrad. *Grundzüge des Verfassungsrechts der Bundesrepublik Deutschland.* 20th edn. Heidelberg: CF Müller, 1995.

Heun, W. 'Die Geburt der Verfassungsgerichtsbarkeit – 200 Jahre Marbury v. Madison'. *Der Staat* 42 (2003): 267.

Higgins, R. 'Time and the Law: International Perspectives on an Old Problem'. ICLQ 46 (1997): 501.

Hilf, M. 'New Frontiers in International Trade: The Role of National Courts in International Trade Relations'. *Mich. J. Int'l. L.* 18 (1997): 321.

Hilf, M. 'The Role of National Courts in International Trade Relations'. In *International Trade Law and the GATT/WTO Dispute Settlement System*, edited by Petersmann, E. London: Kluwer, 1997.

Hilf, M. 'Power, Rules and Principles – Which Orientation for WTO/GATT Law?'. JIEL 4 (2001): 111.

Hirschl, R. 'Symposium: Globalization, Courts, and Judicial Power: The Political Origins of the New Constitutionalism'. *Indian J. Global Leg. Stud.* 11 (2004): 71.

Hogg, P. *Constitutional Law of Canada*. 3rd edn. Ontario: Carswell, 1992.

Hohfeld, W. 'Fundamental Legal Conceptions as Applied in Judicial Reasoning'. *Yale L.J.* 23 (1913): 16. Reprinted in Hohfeld, W. *Fundamental Legal Conceptions as Applied in Judicial Reasoning and other Legal Essays*. New Haven: Yale, 1923.

Howse, R. 'The Legitimacy of the World Trade Organization', unpublished paper on file with the author (1999).

Howse, R., & Regan, D. 'The Product/Process Distinction-An Illusory Basis for Disciplining Unilateralism in Trade Policy'. EJIL 11 (2000): 249.

Howse, R. & Neven, D. 'US – Section 211 Omnibus Appropriations Act of 1998 – A comment', The American Law Institute Reporters' Studies on WTO Case Law <www.ali.org/doc/wto/wto2002/HavanaClub.pdf> (visited 10 October 2007).

Hudec, R. *The GATT Legal System and World Trade Diplomacy*. 2nd edn. Butterworths, 1990.

Hudec, R. *Enforcing International Trade Law*. Butterworths, 1993.

Hudec, R. 'GATT/WTO Constraints on National Regulation: Requiem for an "Aim and Effects" Test'. *The International Lawyer* 32 (1998): 619.

Hudec, R. 'The New WTO Dispute Settlement Procedure: An Overview of the First Three Years'. *Minn J Global Trade* 8 (1999): 1.

Hudson, M. *The Permanent Court of International Justice 1920–1942*. New York: Macmillan, 1943.

International Law Commission, Report on the work of its 48th Session, *Yearbook of the International Law Commission*, vol II, Part 2, A/51/10 (1996).

International Law Commission, 'Draft Articles and Commentaries on Responsibility of States for Internationally Wrongful Acts', *Report of the International Law Commission*, 53rd session, A/56/10 (2001).

International Law Commission, *Report of the International Law Commission*, 54th session, A/57/10 (2002).

International Law Commission, *Report of the International Law Commission*, 58th session, A/61/10 (2006).

Ipsen, J. *Staatsrecht I, Staatsorganisationsrecht*. 5th edn. München: Luchterhand, 2003.

Jackson, J. *The World Trading System: Law and Policy of International Economic Relations*. 2nd edn. MIT Press, 1997.

Jackson, J. 'The WTO Dispute Settlement Understanding-Misunderstandings on the Nature of Legal Obligations'. AJIL 91 (1997): 60.

Jackson, J. *The World Trade Organization: Constitution and Jurisprudence*. London: Pinter/RIIA, 1998.

Jackson, J. 'Global Economics and International Economic Law'. JIEL 1 (1998): 1.

Jackson, J. 'Dispute Settlement and the WTO'. JIEL 1 (1998): 329.

Jackson, J. *The Jurisprudence of GATT and the WTO*. Cambridge: Cambridge University Press, 2000.

Jackson J. 'Comments on Shrimp/Turtle and the Product/Process Distinction'. EJIL 11 (2000): 303.

Jackson J. & Lowenfeld, A. 'Helms-Burton, the U.S., & the WTO'. *ASIL Insight* (1997) <www.asil.org/insights/insight7.htm> (visited 27 August 2007).

Jackson, V. & Tushnet, M. *Comparative Constitutional Law*. New York: Foundation Press, 1999.

Janis, M., Kay, R. & Bradley, T. *European Human Rights Law*. 2nd edn. Oxford: Oxford University Press, 2000.

Jenks, W. *The Prospects of International Adjudication*. London: Steven and Sons, 1964.

Jennings, R. & Watts, A. (eds). *Oppenheim's International Law*. 9th edn. Essex: Longman's, 1992.

Jimenez de Arechaga, E. 'International Responsibility'. In *Manual of Public International Law*, edited by Sørensen. London: Macmillan, 1968, 547–548.

Kahn-Freund, O. 'On Uses and Abuses of Comparative Law'. MLR 37 (1974): 1.

Kazazi, M. *Burden of Proof and Related Issues – A Study on Evidence before International Tribunals*. The Hague: Kluwer, 1995.

Kirk, J. 'Rights, Review and Reasons for Restraint'. *Sydney L Rev* 23 (2001): 19.

Koh, H., 'Transnational Legal Process'. *Neb L Rev* 75 (1996): 181.
Koh, H. 'Why Do Nations Obey International Law?'. *Yale L.J.* 106 (1997): 2599.
Koskenniemi, M. *From Apology to Utopia: The Structure of International Legal Argument.* Helsinki: Finnish Lawyers' Publishing Company, 1989.
Koskenniemi, M. 'The Politics of International Law'. EJIL 1 (1990): 4.
Koskenniemi, M. (ed.). *International Law.* Aldershot: Dartmouth, 1992.
Koskenniemi, M. 'Letter to the Editor of the Symposium'. AJIL 93 (1999): 351.
Koskenniemi, M. (ed.). *Sources of International Law.* Aldershot: Ashgate Publishing Company, 2000.
Krajewski, M. *Verfassungsperspektiven und Legitimation des Rechts der Welthandelsorganisation.* Berlin: Duncker & Humblot, 2001.
Krasner, S. 'What's Wrong With International Law Scholarship?: International Law and International Relations: Together, Apart, Together'. *Chi J Int Law* 1 (2001): 93.
Kunig, P. *Das Rechtsstaatsprinzip.* Tübingen: Mohr, 1986.
Kuyper, P. 'The Law of GATT as a Special Field of International Law'. *Netherlands YIL* 25 (1994): 227.
Kwan Kiat Sim. 'Rethinking the Mandatory/Discretionary Legislation Distinction in WTO Jurisprudence'. *World Trade Review* 2 (2003): 33.
Lachs, M. *The Teacher in International Law.* 2nd edn (The Hague: Martinus Nijhoff, 1986.
Lamy, P. 'The Place of the WTO and its Law in the International Legal Order'. EJIL 17 (2006): 969.
Latane, J. 'Panama Canal Act and the British Protest'. AJIL 7 (1913): 17.
Lauterpacht, H. *The Development of International Law by the International Court.* Cambridge: Cambridge University Press, 1934 (reprinted 1982).
Lennard, M. 'Navigating by the Stars: Interpreting the WTO Agreements'. JIEL 5 (2002): 17.
Lichtenbaum, P. 'Procedural Issues in WTO Dispute Resolution'. *Mich J Int'l L* 19 (1998): 1195.
Lindell, G. 'The Justiciability of Political Questions: Recent Developments'. In *Australian Constitutional Perspectives*, edited by Lee, H. & Winterton, G. Sydney: Law Book, 1992, 180.
Lindsay, P. 'The Ambiguity of GATT Article XXI: Subtle Success or Rampant Failure?'. *Duke L.J.* 52 (2003): 1277.
Luengo, G. *Regulation of Subsidies and State Aids in WTO and EC Law.* Kluwer, 2007.
Lugard, M. 'The Scope of Appellate Review: Objective Assessment of the Facts and Issues of Law'. JIEL 1 (1998): 323.
Mancini, F. 'The Making of a Constitution for Europe'. *CMLR* 26 (1989): 595.
Marceau, G. 'A Call for Coherence in International Law – Praises for the Prohibition Against "Clinical Isolation" in WTO Dispute Settlement'. JWT 33 (1999): 87.
Matsushita, M., Schoenbaum, T. & Mavroidis, P. *The World Trade Organization: Law, Practice, and Policy.* Oxford: Oxford University Press, 2003.

Matsushita, M., Schoenbaum, T. & Mavroidis, P. *The World Trade Organization: Law, Practice, and Policy*. 2nd edn. Oxford: Oxford University Press, 2006.

Mavroidis, P. 'Remedies in the WTO Legal System: Between a Rock and a Hard Place'. EJIL 11 (2000): 763.

Mavroidis, P. *The General Agreement on Tariffs and Trade*. Oxford: Oxford University Press, 2005.

Maxeiner, J. 'Legal Certainty: A European Alternative to American Legal Indeterminacy'. *Tul J Int & Comp Law* 15 (2006–2007): 541.

McRae, D. 'The WTO in International Law: Tradition Continued or New Frontier?'. JIEL 3 (2000): 27.

Mearsheimer, J. 'The False Promise of International Institutions'. *Int'l Security* 19 (1994): 9.

Merryman, J. *The Loneliness of the Comparative Lawyer*. The Hague: Kluwer, 1999.

Meyer, H. *The World Court in Action: Judging among the Nations*. Rowman & Littlefield Publishers, 2002.

Meyer-Ladewig, J. *Konvention zum Schutz der Menschenrechte und Grundfreiheiten*. Baden-Baden: Nomos, 2003.

Mitchell, A. 'Proportionality and Remedies in WTO Disputes'. EJIL 17 (2007): 985.

Morelli, G. *Nozioni di diritto internazionale*. 7th edn. Padua: CEDAM, 1967.

Morse, J. 'Characterization: Shadow or Substance'. *Colum. L Rev* 49 (1949): 1027.

Müllerson, R. *International law, Rights and Politics: Developments in Eastern Europe and the CIS*. London: Routledge, 1994.

Müllerson, R. *Ordering Anarchy: International Law in International Society*. London: Martinus Nijhoff, 2000.

Münch, C. 'Rechtssicherheit als Standortfaktor'. NJW 50 (1996): 3320.

Naiki, Y. 'The Mandatory Discretionary Doctrine in WTO Law: The *US – Section 301* Case and Its Aftermath'. JIEL 7 (2004): 23.

Neumann, J. & Türk, E. 'Necessity Revisited: Proportionality in World Trade Organization Law After Korea – Beef, EC – Asbestos and EC – Sardines'. JWT 37 (2003): 199.

Nolte, G. 'General Principles of German and European Administrative Law – A Comparison in Historical Perspective'. *MLR* 57 (1994): 191.

Oesch, M. 'Standards of Review in WTO Dispute Resolution'. JIEL 6 (2003): 635.

Oesch, M. *Standards of review in WTO Dispute Resolution*. Oxford: Oxford University Press, 2003.

Ovey, C. & White, R. *Jacobs and White: The European Convention on Human Rights*. 3rd edn. Oxford: Oxford University Press, 2002.

Palmeter, D. & Mavroidis, P. 'The WTO Legal System: Sources of Law'. AJIL 92 (1998): 398.

Palmeter, D. & Mavroidis, P. *Dispute Settlement in the World Trade Organization: Practice and Procedure*. Kluwer: The Hague, 1999.

Papier, H. & Möller, J. 'Das Bestimmtheitsgebot und seine Durchsetzung'. *AöR* 122 (1997): 177.

Pauwelyn, J. 'The Concept of a "Continuing Violation" of an International Obligation: Selected Problems'. BYIL 66 (1995): 415.

Pauwelyn, J. 'Evidence, Proof and Persuasion in WTO Dispute Settlement – Who Bears the Burden?'. JIEL 1 (1998): 227.

Pauwelyn, J. 'Enforcement and Countermeasures in the WTO'. AJIL 94 (2000): 335.

Pauwelyn, J. *Conflict of Laws in Public International Law*. Cambridge: Cambridge University Press, 2003.

Pestalozza, C. *Verfassungsprozessrecht*. 3rd edn. München: CH Beck, 1991.

Peters, A. *Einführung in die Europäische Menschenrechtskonvention*. München: CH Beck, 2003.

Petersmann, E. (ed.). *National Constitutions and International Economic Law*. London: Kluwer, 1993.

Petersmann, E. 'Dispute Settlement in International Economic Law – Lessons for Strengthening International Dispute Settlement in Non-economic Areas'. JIEL 2 (1999): 189.

Pieroth, B. & Schlink, B. *Grundrechte*. 19th edn. Heidelberg: CF Müller, 2003.

Pollack, M. *The Engines of European Integration*. Oxford: Oxford University Press, 2003.

Popelier, P. 'Legal Certainty and Principles of Proper Law Making'. *Eur JL Reform* 2 (2000): 321.

Prakash, S. & Yoo, J. 'Symposium: The Constitutional Origins of Judicial Review: Questions for the Critics of Judicial Review'. *Geo Wash LR* 72 (2003): 354.

Preeg, E. *From Here to Free Trade: Essays in Post-Uruguay Round Trade Strategy*. University of Chicago Press, 1998.

Preeg, E. *Traders in a Brave New World: The Uruguay Round and the Future of the International Trading System*. University of Chicago Press, 1998.

Qureshi, A. *Interpreting WTO Agreements: Problems and Perspectives*. Cambridge: Cambridge University Press, 2006.

Radbruch, G. *Rechtsphilosophie*. 2nd edn. Heidelberg: CF Müller, 2003.

Reuter, P. 'La responsabilité internationale', *Droit international public*. Paris: Les Nouvelles Institutes, 1955–1956.

Roach, K. 'Dialogue or defiance: Legislative reversals of Supreme Court decisions in Canada and the United States'. *Int J Constitutional Law* 4 (2006): 347.

Rogowski, R. & Gawron, T. (eds). *Constitutional Courts in Comparison. The U.S. Supreme Court and the German Federal Constitutional Court*. Berghahn Books, 2002.

Sacerdoti, G., Yanovich, A., Bohanes, J. *The WTO at Ten: The Contribution of the Dispute Settlement System*. Cambridge: Cambridge University Press, 2006.

Sachs, M. (ed.). *Grundgesetz*. 3rd edn. München: CH Beck, 2003.

Sachs, M. (ed.). *Grundgesetz*. 4th edn. München: CH Beck, 2007.

Salas, M. & Jackson, J. 'Procedural Overview of the WTO EC – Banana Dispute'. JIEL 3 (2000): 145.

Schachter, O. *International Law in Theory and Practice*. London: Martinus Nijhoff Publishers, 1991.

Scheuner, U. 'L'influence du droit interne sur la formation du droit international'. *Recueil des Cours* 68 (1939): 95.

Schlaich, K., & Korioth, S. *Das Bundesverfassungsgericht*. 6th edn. München: CH Beck, 2004.

Schlaich, K., & Korioth, S. *Das Bundesverfassungsgericht*. 7th edn. München: CH Beck, 2007.

Schlochauer, H. 'Jay Treaty'. In *Encyclopedia of Public International Law*, vol. 3, edited by Bernhardt. R. Amsterdam: Elsevier, 1997, 1140.

Schloemann, H. & Ohlhoff, S. 'Constitutionalization and Dispute Settlement in the WTO: National Security as an Issue of Competence'. AJIL 93 (1999): 424.

Schollendorf, K. *Die Auslegung völkerrechtlicher Verträge in der Spruchpraxis des Appellate Body der Welthandelsorganisation*. Berlin: Duncker & Humblot, 2005.

Schwarzenberger, G. 'The Inductive Approach to International Law'. *Harv LR* 60 (1947): 539.

Schwarzenberger, G. *International Law*, vol. 1. 3rd edn. London: Steven and Sons, 1957.

Schwarzenberger, G. *Power Politics*. 3rd edn. London: Steven and Sons, 1964.

Schwarzenberger, G. *The Inductive Approach to International Law*. London: Steven and Sons, 1965.

Schwarzenberger, G. *The Frontiers of International Law*. London: Steven and Sons, 1962.

Schwarzenberger, G. *A Manual of International Law*. 5th edn. London: Steven and Sons, 1967.

Seddon, N., & Ellinghaus, M. *Cheshire & Fifoot's Law of Contract*. 7th Australian edn. Sydney: Butterworths, 1997.

Senate Legal and Constitutional References Committee, Parliament of Australia, *Trick or Treaty? Commonwealth Power to Make and Implement Treaties* (1995); <www.aph.gov.au/senate/committee/legcon_ctte/treaty/report/index.htm> (visited 27 August 2007).

Sereni, A. *Diritto internazionale*. Milan: Giuffre, 1962.

Shany, Y. 'Toward a General Margin of Appreciation Doctrine in International Law?'. EJIL 16 (2006): 907.

Shaw, M. *International Law*. 5th edn. Cambridge: Cambridge University Press, 2003.

Shell, G. 'Trade Legalism and International Relations Theory: An Analysis of the World Trade Organization'. *Duke L.J.* 44 (1995): 829.

Shelton, D. *Remedies in International Human Rights Law*. Oxford: Oxford University Press, 1999.

Shoyer, A. 'The First Three Years of WTO Dispute Settlement: Observations and Suggestions'. JIEL 1 (1998): 277.

Siedler, N. *Gesetzgeber und Bundesverfassungsgericht*. Hamburg: Dr. Kovač, 1998.

Slaughter, A. 'International Law and International Relations Theory: A Dual Agenda'. AJIL 87 (1993): 205.

Smith, A. 'Executive-Branch Rulemaking and Dispute Settlement in the World Trade Organization: A Proposal to Increase Public Participation'. *Mich LR* 94 (1996): 1267.

Sobota, K. *Das Prinzip Rechtsstaat*. Jena: Mohr, 1997.

Steinle, S. *Völkerrecht und Machtpolitik: Georg Schwarzenberger (1908–1991)*. Baden-Baden: Nomos, 2002.

Stone Sweet, A. 'Proportionality Balancing and Global Constitutionalism' (2007) <www.law.columbia.edu/null/Stone-Sweet+-+Proportionality+Balancing?exclusive=filemgr.download&file_id=101159&showthumb=0> (visited 27 November 2007).

Stuart, A. ' "I tell ya I don't get no respect!": The Policies Underlying Standards of Review in U.S. Courts as a Basis for Deference to Municipal Determinations in GATT Panel Appeals'. *Law & Pol'y Int'l Bus* 23 (1992): 49.

Sykes, A. 'Regulatory Protectionism and the Law of International Trade'. *U Chi LR*. 66 (1999): 1.

Sykes, A. 'Domestic Regulation, Sovereignty and Scientific Evidence Requirements: A Pessimistic View'. *Chi J Int Law* 3 (2002): 353.

Sykes, A. *The WTO Safeguards Agreement – A Legal and Economic Commentary*. Oxford: Oxford University Press, 2006.

Taylor, G. *Characterisation in Federations: Six Countries Compared*. Berlin: Springer, 2006.

Trachtman, J. 'The Domain of WTO Dispute Resolution'. *Harvard Int L.J.* 40 (1999): 333.

Trachtman, J. 'Trade and . . . Problems, Cost-Benefit Analysis and Subsidiarity' (1997) Jean Monnet Working Paper, No. 1/97, New York Uniersity. School of Law, available at <www.jeanmonnetprogram.org/papers/97/97-01.html> (visited 6 September 2007).

Trebilcock, M. & Howse, R. *The Regulation of International Trade*. 2nd edn. London: Routledge, 1999.

Triepel, H. *Völkerrecht und Landesrecht*. Leipzig: Hirschfeld, 1899.

Twomey, A. *Procedure and Practice of Entering and Implementing International Treaties*, Background Paper No. 27, Parliamentary Research Service (1995).

UK Foreign and Commonwealth Office, *The Ponsonby Rule*, January 2001, <www.fco.gov.uk/Files/kfile/ponsonbyrule,0.pdf> (visited 4 August 2004).

Verdross, A. & Simma, B. *Universelles Völkerrecht. Theorie und Praxis*. 3rd edn. Berlin: Duncker & Humblot, 1984.

Verhoosel, G. *National Treatment and WTO Dispute Settlement: Adjudicating the Boundaries of Regulatory Autonomy*. Hart, 2002.

Vermulst, E. *The WTO Anti-Dumping Agreement: A Commentary*. Oxford: Oxford University Press, 2005.

Verzijl, J. *International Law in Historical Perspective*. Leyden: Sijthoff, 1973, vol. 6.

Vitta, E. *La responsibility internazionale dello Stato per atti legislativi*. Milan: Giuffre, 1953.

Waldock, H. 'Plea of Domestic Jurisdiction before International Legal Tribunals'. BYIL 31 (1954): 96.

Watson, A. *Legal Transplants: An Approach to Comparative Law*. Edinburgh, Scottish Academic Press, 1974.

Weiler, J. 'The Rule of Lawyers and the Ethos of Diplomats: Reflections on the Internal and External Legitimacy of WTO Dispute Settlement', Jean Monnet Working Paper 9/00, Harvard Law School (2000).

Wigmore, J. *Wigmore on Evidence*. 3rd edn. Boston: Little Brown, 1940.

Wilson, W. 'Compliance by WTO Members with Adverse WTO Dispute Settlement Rulings: The Record to Date'. JIEL 10 (2007): 397.

Wolfrum, R., Stoll, P. & Seibert-Fohr, A. *WTO – Technical Barriers and SPS Measures*. Brill Academic Publishers, 2007.

WTO Analytical Index – Guide to WTO Law and Practice, <www.wto.org/english/res_e/booksp_e/analytic_index_e/analytic_index_e.htm> (visited 7 April 2008).

Young, P. *Declaratory Orders*. Sydney: Butterworths, 1984.

Zamir I., & Woolf, J. *The Declaratory Judgment*. London: Sweet & Maxwell, 1993.

Zeidler, W., 'Landesbericht Bundesrepublik Deutschland: Die Verfassungsrechtsprechung im Rahmen der Staatliche Funktion'. *EuGRZ* 15 (1988): 207.

Zines, L. *The High Court and the Constitution*. 4th edn. Sydney: Butterworths, 1997.

Zleptnig, S. 'The Standard of Review in WTO Law – An Analysis of Law, Legitimacy and the Distribution of Legal and Political Authority'. *EIoP* 6 (2002) <http://eiop.or.at/eiop/texte/2002-017a.htm> (visited 21 March 2007).

Zweigert, K. & Kötz, H. *An Introduction to Comparative Law*. 3rd edn. Translated by J.A. Weir. Oxford: Oxford University Press, 1998.

Table of WTO Cases

This table is based on the 2008 Annual Report of the WTO Appellate Body, WT/AB/11, 9 February 2009. It represents the official WTO citation method for WTO cases. References to a WTO case in the text of the book use the short title of the case given here.

Short Title	*Full Case Title and Citation*
Argentina – Footwear (EC)	Appellate Body Report, *Argentina – Safeguard Measures on Imports of Footwear*, WT/DS121/AB/R, adopted 12 January 2000, DSR 2000: I, 515.
Argentina – Footwear (EC)	Panel Report, *Argentina – Safeguard Measures on Imports of Footwear*, WT/DS121/R, adopted 12 January 2000, as modified by Appellate Body Report, WT/DS121/AB/R, DSR 2000: II, 575.
Argentina – Hides and Leather	Panel Report, *Argentina – Measures Affecting the Export of Bovine Hides and Import of Finished Leather*, WT/DS155/R and Corr.1, adopted 16 February 2001, DSR 2001: V, 1779.
Argentina – Poultry Anti-Dumping Duties	Panel Report, *Argentina – Definitive Anti-Dumping Duties on Poultry from Brazil*, WT/DS241/R, adopted 19 May 2003, DSR 2003: V, 1727.
Argentina – Textiles and Apparel	Appellate Body Report, *Argentina – Measures Affecting Imports of Footwear, Textiles, Apparel and Other Items*, WT/DS56/AB/R and Corr 1, adopted 22 April 1998, DSR 1998: III, 1003.

Short Title	Full Case Title and Citation
Argentina – Textiles and Apparel	Panel Report, *Argentina – Measures Affecting Imports of Footwear, Textiles, Apparel and Other Items*, WT/DS56/R, adopted 22 April 1998, as modified by Appellate Body Report, WT/DS56/AB/R, DSR 1998: III, 1033.
Australia – Salmon	Appellate Body Report, *Australia – Measures Affecting Importation of Salmon*, WT/DS18/AB/R, adopted 6 November 1998, DSR 1998: VIII, 3327.
Australia – Salmon	Panel Report, *Australia – Measures Affecting Importation of Salmon*, WT/DS18/R and Corr.1, adopted 6 November 1998, as modified by Appellate Body Report, WT/DS18/AB/R, DSR 1998: VIII, 3407.
Australia – Salmon (Article 21.5 – Canada)	Panel Report, *Australia – Measures Affecting Importation of Salmon – Recourse to Article 21.5 of the DSU by Canada*, WT/DS18/RW, adopted 20 March 2000, DSR 2000: IV, 2031.
Brazil – Aircraft	Appellate Body Report, *Brazil – Export Financing Programme for Aircraft*, WT/DS46/AB/R, adopted 20 August 1999, DSR 1999: III, 1161.
Brazil – Aircraft	Panel Report, *Brazil – Export Financing Programme for Aircraft*, WT/DS46/R, adopted 20 August 1999, as modified by Appellate Body Report, WT/DS46/AB/R, DSR 1999: III, 1221.
Brazil – Aircraft (Article 21.5 – Canada)	Appellate Body Report, *Brazil – Export Financing Programme for Aircraft – Recourse by Canada to Article 21.5 of the DSU*, WT/DS46/AB/RW, adopted 4 August 2000, DSR 2000: VIII, 4067.
Brazil – Aircraft (Article 21.5 – Canada)	Panel Report, *Brazil – Export Financing Programme for Aircraft – Recourse by Canada to Article 21.5 of the DSU*, WT/DS46/RW, adopted 4 August 2000, as modified by Appellate Body Report, WT/DS46/AB/RW, DSR 2000: IX, 4093.
Brazil – Desiccated Coconut	Appellate Body Report, *Brazil – Measures Affecting Desiccated Coconut*, WT/DS22/AB/R, adopted 20 March 1997, DSR 1997 :I, 167.
Brazil – Retreaded Tyres	Appellate Body Report, *Brazil – Measures Affecting Imports of Retreaded Tyres*, WT/DS332/AB/R, adopted 17 December 2007.

Short Title	*Full Case Title and Citation*
Brazil – Retreaded Tyres	Panel Report, *Brazil – Measures Affecting Imports of Retreaded Tyres*, WT/DS332/R, adopted 17 December 2007, as modified by Appellate Body Report, WT/DS332/AB/R.
Canada – Aircraft	Appellate Body Report, *Canada – Measures Affecting the Export of Civilian Aircraft*, WT/DS70/AB/R, adopted 20 August 1999, DSR 1999: III, 1377.
Canada – Aircraft (Article 21.5 – Brazil)	Panel Report, *Canada – Measures Affecting the Export of Civilian Aircraft – Recourse by Brazil to Article 21.5 of the DSU*, WT/DS70/RW, adopted 4 August 2000, as modified by Appellate Body Report, WT/DS70/AB/RW, DSR 2000: IX, 4315.
Canada – Autos	Appellate Body Report, *Canada – Certain Measures Affecting the Automotive Industry*, WT/DS139/AB/R, WT/DS142/AB/R, adopted 19 June 2000, DSR 2000: VI, 2985.
Canada – Patent Term	Appellate Body Report, *Canada – Term of Patent Protection*, WT/DS170/AB/R, adopted 12 October 2000, DSR 2000: X, 5093.
Canada – Patent Term	Award of the Arbitrator, *Canada – Term of Patent Protection – Arbitration under Article 21.3(c) of the DSU*, WT/DS170/10, 28 February 2001, DSR 2001: V, 2031.
Canada – Periodicals	Appellate Body Report, *Canada – Certain Measures Concerning Periodicals*, WT/DS31/AB/R, adopted 30 July 1997, DSR 1997: I, 449.
Canada – Periodicals	Panel Report, *Canada – Certain Measures Concerning Periodicals*, WT/DS31/R and Corr.1, adopted 30 July 1997, as modified by Appellate Body Report, WT/DS31/AB/R, DSR 1997: I, 481.
Canada – Wheat Exports and Grain Imports	Appellate Body Report, *Canada – Measures Relating to Exports of Wheat and Treatment of Imported Grain*, WT/DS276/AB/R, adopted 27 September 2004, DSR 2004: VI, 2739.
Canada – Wheat Exports and Grain Imports	Panel Report, *Canada – Measures Relating to Exports of Wheat and Treatment of Imported Grain*, WT/DS276/R, adopted 27 September 2004, upheld

Short Title	Full Case Title and Citation
	by Appellate Body Report, WT/DS276/AB/R, DSR 2004: VI, 2817.
Chile – Alcoholic Beverages	Appellate Body Report, *Chile – Taxes on Alcoholic Beverages*, WT/DS87/AB/R, WT/DS110/AB/R, adopted 12 January 2000, DSR 2000: I, 281.
Chile – Alcoholic Beverages	Panel Report, *Chile – Taxes on Alcoholic Beverages*, WT/DS87/R, WT/DS110/R, adopted 12 January 2000, as modified by Appellate Body Report, WT/DS87/AB/R, WT/DS110/AB/R, DSR 2000: I, 303.
Chile – Price Band System	Appellate Body Report, *Chile – Price Band System and Safeguard Measures Relating to Certain Agricultural Products*, WT/DS207/AB/R and Corr.1, adopted 23 October 2002, DSR 2002: VIII, 3045.
Chile – Price Band System	Panel Report, *Chile – Price Band System and Safeguard Measures Relating to Certain Agricultural Products*, WT/DS207/R, adopted 23 October 2002, as modified by Appellate Body Report, WT/DS207AB/R, DSR 2002: VIII, 3127.
Chile – Price Band System	Award of the Arbitrator, *Chile – Price Band System and Safeguard Measures Relating to Certain Agricultural Products – Arbitration under Article 21.3(c) of the DSU*, WT/DS207/13, 17 March 2003, DSR 2003: III, 1237.
China – Auto Parts	Appellate Body Reports, *China – Measures Affecting Imports of Automobile Parts*, WT/DS339/AB/R, WT/DS340/AB/R, WT/DS342/AB/R, adopted 12 January 2009.
China – Auto Parts	Panel Reports, *China – Measures Affecting Imports of Automobile Parts*, WT/DS339/R, WT/DS340/R, WT/DS342/R and Add.1 and Add.2, adopted 12 January 2009, as upheld (WT/DS339/R), and as modified (WT/DS340/R, WT/DS342/R) by Appellate Body Reports WT/DS339/AB/R, WT/DS340/AB/R, WT/DS342/AB/R.
China – Intellectual Property Rights	Panel Report, *China – Measures Affecting the Protection and Enforcement of Intellectual Property Rights*, WT/DS362/R, circulated 26 January 2009.

Short Title	*Full Case Title and Citation*
Dominican Republic – Import and Sale of Cigarettes	Appellate Body Report, *Dominican Republic – Measures Affecting the Importation and Internal Sale of Cigarettes*, WT/DS302/AB/R, adopted 19 May 2005, DSR 2005: XV, 7367.
Dominican Republic – Import and Sale of Cigarettes	Panel Report, *Dominican Republic – Measures Affecting the Importation and Internal Sale of Cigarettes*, WT/DS302/R, adopted 19 May 2005, as modified by Appellate Body Report, WT/DS302/AB/R, DSR 2005: XV, 7425.
EC – The ACP–EC Partnership Agreement	Award of the Arbitrator, *European Communities – The ACP-EC Partnership Agreement – Recourse to Arbitration Pursuant to the Decision of 14 November 2001*, WT/L/616, 1 August 2005, DSR 2005: XXIII, 11669.
EC – Approval and Marketing of Biotech Products	Panel Report, *European Communities – Measures Affecting the Approval and Marketing of Biotech Products*, WT/DS291/R, WT/DS292/R, WT/DS293/R, Corr.1 and Add.1, 2, 3, 4, 5, 6, 7, 8, and 9, adopted 21 November 2006.
EC – Asbestos	Appellate Body Report, *European Communities – Measures Affecting Asbestos and Asbestos-Containing Products*, WT/DS135/AB/R, adopted 5 April 2001, DSR 2001: VII, 3243.
EC – Bananas III	Appellate Body Report, *European Communities – Regime for the Importation, Sale and Distribution of Bananas*, WT/DS27/AB/R, adopted 25 September 1997, DSR 1997: II, 591.
EC – Bananas III	Award of the Arbitrator, *European Communities – Regime for the Importation, Sale and Distribution of Bananas – Arbitration under Article 21.3(c) of the DSU*, WT/DS27/15, 7 January 1998, DSR 1998: I, 3.
EC – Bananas III (Article 21.5 – Ecuador)	Panel Report, *European Communities – Regime for the Importation, Sale and Distribution of Bananas – Recourse to Article 21.5 of the DSU by Ecuador*, WT/DS27/RW/ECU, adopted 6 May 1999, DSR 1999: II, 803.
EC – Bed Linen (Article 21.5 – India)	Appellate Body Report, *European Communities – Anti-Dumping Duties on Imports of Cotton-Type Bed Linen from India – Recourse to Article 21.5 of the*

Short Title	Full Case Title and Citation
	DSU by India, WT/DS141/AB/RW, adopted 24 April 2003, DSR 2003: III, 965.
EC – Chicken Cuts	Appellate Body Report, *European Communities – Customs Classification of Frozen Boneless Chicken Cuts*, WT/DS269/AB/R, WT/DS286/AB/R, and Corr.1, adopted 27 September 2005, DSR 2005: XIX, 9157.
EC – Computer Equipment	Appellate Body Report, *European Communities – Customs Classification of Certain Computer Equipment*, WT/DS62/AB/R, WT/DS67/AB/R, WT/DS68/AB/R, adopted 22 June 1998, DSR 1998: V, 1851.
EC – Computer Equipment	Panel Report, *European Communities – Customs Classification of Certain Computer Equipment*, WT/DS62/R, WT/DS67/R, WT/DS68/R, adopted 22 June 1998, as modified by Appellate Body Report, WT/DS62/AB/R, WT/DS67/AB/R, WT/DS68/AB/R, DSR 1998: V, 1891.
EC – Hormones	Appellate Body Report, *EC Measures Concerning Meat and Meat Products (Hormones)*, WT/DS26/AB/R, WT/DS48/AB/R, adopted 13 February 1998, DSR 1998: I, 135.
EC – Hormones	Award of the Arbitrator, *EC Measures Concerning Meat and Meat Products (Hormones) – Arbitration under Article 21.3(c) of the DSU*, WT/DS26/15, WT/DS48/13, 29 May 1998, DSR 1998: V, 1833.
EC – Poultry	Appellate Body Report, *European Communities – Measures Affecting the Importation of Certain Poultry Products*, WT/DS69/AB/R, adopted 23 July 1998, DSR 1998: V, 2031.
EC – Sardines	Appellate Body Report, *European Communities – Trade Description of Sardines*, WT/DS231/AB/R, adopted 23 October 2002, DSR 2002: VIII, 3359.
EC – Selected Customs Matters	Appellate Body Report, *European Communities – Selected Customs Matters*, WT/DS315/AB/R, adopted 11 December 2006.
EC – Tariff Preferences	Appellate Body Report, *European Communities – Conditions for the Granting of Tariff Preferences to*

Short Title	*Full Case Title and Citation*
	Developing Countries, WT/DS246/AB/R, adopted 20 April 2004, DSR 2004: III, 925.
EC – Tariff Preferences	Award of the Arbitrator, *European Communities – Conditions for the Granting of Tariff Preferences to Developing Countries – Arbitration under Article 21.3(c) of the DSU*, WT/DS246/14, 20 September 2004, DSR 2004: IX, 4313.
EC – Trademarks and Geographical Indications (Australia)	Panel Report, *European Communities – Protection of Trademarks and Geographical Indications for Agricultural Products and Foodstuffs, Complaint by Australia*, WT/DS290/R, adopted 20 April 2005, DSR 2005: X-XI, 4603.
EC – Tube or Pipe Fittings	Panel Report, *European Communities – Anti-Dumping Duties on Malleable Cast Iron Tube or Pipe Fittings from Brazil*, WT/DS219/R, adopted 18 August 2003, as modified by Appellate Body Report WT/DS219/AB/R, DSR 2003: VII, 2701.
Guatemala – Cement I	Panel Report, *Guatemala – Anti-Dumping Investigation Regarding Portland Cement from Mexico*, WT/DS60/R, adopted 25 November 1998, as modified by Appellate Body Report, WT/DS60/AB/R, DSR 1998: IX, 3797.
Guatemala – Cement II	Panel Report, *Guatemala – Definitive Anti-Dumping Measures on Grey Portland Cement from Mexico*, WT/DS156/R, adopted 17 November 2000, DSR 2000: XI, 5295.
India – Autos	Panel Report, *India – Measures Affecting the Automotive Sector*, WT/DS146/R, WT/DS175/R and Corr.1, adopted 5 April 2002, DSR 2002: V, 1827.
India – Patents (EC)	Panel Report, *India – Patent Protection for Pharmaceutical and Agricultural Chemical Products, Complaint by the European Communities*, WT/DS79/R, adopted 22 September 1998, DSR 1998: VI, 2661.
India – Patents (US)	Appellate Body Report, *India – Patent Protection for Pharmaceutical and Agricultural Chemical Products*, WT/DS50/AB/R, adopted 16 January 1998, DSR 1998: I, 9.

Short Title	Full Case Title and Citation
India – Quantitative Restrictions	Appellate Body Report, *India – Quantitative Restrictions on Imports of Agricultural, Textile and Industrial Products*, WT/DS90/AB/R, adopted 22 September 1999, DSR 1999: IV, 1763.
India – Quantitative Restrictions	Panel Report, *India – Quantitative Restrictions on Imports of Agricultural, Textile and Industrial Products*, WT/DS90/R, adopted 22 September 1999, upheld by Appellate Body Report, WT/DS90/AB/R, DSR 1999: V, 1799.
Japan – Agricultural Products II	Panel Report, *Japan – Measures Affecting Agricultural Products*, WT/DS76/R, adopted 19 March 1999, as modified by Appellate Body Report, WT/DS76/AB/R, DSR 1999: I, 315.
Japan – Alcoholic Beverages II	Appellate Body Report, *Japan – Taxes on Alcoholic Beverages*, WT/DS8/AB/R, WT/DS10/AB/R, WT/DS11/AB/R, adopted 1 November 1996, DSR 1996: I, 97.
Japan – Alcoholic Beverages II	Award of the Arbitrator, *Japan – Taxes on Alcoholic Beverages – Arbitration under Article 21.3(c) of the DSU*, WT/DS8/15, WT/DS10/15, WT/DS11/13, 14 February 1997, DSR 1997: I, 3.
Japan – Apples	Appellate Body Report, *Japan – Measures Affecting the Importation of Apples*, WT/DS245/AB/R, adopted 10 December 2003, DSR 2003: IX, 4391.
Japan – Apples	Panel Report, *Japan – Measures Affecting the Importation of Apples*, WT/DS245/R, adopted 10 December 2003, upheld by Appellate Body Report, WT/DS245/AB/R, DSR 2003: IX, 4481.
Japan – Apples (Article 21.5 – US)	Panel Report, *Japan – Measures Affecting the Importation of Apples – Recourse to Article 21.5 of the DSU by the United States*, WT/DS245/RW, adopted 20 July 2005, DSR 2005: XVI, 7911.
Korea – Alcoholic Beverages	Appellate Body Report, *Korea – Taxes on Alcoholic Beverages*, WT/DS75/AB/R, WT/DS84/AB/R, adopted 17 February 1999, DSR 1999: I, 3.
Korea – Alcoholic Beverages	Panel Report, *Korea – Taxes on Alcoholic Beverages*, WT/DS75/R, WT/DS84/R, adopted 17 February 1999, as modified by Appellate Body

Short Title	Full Case Title and Citation
	Report, WT/DS75/AB/R, WT/DS84/AB/R, DSR 1999: I, 44.
Korea – Alcoholic Beverages	Award of the Arbitrator, *Korea – Taxes on Alcoholic Beverages – Arbitration under Article 21.3(c) of the DSU*, WT/DS75/16, WT/DS84/14, 4 June 1999, DSR 1999: II, 937.
Korea – Commercial Vessels	Panel Report, *Korea – Measures Affecting Trade in Commercial Vessels*, WT/DS273/R, adopted 11 April 2005, DSR 2005: VII, 2749.
Korea – Various Measures on Beef	Appellate Body Report, *Korea – Measures Affecting Imports of Fresh, Chilled and Frozen Beef*, WT/DS161/AB/R, WT/DS169/AB/R, adopted 10 January 2001, DSR 2001: I, 5.
Korea – Various Measures on Beef	Panel Report, *Korea – Measures Affecting Imports of Fresh, Chilled and Frozen Beef*, WT/DS161/R, WT/DS169/R, adopted 10 January 2001, as modified by Appellate Body Report, WT/DS161/AB/R, WT/DS169/AB/R, DSR 2001: I, 59.
Mexico – Anti-Dumping Measures on Rice	Appellate Body Report, *Mexico – Definitive Anti-Dumping Measures on Beef and Rice, Complaint with Respect to Rice*, WT/DS295/AB/R, adopted 20 December 2005, DSR 2005: XXII, 10853.
Mexico – Corn Syrup (Article 21.5 – US)	Appellate Body Report, *Mexico – Anti-Dumping Investigation of High Fructose Corn Syrup (HFCS) from the United States – Recourse to Article 21.5 of the DSU by the United States*, WT/DS132/AB/RW, adopted 21 November 2001, DSR 2001: XIII, 6675.
Mexico – Taxes on Soft Drinks	Appellate Body Report, *Mexico – Tax Measures on Soft Drinks and Other Beverages*, WT/DS308/AB/R, adopted 24 March 2006.
Mexico – Taxes on Soft Drinks	Panel Report, *Mexico – Tax Measures on Soft Drinks and Other Beverages*, WT/DS308/R, adopted 24 March 2006, as modified by Appellate Body Report, WT/DS308/AB/R.
Mexico – Telecoms	Panel Report, *Mexico – Measures Affecting Telecommunications Services*, WT/DS204/R, adopted 1 June 2004, DSR 2004: IV, 1537.

Short Title	Full Case Title and Citation
Thailand – H-Beams	Appellate Body Report, *Thailand – Anti-Dumping Duties on Angles, Shapes and Sections of Iron or Non-Alloy Steel and H-Beams from Poland*, WT/DS122/AB/R, adopted 5 April 2001, DSR 2001: VII, 2701.
Turkey – Rice	Panel Report, *Turkey – Measures Affecting the Importation of Rice*, WT/DS334/R, adopted 22 October 2007.
Turkey – Textiles	Appellate Body Report, *Turkey – Restrictions on Imports of Textile and Clothing Products*, WT/DS34/AB/R, adopted 19 November 1999, DSR 1999: VI, 2345.
US – 1916 Act	Appellate Body Report, *United States – Anti-Dumping Act of 1916*, WT/DS136/AB/R, WT/DS162/AB/R, adopted 26 September 2000, DSR 2000: X, 4793.
US – 1916 Act (EC)	Panel Report, *United States – Anti-Dumping Act of 1916, Complaint by the European Communities*, WT/DS136/R and Corr.1, adopted 26 September 2000, upheld by Appellate Body Report, WT/DS136/AB/R, WT/DS162/AB/R, DSR 2000: X, 4593.
US – 1916 Act (Japan)	Panel Report, *United States – Anti-Dumping Act of 1916, Complaint by Japan*, WT/DS162/R and Add.1, adopted 26 September 2000, upheld by Appellate Body Report, WT/DS136/AB/R, WT/DS162/AB/R, DSR 2000: X, 4831.
US – 1916 Act	Award of the Arbitrator, *United States – Anti-Dumping Act of 1916 – Arbitration under Article 21.3(c) of the DSU*, WT/DS136/11, WT/DS162/14, 28 February 2001, DSR 2001: V, 2017.
US – Anti-Dumping Measures on Oil Country Tubular Goods	Appellate Body Report, *United States – Anti-Dumping Measures on Oil Country Tubular Goods (OCTG) from Mexico*, WT/DS282/AB/R, adopted 28 November 2005, DSR 2005: XX, 10127.
US – Anti-Dumping Measures on Oil Country Tubular Goods	Panel Report, *United States – Anti-Dumping Measures on Oil Country Tubular Goods (OCTG) from Mexico*, WT/DS282/R, adopted 28 November 2005, as modified by Appellate Body Report, WT/DS282/AB/R, DSR 2005: XXI, 10225.

Short Title	Full Case Title and Citation
US – Carbon Steel	Appellate Body Report, *United States – Countervailing Duties on Certain Corrosion-Resistant Carbon Steel Flat Products from Germany*, WT/DS213/AB/R and Corr.1, adopted 19 December 2002, DSR 2002: IX, 3779.
US – Carbon Steel	Panel Report, *United States – Countervailing Duties on Certain Corrosion-Resistant Carbon Steel Flat Products from Germany*, WT/DS213/R and Corr.1, adopted 19 December 2002, as modified by Appellate Body Report, WT/DS213/AB/R and Corr.1, DSR 2002: IX, 3833.
US – Certain EC Products	Appellate Body Report, *United States – Import Measures on Certain Products from the European Communities*, WT/DS165/AB/R, adopted 10 January 2001, DSR 2001: I, 373.
US – Corrosion-Resistant Steel Sunset Review	Appellate Body Report, *United States – Sunset Review of Anti-Dumping Duties on Corrosion-Resistant Carbon Steel Flat Products from Japan*, WT/DS244/AB/R, adopted 9 January 2004, DSR 2004: I, 3.
US – Cotton Yarn	Appellate Body Report, *United States – Transitional Safeguard Measure on Combed Cotton Yarn from Pakistan*, WT/DS192/AB/R, adopted 5 November 2001, DSR 2001: XII, 6027.
US – Cotton Yarn	Panel Report, *United States – Transitional Safeguard Measure on Combed Cotton Yarn from Pakistan*, WT/DS192/R, adopted 5 November 2001, as modified by Appellate Body Report, WT/DS192/AB/R, DSR 2001: XII, 6067.
US – Countervailing Duty Investigation on DRAMS	Appellate Body Report, *United States – Countervailing Duty Investigation on Dynamic Random Access Memory Semiconductors (DRAMS) from Korea*, WT/DS296/AB/R, adopted 20 July 2005, DSR 2005: XVI, 8131.
US – Countervailing Measures on Certain EC Products	Appellate Body Report, *United States – Countervailing Measures Concerning Certain Products from the European Communities*, WT/DS212/AB/R, adopted 8 January 2003, DSR 2003: I, 5.

Short Title	Full Case Title and Citation
US – Countervailing Measures on Certain EC Products	Panel Report, *United States – Countervailing Measures Concerning Certain Products from the European Communities*, WT/DS212/R, adopted 8 January 2003, as modified by Appellate Body Report, WT/DS212/AB/R, DSR 2003: I, 73.
US – DRAMS	Panel Report, *United States – Anti-Dumping Duty on Dynamic Random Access Memory Semiconductors (DRAMS) of One Megabit or Above from Korea*, WT/DS99/R, adopted 19 March 1999, DSR 1999: II, 521.
US – Export Restraints	Panel Report, *United States – Measures Treating Exports Restraints as Subsidies*, WT/DS194/R and Corr.2, adopted 23 August 2001, DSR 2001: XI, 5767.
US – FSC	Appellate Body Report, *United States – Tax Treatment for 'Foreign Sales Corporations'*, WT/DS108/AB/R, adopted 20 March 2000, DSR 2000: III, 1619.
US – FSC	Panel Report, *United States – Tax Treatment for 'Foreign Sales Corporations'*, WT/DS108/R, adopted 20 March 2000, as modified by Appellate Body Report, WT/DS108/AB/R, DSR 2000: IV, 1675.
US – FSC (Article 21.5 – EC)	Appellate Body Report, *United States – Tax Treatment for 'Foreign Sales Corporations' – Recourse to Article 21.5 of the DSU by the European Communities*, WT/DS108/AB/RW, adopted 29 January 2002, DSR 2002: I, 55.
US – FSC (Article 21.5 – EC II)	Appellate Body Report, *United States – Tax Treatment for 'Foreign Sales Corporations' – Second Recourse to Article 21.5 of the DSU by the European Communities*, WT/DS108/AB/RW2, adopted 14 March 2006.
US – Gambling	Appellate Body Report, *United States – Measures Affecting the Cross-Border Supply of Gambling and Betting Services*, WT/DS285/AB/R and Corr.1, adopted 20 April 2005, DSR 2005: XII, 5663.
US – Gambling	Panel Report, *United States – Measures Affecting the Cross-Border Supply of Gambling and Betting*

Short Title	*Full Case Title and Citation*
	Services, WT/DS285/R, adopted 20 April 2005, as modified by Appellate Body Report, WT/DS285/AB/R, DSR 2005: XII, 5797.
US – Gambling (Article 21.5 – Antigua and Barbuda)	Panel Report, *United States – Measures Affecting the Cross-Border Supply of Gambling and Betting Services – Recourse to Article 21.5 of the DSU by Antigua and Barbuda*, WT/DS285/RW, adopted 22 May 2007
US – Gasoline	Appellate Body Report, *United States – Standards for Reformulated and Conventional Gasoline*, WT/DS2/AB/R, adopted 20 May 1996, DSR 1996: I, 3.
US – Gasoline	Panel Report, *United States – Standards for Reformulated and Conventional Gasoline*, WT/DS2/R, adopted 20 May 1996, as modified by Appellate Body Report, WT/DS2/AB/R, DSR 1996: I, 29.
US – Hot-Rolled Steel	Appellate Body Report, *United States – Anti-Dumping Measures on Certain Hot-Rolled Steel Products from Japan*, WT/DS184/AB/R, adopted 23 August 2001, DSR 2001: X, 4697.
US – Lamb	Appellate Body Report, *United States – Safeguard Measures on Imports of Fresh, Chilled or Frozen Lamb Meat from New Zealand and Australia*, WT/DS177/AB/R, WT/DS178/AB/R, adopted 16 May 2001, DSR 2001: IX, 4051.
US – Line Pipe	Appellate Body Report, *United States – Definitive Safeguard Measures on Imports of Circular Welded Carbon Quality Line Pipe from Korea*, WT/DS202/AB/R, adopted 8 March 2002, DSR 2002: IV, 1403.
US – Offset Act (Byrd Amendment)	Appellate Body Report, *United States – Continued Dumping and Subsidy Offset Act of 2000*, WT/DS217/AB/R, WT/DS234/AB/R, adopted 27 January 2003, DSR 2003: I, 375.
US – Offset Act (Byrd Amendment)	Panel Report, *United States – Continued Dumping and Subsidy Offset Act of 2000*, WT/DS217/R, WT/DS234/R, adopted 27 January 2003, as modified by Appellate Body Report, WT/DS217/AB/R, WT/DS234/AB/R, DSR 2003: II, 489.
US – Offset Act (Byrd Amendment)	Award of the Arbitrator, *United States – Continued Dumping and Subsidy Offset Act of 2000 –*

Short Title	Full Case Title and Citation
	Arbitration under Article 21.3(c) of the DSU, WT/DS217/14, WT/DS234/22, 13 June 2003, DSR 2003: III, 1163.
US – Oil Country Tubular Goods Sunset Reviews	Appellate Body Report, *United States – Sunset Reviews of Anti-Dumping Measures on Oil Country Tubular Goods from Argentina*, WT/DS268/AB/R, adopted 17 December 2004, DSR 2004: VII, 3257.
US – Oil Country Tubular Goods Sunset Reviews	Panel Report, *United States – Sunset Reviews of Anti-Dumping Measures on Oil Country Tubular Goods from Argentina*, WT/DS268/R and Corr.1, adopted 17 December 2004, as modified by Appellate Body Report, W/DS/268/AB/R, DSR 2004: VIII, 3421.
US – Oil Country Tubular Goods Sunset Reviews	Award of the Arbitrator, *United States – Sunset Reviews of Anti-Dumping Measures on Oil Country Tubular Goods from Argentina – Arbitration under Article 21.3(c) of the DSU*, WT/DS268/12, 7 June 2005, DSR 2005: XXIII, 11619.
US – Section 110(5) Copyright Act	Panel Report, *United States – Section 110(5) of the US Copyright Act*, WT/DS160/R, adopted 27 July 2000, DSR 2000: VIII, 3769.
US – Section 110(5) Copyright Act	Award of the Arbitrator, *United States – Section 110(5) of the US Copyright Act – Arbitration under Article 21.3(c) of the DSU*, WT/DS160/12, 15 January 2001, DSR 2001: II, 657.
US – Section 129(c)(1) URAA	Panel Report, *United States – Section 129(c)(1) of the Uruguay Round Agreements Act*, WT/DS221/R, adopted 30 August 2002, DSR 2002: VII, 2581.
US – Section 211 Appropriations Act	Appellate Body Report, *United States – Section 211 Omnibus Appropriations Act of 1998*, WT/DS176/AB/R, adopted 1 February 2002, DSR 2002: II, 589.
US – Section 301 Trade Act	Panel Report, *United States – Sections 301–310 of the Trade Act of 1974*, WT/DS152/R, adopted 27 January 2000, DSR 2000: II, 815.
US – Shrimp	Appellate Body Report, *United States – Import Prohibition of Certain Shrimp and Shrimp Products*, WT/DS58/AB/R, adopted 6 November 1998, DSR 1998: VII, 2755.

Short Title	Full Case Title and Citation
US – Shrimp	Panel Report, *United States – Import Prohibition of Certain Shrimp and Shrimp Products*, WT/DS58/R and Corr.1, adopted 6 November 1998, as modified by Appellate Body Report, WT/DS58/AB/R, DSR 1998: VII, 2821.
US – Shrimp (Article 21.5 – Malaysia)	Appellate Body Report, *United States – Import Prohibition of Certain Shrimp and Shrimp Products – Recourse to Article 21.5 of the DSU by Malaysia*, WT/DS58/AB/RW, adopted 21 November 2001, DSR 2001: XIII, 6481.
US – Shrimp (Article 21.5 – Malaysia)	Panel Report, *United States – Import Prohibition of Certain Shrimp and Shrimp Products – Recourse to Article 21.5 of the DSU by Malaysia*, WT/DS58/RW, adopted 21 November 2001, upheld by Appellate Body Report, WT/DS58/AB/RW, DSR 2001: XIII, 6529.
US – Softwood Lumber IV	Appellate Body Report, *United States – Final Countervailing Duty Determination with Respect to Certain Softwood Lumber from Canada*, WT/DS257/AB/R, adopted 17 February 2004, DSR 2004: II, 571.
US – Softwood Lumber VI (Article 21.5 – Canada)	Appellate Body Report, *United States – Investigation of the International Trade Commission in Softwood Lumber from Canada – Recourse to Article 21.5 of the DSU by Canada*, WT/DS277/AB/RW and Corr.1, adopted 9 May 2006.
US – Softwood Lumber VI (Article 21.5 – Canada)	Panel Report, *United States – Investigation of the International Trade Commission in Softwood Lumber from Canada – Recourse to Article 21.5 of the DSU by Canada*, WT/DS277/RW, adopted 9 May 2006, as modified by Appellate Body Report, WT/DS277/AB/RW
US – Steel Plate	Panel Report, *United States – Anti-Dumping and Countervailing Measures on Steel Plate from India*, WT/DS206/R and Corr.1, adopted 29 July 2002, DSR 2002: VI, 2073.
US – Steel Safeguards	Appellate Body Report, *United States – Definitive Safeguard Measures on Imports of Certain Steel Products*, WT/DS248/AB/R, WT/DS249/AB/R,

Short Title	*Full Case Title and Citation*
	WT/DS251/AB/R, WT/DS252/AB/R, WT/DS253/AB/R, WT/DS254/AB/R, WT/DS258/AB/R, WT/DS259/AB/R, adopted 10 December 2003, DSR 2003: VII, 3117.
US – Steel Safeguards	Panel Reports, *United States – Definitive Safeguard Measures on Imports of Certain Steel Products*, WT/DS248/R, WT/DS249/R, WT/DS251/R, WT/DS252/R, WT/DS253/R, WT/DS254/R, WT/DS258/R, WT/DS259/R, and Corr.1, adopted 10 December 2003, as modified by Appellate Body Report, WT/DS248/AB/R, WT/DS249/AB/R, WT/DS251/AB/R, WT/DS252/AB/R, WT/DS253/AB/R, WT/DS254/AB/R, WT/DS258/AB/R, WT/DS259/AB/R, DSR 2003: VIII, 3273.
US – Underwear	Appellate Body Report, *United States – Restrictions on Imports of Cotton and Man-made Fibre Underwear*, WT/DS24/AB/R, adopted 25 February 1997, DSR 1997: I, 11.
US – Upland Cotton	Appellate Body Report, *United States – Subsidies on Upland Cotton*, WT/DS267/AB/R, adopted 21 March 2005, DSR 2005: I, 3.
US – Upland Cotton	Panel Report, *United States – Subsidies on Upland Cotton*, WT/DS267/R, and Corr.1, adopted 21 March 2005, as modified by Appellate Body Report, WT/DS267/AB/R, DSR 2005: II-VI, 299.
US – Wheat Gluten	Appellate Body Report, *United States – Definitive Safeguard Measures on Imports of Wheat Gluten from the European Communities*, WT/DS166/AB/R, adopted 19 January 2001, DSR 2001: II, 717.
US – Wool Shirts and Blouses	Appellate Body Report, *United States – Measure Affecting Imports of Woven Wool Shirts and Blouses from India*, WT/DS33/AB/R and Corr.1, adopted 23 May 1997, DSR 1997: I, 323.
US – Wool Shirts and Blouses	Panel Report, *United States – Measure Affecting Imports of Woven Wool Shirts and Blouses from India*, WT/DS33/R, adopted 23 May 1997, upheld by Appellate Body Report, WT/DS33/AB/R, DSR 1997: I, 343.

Short Title	*Full Case Title and Citation*
US – Zeroing (EC)	Appellate Body Report, *United States – Laws, Regulations and Methodology for Calculating Dumping Margins ('Zeroing')*, WT/DS294/AB/R and Corr.1, adopted 9 May 2006.
US – Zeroing (EC)	Panel Report, *United States – Laws, Regulations and Methodology for Calculating Dumping Margins ('Zeroing')*, WT/DS294/R, adopted 9 May 2006, as modified by Appellate Body Report, WT/DS294/AB/R.

Index

I

J

K

L

M

N

O

P

GLOBAL TRADE LAW SERIES

1. Emmanuel T. Laryea, *Paperless Trade: Opportunities, Challenges and Solutions*, 2002 (ISBN 90-411-9897-0).
2. Xiang Gao, *The Fraud Rule in the Law of Letters of Credit: A Comparative Study*, 2002 (ISBN 90-411-9898-9).
3. Yuwa Wei, *Comparative Corporate Governance: A Chinese Perspective*, 2003 (ISBN 90-411-9908-X).
4. Ross P. Buckley (ed.), *The WTO and the Doha Round: The Changing Face of World Trade*, 2003 (ISBN 90-411-9947-0).
5. Bradley J. Condon, Joyce C. Sadka, Tapen Sinha (eds), *Insurance Regulation in North America: Integrating American, Canadian and Mexican Markets*, 2003 (ISBN 90-411-2301-6).
6. Jan Hoogmartens, *EC Trade Law Following China's Accession to the WTO*, 2004 (ISBN 90-411-2301-6).
7. Yang Guohua, Bryan Mercurio, Li Yongjie, *WTO Dispute Settlement Understanding: A Detailed Interpretation*, 2005 (ISBN 90-411-2361-X).
8. Jan Job de Vries Robbé, Paul U. Ali, *Securitisation of Derivatives and Alternative Asset Classes, Yearbook*, 2005 (ISBN 90-411-2375-X).
9. Markus W. Gehring, Marie-Claire Cordonier Segger, *Sustainable Development in World Trade Law*, 2005 (ISBN 90-411-2366-0).
10. Yann Aubin, Arnaud Idiart. *Export Control Law and Regulations Handbook: A Practical Guide to Military and Dual-Use Goods Trade Restrictions and Compliance*, 2007 (ISBN 90-411-2601-5).
11. Henry Kibet Mutai, *Compliance with International Trade Obligations: The Common Market for Eastern and Southern Africa*, 2007 (ISBN 978-90-411-2664-1).
12. Yong-Shik Lee, *Economic Development through World Trade: A Developing World Perspective*, 2007 (ISBN 978-90-411-2681-8).
13. Yanning Yu, *Circumvention and Anti-Circumvention Measures: The Impact on Anti-Dumping Practice in International Trade*, 2007 (ISBN 978-90-411-2686-3).
14. Ross Buckley, Vai Io Lo, Laurence Boulle, *Challenges to Multilateral Trade:The Impact of Bilateral, Preferential and Regional Agreements*, 2008 (ISBN 978-90-411-2711-2).
15. K.D. Raju, *World Trade Organization Agreement on Anti-dumping: A GATT/WTO and Indian Jurisprudence*, 2008 (ISBN 978-90-411-2780-8).
16. Xiaochen Wu, *Anti-dumping Law and Practice in China*, 2008 (ISBN 978-90-411-2790-7).
17. Amin Alavi, *Legalization of Development in the WTO: Between Law and Politics*, 2008 (ISBN 978-90-411-2795-2).
18. Henrik Andersen, *EU Dumping Determinations and WTO Law*, 2009 (ISBN 978-90-411-2827-0).

19. Sherzod Shadikhodjaev, *Retaliation in the WTO Dispute Settlement System*, 2009 (ISBN 978-90-411-2811-9).
20. Yi Shin Tang, *The International Trade Policy for Technology Transfers: Legal and Economic Dilemmas on Multilateralism versus Bilateralism*, 2009 (ISBN 978-90-411-2825-6).
21. Reem Anwar Ahmed Raslan, *Antidumping: A Developing Country Perspective*, 2009 (ISBN 978-90-411-3128-7).
22. Pietro Poretti, *The Regulation of Subsidies within the General Agreement on Trade in Services of the WTO: Problems and Prospects*, 2009 (ISBN 978-90-411-3162-1).
23. Esther Lam, *China and the WTO: A Long March towards the Rule of Law*, 2009 (ISBN 978-90-411-3144-7).
24. Jorge Alberto Huerta Goldman, *Mexico in the WTO and NAFTA: Litigating International Trade Disputes*, 2009 (ISBN 978-90-411-3169-0).
25. Laurence Boulle, *The Law of Globalization: An Introduction*, 2009 (ISBN 978-90-411-2828-7).
26. Daniel Lovric, *Deference to the Legislature in WTO Challenges to Legislation*, 2010 (ISBN 978-90-411-3145-4).